PHILOSOPHY OF
MIND

PHILOSOPHY OF
MIND

SECOND EDITION

JAEGWON KIM

A Member of the Perseus Books Group

Copyright © 2006 by Westview Press, a Member of the Perseus Books Group.

Published in the United States of America by Westview Press, A Member of the Perseus Books Group.

Find us on the world wide web at www.westviewpress.com

Westview Press books are available at special discounts for bulk purchases in the United States by
corporations, institutions, and other organizations. For more information, please contact the Special
Markets Department at the Perseus Books Group, 11 Cambridge Center, Cambridge, MA 02142, or call
(617) 252-5298, (800) 255-1514 or email special.markets@perseusbooks.com.

A Cataloging-in-Publication data record for this book is available from the Library of Congress.

ISBN-13 978-0-8133-4269-6 (paperback)
ISBN 0-8133-4269-4 (paperback)

The paper used in this publication meets the requirements of the American National Standard for
Permanence of Paper for Printed Library Materials Z39.48–1984.

10   9   8   7   6   5   4   3   2   1

Contents

Preface to the Second Edition

The generally warm and positive responses to the first edition, from readers and reviewers alike, have encouraged me to prepare this revised edition. Since the publication of the earlier edition, the field has continued to thrive, and there have been many significant new developments that have deepened and enriched our understanding of the mind. Revising the book has made me realize how much the field has changed—there are many new perspectives on the issues, and some of the issues have undergone substantial transformation. There are new claims and options, and new problems growing out of the old. In spite of all that, though, the general shape of the field has remained remarkably stable, attesting to both the continuity and the evolving nature of the central problematics of the mind. In any case, eight years have passed since the publication of the first edition, and this seemed like a good time for an update. I cannot claim that this update is fully comprehensive or complete; there is too much material to cover—far more so than when the first edition was prepared.

One new feature of this edition is the addition of a chapter on substance dualism, the position that our mentality consists in possessing an immaterial mind. Although there are only a handful of substance dualists today, I believe this traditional viewpoint deserves attention, for its philosophical as well as historical interest. The new chapter presents various arguments pro and con, although the discussion in the end points to a negative conclusion. I hope the coverage of "serious" dualism has broadened the scope and interest of the book. Many of the chapters have been substantially rewritten; this is especially true of the chapters on the psychoneural ("mind-brain") identity theory, mental causation, and consciousness. The last chapter of the first edition ("Reductive and Nonreductive Physicalism") has been replaced with a new chapter dealing with more current issues.

This book is intended to be something more than a passively descriptive—or "objective"—survey of the field. (Such a book would have been much less rewarding to write.) On many issues I have my own ideas and perspectives, and it will not be difficult for the reader to see where my sympathies lie. This makes the book argument-oriented (you might even say "polemical"). The book has a point of view, but I have no interest in making this a piece of philosophical advocacy. I have made an effort to present, within limits of available space, a fair and balanced picture of the competing approaches and arguments. Instructors using this book in a college course could set up the perspectives and arguments found here as foils against which to deploy and discuss their own views. The argumentative approach of the book, it is hoped, gives a focus and direction to the discussion and helps to enliven it, providing the reader with something to react against.

One more note on the writing of this book: I have tried throughout not to present the reader merely with a *list* of problems, claims, arguments, objections, and so on; rather, my aim has been to tell an intelligible *story*, a continuous narrative, that motivates a problem and various rival approaches to it. My hope has been to relate to readers the way I have come to understand the issues myself—to tell them a story that, above all, makes sense to me.

Finally, I want to thank Sarah Warner, my former editor at Westview, and Steve Catalano, my present editor, for their support and encouragement. My assistant at Brown, Maura Geisser, has again provided me with valuable help throughout the process.

Providence, Rhode Island
January 2005

Preface to the First Edition

This book is an introductory survey of philosophy of mind, with brief incursions into the overlapping and adjoining field of philosophy of psychology. It covers many of the central issues currently debated in the field in a way that is intended to be accessible to those without a formal background in philosophy.

But the distance between what one hopes and what one actually has to settle for can be great, and I will have to leave it to the reader to judge to what extent I have been successful. In the course of writing this book, I was constantly reminded of what Sir Peter Strawson once said, namely, that there is no such thing as "elementary philosophy." It has remained my intention and hope, though, to present the issues, claims, and arguments concerning the mind in a way that will make them intelligible, interesting, and challenging to the beginning students of philosophy as well as those who are first coming to the philosophy of mind with some general philosophical background. I hope too that those with some familiarity with the field will also find something of interest here.

A book like this must deal with a number of diverse topics that are closely connected and yet relatively independent of one another. This has affected the structure of the book in two ways: First, it seemed to me desirable to make each chapter as self-sufficient as possible so that it could be read as an independent essay on the issues under discussion. To accomplish this I thought it important to preserve, within each chapter, as much narrative continuity and flow of argument as possible. Second, in the course of pursuing this goal, I have found it desirable, and sometimes even necessary, to tolerate some overlap and repetition of material from chapter to chapter; for example, issues concerning mental causation, mind-body supervenience, content, qualia, and reduction are discussed in various places, and similar or closely related points and arguments make more than one appearance throughout the book.

Over the past two decades or so, philosophy of mind has been an unusually active and exciting area. The field has grown enormously, and I believe there have been significant advances in our understanding of the issues concerning the mind. A large body of literature has built up during this period, and the rate of research publication shows no signs of abating. In part this boom has been due to the impetus provided by the explosive growth, since around midcentury, of "cognitive science"—a loosely allied group of disciplines, including psychology, linguistics, neuroscience, and artificial intelligence, with aspirations to enhance the scientific understanding of mentality. This has, to some extent (some will say fundamentally), changed the character of philosophy of mind, and there are areas where philosophical work on the nature of mind is continuous with scientific work. These include such topics as mental representation, mental imagery, rationality and decision-making, language and language acquisition, the nature of "folk psychology" and its relationship to systematic psychology, and the controversy concerning classical artificial intelligence and connectionism. A separate volume devoted to philosophy of psychology and cognitive science is needed to provide proper coverage of these topics. (Such a volume, I understand, is forthcoming in the Dimensions of Philosophy series.) In this book I have tried to stay with the issues that are standardly and traditionally regarded as falling squarely within philosophy of mind, rather than those that emerge primarily from the recent developments in the sciences.

I am indebted to Marian David and Fred Feldman, who have given me helpful comments on earlier versions of various chapters. Lynne Rudder Baker and John Heil, who read the manuscript for Westview, provided me with many useful comments and suggestions that have improved the book. Maura Geisser, my research assistant at Brown, has given me invaluable help with many tedious chores. Spencer Carr, my editor, has treated me with great patience and tact in the face of repeated delays. It goes without saying that I owe intellectual debts to a great many philosophers, too numerous for individual acknowledgments. But it should be apparent from the text and references who many of them are. My thanks go to them all.

Jaegwon Kim

1

Introduction

In coping with the myriad things and events that come our way at every moment of our waking life, we try to organize and structure them into manageable chunks. A principal way of doing this is to sort things into groups—categorizing them as "rocks," "trees," "fish," "birds," "bricks," "fires," "rains," and countless other kinds, and describing them in terms of their properties and features as "large" or "small," "tall" or "short," "red" or "yellow," "slow" or "swift," and so on. A distinction that we almost instinctively, though usually without conscious awareness, apply to just about everything is whether or not it is a *living* thing. (It might be a dead bird, but still we know it is the *kind* of thing that lives, unlike a rock or a pewter vase, which couldn't be "dead.") There are exceptions, of course, but it is unusual for us to know what something is without at the same time knowing, or having some ideas about, whether or not it is a living thing. Another example: When we *know a person*, we almost always know whether the person is male or female.

The same is true of the distinction between things or creatures with a "mind," or "mentality," and those without a mind. This is probably one of the most basic contrasts we use in our thoughts about things in the world. Our attitudes toward creatures that are conscious and capable of experiencing sensations like pain and pleasure, however lowly they may be in the biological hierarchy, are importantly different from our attitudes toward things lacking such capacities, mere chunks of matter or insentient plants, as witness the controversy about vegetarianism and medical experiments performed on live animals. And we are apt to regard ourselves as occupying a special and distinctive place in the natural world on account of our particularly highly developed mental capacities and functions, such as the capacity for abstract thoughts, self-consciousness, artistic sensibilities, complex emotions, and a capacity for rational deliberation and action. Much as we admire the miracle of the flora and fauna, we do not think that every living thing has a mind or that we need a psychological theory to understand the life cycles of elms and birches or the behavior and reproductive patterns of amoebas. Except those few of us with certain mystical inclinations, we do not think that members of the plant world are endowed with mentality, and we would exclude many members of the animal kingdom from the mental realm as well. We would not think that planarians and gnats have a mental life that is fit for serious psychological inquiry. When we come to higher forms of animal life, such as cats, dogs, and chimpanzees, we are willing to grant them a fairly rich mental life. They are surely *conscious* in that they experience *sensations*, like pain, itch, and pleasure; they *perceive* their surroundings more or less the way we do and use the information gained to guide their behavior. They surely *remember* things—that is, store and use information about their surroundings—and *learn* from experience, and they certainly appear to have *feelings* and *emotions*, such as fear, frustration, and anxiety. We describe their psychological life using the expressions we normally use for fellow human beings: "Phoebe is feeling too cramped inside the pet carrier, and all that traffic noise has made her nervous. The poor thing is dying to be let out."

But are the animals, even the more intelligent ones like horses and dolphins, capable of complex social emotions like embarrassment and shame? Are they capable of forming intentions, engaging in deliberation and making decisions, or performing logical reasoning? When we go down the ladder of animal life to, say, oysters, crabs, and earthworms, we would think that their mental life is considerably impoverished in comparison with that of, say, a domestic cat. Surely these creatures have sensations, we think, for they react in appropriate ways to noxious stimuli, and they have sense organs through which they gain information about what goes on around them and adjust and modify their behavior accordingly. But do they have minds? Are they conscious? Do they have mentality? What is it to have a mind, or mentality?

Philosophy of Mind

Philosophy of mind, like any other field of inquiry, is defined by a group of problems. As we expect, the problems that constitute this field concern mentality and mental properties. What are some of these problems? And how do they differ from the scientific problems about mentality and mental properties, those that psychologists, cognitive scientists, and neuroscientists investigate in their research?

There is, first of all, the problem of answering the question raised earlier: What is it to be a creature with a mind? Before we can fruitfully consider questions like whether inorganic electromechanical devices (for example, computers and robots) can have a mind, or whether speechless animals are capable of having thoughts, we need a reasonably clear idea about what mentality is and what having a thought consists in. What conditions must a creature or system meet if we are to attribute to it a "mind" or "mentality"? We commonly distinguish between mental phenomena, like thoughts and sensory experiences, and those that are not mental, like digestive processes or the circulation of blood through the arteries. Is there a general characteristic that distinguishes mental phenomena from nonmental, or "merely" physical, phenomena? We canvass some suggestions for answering these questions later in this chapter.

There are also problems concerning specific mental properties or kinds of mental states and their relationship to one another. Are pains only sensory events (they hurt), or must they also have a motivational component (such as aversiveness)? Can there be pains of which we are not aware? Do emotions like anger and jealousy necessarily involve felt qualities? Do they involve a cognitive component, like belief? What is a belief anyway, and how does a belief come to have the content it has (say, that it is raining outside, or that $7 + 5 = 12$)? Do beliefs and thoughts require a capacity for speech?

A third group of problems concerns the relation between minds and bodies, or between mental and physical phenomena. Collectively called "the mind-body problem," this has been a central problem of philosophy of mind since Descartes formulated it more than 350 years ago. It is a central problem for us in this book as well. The task here is to clarify and make intelligible the relation between our mentality and the physical nature of our being—or more generally, the relationship between mental and physical properties. But why should we think there is a philosophical problem here? Just what needs to be clarified and explained?

A simple answer might go like this: On the one hand, the mental seems so utterly different from the physical, and yet the two seem intimately related to each other. When you think of conscious experiences—such as the smell of basil, a pang of remorse, or the burning painfulness of a freshly bruised elbow—it is hard to imagine anything that could be more different from mere configurations and motions, however complex, of material particles, atoms and molecules, or mere physical changes involving cells and tissues. On the other hand, these conscious phenomena seem to arise from just these configurations of physical-biological phenomena—that is, from neural processes in the brain. We are at bottom physical-biological systems—complex biological structures wholly made up of bits of matter. (In case you disagree, we consider Descartes' contrary proposal in chapter 2.) How can biological-physical systems come to have states like thoughts, fears, and hopes, experience feelings like guilt and shame, act for reasons, and be morally responsible? It strikes many of us that there is a fundamental, seemingly unbridgeable gulf between mental and physical phenomena and that this makes their apparently intimate relationships puzzling and mysterious.

But it seems beyond doubt that phenomena of the two kinds are intimately related. For one thing, there is reason to believe that mental events occur as a result of physical-neural processes. Stepping barefoot on an upright thumbtack causes a sharp pain in your foot. It is likely that the proximate basis of the pain is some event in your brain: A bundle of neurons deep in your hypothalamus or cortex discharges, and as a result you experience a sensation of pain. Impingement of photons on your retina starts off a chain of events, and as a result you have a certain visual experience, which in turn leads you to form the belief that there is a tree in front of you. How could a series of physical events—little particles jostling against one another, electric current rushing to and fro, and so on—blossom all of a sudden into a conscious experience, like the burning hurtfulness of a badly scalded hand, the brilliant red and purple sunset you see over the dark green ocean, or the smell of freshly mown lawn? We are told that when certain special neurons (nociceptive neurons) discharge, we experience pain, and presumably there is another group of neurons that fire when we experience an itch. Why are pain and itch not switched around? That is, why is it that we feel pain, rather than itch, when just these neurons fire and we experience itch, not pain, when those other neurons fire? Why is it not the other way around? Why should any experience emerge from molecular-biological processes?

Moreover, we take it for granted that mental events have physical effects. It seems essential to our concept of ourselves as agents that our bodies are moved in appropriate ways by our wants and beliefs. You see a McDonald's sign across the street and you want to get a burger, and the perception and desire apparently cause your limbs to move in such a way that you now find your body at the doors of the McDonald's. Cases like this are among the familiar facts of life and are too boring to mention. But how did your perception and desire manage to move your body, all of it, all the way across the street? You say, that is easy: Beliefs and desires first cause certain neurons in the motor cortex of my brain to discharge, these neural impulses are transmitted through the network of neural fibers all the way down to the peripheral control systems, which cause the appropriate muscles to contract, and so on. All that might be a complicated story, you say, but it is something that brain science, not philosophy, is in charge of explaining. But how do beliefs and desires manage to cause those little neurons to fire to begin with? How can this happen unless beliefs and desires are themselves just physical happenings in the brain? But is it coherent to suppose that these mental states are simply physical processes in the brain? These questions do not seem to be questions that can be answered just by doing more research in neuroscience; they seem to require philosophical reflection and analysis beyond what we can learn from science alone. This is what is called the problem of mental causation, one of the most important issues concerning the mind ever since Descartes first formulated the mind-body problem.

In this book, we are chiefly, though not exclusively, concerned with the mind-body problem. We begin, in the next chapter, with an examination of Descartes' mind-body dualism—a dualism of material things and immaterial minds. In contemporary philosophy of mind, however, the world is conceived to be fundamentally material: There are persuasive (some will say compelling) reasons to believe that the world we live in is made up wholly of material particles and their structured aggregates, all behaving strictly in accordance with physical laws. How can we accommodate minds and mentality in such an austerely material world? That is our main question.

But before we set out to consider specific doctrines concerning the mind-body relationship, it will be helpful to survey some of the basic concepts, principles, and assumptions that guide the discussions to follow.

Properties, Events, and Processes

Descartes had a literal reading of "having a mind." For him, having a mind amounts to having an immaterial soul, outside physical space, whose essence consists in thinking. We examine this view of minds as substances of a special sort in chapter 2. A substantival view of mentality like Descartes' is not widely accepted today. However, to reject minds as substances or objects in their own right is not to deny that each of us "has a mind"; it is only that we should not think of "having a mind" as there being some object or substance called a "mind" that we literally "have." Having a mind is not like having brown eyes or a sore elbow. Think of "dancing a waltz" or "taking a walk": When we say, "Sally danced a waltz," or, "Sally took a leisurely walk along the river," we do not mean—at least we do not need to mean—that there are *things* in this world called "waltzes" or "walks" such that Sally picked out one of them and danced it or walked it. Where are these dances and walks when no one is dancing or walking them? Having a mind or dancing a waltz is not like owning an SUV or kicking a tire. Dancing a waltz is merely a *manner* of dancing, and taking a walk is a *manner* of moving your limbs in a certain relationship to the physical surroundings. In using these expressions, we need not accept the existence of entities like waltzes and walks; all we need to admit into our ontology are persons who waltz and persons who walk.

Similarly, when we use such expressions as "having a mind," "losing one's mind," "being out of one's mind," and the like, there is no need to suppose there are objects in this world called "minds" that we have, lose, or are out of. Having a mind can be construed simply as having a certain group of *properties, capacities,* and *features* that are possessed by humans and some higher animals but absent in things like pencils and rocks. To say that something "has a mind" is to classify it as a certain sort of thing, capable of certain characteristic sorts of behaviors and functions—sensation, perception, memory, learning, reasoning, consciousness, action, and the like. It is less misleading, therefore, to speak of "mentality" than of "having a mind"; the surface grammar of the latter abets the problematic idea of a substantival mind—mind as an object of a special kind.

Mentality is a broad and complex property. As we just saw, there are numerous specific properties and functions through which mentality manifests itself, such as experiencing sensations, entertaining thoughts, reasoning and judging, making decisions, and feeling emotions. There are also more specific properties that fall within these categories, such as experiencing a throbbing pain in the right elbow, believing that Kabul is in Afghanistan, wanting to visit Tibet, and being angry at your roommate. In this book, we often talk in terms of "instantiating" or "exemplifying" this or that property. When you shut a door on your thumb, you *instantiate* or *exemplify* the property of being in pain; most of us *have,* or instantiate, the property of believing that snow is white; some of us have the property of wanting to visit Tibet; and so on. Admittedly this is a somewhat cumbersome way of talking, but it gives us a uniform and simple way of referring to certain entities in our discussion. (Throughout this book, the expressions "mental" and "psychological" and their respective cognates are used interchangeably. In most contexts, the same goes for "physical" and "material.")

We now set out in more general terms the kind of ontological scheme that we presuppose in this book and explain how we use certain terms associated with the scheme. We suppose, first, that our scheme includes *things* or *objects* (including persons, biological organisms and their organs, molecules, computers, and such) and that they have various *properties* and stand in various *relations* to each other. (Properties and relations are together called *attributes*.) Some of these are physical, like having a certain mass or temperature, being one meter long, or being heavier than some other objects. Some things—in particular, persons and certain biological organisms—can also instantiate mental properties, like being in pain and liking the taste of avocado. We also speak of mental or physical *events*, *states*, and *processes* and sometimes of *facts*. A process can be thought of as a (causally) connected series of events and states; events differ from states only in that they suggest *change*, whereas states do not. The terms "phenomenon" and "occurrence" can be used to cover both events and states. We often use one or another of these terms in a broad sense inclusive of the rest. (For example, when we say "events," we are not excluding states, phenomena, and the rest.) How events and states are related to objects and their properties is a question of some controversy in metaphysics. We simply assume here that when a person instantiates, at time *t*, a mental property—say, being in pain—then there is the event (or state) of that person's being in pain at *t*, and there is also the fact that the person is in pain at *t*. Some events are psychological events, such as pains, beliefs, and onsets of anger, and these are instantiations by persons and other organisms of mental properties. Some events are physical, such as earthquakes, hiccups and sneezes, and the motion of your limbs when you walk to the library, and these are instantiations of physical properties. (Note that in the context of the mind-body problem, the physical usually goes beyond the properties and phenomena studied in physics; the biological, the chemical, the geological, and so on, also count as physical.) Events too have properties and stand in relation to other events. Take a particular occurrence of pain (someone just stepped on your toe): Being a pain (that is, falling under the event kind of pain) is a property of that event. It bears the relation of *occurring an instant later than* to your toe's being stepped on and stands in the relation of *being a cause of* with respect to your crying "Ouch!" Sometimes clarity and precision demand attention to ontological details, but as far as possible we try to avoid general metaphysical issues that are not directly germane to our concerns about the nature of mind.

Mind-Body Supervenience

Consider the apparatus called the "transporter" in the science-fiction television series *Star Trek*. You walk into a booth. When the transporter is activated, your body is instantly disassembled; exhaustive information concerning your bodily composition, down to the last molecule, is transmitted, apparently instantaneously, to another location, often a great distance away, where a body that is exactly like yours is reconstituted (presumably with locally available material). And someone who looks exactly like you walks out of the receiving booth and starts doing the tasks you were assigned to do there.

Let us not worry about whether the person who walks out of the destination booth is really you or only an exact duplicate who replaces you. In fact, we can avoid this issue by slightly changing the story: Exhaustive information about your bodily structure is obtained by a scanner that does no harm to the object scanned, and on the basis of this information, an exact physical replica of your body—a molecule-for-molecule identical replica—is created at another location. By assumption, you and your replica have exactly the same *physical* properties; you and your replica could not be distinguished by any *current intrinsic* physical differences. (We say "current" to rule out the obvious possibility of distinguishing you from your duplicate by tracing the causal chains backward to the past. We say "intrinsic" because you and your replica have different relational, or extrinsic, properties; for example, you have a mother but your replica does not.)

Given that your replica is your *physical* replica, will she also be your *psychological* replica? That is, will she be identical with you in all mental respects as well? Will she be as smart and witty as you are, or as prone to daydream? Will she share your likes and dislikes in food and music and behave just as you would when angry or irritable? Will she prefer blue to green and have a visual experience exactly like yours when you and she both look at a Van Gogh landscape of yellow wheat fields drenched in sunlight against a dark blue sky? Will her twinges, itches, and tickles feel to her just the way yours feel to you? Well, you get the idea. An unquestioned assumption of *Star Trek* and similar science-fiction fantasies seems to be that the answer is yes to each of these questions. If you are like the many *Star Trek* fans in going along with this assumption, that is because you have tacitly accepted the following "supervenience" thesis:

Mind-Body Supervenience I. The mental supervenes on the physical in that things (objects, events, organisms, persons, and so on) that are exactly alike in all physical properties cannot differ with respect to mental properties. That is, physical indiscernibility entails psychological indiscernibility.

Or as it is sometimes put: No mental difference without a physical difference. Notice that this principle does not say that things that are alike in psychological respects must be alike in physical respects. We seem to be able coherently to imagine intelligent extraterrestrial creatures whose biochemistry is different from ours (say, their physiology is not carbon-based) and yet who share the same psychology with us. If so, the converse of the supervenience thesis is false: Creatures could be physically different and yet psychologically alike. Mind-body supervenience asserts only that creatures could not be psychologically different and yet physically identical.

There are two other important ways of explaining the idea that the mental supervenes on the physical. One is the following, known as "strong supervenience":

Mind-Body Supervenience II. The mental supervenes on the physical just in case if anything *x* has a mental property M, there is a physical property P such that *x* has P, and necessarily any object that has P has M.

Suppose that some creature is in pain (that is, it has the mental property of being in pain). This supervenience principle says that in that case there is some physical property P that the creature has that "necessitates" its being in pain. That is to say, pain has a physical substrate (or "supervenience base") such that anything that has this underlying physical property must be in pain. Thus, this formulation of mind-body supervenience captures the idea that the instantiation of a mental property in something "depends" on its instantiating an appropriate physical "base" property (that is, a neural correlate or substrate). How is this new statement of mind-body supervenience related to the earlier statement? It is pretty straightforward to show that the supervenience principle (II) entails (I); that is, if the mental supervenes on the physical according to (II), it will also supervene according to (I). Whether (I) entails (II) is more problematic.[1] For practical purposes, however, the two principles can be considered equivalent, and we make use of them in this book without worrying about their subtle differences.

There is a third way of understanding the supervenience relationship:

Mind-Body Supervenience III. The mental supervenes on the physical in that worlds that are alike in all physical respects are alike in all mental respects; in fact, worlds that are physically alike are exactly alike overall.[2]

This formulation of supervenience, standardly called "global" supervenience, is that if there were another world that is just like our world in all physical respects, with the same molecules in the same places, the two could not differ in any mental respects. If God created this world, all he had to do was to put the right basic particles in the right places, and all else, including all aspects of mentality, would just come along. Once the basic physical structure is put in place, his job would be finished; he does not *also* have to create minds or mentality, any more than he has to create trees and refrigerators. The question whether this formulation of supervenience is equivalent to either of the earlier two is a somewhat complicated one; let it suffice to say that the second formulation entails this version, and that there are close relationships between all three. In this book, we do not have occasion to use (III); however, it is stated here because this is the formulation some philosophers favor, and the reader may come across it in the philosophy of mind literature.

To put mind-body supervenience in perspective, it might be instructive to look at it in other areas—in ethics and aesthetics. Most moral philosophers would accept the thesis that the ethical, or normative, properties of persons, acts, and the like are supervenient on their nonmoral, descriptive properties. That is, if two persons, or two acts, are exactly alike in all factual, nonmoral respects (say, the persons are both honest, courageous, kind, sensitive, and so on), they could not differ in moral respects (say, one of them is a morally good person but the other is not). Supervenience seems to apply to aesthetic qualities as well: If two pieces of sculpture are physically exactly alike (the same shape, size, color, texture, and all the rest), they cannot differ in some aesthetic respect (say, one of them is elegant, noble, and beautiful while the second has none of these properties). A world physically just like our world will contain works of art just as beautiful, noble, and touching as our Michelangelos, Vermeers, and Cézannes. One more example: Just as mental properties are thought to supervene on physical properties, most consider biological properties to supervene on more basic physicochemical properties. It seems natural to suppose that if two things are exactly alike in basic physical and chemical features, including, of course, their material composition and structure, it could not be the case that one of them is a living thing and the other is not, or that one of them has a certain biological function and the other does not. That is to say, physicochemically indiscernible things must be biologically indiscernible.

As noted, most philosophers accept these supervenience theses; however, whether they are true, or why they are true (if true), are philosophically non-trivial questions. And each supervenience thesis must be evaluated and assessed on its own merit. Mind-body supervenience, of course, is our present concern. Our ready acceptance of the idea of the *Star Trek* transporter shows the strong intuitive attraction of mind-body supervenience. Should we accept it? Is it true? What is the evidence in its favor? These are deep and complex questions. The reason is that, in spirit and substance, they amount to the following questions: Should we accept physicalism? Is physicalism true?

Physicalism

Since physicalism broadly understood is the basic framework in which contemporary philosophy of mind has been debated, it is useful for us to begin with some idea of what it is. If you are comfortable with the idea of the *Star Trek* transporter, that means you are comfortable with physicalism as a perspective on the mind-body problem. The wide and seemingly natural acceptance of the transporter idea shows how deeply physicalism has penetrated modern Western culture, although when this is made explicit some people would no doubt protest and proclaim themselves to be against physicalism.

What is the relationship between mind-body supervenience and physicalism? We have not so far defined what physicalism is, but the term itself suggests that it is a doctrine that affirms the priority or basicness of what is physical. With this very rough idea in mind, let us see what mind-body supervenience implies for the dualist view (to be discussed in more detail in chapter 2) associated with Descartes that minds are immaterial substances with no physical properties whatever (like mass and motion). Take two immaterial minds: We have to say that they are exactly alike in all physical respects since neither has any physical property and it is not possible to distinguish them from a physical perspective. So if mind-body supervenience, in the form of (I), holds, it follows that they are alike in all mental respects. That is, under mind-body supervenience (I), all Cartesian immaterial souls are exactly alike in all mental respects, and they must be exactly alike in all possible respects! This in turn seems to mean that there can be at most one immaterial soul if mind-body supervenience is true. A serious mind-body dualist—someone who believes in minds and bodies as separate entities—should find these consequences of mind-body supervenience intolerable. This is one way of seeing how the supervenience thesis puts pressure on us to move toward physicalism.

To appreciate the physicalist implication of mind-body supervenience we must consider one aspect of supervenience that we have not so far discussed. Many philosophers regard the supervenience thesis as affirming a relation of *dependence* or *determination* between the mental and the physical; that is, the mental properties a given thing has depend on, or are determined by, the physical properties it has. Consider version (II) of mind-body supervenience: It says that for every mental property M, if anything has M, it has some physical property P that *necessitates* M—if anything has P, it *must* have M. This captures the idea that mental properties must have neural, or other physical, "substrates" from which they arise or emerge and that there can be no instantiation of a mental property not grounded or anchored in some physical property. So a dependence relation can naturally be read into the claim that the mental supervenes on the physical, although, strictly speaking, the supervenience theses as stated only make claims about how mental properties *covary* with physical properties. In any case, many physicalists interpret supervenience as implying mind-body dependence in something like the following sense:

> *Mind-Body Dependence.* The mental properties a given thing has depend on, and are determined by, the physical properties it has. That is to say, our psychological character is wholly determined by our physical nature.

The dependence thesis is important because it is an explicit affirmation of the *ontological primacy*, or *priority*, of the physical in relation to the mental. The thesis seems to accord well with the way we ordinarily think of the mind-body relation, as well as with scientific assumptions and practices. For very few of us would think that there can be mental events and processes that float free, so to speak, of physical processes; most of us believe that what happens in our mental life, including the fact that we have a mental life at all, is dependent on what happens in our body, in particular in our nervous system. Furthermore, it is because mental states depend on what goes on in the brain that it is possible to intervene in the mental goings-on. To ease your headache, you take aspirin—the only way you can affect the headache is to alter the neural base on which it supervenes. There apparently is no other way.

For these reasons, we can think of the mind-body supervenience thesis, in one form or another, as *minimal physicalism*, in the sense that it is one commitment that all who consider themselves physicalists must accept. But is it sufficient as physicalism? That is, can we say that anyone who accepts mind-body supervenience is ipso facto a full physicalist? Opinions differ on this question. We saw earlier that supervenience does not by itself completely rule out the existence of immaterial minds, something antithetical to physicalism. But we also saw that supervenience has consequences that no serious dualist can accept. Whether supervenience itself suffices to deliver physicalism depends, by and large, on what we consider to be full and robust physicalism. As our starting options, then, let us see what varieties of physicalism are out there. First, there is an ontological claim about what objects there are in this world:

Ontological Physicalism. All that exists in this world are bits of matter in space-time and aggregate structures composed exclusively of bits of matter. There is nothing else in the spacetime world.

This thesis, though it is disputed by Descartes and other substance dualists, is accepted by most contemporary philosophers of mind. The main point of contention concerns the *properties* of material or physical things. Certain complex physical systems are also psychological systems; they exhibit mental or psychological properties and functions as well as physical properties. How are the psychological properties and physical properties of a system related to each other? Broadly speaking, an ontological physicalist has a choice between the following two options:

Property Dualism, or Nonreductive Physicalism. The psychological properties of a system are distinct from, and irreducible to, its physical properties.[3]

Property Monism, or Reductive Physicalism. Psychological properties are reducible to, and reductively identifiable with, physical properties. There are only properties of one sort exemplified in this world, and they are physical properties.

Remember that for our purposes "physical" properties include chemical, biological, and neural properties, not just those properties investigated in basic physics (such as energy, mass, or charm). You could be a property dualist because you reject mind-body supervenience, but then you would not count as a physicalist since, as we argued, mind-body supervenience is a necessary element of physicalism. So the physicalist we have in mind is someone who accepts mind-body supervenience. However, it is generally supposed that mind-body supervenience is consistent with property dualism, the claim that the supervenient psychological properties are irreducible to, and not identical with, the underlying physical base properties. In defense of this claim, some point to the fact that philosophers who accept the supervenience of ethical properties on nonethical, factual properties for the most part reject the reducibility of ethical properties, like being good or being right, to nonethical properties. The situation seems the same with the case of aesthetic supervenience and aesthetic properties.

What we have called reductive physicalism is also called "type" physicalism because it says psychological properties and kinds—that is, types of psychological events and states—are in fact physical properties and kinds. Some philosophers who reject type physicalism as too strong and too ambitious embrace "token" physicalism—the thesis that although psychological types are not identical with physical types, each and every individual psychological event, or event-token, is a physical event. So pain, as a mental kind, is not identical with, or reducible to, a kind of physical event or state, and yet each individual instance of pain—this pain here now—is in fact a physical event. Token physicalism therefore is a form of nonreductive physicalism. The continuing debate between nonreductive physicalists and reductive physicalists has largely shaped the contemporary debate on the mind-body problem. We consider this issue in detail in chapter 10.

Varieties of Mental Phenomena

It is useful at this point to look at some major categories of mental events and states. This will give us a rough idea about the kinds of phenomena we are concerned with and also remind us that the phenomena that come under the rubric "mental" or "psychological" are extremely diverse and variegated. The following list is not intended to be complete or systematic, and some of the categories obviously overlap with one another.

First, we may distinguish those mental phenomena that involve *sensations* or *sensory qualities*: pains, itches, tickles, afterimages, seeing a round green patch, smelling ammonia, feeling nauseous, and so on. These mental states are thought to have a "phenomenal" or "qualitative" character—the way they *feel* or the way they *look* or *appear*. To use a popular term, there is *something it is like* to experience such phenomena or be in such states. Thus, pains have a special qualitative feel that is distinctive of pains—they hurt. Similarly, itches itch and tickles tickle. When you look at a green patch, there is a distinctive way the patch looks to you: It *looks green*, and your visual experience involves this green look. Each such sensation has its own distinctive feel and is characterized by a sensory quality that we seem to be able to identify in a direct way, at least as to the general type to which it belongs (for example, pain, itch, or seeing green). These items are sometimes called "raw feels." However, "qualia" has now become the standard term for these sensory, qualitative states, or the sensory qualities experienced in such states. Collectively, these mental phenomena are said to constitute "phenomenal consciousness."

Second, there are mental states that are attributed to a person by the use of embedded that-clauses: for example, President Bush *hopes that* Congress will pass another tax-cut bill this year, Senator Reid *doubts that* that will happen, and Senator Kerry *fears that* Bush may get what he wants. Such states are called "propositional attitudes." The idea is that these states consist in a subject's having an "attitude" (for example, thinking, hoping, fearing) toward a "proposition" (for example, that tuna is more healthful than beef or that Congress will pass a tax-cut bill). These propositions are said to constitute the "content" of the propositional attitudes, and that-clauses that specify these propositions are called "content sentences." Thus, the content of Bush's hope is the proposition that Congress will pass a tax-cut bill, which is also the content of Reid's doubt, and this content is expressed by the sentence "Congress will pass a tax-cut bill." These states are also called "intentional" or "content-bearing" states.

Do these mental states have a phenomenal, qualitative aspect? We do not normally associate a specific feel with beliefs, another specific feel with desires, and so on. There does not seem to be any special belieflike feel, a certain sensory quality, associated with your belief that Providence is south of Boston or that 2 is the smallest prime number. At least it seems that we can say this much: If you believe that 2 is the smallest prime and I do too, there does not seem to be—nor need there be—any common sensory quality that both of us experience in virtue of sharing this belief. Much of our ordinary psychological thinking and theorizing ("commonsense" or "folk" psychology) involves propositional attitudes; we make use of them all the time to explain and predict what people will do. Why did Mary cross the street?

Because she wanted some coffee and thought that she could get it at the Starbucks across the street.

And then there are various mental states that come under the broad and somewhat vague heading of *feelings* and *emotions*. They include anger, joy, sadness, depression, elation, embarrassment, remorse, regret, and the like. Notice that emotions are often attributed to persons with a that-clause. In other words, some states of emotions involve propositional attitudes: for example, Bush was *annoyed that* several reporters were overly persistent with their questions about the weapons of mass destruction, and he was *embarrassed that* he showed his irritation in public. Further, some emotions involve belief: If the president was *embarrassed that* he showed his irritation, he must have had the belief that he showed his irritation. As the word *feeling* suggests, there is often a special qualitative component we seem to associate with some kinds of emotions, such as anger and pride, although it is far from certain that all instances of emotion or feeling are accompanied by such a qualitative feel or that there is a single specific sensory feel to each type of emotion.

There are also what some philosophers call "volitions," like intending, deciding, and willing. These states are propositional attitudes; intentions and decisions have content. For example, I may intend to take the ten o'clock train to New York tomorrow; here the content is expressed by an infinitive construction ("to take"), but it is easily spelled out in a full content sentence, as in "I intend that I take the ten o'clock train to New York tomorrow." In any case, these states are closely related to actions. When I intend to raise my arm *now*, I must *now* undertake to raise my arm; when you intend, or decide, to do something, you commit yourself to doing it. You must be prepared not only to take the necessary steps toward doing it but also to initiate them at an appropriate time. This is not to say that you cannot change your mind, or that you will necessarily succeed; it is to say that you need to change your intention to be released from the commitment to action. According to some philosophers, all intentional actions must be preceded by an act of volition.

Actions typically involve motions of our bodies, but they do not seem to be mere bodily motions. My arm is going up, and so is yours. However, you are raising your arm, but I am not—my arm is being pulled up by someone else. The raising of your arm is an action; it is something you do. But the rising of my arm is not an action; it is not something that I do but something that happens to me. There appears to be something mental about your raising your arm that is absent from the mere rising of an arm; perhaps it is the involvement of your desire, or intention, to raise your arm, but exactly what distinguishes actions from "mere bodily motions" has been a matter of philosophical dispute. Or consider something like buying a loaf of bread. Evidently someone who can engage in the act of buying a loaf of bread must have certain appropriate beliefs and desires; she must, for example, have a desire to buy bread, or at least a desire to buy something (for you could buy a loaf of bread by mistake, thinking that it is something else that you wanted). And to do something like buying, you must have knowledge, or beliefs, about what constitutes buying rather than, say, borrowing or simply taking, about money and exchange of goods, and so on. That is to say, only creatures with beliefs and desires and an understanding of appropriate social conventions and institutions can engage in activities like buying and selling. The same goes for much of what we do as social beings; actions like promising, greeting, and apologizing presuppose a rich and complex background of beliefs, desires, and intentions, as well as an understanding of social relationships and arrangements.

There are other items that are ordinarily included under the rubric of "psychological," such as traits of character and personality (being honest, obsessive, witty, introverted), habits and propensities (being industrious, punctual), intellectual abilities, artistic talents, and the like. But we can consider them to be mental in an indirect or derivative sense: Honesty is a mental characteristic because it is a tendency, or disposition, to form desires of certain sorts (for example, the desire to tell the truth, or not to mislead others) and to act in appropriate ways (in particular, saying only what you sincerely believe).

In the chapters to follow, we focus on sensations and intentional states. They provide us with examples of mental states when we discuss the mind-body problem and other issues. We also discuss some specific philosophical problems about these two principal types of mental states. We will largely bypass detailed questions, however, such as what types of mental states there are, how they are interrelated, and the like.

But in what sense are all these variegated items "mental" or "psychological"? Is there some single property or feature, or a reasonably simple and perspicuous set of them, by virtue of which they all count as mental?

Is There a "Mark of the Mental"?

Various characteristics have been proposed by philosophers to serve as a "mark of the mental," a criterion that would separate mental phenomena or properties from those that are not mental. Each has a certain degree of plausibility and can be seen to cover a range of mental phenomena, but as we will see, none seems to be adequate for all the diverse kinds of events and states, functions and capacities, that we normally classify as "mental" or "psychological." Although we do not try to formulate our own criterion of the mental, a review of some of the prominent proposals will give us an understanding of the principal ideas traditionally associated with the concept of mentality and highlight some of the important characteristics of mental phenomena, even if, as noted, no single one of them seems capable of serving as a universal, necessary and sufficient condition of mentality.

Epistemological Criteria

You are experiencing a sharp toothache caused by an exposed nerve in a molar. The toothache that you experience, but not the condition of your molar, is a mental occurrence. But what is the basis of this distinction? One influential answer says that the distinction consists in certain fundamental differences in the way you come to have *knowledge* of the two phenomena.

Direct or Immediate Knowledge.   Your knowledge that you have a toothache, or that you are hoping for rain tomorrow, is "direct" or "immediate"; it is not based on evidence or inference. There is no other thing that you know or need to know from which you infer that you have a toothache; that is, your knowledge is not mediated by other beliefs or knowledge. This is seen in the fact that in cases like this the question "How do you know?" seems to be out of place ("How do you know you are hoping for rain and not snow?"). The only possible answer, if you take the question seriously, is that you *just* know. This shows that here the question of "evidence" is inappropriate: Your knowledge is direct and immediate, not based on evidence. Yet your knowledge of the physical condition of your tooth is based on evidence: That kind of knowledge is often based on the testimonial evidence provided by a third party, for example, your dentist. And your dentist's knowledge presumably depends on the evidence of X-ray pictures, visual inspection of your teeth, and so on. The question "How do you know that you have an exposed nerve in a molar?" makes good sense and can be given an informative answer.

But isn't our knowledge of certain simple physical facts just as "direct" and "immediate" as knowledge of mental events like toothaches and itches? Suppose you are looking at a large red circle painted on a wall directly in front of you: Doesn't it seem that you would know, directly and without the use of any further evidence, that there is a round red patch in front of you? Don't I know, in the same way, that here is a piece of white paper in front of me or that there is a tree just outside my window?

Privacy, or First-Person Privilege.　　One possible response to the foregoing challenge is to invoke the privacy of our knowledge of our own mental states, namely, the apparent fact that this direct access to a mental event is enjoyed by a single subject, the person to whom the event is occurring. In the case of the toothache, it is only you, not your dentist or anyone else, who is in this kind of specially privileged position. But this does not hold in the case of seeing the red patch. If you can know "directly" that there is a round red spot on the wall, so can I and anyone else who is suitably situated in relation to the wall. There is no single person with a specially privileged epistemic access to the round red spot. In this sense, knowledge of certain mental events exhibits an *asymmetry* between first person and third person, but knowledge of physical states shows no such asymmetry. Moreover, this asymmetry holds only for knowledge of *current* mental occurrences, not for knowledge of *past* ones: You know that you had a toothache yesterday, a week ago, or two years ago, from the evidence of memory, an entry in your diary, your dental record, and the like.

But what about those bodily states we are said to detect through "proprioception," such as the positions of our limbs and the spatial orientation of our bodies (for example, knowing whether your legs are crossed or whether you are lying down or standing)? Our proprioceptive sense organs and associated neural machinery are in the business of keeping us *directly* informed of certain physical conditions of our bodies, and proprioception is, in general, highly reliable. Moreover, first-person privilege seems to hold for such cases: It is only I who know, through proprioception, that my right knee is bent; no third party has similar access to this fact. And yet it is knowledge of a bodily condition, not of a mental occurrence. Perhaps this counterexample could be handled by appealing to the following criterion.

Infallibility and Transparency (Self-Intimacy).　　Another epistemic feature sometimes associated with mentality is the idea that in some sense your knowledge of your own current mental states is "infallible" or "incorrigible," or that it is "self-intimating" (or that your mind is "transparent" to you). The main idea is that mental events—especially events like pains and other sensations—have the following property: You cannot be mistaken about whether or not you are experiencing them. That is, if you *believe* that you are in pain, then it follows that you *are* in pain, and if you believe that you are not in pain, then you are not; it is not possible to have false beliefs about your own pains. In this sense, your knowledge of your own pain is *infallible*. So-called psychosomatic pains are pains nonetheless. The same may hold for your knowledge of your own propositional attitudes like belief; Descartes famously said that you cannot be mistaken about the fact that you doubt, or that you think.[4] In contrast, when your belief concerns a physical occurrence, there is no guarantee that your belief is true: Your belief that you have a decayed molar may be true, but its truth is not entailed by the mere fact that you believe it. Or so goes the claim, at any rate. Returning briefly to knowledge gained through proprioception, the reply would be that such knowledge may be reliable but not infallible; there can be incorrect beliefs about your bodily position based on proprioception.

"Self-intimacy" is the converse of infallibility: A state or event *m* is said to be "self-intimating" to a person just in case, necessarily, if *m* occurs, the person is aware that *m* occurs—that is, she knows that *m* occurs.[5] The claim, then, is that mental events are self-intimating to the subjects to whom they occur. If pains are self-intimating in this sense, there could not be *hidden* pains—pains that the subject is unaware of. Just as the infallibility of beliefs about your own pains implies that pains with no physiological cause are at least conceivable, the self-intimating character of pain would imply that even if all normal physical and physiological causes of pain are present, if you are not aware of any pain, then you are not in pain. There are reports about soldiers in combat and athletes in the heat of competition that they experienced no pain in spite of severe physical injuries; if we assume pains are self-intimating, we would have to conclude that pain, as a mental event, is not occurring to these subjects. We may define "the doctrine of the transparency of mind" as the joint claim that our knowledge of our own mental occurrences is infallible and that all our mental occurrences are self-intimating. On this doctrine, the mind is a totally transparent medium, but only to a single person. This is a doctrine often associated with the traditional conception of the mind, especially Descartes'.

Infallibility and self-intimacy are extremely strong properties. It would be no surprise if physical events and states did not have them; a more interesting question is whether all or even most mental events satisfy them. Evidently, not all mental events or states have these special epistemic properties. In the first place, it is now commonplace to speak of "unconscious" or "subconscious" beliefs, desires, and emotions, like repressed desires and angers—psychological states that the subject is not aware of and would even vehemently deny having but that evidently shape and influence his overt behavior. Second, it is not always easy for us to determine whether an emotion that we are experiencing is, say, one of embarrassment, remorse, or regret—or one of envy, jealousy, or anger. And we are often not sure whether we "really" believe or desire something. Do I believe that globalization is a good thing? Do I believe that I am by and large a nice person? Do I want to be popular and gregarious, or do I want to be seen as somewhat aloof and distant? If you reflect on such questions, you may not be sure what the answers are. It is not as though you have suspended judgment about them—you may not even know *that*. Epistemic uncertainties can happen with sensations as well. Does this overripe avocado smell a little like a rotten egg, or is it okay for the salad? Special epistemic access is perhaps most plausible for sensations like pains and itches, but here again, not all our beliefs about pains appear to have the special authoritative character indicated by the epistemic properties we have surveyed. Is the pain I am now experiencing more intense than the pain I felt a moment ago in the same elbow? Just where in my elbow is the pain? Clearly there are many characteristics of pains, even introspectively identifiable ones, about which I could be mistaken and feel uncertain.

It is also thought that you can misclassify, or misidentify, the type of sensation you are experiencing: for example, you may report that you are itchy in the shoulder when the correct description would be that you have a ticklish sensation there. However, it is not clear just what such cases show. It might be replied, for example, that the error is a verbal one, not one of belief. Although you are using the sentence "My left shoulder is itchy" to report your belief, your belief *is* to the effect that your left shoulder tickles, and this belief, you might claim, is true.

Thus, exactly how the special epistemic character of mental events is to be characterized can be a complex and controversial business, and unsurprisingly there is no agreement in this area. There are some philosophers, especially those who are physicalistically minded, who would take pains to minimize these prima facie differences between mental and bodily events. But it is apparent that there are important epistemological differences between the mental and the nonmental, however these differences are to be precisely described. Especially important is the first-person epistemic authority noted earlier: We seem to have special access to our own mental states—or at least to an important subclass of them if not all of them. Our knowledge of our own minds may fall short of infallibility or incorrigibility, and it seems beyond doubt that our minds are not wholly transparent to us. But the differences we have noted, even if they are not quite the way described, do seem to point to a crucial qualitative difference between what is physical and an important subclass of the mental. It may well be that we get our initial purchase on the concept of mentality through the core class of mental states for which some form of special first-person authority holds and that we derive the broader class of mental phenomena by extending and generalizing this core in various ways.[6]

Mentality as Nonspatial

For Descartes, the essential nature of a mind is that it is a thinking thing ("res cogitans"), and the essential nature of a material thing is that it is a spatially extended thing. A corollary of this, for Descartes, is that the mental is essentially nonspatial and the material is essentially lacking in the capacity for thinking. Most physicalists would reject this corollary even if they accept the thesis that the mental is definable as thinking. But there may be a way of developing the idea that the mental is nonspatial that leaves the question of physicalism open.

For example, we might attempt something like this: To say that M is a mental property is to say that the proposition that something, x, has M *does not imply* that x is spatially extended ("spatial" for short). This is consistent with saying that anything that has M is in fact a spatial thing; that is, the notion of mentality does not *require* that anything with mentality be a spatially extended material thing, although *as a matter of contingent fact*, all things that have any mental property are spatially extended things, like humans and other biological organisms.

Thus, from the proposition that something x believes that 4 is an even number, it does not seem to follow that x is a spatially extended thing. There may be no immaterial angels in this world, but it seems at least logically consistent to say that there are angels and that angels have beliefs as well as perhaps other mental states, like desires and hopes. But it evidently is a contradiction to say that something has a physical property—say, the color red, a triangular shape, or a rough texture—and at the same time to deny that it has spatial extensions. What about being located at a geometric point? Or *being* a geometric point for that matter? But no physical *thing* is a geometric point; geometric points are not physical objects, and no physical object has the property of being a point or being located wholly at a point in space.

But what of *abstract objects* such as numbers and propositions? Take the property of being divisible by 4. The number 16 has it, but no number is spatially extended; numbers, if they exist, are not in physical space at all. To take account of numbers, propositions, and other abstracta, we may simply exclude them from the criterion as follows: Property M is a mental property just in case the proposition that x has M, where x is not an abstract object, does not logically entail that x is spatially extended.

Perhaps there are other complications that call for further adjustments. But how useful is this general approach toward a mark of the mental? It would seem that if you take this approach seriously, you must also take the idea of mental substance seriously. For you must allow the existence of possible worlds in which mental properties are instantiated by nonphysical beings (beings without spatial extension). The reasoning leading to this conclusion is straightforward: Any mental property M is such that something can instantiate M without being spatially extended—that is, without being a physical thing. So apparently M can be instantiated even if there is no physical thing. That is, there is a possible world in which mental properties are instantiated even though no physical things exist. Since it makes no sense to think of abstract entities, like numbers, as subjects of mental properties, the only remaining possibility is Cartesian mental substances. Thus, anyone who accepts the criterion of the mental as nonspatial must accept the idea of mental substance as a coherent one, an idea that makes sense. This means that if you have qualms about the coherence of the Cartesian conception of minds as pure mental substances, you should be very cautious about the nonspatiality criterion of mentality (see chapter 2).

Intentionality as a Criterion of the Mental

Schliemann sought the site of Troy. He was fortunate; he found it. Ponce de León sought the fountain of youth, but he never found it. He could not have found it, since it does not exist and never did. It remains true, though, that he looked for the fountain of youth. The nonexistence of Bigfoot or the Loch Ness Monster has not prevented people from looking for them. Not only can you *look for* something that in fact does not exist, but you can apparently also *believe in, think of, write about,* and even *worship* a nonexistent object. Even if God should not exist, he could be, and has been, the object of these mental acts or attitudes on the part of many people. Contrast these mental acts and states with physical ones, like cutting, kicking, and being to the left of. You cannot cut a nonexistent piece of wood, kick nonexistent tires, or be to the left of a nonexistent tree. That you kick something x logically entails that x exists. That you are thinking of x does not entail the existence of x. Or so it seems.

The Austrian philosopher Franz Brentano called this feature "the intentional inexistence" of psychological phenomena, claiming that it is this characteristic that separates the mental from the physical. In an often quoted passage, he wrote:

> Every mental phenomenon is characterized by what the Scholastics of the Middle Ages called the intentional (or mental) inexistence of an object, and what we might call, though not wholly unambiguously, reference to a content, direction toward an object (which is not to be understood here as meaning a thing), or immanent objectivity. Every mental phenomenon includes something as object within itself, although they do not all do so in the same way. In presentation something is presented, in judgement something is affirmed or denied, in love loved, in hate hated, in desire desired and so on.[7]

This feature of the mental—namely, that mental states are about, or are directed upon, objects that may not exist or contents that may be false—has been called "intentionality."

The concept of intentionality may be subdivided into *referential intentionality* and *content intentionality*. Referential intentionality concerns the "aboutness" or reference of our thoughts, beliefs, intentions, and the like. When Ludwig Wittgenstein asked, "What makes my image of him into an image of *him*?"[8] he was asking for an explanation of what makes it the case that a given mental state (my "image of him") is *about*, or *refers to*, a particular object—him—rather than someone else. (That person may have an identical twin, and your image may fit his twin just as well, perhaps even better, but your image is of him, not of his twin. You may not even know that he has a twin.) Our words, too, refer to, or are directed upon, objects; "Mount Everest" refers to Mount Everest, and "horse" refers to horses.

Content intentionality concerns the fact that, as we saw, an important class of mental states—that is, propositional attitudes such as beliefs, hopes, and intentions—have contents or meanings, which are often expressed by full sentences. It is in virtue of having contents that our mental states *represent* states of affairs both inside us and in the external world. My perceiving that there are flowers in the field represents the fact, or state of affairs, of there being flowers in the field, and your remembering that there was a thunderstorm last night represents the state of affairs of there having been a thunderstorm last night. The capacity of our mental states to represent things external to them—that is, the fact that they have *representational content*—is clearly a very important fact about them. It is because we have mental states with the capacity to represent that we can have knowledge. For on a standard account, having knowledge is a matter of having mental representations with true contents—that is, representations that correctly represent.

But can intentionality be taken as the mark of the mental? There are at least two apparent difficulties. The first is that some mental phenomena—in particular, sensations like pains and tickles—do not seem to exhibit either kind of intentionality. The sensation of pain does not seem to be "about," or to refer to, anything; nor does it have a content in the way that beliefs and intentions do. Doesn't the pain in my knee "mean," or "represent," the fact that I have strained the torn ligament in the knee again? But the sense of "meaning" involved here seems something like causal indication; the pain "means" a damaged ligament in the same sense in which your nice new suntan means that you spent the weekend on the beach. Some philosophers have recently advanced the view that all states of consciousness, including sensations, are representational (we discuss this approach in chapter 8). In any case, there seem to be mental states that are not unproblematically characterized by either type of intentionality. Second, it may be argued that mental states are not the only things that exhibit intentionality. In particular, words and sentences can refer to things and have content and meaning. The word "London" refers to London, and the sentence "London is large" refers to, or represents, the fact, or state of affairs, that London is large. A string of 0s and 1s in a computer data structure can mean your name and address, and such strings are ultimately electronic states of a physical system. If these physical items and states are capable of reference and content, how can intentionality be considered an exclusive property of mentality?

The following line of reply seems open, however. As some have argued, we might distinguish between *genuine*, or *intrinsic*, intentionality, which our minds and mental states have, and *make-believe*, or *derived*, intentionality, which we attribute to objects and states that do not have intentionality in their own right.[9] When I say that my computer printer "likes" to work with Windows but not with the Mac OS, I am not really saying that my printer has likes and dislikes. It is at best an "as-if" or metaphorical use of language, and no one will take my statement to imply the presence of mentality in the machine. And it is not implausible to argue that the word "London" refers to London only because language users use the word to refer to London. If we used it to refer to Paris, it would mean Paris, not London. Or if the inscription "London" were not a word in a language, it would just be meaningless scribbles with no referential function. Similarly, the sentence "London is large" represents the state of affairs it represents only because speakers of English use this sentence to represent that state of affairs—for example, in affirming this sentence, they express the belief that London is large. The point, then, is that the intentionality of language depends on, and is derived from, the intentionality of language users and their mental processes. It is the latter that have intrinsic intentionality, intentionality that is not derived from, or borrowed from, anything else. Or so we could argue.[10]

A second and perhaps more direct reply may go as follows: To the extent that some physical systems can be said to refer to things, represent states of affairs, and have meanings, they should be considered as exhibiting mentality and be dealt with on that basis. No doubt, as the first reply indicates, analogical or metaphorical uses of intentional idioms abound, but this fact should not blind us to the possibility that physical systems and their states possess genuine intentionality and hence mentality. After all, some would argue, we too are complex physical systems, and the physical-biological states of our brains are capable of referring to things and states of affairs external to them and of storing their representations in memory. Of course, it may turn out not to be possible for purely physical states to have such capabilities, but that would only show that they are not capable of mentality. It remains true, the reply goes, that intentionality is at least a sufficient condition for mentality.

A Puzzle

In surveying these candidates for "the mark of the mental," we realize that our notion of the mental is far from unified and monolithic and that it is in fact a cluster of many ideas. Some of the ideas are fairly closely related to one another, but others appear independent of each other. (Why should there be a connection between special epistemic access and nonspatiality?) The diversity and possible lack of unity in our conception of the mental imply that the class of things and their states that we classify as mental is also likely to be a varied and heterogeneous lot. It is standardly thought that there are two broad categories of mental phenomena: sensory or qualitative states (those with qualia), like pains and sensings of colors and textures, and intentional states, like beliefs, desires, and intentions. The former seem to be paradigm cases of states that satisfy the epistemic criteria of the mental, such as direct access and privacy, and the latter are the prime examples of mental states that satisfy the intentionality criterion. A question to which we do not as yet have an answer is this: In virtue of *what common property* are both sensory states and intentional states "mental"?[11] What do our pains and beliefs have in common in virtue of which they fall under the single rubric of "mental phenomena"? They of course satisfy the disjunctive property "qualitative or intentional," but that would be like trying to find a commonality between red and round by saying that both red things and round things satisfy "red or round." To the extent that we lack a satisfying answer to this question we fail to have a unitary conception of what mentality consists in.

Further Readings

Readers interested in issues of cognitive science may consult Barbara von Eckardt, *What Is Cognitive Science?*; Robert M. Harnish, *Minds, Brains, Computers: The Foundations of Cognitive Science*; or Paul Thagard, *Mind: Introduction to Cognitive Science*. Also useful are two anthologies: *Minds, Brains, and Computers*, edited by Denise Dellarosa Cummins and Robert Cummins, and *Readings in Philosophy and Cognitive Science*, edited by Alvin Goldman.

Readers will also find the following reference works useful; *A Companion to Philosophy of Mind*, edited by Samuel Guttenplan; *The Oxford Handbook of Philosophy of Mind*, edited by Brian McLaughlin and Ansgar Beckermann; and *The MIT Encyclopedia of the Cognitive Sciences*, edited by Robert A. Wilson and Frank C. Keil. The following general encyclopedias of philosophy include many fine articles (some with extensive bibliographies) on topics in philosophy of mind and related philosophical fields: *Stanford Encyclopedia of Philosophy* (http://plato.stanford.edu/); *Macmillan Encyclopedia of Philosophy*, second edition, edited by Donald Borchert; and *Routledge Encyclopedia of Philosophy*, edited by Edward Craig.

There are many good general anthologies of writings on philosophy of mind. To mention a sample: *Philosophy of Mind: Classical and Contemporary Readings*, edited by David J. Chalmers; *Problems in Mind*, edited by Jack S. Crumley II; *Philosophy of Mind: A Guide and Anthology*, edited by John Heil; *Mind and Cognition*, second edition, edited by William G. Lycan; *Philosophy of Mind: Contemporary Readings*, edited by Timothy O'Connor and David Robb; and *The Nature of Mind*, edited by David M. Rosenthal.

Notes

1. For details see Brian McLaughlin, "Varieties of Supervenience."

2. Sometimes this version of supervenience is formulated as follows: "Any minimal physical duplicate of this world is a duplicate *simpliciter* of this world." See, for example, Frank Jackson, "Finding the Mind in the Natural World." The point of the qualifier "minimal" is to exclude the following kind of situation: Consider a world that is like ours in all physical respects but in addition contains ectoplasms and immaterial spirits. (We are assuming these things do not exist in the actual world.) There is a sense in which this world and our world are physically alike, but they are clearly not alike overall. A case like this is ruled out by the qualifier "minimal" because this strange world is not a minimal physical duplicate of our world.

3. Nonreductive physicalism as standardly understood also includes mind-body supervenience; property dualism as such is not committed to supervenience. See chapter 10.

4. René Descartes, *Meditations on First Philosophy*, Meditation II.

5. This is so because the belief is guaranteed true and there seems to be no question about the person's entitlement to such a belief.

6. It is worth noting that cognitive scientists are in general quite skeptical about our having specially privileged access to the contents of our minds. See, for example, Alison Gopnik, "How We Know Our Minds: The Illusion of First-Person Knowledge of Intentionality."

7. Franz Brentano, *Psychology from an Empirical Standpoint*, p. 88.

8. Ludwig Wittgenstein, *Philosophical Investigations*, p. 177.

9. See, for example, John Searle, *Intentionality* and *The Rediscovery of the Mind*.

10. This point has been disputed. Other possible positions are these: First, we might hold that linguistic intentionality is in fact prior to the intentionality of mental states, the latter deriving from the former (Wilfrid Sellars); second, the two types of intentionality are distinct but interdependent, neither being prior to the other and neither being derivable from the other (Donald Davidson); and third, the very distinction between "intrinsic" and "derived" intentionality is bogus and incoherent (Daniel C. Dennett).

11. Philosophers who take sensory states as essentially representational have a potential answer: All mental states are representational, and this is what makes them all mental. We discuss the representational view of sensory states in chapter 8.

2

Substance Dualism

What is it for something to "have a mind," or "have mentality"? When the ancients reflected on the contrast between us and mindless creatures, they sometimes described the difference in terms of having a "soul." For example, according to Plato, each of us has a soul that is simple, divine, and immutable, unlike our bodies, which are composite and perishable. In fact, before we were born into this world, our souls preexisted in a pure, disembodied state, and on Plato's doctrine of recollection, what we call "learning" is merely a process of recollecting what we already knew in our prenatal existence as pure souls. Bodies are merely vehicles of our existence in this earthly world, a transitory stage in our soul's eternal journey. The general idea, then, is that because each of us has a soul, we are the kind of conscious, intelligent, and rational creature that we are. Strictly speaking, we do not really "have" souls, since we are in an important sense *identical with* our souls—that is, each of us *is* a soul. My soul is the thing that I am. Each of us "has a mind," therefore, because each of us *is* a mind.

All that is probably a bit too speculative, if not totally fantastical, for most of us to swallow. However, many of us seem to accept, or to have internalized, a kind of mind-body dualism according to which, although each of us has a body that is fully material, we also have a mental or spiritual dimension that no "mere" material things can have. When we see the term "material,"

29

we are apt to think "not mental" or "not spiritual," and when we see the term "mental," we tend to think "not material" or "not physical." This does not amount to a clearly delineated perspective or point of view, but it seems fair to say that some such dualism of the mental and the material is entrenched in our ordinary thinking and that dualism is a kind of "folk" theory of our nature as creatures with minds.

But folk dualism often goes beyond a mere duality of mental and physical events and processes. It is part of folklore in many cultures and of most established and developed religions that, as Plato claimed, each of us has a soul, or spirit, that survives bodily death and decay and that we are really our souls, not our bodies, in that when we die we continue to exist in virtue of the fact that our souls continue to exist. Your soul defines your identity as an individual person; as long as it exists—and only so long as it exists—you exist. And it is our souls in which our mentality inheres; thoughts, consciousness, rational will, and other mental events, functions, and capacities belong to souls, not to material bodies. Ultimately, to have a mind, or to be a creature with mentality, is to have a soul.

In this chapter, we examine a philosophical theory of mind, due to René Descartes, which is built on a view of this kind. One caveat before we begin: Our goal here is not so much a historical exegesis of Descartes as it is an examination of a point of view often associated with him; as with other great philosophers, the interpretation of what he "really" said, or meant to say, continues to be controversial. For this reason, the dualist view of the mind we discuss is better regarded as Cartesian rather than as the historical Descartes'.

Cartesian Dualism

The dualist view of persons that Descartes formulated and defended is a form of substance dualism. Substance dualism is the thesis that there are substances of two fundamentally and irreducibly distinct kinds in this world, namely, minds and bodies—or mental stuff and material stuff—and that a human person is a composite entity consisting of a mind and a body, each of which is an entity in its own right. Dualism of this form contrasts with monism, according to which all things in the world are substances of one kind. We later encounter various forms of material monism that claim that our world is fundamentally material, consisting only of bits of matter and complex structures exclusively made up of bits of matter, all behaving in accordance with physical laws. This is materialism or physicalism. (These terms are often used interchangeably, although there are subtle differences: We may think of physicalism as a modern version of materialism—materialism informed by modern physics.) There is also a mental version of monism, somewhat uninformatively called "idealism." This is the view that minds, or mental items at any rate ("ideas"), constitute the fundamental reality of the world and that material things are mere constructs out of thoughts and other mental experiences. This form of monism has not been very much in evidence for some time, though there are reputable philosophers who still defend it.[1] We will not be further concerned with mental monism in this book.

So substance dualism claims that minds and bodies are two different sorts of substance. But what is a substance? Traditionally, two ideas have been closely associated with the concept of a substance. First, a substance is something in which properties "inhere"; that is, it is what has, or exemplifies, properties.[2] Consider this vase on my table. It is something that has a weight, shape, color, and volume; it has further properties like fragility and beauty. But a substance is not in turn something that other things can exemplify or have as a property. Linguistically, this idea is sometimes expressed by saying that a substance is the subject of predication, something to which we can attribute predicates like "red," "heavy," and "fragile," whereas it cannot in turn be predicated of anything else.

Second, and this is more important for us, a substance is thought to be something that has the capacity for independent existence.[3] What does this mean? Consider the vase and the pencil holder to its right. Both are substances in that either can exist without the other existing. In fact, we could conceive of a world in which only the vase (with all its constituent parts) exists and nothing else, and a world in which only the pencil holder exists and nothing else. It is in that sense that a substance is capable of independent existence. This means that if my mind is a substance, it can exist without any body existing, or any other mind existing. There seems to be a further sense in which a substance is an independent existent. Consider the vase again: There is an intuitively intelligible sense in which its color and shape cannot exist apart from the vase, whereas the vase is something that exists in its own right. (The color and shape would be "modes" that belong to the vase.) The same seems to hold when we compare the vase and its surface. Surfaces are "dependent entities," as we might say; their existence depends on the existence of the objects of which they are surfaces, whereas an object could exist without the particular surface it has at a given time. As we noted, there is a possible world of which the vase is the sole inhabitant. Compare the evidently absurd claim that there is a possible world in which the surface of the vase exists but nothing else; in fact, there is no possible world in which only surfaces exist and nothing else. For surfaces to exist they must be surfaces of some objects—existing objects.[4]

Thus, the thesis that minds are substances implies that minds are objects, or things, in their own right, just like material objects. They have properties and engage in activities of various sorts, like thinking, sensing, judging, and willing. Most importantly, they are capable of independent existence, and this means that there is a possible world in which only minds exist and nothing else. That is to say, on the further Cartesian thesis that minds are not identical with material things, minds could exist even if no material thing existed—there is a possible world in which only minds, and no material bodies, exist. So my mind, as a substance, can exist apart from my body, and so of course could your mind even if your body perished.

Let us then put down these major tenets of Cartesian substance dualism (there is more to come):

1. There are substances of two fundamentally different kinds in the world, minds and bodies. The essential nature of a body is to be extended in space; the essence of a mind is to think and engage in other mental activities.
2. A human person is a composite being ("union," as Descartes called it) of a mind and a body.
3. Minds are diverse from bodies; no mind is identical with a body.

What distinguishes Descartes' philosophy of mind from the positions of many of his contemporaries, including Leibniz, Malebranche, and Spinoza, is his eminently commonsensical claim that minds and bodies are in causal interaction with each other. When we perform a voluntary action, the mind causes the body to move in appropriate ways, as when my desire for water causes my hand to reach for a glass of water. To see a tree, the tree must cause in us a visual experience as of a tree; that is the difference between seeing a tree and merely imagining or hallucinating one. Thus, we have the following thesis of mind-body causal interaction:

4. Minds and bodies causally influence each other. Some mental phenomena are causes of physical phenomena and vice versa.

The only way we can influence the objects and events around us, as far as we know, is first to move our limbs or vocal cords in appropriate ways and thereby start a chain of events culminating in the effects we desire—like opening a window, retrieving the cat from the roof, or starting a war. But as we will see, it is this most plausible thesis of mind-body causal interaction that brought down Cartesian dualism. The question was not whether the interactionist thesis was in itself acceptable; rather, the main question was whether it was compatible with the radical dualism of minds and bodies— that is, whether minds and bodies, sundered apart by the dualist thesis (3), could be brought together in causal interaction as claimed in (4).

Arguments for the Thesis That Minds and Bodies Are Distinct

Before we consider the supposed difficulties for Descartes' interactionist dualism, let us first consider arguments that seem to favor the dualist thesis that minds are substances distinct from bodies. The arguments we consider are Cartesian—some of them perhaps only vaguely so—in the sense that most of them can be traced one way or another to Descartes' *Second* and *Sixth Meditations* and that all are at least Cartesian in spirit. It is not claimed, however, that these are in fact the arguments that Descartes offered or that they were among the considerations that moved Descartes to advocate substance dualism. You might want to know first of all why anyone would think of minds as substances—why we should countenance minds as entities in addition to people and creatures with mentality. As we will see, some of the arguments do address this issue, though not directly.

At the outset of his *Second Meditation*, Descartes offers his famous "cogito" argument. As every student of philosophy knows, the argument goes "I think, therefore I am." This inference convinces him that he can be absolutely certain about his own existence; his existence is one perfectly indubitable bit of knowledge he has, or so he is led to think. Now that he knows he exists, he wonders what kind of thing he is, asking, "But what then am I?" A good question! Descartes answers: "A thinking thing" ("sum res cogitans"). How does he know that? Because he has proved his existence from the premise that he thinks; it is through his knowledge of himself as something that thinks that he knows that he exists. To get on with his dualist arguments we will grant him the metaphysical point that if there is thinking, there must be some thing that does the thinking. So we are granting him the proposition that he is a thinking thing. The main issue for him, and for us, is the question whether the thinking thing can be his body—that is, why we should not take his body as the thing that does the thinking.

We first consider two arguments based on epistemological considerations. The simplest—perhaps a bit simplistic—argument of this form would be something like this:

Argument 1

I am such that my existence cannot be doubted.
My body is not such that its existence cannot be doubted.
Therefore, I am not identical with my body.
Therefore, the thinking thing that I am is not identical with my body.

This argument is based on the supposed asymmetry between knowledge of one's own existence and knowledge of one's body: While I cannot doubt that I exist, I can doubt that my body exists. We could also put the point this way: I know immediately and directly that I exist as a thinking thing, but my knowledge that my body exists, or that I have a body, is not direct and immediate in the same sense. I must make observations to know that I have a body—a body of the kind that I have.

What does Descartes mean by "thinking"? He says that a thinking thing is "a thing that doubts, understands, affirms, denies, is willing, is unwilling, and also imagines and has sensory perceptions."[5] For Descartes, "thinking" is a generic term, roughly meaning "mental activity," and specific mental states and activities, like believing, doubting, affirming, sensing a color, hearing a sound, or thinking in narrower senses, fall under the broad rubric of thinking. Or in Descartes' own terms, thinking is the general essence of minds and the specific kinds of mental activities and states are its various "modes." Our second epistemological argument attempts to exploit the widely acknowledged epistemological asymmetry between our knowledge of our own minds and our knowledge of our bodies.

Argument 2

My mind is transparent to me—that is, nothing can be in my mind
    without my knowing that it is there.
My body is not transparent to me in the same sense.
Therefore, my mind is not identical with my body.

As stated, the first premise is quite strong and likely not to be generally true. Most of us would accept the view that at least some of our beliefs, desires, and emotions are beyond our cognitive reach—that is, that there are "unconscious" or "subconscious" mental states (beliefs and desires, angers and resentments) of which the subject is not aware. But for this argument the premise could be stated in a weaker form, to the effect that my mind is transparent at least with respect to *some* of the events that occur in it. This weaker premise suffices as long as we understand the second premise as asserting that *none* of my bodily events have this "self-intimating" character. To find out any fact about my body, I must make observations and sometimes make inferences from the evidence gained through observations. Often a third person —my physician or dentist—is in a better position to know the conditions of my body than I am. We can safely say that what I know about my body is an infinitesimally small fraction of the totality of facts about my body.

We now consider our last epistemological argument for substance dualism:

Argument 3

Each mind is such that there is a unique subject who has direct and privileged access to its contents.

No material body has a specially privileged knower—knowledge of material things is in principle public and intersubjective.

Therefore, minds are not identical with material bodies.

This argument makes use of a related epistemological asymmetry between minds and bodies—the supposed privacy and subjectivity of knowledge of the former and the intersubjectivity of knowledge of the latter.

What should we think of these arguments? We will not formulate and discuss specific objections to them; that is left to the reader. But one observation is in order: It is widely believed that there is a problem with using epistemic (or more broadly, "intentional") properties to differentiate things. To show that X ≠ Y, it is necessary and sufficient to come up with a property P such that X has P but Y lacks it, or Y has P but X lacks it. Such a property P can be called a *differential property* for X and Y. The question, then, is whether epistemic properties, like being known with certainty (or an intentional property like being believed to be such-and-such), can be used as a differential property. Consider the property of being known to the police to be the hit-and-run driver. The man who sped away in a black SUV is known to the police to be the hit-and-run driver. The man who drove away in a black SUV is identical with my neighbor, and yet my neighbor is not known to the police to be the hit-and-run driver (or else the police would have him in custody already). The epistemic properties invoked in the foregoing three arguments are not the same—or exactly of the same sort—as the one just used. But the reader is invited to examine the arguments in light of this and similar examples.

We now turn to metaphysical arguments, which instead of appealing to epistemic differences between minds and bodies attempt to invoke real metaphysical differences between them. Throughout the *Second* and *Sixth Meditations*, there is a constant reference to the essence of mind as thinking (and something unextended) and the essence of body as being extended in space. By extension in space Descartes means three-dimensional extension, that is, bulk. Surfaces or geometric lines do not count as material substances; only things that have a bulk count as material substances. Perhaps an argument could be formulated in terms of essences or essential natures, like this:

Argument 4

My essential nature is to be a thinking thing.
My body's essential nature is to be an extended thing in space.
My essential nature does not include being an extended thing in space.
Therefore, I am not identical with my body. And since I am a thinking
    thing (namely a mind), my mind is not identical with my body.

How could the first and third premises be defended? Perhaps a Cartesian dualist could make two points in defense of the first premise. First, as the "cogito" argument shows, I know that I exist solely as a thinking thing, and this means that my existence is inseparably tied to the fact that I am a thinking thing. An essential nature of something is a property without which the thing cannot exist; when something loses its essential nature, that is when it ceases to exist. Second, on this understanding of essential nature, being a thinking thing is my essential nature; when I cease to be a thinking thing, that is when I cease to be. On the other hand, I can "clearly and distinctly" conceive of myself as existing without a body; there is no inherent incoherence, or contradiction, in the idea of my disembodied existence. Hence, being an extended object in space is not part of my essential nature.

This argument has some weak points, which at least need strengthening. For one thing, the argument seems to need a stronger first premise, to the effect that thinking is my *whole* essence. For another, it seems to move too quickly from the statement that a state of affairs (for example, my disembodied existence) is *conceivable* to the conclusion that it could really be so. The second point can lead—and has led—to an extended series of considerations too complex to enter into here.[6] We should note, though, that something like this assumption—to the effect that conceivability is the best guide to possibility—is difficult to avoid when we try to formulate arguments based on considerations of what is possible and what is not, of what is necessarily the case and what is only contingently so.

Let us say that something is "essentially" or "necessarily" F, where F denotes a property, just in case whenever or wherever (in any "possible" world) it exists, it must be F. In the terminology of the preceding paragraph, for something to have property, F essentially or necessarily is to have F as part of its essential nature. Consider, then, the following argument:

Argument 5

If anything is material, it is essentially material.

However, I am possibly immaterial—that is, there is a world in which I exist without a body.

Hence, I am not essentially material.

Hence, it follows (with the first premise) that I am not material.

This is an interesting argument. There seems to be a lot to be said for the first premise. Take something material, say, a bronze bust of Beethoven: This object could perhaps exist without being a bust of Beethoven—it could have been fashioned into a bust of Brahms. In fact, it could exist without being a bust of anyone; it could be melted down and made into a door stopper. If transmutation of matter were possible (surely this is not something a priori impossible), it could even exist without being bronze. But could this statue exist without being a material thing? The answer seems a clear no. If anything is a material object, being material is part of its essential nature; it cannot exist without being a material thing. So it appears that the acceptability of the argument depends crucially on the acceptability of the second premise. Is it possible that I exist without a body? That surely is conceivable, Descartes would insist. But again, is something possible just because it is conceivable? Can we say more about the possibility of our disembodied existence?

Consider the bronze bust again. There is here a piece of sculpture and a quantity of bronze. Is the sculpture the very same thing as the bronze? Many philosophers would say no: Although the two share many properties in common (such as weight, density, and location), they differ at least in one respect, namely, their persistence condition. If the bust is melted down and shaped into a cube, the bust is gone but the bronze continues to exist. According to the next dualist argument, my body and I differ in a somewhat similar way.

Argument 6

Suppose I am identical with this body of mine.
In 1995 I existed.
In 1995 this body did not exist.
Hence, from the first premise, it follows that I did not exist in 1995.
But this contradicts the second premise, and the supposition is false.
Hence, I am not identical with my body.

In 1995 this body did not exist because all the molecules making up a human body are cycled out every six or seven years. When all the molecular constituents of a body are replaced, we have a new material body. The body that I now have shares no constituents with the body I had in 1995. The person that I am, however, persists through changes of material constituents. So even if I have to have some material body or other, I do not have to have any particular body. But if I am identical with a body, I must be identical with a particular body. That is the argument. (This probably was not one of Descartes' actual arguments.)

An initial response to argument 6 could run as follows: When I say I am identical with this body of mine, I do not mean that I am identical with the "time slice"—that is, a temporal cross section—of my body at this instant. What I mean is that I am identical with the temporally elongated "worm" of a three-dimensional biological organism that came into existence at my birth and will cease to exist when my biological death occurs. This four-dimensional object—a three-dimensional object stretched along the temporal dimension—has different material constituents at different times, but it is a clearly delineated system with a substantival unity and integrity. It is this material structure with a history with which I claim I am identical.

Another reply, related to the first, might go as follows: My body is not a mere assemblage or structure made up of material particles; rather, it is a biological organism, a human animal. And the persistence condition appropriate to mere material things is not necessarily appropriate for animals. In fact, animals can retain their identities even though the matter constituting them may change over time (this may well be true of nonanimal biological systems, such as trees), just as in the case of persons. The criterion of identity over time for animals (however it is to be spelled out in detail) is the one that should be applied to human bodies.[7] Does the substance dualist have a reply to this? I believe an answer may be implicit in the next and final dualist argument we consider.

Tully is the same person as Cicero. There is one person here, not two. Can there be a time at which Tully exists but not Cicero? Obviously not—that is no more possible than for Tully to be at a place where Cicero is not. Given that Cicero = Tully in this world, is there a possible world in which Cicero is not identical with Tully? That is, given that Cicero is Tully, is it possible that Cicero is not Tully? (Given that Cicero is sitting, it is possible that Cicero is not sitting; he could be standing.) Suppose world W is such a world: Cicero ≠ Tully in W. So there must be some property, F, such that, in W, Cicero has it but Tully does not. Let's say that F is the property of being tall. But *being tall in world W* is a property that things can have *in this world*; for example, I am tall in world W, but you are not. We said: Cicero is tall in W, and Tully is not tall in W, and that is a fact about Cicero and Tully in this world. But given that Cicero = Tully, how is that possible? Isn't it necessarily the case that Cicero is tall in W if and only if Tully is tall in W? So the alleged fact is a contradiction. We therefore have the following principle ("NI" for "necessity of identities"):

(NI) If X = Y, then necessarily X = Y—that is, X = Y in every possible world.

Given this widely accepted principle, our last dualist argument may be formulated as follows:

Argument 7

Suppose I am identical with this body of mine.
Then, by (NI), I am necessarily identical with this body—that is, I am identical with it in every possible world.
But that is false, for (a) in some possible worlds I could be disembodied and have no body, or at least (b) I could have a *different* body in another possible world.

So it is false that I am identical with this body in every possible world, and this contradicts the second line.

Therefore, I am not identical with my body.

The principle (NI) is considered unexceptionable. So if there is a vulnerability in this argument, it would have to be the third line; to criticize this premise effectively, we would have to eliminate both (a) and (b) as possibilities. Arguing against (b), I believe, would require some ingenuity and creative thinking on the part of the critic.

The leading idea driving all of these metaphysical arguments is the thought that although I may be a composite being consisting of a mind and a body, my relation to my mind is more intimate and essential than my relation to my body and that I am "really" my mind and could not exist apart from it, while it is a contingent fact that I have the body that I happen to have. Descartes' interest in defending minds as immaterial substances was apparently motivated in part by his desire to allow for the possibility of survival after bodily death.[8] Most established religions have a story to tell about the afterlife, and the conceptions of an afterlife in some of them seem to require, or at least allow, the possibility of our existence without a body. But all that is a wish list; it does not make the possibility of our disembodied existence a real one (Descartes was under no such illusion). The arguments we have looked at must earn their plausibility on their own merits, not from the allure of their conclusions.

Princess Elisabeth Versus Descartes: Dualism and Mental Causation

As will be recalled, the fourth component of Descartes' dualism is the thesis that minds and bodies causally influence each other. In voluntary action, the mind's volition causes our limbs to move; in perception, physical stimuli impinging on sensory receptors cause perceptual experiences in the mind. This view is not only commonsensical but also absolutely essential to our conception of ourselves as agents and cognizers: Unless our minds, in virtue of having certain desires, beliefs, and intentions, are able to cause our bodies to move in appropriate ways, how could human agency be possible? How could we be agents who act and take responsibility for our actions? If objects and events in the physical world do not cause us to have perceptual experiences and beliefs, how could we have any knowledge of what is happening around us? How could we know that we are holding a tomato in our hand, that we are coming up on a stop sign, or that a big bear is approaching us from our left?

Descartes has something to say about how mental causation works. In the *Sixth Meditation*, he writes:

> The mind is not immediately affected by all parts of the body, but only by the brain, or perhaps just by one small part of the brain. . . . Every time this part of the brain is in a given state, it presents the same signals to the mind, even though the other parts of the body may be in a different condition at the time. . . . For example, when the nerves in the foot are set in motion in a violent and unusual manner, this motion, by way of the spinal cord, reaches the inner parts of the brain, and there gives the mind its signal for having a certain sensation, namely the sensation of a pain as occurring in the foot. This stimulates the mind to do its best to get rid of the cause of the pain, which it takes to be harmful to the foot.[9]

In *The Passions of the Soul*, Descartes identifies the pineal gland as the "seat of the soul," the locus of direct mind-body interaction. This gland, Descartes maintains, can be moved directly by the soul, thereby moving the "animal spirits" (bodily fluids in the nerves), which then transmit causal influence to appropriate parts of the body:

> And the activity of the soul consists entirely in the fact that simply by willing something it brings it about that the little gland to which it is closely joined moves in the manner required to produce the effect corresponding to this desire.[10]

In the case of physical-to-mental causation, this process is reversed: Disturbances in the animal spirits surrounding the pineal gland make the gland move, which in turn causes the mind to experience appropriate sensations and perceptions. For Descartes, then, each of us is a "union" or "intermingling" of a mind and a body in direct causal interaction.

In what must be one of the most celebrated letters in the history of philosophy, Princess Elisabeth of Bohemia, an immensely astute pupil of Descartes', wrote to him in May 1643, challenging him to explain

> how the mind of a human being, being only a thinking substance, can determine the bodily spirits in producing bodily actions. For it appears that all determination of movement is produced by the pushing of the thing

being moved, by the manner in which it is pushed by that which moves it, or else by the qualification and figure of the surface of the latter. Contact is required for the first two conditions, and extension for the third. [But] you entirely exclude the latter from the notion you have of the body, and the former seems incompatible with an immaterial thing.[11]

(For "determine," read "cause"; for "bodily spirits," read "fluids in the nerves and muscles.") Elisabeth's demand is clearly understandable. First, see what Descartes has said about bodies and their motion in the *Second Meditation*:

By a body I understand whatever has determinate shape and a definable location and can occupy a space in such a way as to exclude any other body; it can be perceived by touch, sight, hearing, taste or smell, and can be moved in various ways, not by itself but by whatever else comes into contact with it.[12]

For Descartes, minds are immaterial; that is, minds have no spatial extension and are not located in physical space. If bodies can be moved only by contact, how could an unextended mind, which is not in space, come into contact with an extended material thing, even the finest and lightest particle in animal spirits, thereby causing it to move? This is a perfectly reasonable question.

In modern terminology we can put Elisabeth's challenge as follows: For anything to cause a physical object to move, or cause any change in one, there must be a flow of energy, or transfer of momentum, from the cause to the physical object. But how could there be an energy flow from an immaterial mind to a material thing? What kind of energy could it be? How could anything "flow" from something *outside space* to something *in space*? If an object is going to impart momentum to another, it must have mass and velocity. But how could an unextended mind outside physical space have either mass or velocity? The question does not concern the truth or plausibility of Descartes' thesis of mind-body interaction; the question is whether this commonsensical interactionist thesis is tenable within the dualist ontology of nonspatial immaterial minds and material things in a spatial world.

Descartes responded to Elisabeth in a letter written in the same month:

I observe that there are in us certain primitive notions which are, as it were, the originals on the pattern of which we form all of other thoughts, . . . as regards the mind and body together, we have only the primitive notion of their union, on which depends our notion of the mind's power to move the body, and the body's power to act on the mind and cause sensations and passions.[13]

Descartes is defending the position that the idea of mind-body union is a "primitive" notion—a fundamental notion that is intelligible in its own right and cannot be explained in terms of other more basic notions—and that the idea of mind-body causation "depends" on that of mind-body union. What does this mean? Although, on Descartes' view, minds and bodies seem on an equal footing causally, there is an important asymmetry between them: My mind can exercise its causal powers—on other minds as well as on bodies around me—only by first causally influencing my own body, and nothing can influence my mind except by influencing my body. But my body is different: It can causally interact with other bodies quite independently of my mind. My body—or my pineal gland—is the necessary causal intermediary between my mind and the rest of the world; in a sense, my mind is causally isolated from the world by being united with my body. To put it another way, my body is the enabler of my mind's causal powers; it is by being united with my body that my mind can exercise its causal powers in the world—on other minds as well as on other bodies. Looked at this way, the idea of mind-body union does seem essential to understanding the mind's causal powers.

Elisabeth was not satisfied. She immediately fires back:

> And I admit that it would be easier for me to concede matter and extension to the mind than it would be for me to concede the capacity to move a body and be moved by one to an immaterial thing.[14]

This is a remarkable statement; it may well be the first appearance of the causal argument for materialism (see chapters 4, 7, and 10). For she is in effect saying that to allow for the possibility of mental causation, she would rather accept materialism concerning the mind ("it would be easier to concede matter and extension to the mind") than accept what she regards as the wholly implausible dualist account offered by her mentor.

Why should anyone find Descartes' story so implausible? A couple of paragraphs back, it was pointed out that my mind's forming a "union" with my body amounts to the fact that my body serves as a necessary and omnipresent proximate cause and effect of changes in my mind and that my body is what makes it possible for my mind to have a causal influence on the outside world. Descartes, however, would reject this characterization of a mind-body union, for the simple reason that it would beg the question as far as the possibility of mind-body causation is concerned. That is presumably why Descartes claimed that the notion of mind-body union is a "primitive"—one that is intelligible per se but that is neither further explainable nor in need of an explanation. Should this answer have satisfied Elisabeth, or anyone else? A plausible case can be made for a negative answer. For when we ask what makes this body my body, not someone else's, a causal answer seems the most natural one and the only correct one. This is my body because it is the only body that I, or my desires and volitions, can directly move—that is, without moving or causally influencing anything else, whereas I can move other bodies, like this pen on my desk or the door to the hallway, only by moving my body first. Moreover, any changes in my mind—or my mental states—can be brought about only by bringing about appropriate changes in my body (presumably in my brain). What could be a more natural account of how my mind and my body form a "union"? But this explanation of mind-body union presupposes the possibility of mind-body causation, and it would be circular to turn around and say that an understanding of mind-body causation "depends" on the idea of mind-body union. Descartes' declaration that the idea of a union is a "primitive" and hence not in need of an explanation is unlikely to impress someone seeking an understanding of mental causation; it is liable to strike his critics simply as a dodge—a refusal to acknowledge a deep difficulty confronting his approach.

The "Pairing Problem": Another Causal Argument

We will develop another causal argument against Cartesian substance dualism. If this argument works, it will show not only that immaterial minds cannot causally interact with material things situated in space but also that they are not able to enter into causal relations with anything else, including other immaterial minds. Immaterial objects would be causally impotent and hence explanatorily useless; positing them would be philosophically unmotivated.

Here is the argument.[15] To set up an analogy and a point of reference, let us begin with an example of physical causation. A gun, call it A, is fired, and this causes the death of a person, X. Another gun, B, is fired at the same time (say, in A's vicinity, but this is unimportant), and this results in the death of another person, Y. What makes it the case that the firing of A caused X's death and the firing of B caused Y's death, and not the other way around? That is, why did A's firing not cause Y's death and B's firing not cause X's death? What principle governs the "pairing" of the right cause with the right effect? There must be a relation R that grounds and explains the cause-effect pairings, a relation that holds between A's firing and X's death and also between B's firing and Y's death, but not between A's firing and Y's death or between B's firing and X's death. What is this R, the "pairing relation," as we might call it? We are not necessarily supposing at this point that there is a single such R for all cases of physical causation, only that some relation must ground the fact that a given cause is a cause of the particular effect that is caused by it.

Two ideas come to mind. First, there is the idea of a *causal chain*: There is a continuous causal chain between A's firing and X's death, as there is between B's firing and Y's death, whereas no such chains exist between A's firing and Y's death or between B's firing and X's death. Indeed, with a high-speed video camera, we could trace the bullet's flight from each rifle to its impact point on the target. The second idea is the thought that each gun when it fired was at a certain distance and in appropriate orientation in relation to the person it hit, but not to the other person. That is, *spatial relations* do the job of pairing causes with their effects.

A moment's reflection shows that the causal chain idea does not work as an independent solution to the problem. A causal chain, after all, is a series of events related as cause to effect, and interpolating more cause-effect pairs does not solve the pairing problem. For obviously it begs the question: We would need to explain what pairing relations ground these interpolated cause-effect pairs. Interpolating intermediate causal links only multiplies the problem. It seems plausible that spatial relations—and more broadly, spatiotemporal relations—are the only possible way of generating pairing relations. Space appears to have nice causal properties; for example, as distance increases, causal influence diminishes, and it is often possible to set up barriers at intermediate positions to block or impede the propagation of causal influence. In any case, we can now state a fundamental assumption that will be used in the argument to be presented:

(M) It is metaphysically possible for there to be two distinct physical objects, a and b, with the same intrinsic properties and hence the same causal potential or powers; one of these, say, a, causes a third object, c, to change in a certain way, but object b has no causal influence on c.

The fact that a but not b causes c to change must be grounded in some fact about a, b, and c. Since a and b have the same intrinsic properties, it must be their *relational properties* with respect to *c* that provide the desired explanation of their different causal roles. What relational properties or relations can do this job? It is plausible to think that when *a*, *b*, and *c* are physical objects, it is the spatial relation between *a* and *c* and that between *b* and *c* that are responsible for the causal difference between *a* and *b* vis-à-vis *c*. (*a* was in the right spatial relation to *c*; *b* was "too far away" to exert any influence on it.) At least, there seems no other obvious candidate that comes to mind. Later we give an explanation of what it is about spatial relations that enables them to do the job.

Consider the possibility of immaterial souls, outside physical space, causally interacting with material objects in space. The dualist who believes in mind-body causal interaction must accept the following companion principle to (M), and if she does not, she should give a principled explanation why not.

(M*) It is metaphysically possible for there to be two souls, A and B, with the same intrinsic properties[16] such that they both act in a certain way at the same time and as a result a material object, C, undergoes a change. Moreover, it is the action of A, not that of B, that is the cause of the physical change in C.

What makes it the case that this is so? What pairing relation pairs the first soul, but not the second soul, with the physical object? Since souls, as immaterial substances, are outside physical space and cannot bear spatial relations to anything, it is not possible to invoke spatial relations to ground the pairing. What possible relations could provide causal pairings across the two domains, one of spatially located material things and the other of immaterial minds outside space?

Consider a variation on the foregoing example: There are two physical objects, P_1 and P_2, with the same intrinsic properties, and an action of an immaterial soul causally affects one of them, say, P_1, but not P_2. How can we explain this? Since P_1 and P_2 have identical intrinsic properties, they must have the same causal capacity ("passive" causal powers as well as "active" causal powers), and it would seem that the only way to make them discernible in a causal context is their spatial relations to other things. Doesn't that mean that any pairing relation that can do the job must be a spatial relation? If so, the pairing problem for this case is unsolvable since the soul is not in space and bears no spatial relation to anything. The soul cannot be any "nearer" to, or "more properly oriented" toward, one physical object than another. Nor could we say that there was a causal barrier "between" the soul and one of the physical objects but not the other, for what could "between" mean as applied to something in space and something outside it? It is a total mystery what nonspatial relations there could be that might help distinguish, from the point of view of an immaterial soul, between two intrinsically indiscernible physical objects.

Could there be causal interactions among immaterial substances? Ruling out mind-body causal interaction does not in itself rule out the possibility of a causally autonomous domain of immaterial minds in which minds are in causal commerce with other minds. Perhaps that is the picture of a purely spiritual afterlife envisioned in some religions and theologies. Is that a possibility? The pairing problem makes such an idea a dubious proposition. Again, any substance dualist who wants causation in the immaterial realm must allow the possibility of there being three mental substances, M_1, M_2, and M_3, such that M_1 and M_2 have the same intrinsic properties, and hence the same causal powers, and yet an action by M_1, but not the same action by M_2 at the same time, is causally responsible for a change in M_3. If such is a metaphysically possible situation, what pairing relation could connect M_1 with M_3 but not M_2 with M_3? If causation is to be possible within the mental domain, there must be an intelligible and motivated answer to this question. But what mental relations could serve this purpose? It is difficult to think of any.

Consider what space does for physical causation. In the kind of picture envisaged, where a physical thing or event causally acts on only one of the two objects with identical intrinsic properties, what distinguishes these two objects has to be their spatial locations with respect to the cause. Space provides a "principle of individuation" for material objects. Pure qualities and causal powers do not. And what enables space to serve this role is the fact that physical objects occupying exactly the same location in space at the same time are one and the same object.[17] This is in effect the venerable principle of "impenetrability of matter," which can usefully be understood as a sort of "exclusion" principle for space: Material things compete for, and exclude one another from, spatial regions. From this it follows that if physical objects a and b bear the same spatial relations to a third object c, a and b are one and the same object. This principle is what enables space to individuate material things with identical intrinsic properties. The same goes for causation in the mental domain. What is needed to solve the pairing problem for immaterial minds is a kind of mental coordinate system, a "mental space," in which these minds are each given a unique "location" at a time. Further, a principle of "impenetrability of minds" must hold in this mental coordinate system; that is, minds that occupy the same "location" in this space must be one and the same. It seems fair to say that we do not have any idea how a mental space of this kind could be constructed. Moreover, even if we could develop such a space for immaterial minds, that still would fall short of a complete solution to the pairing problem; to solve it for causal relations across the mental and physical domains we need to somehow coordinate or fuse the two spaces, the mental and the physical, to yield unitary pairing relations across the domains. It is not clear that we even know where to begin.

If there are Cartesian minds, therefore, they are threatened with total causal isolation—from each other as well as from the material world. The considerations presented do not show that causal relations cannot hold within a single mental substance (even Leibniz, famous for disallowing causation between monads, allowed it within a single monad). However, what has been shown seems to raise serious challenges for substance dualism. If this is right, we have a causal argument for monistic physicalist ontology. Causality requires a spacelike structure, and as far as we know, the physical domain is the only domain with a structure of that kind.

Immaterial Minds in Space?

All these difficulties with the pairing problem arise because of the radically nonspatial nature of minds in traditional substance dualism. According to Descartes, not only do minds lack spatial extension but also they are not in space at all. So why not bring minds into space, enabling them to have spatial locations and thereby solve the pairing problem? Most popular notions of minds as immaterial spirits do not seem to conceive them as wholly nonspatial. For example, when a person dies, her soul is thought to "rise" from the body, or otherwise "leave" it, implying that before the death the soul was inside the body and that the soul is capable of moving in space and changing its locations. Sometimes the departed souls of our loved ones are thought to be able to make their presence known to us in various ways, including in a visible form (think of Hamlet's ghostly father). It is probably impossible to make coherent sense of these popular ideas, but is there anything in principle wrong with locating immaterial minds in physical space and thereby making it possible for them to participate in the causal transactions of the world?

As we will see, the proposal to bring immaterial minds into space is fraught with complications and difficulties and probably not worth considering as an option. First there is the question of just where in space to put them. Is there a principled and motivated way of assigning a location to each soul? We might suggest that I locate my soul in my body, you locate your soul in your body, and so on. That may sound like a natural and reasonable suggestion, but it faces a number of difficulties. First, what about disembodied souls, souls that are not "united" with a body? Since souls are supposed to be substances in their own right, such souls are metaphysically possible. Second, if your soul is located in your body, exactly where in your body is it located? In the brain, we might reply. But exactly where in the brain? It could not be spread all over the brain because minds are not supposed to be extended in space. If it has a location, the location has to be a geometric point. Is it coherent to think that there is a geometric point somewhere in your brain at which your mind is located? Descartes called the pineal gland the "seat of the soul," presumably because the pineal gland is where mind-body causal interaction was supposed to take place, although of course his official doctrine was that the soul is not in space at all.

Following Descartes' strategy here, however, does not seem to make much sense. For one thing, there is no evidence that there is any single place in the brain—a dimensionless point at that—at which mind-body causation takes place. As far as we know, various mental states and activities are distributed over the entire brain and nervous system, and it does not make scientific sense to think, as Descartes did in regard to the pineal gland, that there is a single small organ responsible for all mind-body causal interaction. Second, how could an entity occupying a single geometric point cause all the physical changes in the brain that are involved in mind-body causation? By what mechanism could this happen? How is energy transmitted from this geometric point to the neural fibers making up the brain? And there is this further question: What keeps the soul at that particular location? When I stand up from my chair in the study and go downstairs to the living room, somehow my soul tags along and moves exactly on the same trajectory as my body. When I board an airplane and the airplane accelerates on the runway and takes off, somehow my pointlike immaterial mind manages to gain speed exactly at the same rate and begins to cruise at the speed of 560 miles an hour! It seems that the soul is somehow firmly glued to some part of my brain and moves as my brain moves, and when I die it miraculously unglues itself from my body and migrates to a better (or perhaps worse) place in the afterlife. Does any of this make sense? Descartes was probably wise to keep immaterial minds wholly outside physical space.

In any case, giving locations to immaterial minds will not in itself solve the pairing problem. As we saw, spatial locations of physical objects help solve

the pairing problem in virtue of the principle that physical objects can be individuated in terms of their locations. As was noted, this is the principle of
impenetrability of matter: Distinct objects exclude one another from spatial
regions. That is how the causal roles of two intrinsically indiscernible physical objects could be differentiated. For the spatial locations of immaterial
minds to help, therefore, we need a similar principle of spatial exclusion for
immaterial minds—or the principle of impenetrability of mental substance—to the effect that distinct minds cannot occupy exactly the same
point in space. What reason is there to think such a principle holds? Why
cannot a single point be occupied by all the souls that exist, like the thousand
angels dancing on the head of a pin? Such a principle is needed if we are to
make sense of causation for spatially located pointlike souls. But this does
not mean that the principle is available; we must be able to produce independently plausible evidence or give a credible argument to show that the principle holds.

When we see all the difficulties and puzzles to which the idea of an immaterial mind, or soul, appears to lead, it is understandable why Descartes declared the notion of mind-body union to be primitive and not further
explainable in terms of more fundamental ideas. Even a contemporary writer
has invoked God and theology to make sense of how a particular mind (say,
your mind) gets united to a particular body (your brain).[18] The reader is
urged to think about whether such an appeal to theology gives us real help
with the problems the dualist faces.

Substance Dualism and Property Dualism

It has seemed to most contemporary philosophers that the concept of
mind as a mental substance gives rise to too many difficulties and puzzles
without compensating explanatory gains. In addition, the idea of an immaterial and immortal soul usually carries with it various, often conflicting, religious and theological constraints and associations that many of us
would rather avoid. For example, the traditional conception of the soul involves a sharp and unbridgeable gap between humans and the rest of animal life. Even if our own mentality could be explained as consisting in the
possession of a soul, what might explain the mentality of nonhuman animals? It is not surprising that substance dualism has not been a prominent
alternative in contemporary philosophy of mind. But there is no call to exclude it a priori, without serious discussion; some highly reputable and re-

spected philosophers continue to defend it as a realistic—perhaps the only—option (see "Further Readings").

To reject the substantival view of mentality is not to deny that each of us "has a mind"; it is only that we should not think of "having a mind" literally—that is, as there being some object or substance called a "mind" that we literally possess. As discussed earlier (in chapter 1), having a mind is not like—at least, it need not be like—having brown eyes or a good throwing arm. To have brown eyes, there must be brown eyes that one has. To "be out of your mind" or to "keep something in mind," you do not have to *have* some object—namely, a mind—of which you are out of, or in which you keep something. If you have set aside substance dualism, at least for now, you can take having a mind simply as having a certain special set of *properties, capacities,* and *characteristics,* something that humans and some higher animals possess but flowerpots and rocks do not. To say that something "has a mind" is to classify it as a certain sort of thing—as a thing with capacities for certain characteristic sorts of behavior and functions, such as sensation, perception, memory, learning, consciousness, and purposeful action. From this perspective, it is less misleading to speak of "having mentality" than "having a mind."

In any case, the fact is that substance dualism has played a very small role in contemporary discussions in philosophy of mind. Philosophical attention has focused instead on mental activities and functions—or mental events, states, and processes—and the mind-body problem has turned into the problem of understanding how these mental events, states, and processes are related to physical and biological events, states, and processes, or how our mental or psychological capacities and functions are related to the nature of our physical structure and capacities. In regard to this question, there are two principal positions: dualism and physical monism. Dualism is no longer a dualism of two sorts of substances; it is now a dualism of two sorts of properties, mental and physical. "Property" is used here in a broad sense: Mental properties comprise mental functions, capacities, events, states, and the like, and similarly for physical properties. It is a catchall term referring to events, activities, states, and the rest. So property dualism is the claim that mental properties are diverse from and irreducible to physical properties. In contrast, physical monism (more often called reductionist, or reductive, physicalism, type physicalism, or just physicalism) is the position that mental properties are reducible to, and therefore can be identified with, physical properties. As we will see, there are various forms of both property dualism and reductionist physicalism. However, they all share one thing in common: the rejection of immaterial minds. Contemporary property dualism and reductive physicalism acknowledge only objects of one kind in the world—bits of matter and increasingly complex structures aggregated out of bits of matter. Some of these complex physical systems exhibit complex behaviors and activities, like perceiving, sensing, reasoning, and consciousness. But these are only properties of material structures. The main point of dispute concerns the relationship between these mental properties and the structures' physical properties. This is the central question for the remainder of this book.

Further Readings

The primary source of Descartes' interactionist dualism is his *Meditations on First Philosophy*, first published in 1641. There are numerous English editions; see, for example, the version (including *Objections and Replies*) in *The Philosophical Writings of Descartes*, vol. 2, translated and edited by John Cottingham, Robert Stoothoff, and Dugald Murdoch. Helpful historical and interpretive literature on Descartes' philosophy of mind includes: Richard A. Watson, *The Breakdown of Cartesian Metaphysics*; Daniel Garber, *Descartes Embodied* (especially chapter 8, "Understanding Causal Interaction: What Descartes Should Have Told Elisabeth"); Marleen Rozemond, *Descartes' Dualism*, chapter 1; and Lilli Alanen, *Descartes's Concept of Mind*, chapter 2.

For some contemporary defenses of substance dualism, see John Foster, *The Immaterial Self*; W. D. Hart, *The Engines of the Soul*; and Richard Swinburne, *The Evolution of the Soul*. Also recommended are Noa Latham, "Substance Physicalism," and Tim Crane, "Mental Substances."

Notes

1. See, for example, John Foster, *The Case for Idealism*.

2. Descartes writes: "Substance: this term applies to every thing in which whatever we perceive immediately resides, as in a subject. . . . By 'whatever we perceive' is meant any property, quality or attribute of which we have a real idea." See "Author's Replies to the Second Set of Objections," p. 114.

3. In his "Author's Replies to the Fourth Set of Objections" (p. 159), Descartes writes: "The notion of a substance is just this—that it can exist by itself, that is without the aid of any other substance."

4. Many philosophers in Descartes' own time, including Descartes himself, held that, strictly speaking, God is the only being capable of independent existence and therefore that the only true substance is God, all others being "secondary" or "derivative" substances.

5. René Descartes, *Meditations on First Philosophy*, Meditation II, p. 19.

6. See some of the essays in *Conceivability and Possibility*, edited by Tamar Szabo Gendler and John Hawthorne.

7. This approach, called "animalism," has recently been receiving much attention. See, for example, Eric T. Olson, *The Human Animal: Personal Identity Without Psychology*.

8. As noted by Marleen Rozemond in her *Descartes' Dualism*, p. 3.

9. René Descartes, *Meditations on First Philosophy*, Meditation VI, pp. 59–60.

10. René Descartes, *The Passions of the Soul*, I, 41, p. 343.

11. Daniel Garber, "Understanding Interaction: What Descartes Should Have Told Elisabeth," p. 172. This and other quotations from the correspondence between Elisabeth and Descartes are taken from this chapter of Garber's book, *Descartes Embodied*.

12. René Descartes, *Meditations on First Philosophy*, Meditation VI, p. 17.

13. René Descartes to Princess Elisabeth of Bohemia, May 21, 1643, in Garber, *Descartes Embodied*, p. 173.

14. Princess Elisabeth of Bohemia to René Descartes, June 1643, in Garber, *Descartes Embodied*, p. 172.

15. For a fuller presentation and discussion of this argument, see my *Physicalism, or Something Near Enough*, ch. 2. For a dualist response to the pairing problem, see John Foster, "A Defense of Dualism."

16. If you are inclined to invoke the identity of intrinsic indiscernibles for souls to dissipate the issue, the next situation we consider involves only one soul and this remedy does not apply. Moreover, the pairing problem can be generated without assuming that there can be distinct intrinsic indiscernibles. This assumption, however, helps to present the problem in a simple and compelling way.

17. There is the familiar problem of the statue and the lump of clay of which it is made (the problem of coincident objects). Some claim that although these occupy the same region of space and coincide in many of their properties (for example, weight, shape, size), they are distinct objects because their persistence conditions are different (for example, if the clay is molded into a cube, the clay, but not the statue, continues to exist). We must set this problem aside, but it should be noted that the statue and the lump of clay share the same causal powers and suffer the same causal fate (except perhaps coming into being and going out of existence).

18. John Foster, "A Brief Defense of the Cartesian View."

3

Mind as Behavior

Behaviorism

Behaviorism arose early in the twentieth century as a doctrine on the nature and methodology of psychology, in reaction to what some psychologists took to be the subjective and unscientific character of introspectionist psychology. In his classic *Principles of Psychology*, published in 1890, William James, who had a major role in establishing psychology as an independent field of science, begins with the following definition of the scope of psychology:

> Psychology is the Science of Mental Life, both of its phenomena and of their conditions. The phenomena are such things as we call feelings, desires, cognitions, reasonings, decisions, and the like.[1]

For James, then, psychology was the scientific study of mental phenomena, and he took the study of conscious mental processes as a core task of psychology. As for the method of investigation of these processes, James states: "Introspective Observation is what we have to rely on first and foremost and always."[2]

Compare this with the declaration in 1913 by J. B. Watson, who is considered the founder of the behaviorist movement: "Psychology . . . is a purely objective experimental branch of natural science. Its theoretical goal is the prediction and control of behavior."[3] This view of psychology as the study of publicly observable human and animal behavior, not of inner mental life, dominated scientific psychology and associated fields until the 1960s and made the term "behavioral science" a preferred name for psychology in universities and research centers around the world, especially in North America.

The rise of behaviorism and the influential position it attained was no fluke. Even James saw the importance of behavior to mentality; in *The Principles of Psychology*, he also writes:

> *The pursuance of future ends and the choice of means for their attainment are thus the mark and criterion of the presence of mentality* in a phenomenon. We all use this test to discriminate between an intelligent and a mechanical performance. We impute no mentality to sticks and stones, because they never seem to move for *the sake of* anything.[4]

It can be agreed on all sides that behavior has a lot to do with mentality. But what precisely is the relationship? Does behavior merely serve, as James seems to be suggesting, as an *indication*, or a *sign*, that a mind is present? And if behavior is a sign of mentality, what makes it so? If something serves as a sign of something else, there must be an underlying relationship that explains why the first is a sign of the second. Or is the relationship between behavior and mentality a more intimate one? Philosophical behaviorism takes behavior as *constitutive* of mentality: Having a mind just *is* a matter of exhibiting, or having a *propensity* or *capacity* to exhibit, appropriate patterns of behavior. Although behaviorism, in both its scientific and philosophical forms, has lost the sweeping influence it once enjoyed, it is a doctrine that we need to know and understand, since not only does it form the historical backdrop of much of the subsequent thinking about the mind, but its influence lingers on and can be discerned in some important current philosophical positions. In addition, a proper appreciation of its motivation and arguments will help us gain a better understanding of the relationship between behavior and mentality.

Reactions Against the Cartesian Conception of the Mind

On the traditional conception of the mental deriving from Descartes, the mental is essentially private and subjective: For any mental phenomenon, be it a sensation of pain or an intentional state such as believing or doubting, only a single subject, the one to whom it occurs, has direct and authoritative cognitive access to it. Others must depend on the subject's verbal reports or other observable behavioral clues and infer that she is experiencing a pain or thinking a certain thought. We see a person holding up a bleeding thumb and groaning and infer that she must be experiencing a very bad pain in her thumb. You see your roommate leaving the apartment with her raincoat on and carrying an umbrella, and you infer that she believes it is going to rain today. So there apparently is a clear-cut asymmetry between the first person and the third person where knowledge of mental states is concerned: Our knowledge of our own current mental states is direct and, in normal circumstances, immune to the third person's challenge "How do you know?" You do not *infer* that your thumb hurts, or that you believe it will rain; you apparently just know such things. But that is just what you do to gain knowledge of what goes on in other people's minds: Your knowledge is based on inference from observable physical and behavioral evidence. Early in the twentieth century, however, some philosophers and psychologists began to question this traditional conception of mentality; they thought that it led to absurd consequences.

The difficulty with this conception of how we come to know other minds is *not* that such knowledge, based as it is only on "outer" signs, is liable to error and cannot attain the kind of certainty with which we supposedly know our own minds. The problem, as some saw it, goes deeper: It makes knowledge of other minds not possible at all! Take a standard case of inductive inference—inference based on premises that are less than logically conclusive—such as this: You find your roommate listening to the weather report on the radio, which is predicting heavy rain later today, and say to yourself, "She is going to be looking for her old umbrella!" This inference too is liable to error: Perhaps she misunderstood the weather report or was not really paying attention, or she has already packed the umbrella in her backpack, or she does not mind getting wet. Now compare this with our inference of a person's pain on the basis of her "pain behavior." You notice the following apparent difference: With the former, you can check by further observation whether your inference was correct (you can wait and see whether she looks for her umbrella), but with the latter, further observation yields only more observations of her behavior, never an observation of her pain. Only she can experience her pains; all you can do is to see what she does and says. And what she *says* is only behavior of another kind. (How do you know that by "pain" she means pain?) So what reason is there for thinking that she has an inner mental life at all?

We can illustrate this point further with a striking analogy due to Wittgenstein, "the beetle in the box." Suppose that each of us has a little box with something in it and that we can look at what is in our own box but never at the inside of another person's box. As it happens, you have a beetle in your box, and everyone else says that they too have a beetle in their box.[5] But what can you know from their utterances, "I have a beetle in my box"? How do you know what they mean by the word "beetle"?

It is clear that you cannot know what others mean by "beetle": For all you know, some may have a butterfly, some may have a little rock, and perhaps others have nothing at all in their boxes. Nor can others know what you mean when they hear you say, "I have a beetle in my box." As Wittgenstein says, the thing in the box "cancels out whatever it is." It is difficult to see how the word "beetle" can have a role in interpersonal communication.

In the same way, it is mysterious how, on the Cartesian conception of the mental, we could ever learn the meaning of, say, the word "pain" and be able to use utterances like "I have a sharp pain in my elbow" to impart information to another person. For the pain case seems exactly analogous to the beetle in the box: Suppose that you and your friends all take a fall while running on a track and all of you have your knees badly bruised. Each of you says that she has a pain in the knee, a pain that only she can introspectively observe. Is there any reason to think that there is something common, some identical sensory experience, going on in each person's mind? Pain in the mind seems just like the beetle in the box. The apparently evident fact, however, is that utterances like "My knee hurts" can be used to transmit information from person to person and that expressions like "pain" and "the thought that it's going to rain" have intersubjective meanings, meanings that can be shared by different persons. This seems to flatly discredit the Cartesian picture of the mind as a private inner theater for an audience of one.

Behaviorism, in one form or another, is a reaction to these seemingly unacceptable implications of the Cartesian conception. It attempts to construe the meanings of our mental expressions not as referring to private inner episodes but as referring to publicly accessible and intersubjectively verifiable facts and conditions about people. According to the behaviorist approach, in short, the meanings of mental expressions, such as "pain" and "thought," are to be explained by reference to facts about publicly observable behavior, not inner occurrences in private minds. But what is meant by "behavior"?

What Is Behavior?

We may take "behavior" to mean whatever people or organisms, or even mechanical systems, *do* that is *publicly observable*. "Doing" is to be distinguished from "having something done." If you grasp my arm and pull it up, the rising of my arm is not something I do; it is not my behavior (although your pulling up my arm is behavior—your behavior). It is not something that a psychologist would be interested in investigating. But if I raise my arm—that is, if I cause it to rise—then it is something I do, and it counts as my behavior. It is not assumed here that the doing must in some sense be "intentional" or done for a purpose; it is only required that it is proximately caused by some occurrence internal to the behaving system. If a robot moves toward a table and picks up a book, its movements are part of its behavior, whether or not the robot "knows" what it is doing. If a bullet punctures its skin, that is not part of its behavior, not something it does; that is only something that happens to it.[6]

What are some examples of things that humans and other behaving organisms do? Let us consider the following four possible types:

i. *Physiological reactions and responses*: for example, perspiration, salivation, increase in the pulse rate, increase in blood pressure
ii. *Bodily movements*: for example, raising and waving a hand, opening a door, throwing a baseball, a cat scratching at the door, a rat turning left in a T-maze
iii. *Actions involving bodily motions*: for example, typing an invitation, greeting a friend, checking a book out of the library, going shopping, writing a check, signing a contract
iv. *Actions not involving overt bodily motions*: for example, reasoning, guessing, calculating, judging, deciding

Behaviors falling under (iv), sometimes called "mental acts," are "inner" events that are not, strictly speaking, publicly observable, and behaviorists do not consider them "behavior" in their sense. (This, of course, does not necessarily rule out behavioral analyses of these activities.) Those falling under (iii), although they involve bodily movements, also have clear and substantial mental components. Consider the act of writing a check: Only if you have certain cognitive capacities, beliefs, desires, and an understanding of relevant social institutions can you write a check. You must have a desire to make a payment and the belief that writing a check is a means toward that end. You must also have some understanding of exchange of money for goods and services and the institution of banking. A person whose overt behavior is observationally indistinguishable from yours when you are writing a check is not necessarily writing a check (try to think how that can happen). Something like this is true of other examples listed under (iii), and this means that none of them can count as behavior for behaviorists.

Since public observability is of central concern to behaviorists, they exclude items under (iii) and (iv) as behavior, counting only those under (i) and (ii)—what Gilbert Ryle, a leading behaviorist in the midtwentieth century, called "motions and noises"—as meeting their requirements. In much behaviorist literature, there is an implicit assumption that only physiological responses and bodily motions that are in a broad sense "overt" and "external" are to count as behavior. This would rule out events and processes occurring in the internal organs; thus, internal physiological states, including states of the brain, would not, on this view, count as behavior, although they are, of course, among the physical states and conditions that are intersubjectively accessible. The main point to remember, though, is that however the domain of behavior is circumscribed, behavior is taken to be bodily events and conditions that are publicly observable and that do not give rise to the kind of first-person epistemic asymmetry noted earlier for supposedly private mental phenomena.

Logical Behaviorism: Hempel's Argument

Writing in 1935, Carl Hempel, a leading logical positivist, said: "We see clearly that the meaning of a psychological statement consists solely in the function of abbreviating the description of certain modes of physical response characteristic of the bodies of men and animals."[7] A claim of this kind, usually called "logical behaviorism" or "analytical behaviorism," is about the translatability of psychological sentences, which can be put as follows:

Logical Behaviorism I. Any meaningful psychological statement, that is, a statement purportedly describing a mental phenomenon, can be *translated*, without loss of content, into a statement solely about behavioral and physical phenomena.

And the claim can be formulated somewhat more broadly as a thesis about the behavioral definability of all meaningful psychological expressions:

Logical Behaviorism II. Every meaningful psychological expression can be *defined* solely in terms of behavioral and physical expressions, that is, those referring to behavioral and physical phenomena.

Here "definition" is to be understood in the following fairly strict sense: If an expression E is defined as E^*, then E and E^* must be either synonymous or necessarily equivalent (that is, there is no conceivable situation to which one of the expressions applies but the other does not).[8] Assuming translation to involve synonymy or at least necessary equivalence, we see that logical behaviorism (II) entails logical behaviorism (I).

Why should anyone accept logical behaviorism? The following argument extracted from Hempel represents one important line of thinking that led to the behaviorist position:

1. The content, or meaning, of any meaningful statement is exhausted by the conditions that must be verified to obtain if we are to consider that statement true (we may call them "verification conditions").
2. If a statement is to have an intersubjective content—that is, a meaning that can be shared by different persons—its verification conditions must be publicly observable.
3. Only behavioral and physical phenomena are publicly observable.
4. Therefore, the content of any meaningful psychological statement must be specifiable by statements of publicly observable verification conditions, that is, statements describing appropriate behavioral and physical conditions that must hold if and only if the psychological statement is to count as true.

Premise (1) is called "the verifiability criterion of meaning," a central doctrine of the philosophical movement in the early twentieth century known as logical positivism. The idea that meanings are verification conditions is no longer accepted by most philosophers, though it is by no means dead. However, we can see and appreciate the motivation to go for something like the intersubjective verifiability requirement in the following way. We want our psychological statements to have public, sharable meanings and to serve as vehicles of interpersonal communication. Suppose someone asserts a sentence S. For me to understand what S means, I must know what state of affairs is represented by S (for example, whether S represents snow's being white or the sky's being blue). But for me to know what state of affairs this is, it must be one that is accessible to me; it must be the kind of thing that I could in principle determine to obtain or not to obtain. This means that if the meaning of S—namely, the state of affairs that S represents—is intersubjectively sharable, it must be specifiable by conditions that are intersubjectively accessible. Therefore, if psychological statements and expressions are to be part of public language suitable for intersubjective communication, their meanings must be governed by publicly accessible criteria, and only behavioral and physical conditions qualify as such criteria. And if anyone insists that there are inner subjective criteria for psychological expressions as well, we should reply, the behaviorist would argue, that even if such existed, they (like Wittgenstein's beetles) could not be part of the meanings that can be understood and shared by different persons. Summarizing all this, we could say: Insofar as psychological expressions have interpersonal meanings, they must be definable in terms of behavioral and physical expressions.

A Behavioral Translation of "Paul Has a Toothache"

As an example of behavioral and physical translation of psychological statements, let us see how Hempel proposes to translate "Paul has a toothache" in behavioral terms. His translation consists in the following five conditions:[9]

a. Paul weeps and makes gestures of such and such kinds.
b. At the question "What is the matter?" Paul utters the words, "I have a toothache."
c. Closer examination reveals a decayed tooth with exposed pulp.
d. Paul's blood pressure, digestive processes, the speed of his reactions, show such and such changes.
e. Such and such processes occur in Paul's central nervous system.

Hempel suggests that we regard this list as open-ended; there may be many other such "test sentences" that would help to verify the statement that Paul is having a toothache. But how plausible is the claim that these sentences together constitute a behavioral-physical translation of "Paul has a toothache"?

It is clear that as long as translation is required to preserve "meaning" in the ordinary sense, we must disqualify (d) and (e): It is not a condition on the mastery of the meaning of "toothache" that we know anything about blood pressure, reaction times, and conditions of the nervous system. (The latter would be disqualified by some behaviorists as well.) Even (c) is questionable: Why cannot someone experience toothache (that is, have a "toothachy" pain) without having a decayed tooth or in fact any tooth at all? (Think about "phantom pains" in an amputated limb.) (If "toothache" means "pain caused by an abnormal physical condition of a tooth," then "toothache" is no longer a purely psychological expression.) This leaves us with (a) and (b).

Consider (b): It associates *verbal behavior* with toothache. Unquestionably, verbal reports play an important role in our finding out what other people are thinking and feeling, and we might think that verbal reports, and verbal behavior in general, are observable behavior that we can depend on to yield knowledge of other minds. But there is a problem: Verbal behavior is not pure physical behavior, behavior narrowly so called. In fact, it can be seen that verbal behavior, such as responding to a question with an utterance like "I have a toothache," presupposes much that is robustly psychological; it is a behavior of kind (iv) distinguished earlier. For Paul's response to be relevant here, he must *understand* the question "What is the matter?" and *intend to express the belief* that he has a toothache, by uttering the sentence "I have a toothache." That is, Paul must be a speaker of English and be able to perform speech acts (for example, asserting, expressing a belief). Understanding a language and being able to use it for interpersonal communication is a sophisticated, highly complex cognitive ability, not something we can subsume under "motions and noises." Moreover, given that Paul is having a toothache, he responds in the way specified in (b) *only if he wants to tell the truth*. But "want" is a psychological term, and building this clause into (b) would again destroy its behavioral-physical character. We must conclude that (b) could hardly count as an eligible behavioral-physical "test sentence"; it makes huge assumptions about Paul's psychological and cognitive capacities. We return in the next section to condition (a) of Hempel's translation.

Difficulties with Behavioral Translation

Let us consider beliefs: How might we define "S believes that there are no native leopards in North America" in terms of *S*'s behavior? Pains are associated with a rough but distinctive range of behavior patterns, such as winces, groans, screams, characteristic ways in which we favor the affected bodily parts, and so on, which we may collectively call "pain behavior" (recall Hempel's condition [a]). However, it is much more difficult to associate higher cognitive states with specific patterns of behavior. Is there even a loosely definable range of bodily behavior that is characteristically and typically exhibited by all people who believe, say, that an independent judiciary system is essential to democracy, or that there is no largest prime number? Surely the very idea of looking for bodily behaviors correlated with these beliefs makes little sense.

This is why it is tempting, perhaps necessary, to resort to the idea of *verbal behavior*—the disposition to produce appropriate verbal responses when prompted in certain ways. A person who believes that there are infinitely many prime numbers has a certain linguistic disposition—for example, he would tend to utter the sentence "There are infinitely many primes," or its synonymous variants, under certain specifiable conditions. This leads to the following schematic definition:

S believes that p = $_{def}$ If S is asked, "Is it the case that p?" S will answer, "Yes, it is the case that p."

The right-hand side of this formula (the "definiens") states a *dispositional* property (*disposition* for short) of S: S has a disposition, or propensity, to produce behavior of an appropriate sort under specified conditions. It is in this sense that properties like being soluble in water or being magnetic are called dispositions: Water-soluble things dissolve when immersed in water, and magnetic objects attract iron filings that are placed nearby. To be soluble at time t, it need not be dissolving at t, or ever. To have the belief that p at time t, you only need to be disposed, at t, to respond appropriately if prompted in certain ways; you need not actually produce any of the specified responses at t.

There is no question that something like the above definition plays a role in finding out what other people believe. And it should be possible to formulate similar definitions for other propositional attitudes, like desiring and hoping. The importance of verbal behavior in the ascription of beliefs can be seen when we reflect on the fact that we are willing to ascribe to nonverbal animals only crude and rudimentary beliefs. We routinely attribute to a dog beliefs like "The food bowl is empty" and "There is a cat sitting on the fence," but not beliefs like "Either the food bowl is empty or there is no cat sitting on the fence" and "Next Sunday that cat will be sitting on the fence again." It is difficult to think of nonverbal behavior on the basis of which we can attribute beliefs with logically complex contents, say, those expressed by "Everyone can be fooled some of the time, but no one can be fooled all of the time," or "Since tomorrow is Monday, my master will head for work in Manhattan as usual, unless his cold gets worse and he decides to call in sick," and the like. It is arguable that in order to have beliefs or entertain thoughts like these, you must be a language speaker with a capacity to generate and understand sentences with complex structures.

Confining our attention to language speakers, then, let us see how well the proposed definition of belief works as a behaviorist definition. Serious difficulties immediately come to mind. First, as we saw with Hempel's "toothache" example, the definition presupposes that the person in question *understands* the question "Is it the case that *p*?"—and understands it *as a request for* an answer of a certain kind. (The definition as stated presupposes that the subject understands English, but this feature of the definition can be eliminated by modifying the antecedent, thus: "S is asked a question in a language S understands that is synonymous with the English sentence 'Is it the case that *p*?'") But understanding is a psychological concept, and if this is so, the proposed definition cannot be considered behaviorally acceptable (unless we have a prior behavioral definition of "understanding" a language). The same point applies to the consequent of the definition: In uttering the words "Yes, it is the case that *p*," S must *understand what these words mean* and *intend them to be understood by her hearer to have that meaning*. It is clear that speech acts like saying something and uttering words with an intention to communicate a particular meaning carry very substantial psychological presuppositions about the subject. If they are to count as "behavior," it would seem that they must be classified as type (iii) or (iv) behavior, not as "motions and noises."

A second difficulty (this too was noted in connection with Hempel's example): When S is asked the question "Is it the case that *p*?" S responds in the desired way only if S *wants* to tell the truth. Thus, the condition "if S wants to tell the truth" must be added to the antecedent of the definition, but this again threatens its behavioral character. The belief that *p* leads to an utterance of a sentence expressing *p* only if we combine the belief with a certain desire, the desire to tell the truth. The point can be generalized: Often behavior or action issues from a complex of mental states, not from a single, isolated mental state. As a rule, beliefs alone do not produce any specific behavior unless they are combined with appropriate desires.[10] Nor will desires: If you want to eat a ham sandwich, this will lead to your ham-sandwich-eating behavior only if you believe that what you are handed is a ham sandwich; if you believe that it is a beef-tripe sandwich, you may very well pass it up. If this is so, it seems not possible to define belief in behavioral terms without building desire into the definition, and if we try to define desire behaviorally, we find that that is not possible unless we build belief into *its* definition.[11] This would indeed be a very small definitional circle.

The complexity of the relationship between mental states and behavior can be appreciated in a more general setting. Consider the following schema relating desire, belief, and action:

Desire-Belief-Action Principle (DBA). If a person desires that *p* and believes that doing A is an optimal way to secure that *p*, she will do A.

There are various ways of sharpening this principle: For example, it is probably more accurate to say, "She will try to do A," or, "She will tend to do A," rather than, "She will do A." In any event, some such principle as DBA underlies our "practical reasoning"—the means-ends reasoning that issues in action. It is by appeal to such a principle that we "rationalize" actions—that is, give reasons that explain why people do what they do. DBA is also useful as a predictive tool: When we know that a person has a certain desire and that she takes a certain action as a good way of securing what she desires, we can reasonably predict that she will do, or attempt to do, the required action. Something like DBA is often thought to be fundamental to the very concept of "rational action."

Consider now an instance of DBA:

1. If Mary desires that fresh air be let into the room and believes that opening the window is a good way to make that happen, she will open the window.

Is (1) true? If Mary does open the window, we could explain her behavior by appealing to her desire and belief as specified in (1). But it is clear that she may have the desire and belief but not open the window—not if, for example, she thinks that opening the window will also let in the horrible street noise that she abhors. So perhaps we could say:

2. If Mary desires fresh air to be let in and believes that opening the window is a good way to make that happen, but if she also believes that by opening the window she will let in the horrible street noise, she will not open the window.

But can we count on (2) to be true? Even given the three antecedents of (2), Mary will still open the window if she also believes that her ill mother very badly needs fresh air. It is clear that this process could go on indefinitely.

This suggests something interesting and very important about the relationship between mental states and behavior, which can be stated like this:

Defeasibility of Mental-Behavioral Entailments. If there is a plausible entailment of behavior B by mental states $M_1, \ldots, M_n$, there always is a further mental state M_{n+1} such that $M_1, \ldots, M_n, M_{n+1}$ together plausibly entail not-B.

If we assume not-B (that is, the failure to produce behavior B) to be behavior as well, the principle can be iteratively applied, without end, as we saw with Mary and the window opening: There exists some mental state M_{n+2} such that $M_1, \ldots, M_n, M_{n+1}, M_{n+2}$ together plausibly entail B. And so on without end.[12]

This shows that the relationship between mental states and behavior is highly complex: The moral is that mind-to-behavior connections are always *defeasible*—and defeasible by the occurrence of a *further mental state*, not merely by physical barriers and hindrances (as when Mary cannot open the window because her arms are paralyzed or the window is nailed shut). This makes the prospect of producing for each mental expression a purely behavioral-physical definition extremely remote. But we should not lose sight of the important fact that the defeasibility thesis does state an important and interesting connection between mental phenomena and behavior. Strictly speaking, this thesis does not say that there are no mental-behavioral entailments. What it does do is to give us a way of understanding DBA and other such principles connecting mind with behavior: It says that any such entailments have mental defeaters, not just physical defeaters.

What Kinds of Behavior Are Entailed by Mental States?

Suppose you want to greet someone. What behavior is entailed by this want? We might say: Greeting desires issue in greeting behavior. But what is greeting behavior? When you see Mary across the street and want to greet her, you will, for instance, wave your hand. The entailment is defeasible since you would not greet her, even though you want to, if you also thought that by doing so you might cause her embarrassment. Be that as it may, saying that wanting to greet someone issues in a *greeting* does not say much about the *observable physical behavior*, because greeting is an action that includes a robustly psychological component (behavior of type [iii] distinguished earlier). Greeting Mary involves *noticing* and *recognizing* her, *believing* (or at least *hoping*) that she will *notice* your physical gesture and *recognize* it as expressing your *intention* to greet her, and so on. Greeting obviously will not count as behavior of kind (i) or (ii)—that is, a physiological response or bodily movement.

But does wanting to greet entail any bodily movements? If so, what bodily movements? There are innumerable ways of greeting: You can greet by waving your right hand, waving your left hand, or waving both; by saying "Hi!" or "How are you?" or "Hey, how're you doing, Mary?"; by saying these things in French or Chinese (Mary is from France, and you and Mary are taking a Chinese class); by rushing up to Mary and shaking her hand or giving her a hug; and countless other ways. In fact, any physical gesture will do as long as it is socially recognized as a way of greeting.[13]

And there is a flip side to this. As travel books often warn us, a gesture that is recognized as a friendly and respectful greeting in one culture may be one of insult and an expression of disdain in another. Indeed, within our own culture the very same physical gesture could count as greeting someone, cheering your basketball team, bidding at an auction, signaling for a left turn, and any number of other things. The factors that determine exactly what it is that you are doing when you produce a physical gesture include the customs, habits, and conventions that are in force as well as the particular circumstances—a complex network of entrenched habits and customs, mutual expectations based on them, the agent's beliefs and intentions, and numerous other social and psychological factors and relationships.

Considerations like these make it seem exceedingly unlikely that anyone could ever produce correct behavioral definitions of mental terms that link each mental expression with an equivalent behavioral expression referring solely to pure physical behavior ("motions and noises"). In fact, we have seen here how futile it would be to look for interesting generalizations, much less definitions, connecting mental states, like wanting to greet someone, with physical behavior. To have even a glimmer of success, we would need, it seems, to work at the level of intentional action, not of physical behavior—that is, at the level of actions like greeting a friend, buying and selling, and reading the morning paper, not behavior at the level of motions and noises.

Do Pains Entail Pain Behavior?

Nevertheless, as noted earlier, some mental phenomena seem more closely tied to physical behavior—occurrences like pains and itches that have "natural expressions" in behavior. When you experience pain, you wince and groan and try to get away from the source of the pain; when you itch, you scratch. This perhaps is what gives substance to the talk of "pain behavior"; it is probably easier to recognize pain behavior than, say, greeting behavior, in an alien culture. We sometimes try to hide our pains and may successfully suppress winces and groans; nonetheless, pains do seem, under normal conditions, to issue in a roughly identifiable range of physical behavior. Does this mean that pains entail certain specific types of physical behavior?

Let us first get clear about what "entailment" is to mean for present purposes. When we say that pain "entails" winces and groans, we are saying that "Anyone in pain winces and groans" is *analytically*, or *conceptually*, *true*—that is, like "Bachelors are unmarried" and "Vixens are females," it is true *solely in virtue of the meanings of the terms involved* (or *the concepts expressed by these terms*). If "toothache" is definable, as Hempel claims, in terms of "weeping" and "making gesture G" (where we leave it to Hempel to specify G), toothache entails weeping and making gesture G in our sense. And if pain entails winces and groans, no organism could count as "being in pain" unless it could evince wincing and groaning behavior. That is, there is no "possible world" in which something is in pain but does not wince and groan.[14]

Some philosophers have argued that there is no pain-behavior entailment because pain behavior can be completely and thoroughly suppressed by some people, those "super-Stoics" and "super-Spartans" who have trained themselves not to manifest their pains in overt behavior.[15] This objection can be met, at least partially, by pointing out that super-Spartans, although they do not actually exhibit pain behavior, can still be said to have a *propensity*, or *disposition*, to exhibit pain behavior—that is, they *would* exhibit overt pain behavior *if certain conditions were to obtain*. It is only that some of these conditions do not obtain for them, and so the behavior disposition associated with pain remains unrealized. Thus, there is this crucial difference between a super-Spartan who is in pain and another super-Spartan who is not in pain: It is true of the former, but not the latter, that if certain conditions were to obtain for him (for example, he has renounced his super-Spartan code of conduct), he would wince and groan. It seems, therefore, that the objection based on the conceivability of super-Spartans can be substantially mitigated by formulating the entailment claim in terms of behavior dispositions or propensities rather than actual behavior production. This would be completely consistent with the behaviorist approach.

So the modified entailment thesis says this: It is an analytic, conceptual truth that anyone in pain has a propensity to wince or groan. Is this true?

Consider animals: Dogs and cats can surely feel pain. Do they wince or groan? Perhaps. How about squirrels or bats? How about snakes and octopuses? Evidently, in order to groan or wince or emit a specified type of behavior (such as screaming and writhing in pain), an organism needs a certain sort of body and bodily organs with specific capacities and powers. Only animals with vocal cords can groan or scream; presumably no one has ever observed a groaning snake or octopus! Thus, the entailment thesis under consideration has the consequence that organisms without vocal cords cannot be in pain, which is absurd. The point can be generalized: Whatever behavior type is picked, we can coherently imagine a pain-capable organism that is physically unsuited to produce behavior of that type.[16]

If this is the case, there is no specific behavior type that is entailed by pain. More generally, the same line of consideration should show that no specific behavior type is entailed by any mental state. And yet a weaker thesis, perhaps something like the following, may be true:

> *Weak Behavior Entailment Thesis.* For any pain-capable species[17] there is a certain behavior type B such that, for that species, being in pain entails a propensity to emit behavior of type B.

According to this thesis, then, each species may have its own special way of expressing pain behaviorally, although there are no universal and species-independent pain-to-behavior entailments. If this is correct, the concept of pain involves the concept of behavior only in this sense: Any organism in pain must be disposed to behave in some specific way or other. But there is no behavior pattern that can count as "pain behavior" across all pain-capable organisms (and perhaps also inorganic systems). Again, this makes the prospect of defining pain in terms of behavior exceedingly remote.

Ontological Behaviorism

Logical behaviorism is a claim about the meanings of psychological expressions; as you recall, the claim is that the meaning of every psychological term is definable exclusively on the basis of behavioral-physical terms. But we can also consider a behaviorist thesis about psychological states or phenomena as such, independently of the language in which they are described. Thus, a behaviorist might claim:

There are no psychological facts over and above behavioral facts; and there are no psychological states or events over and above actual and possible behavior.

Compare the following two claims about pain:

1. Pain = winces and groans.
2. Pain = the cause of winces and groans.

Claim (1) expresses what we may call "ontological behaviorism" about pain; if it is true, there indeed is nothing more to pain than pain behavior—that is, winces and groans. But (2) is not a form of ontological behaviorism, since the *cause* of winces and groans need not be just more behavior. Clearly (2) may be affirmed by someone who thinks that it is the *internal states* of organisms (say, certain neural states) that cause them to display pain behavior. Moreover, a dualist—whether she is a substance dualist or property dualist—can accept (2): She would take a private mental event, an inner pain experience, to be the cause of pain behavior. Moreover, we might even claim that (2) is analytically or conceptually true: The concept of pain is that of an internal state apt to cause characteristic pain behaviors like winces and groans.[18] Thus, (2) can be taken as a somewhat unexpected form of logical behaviorism about the expression "pain," since it allows us to eliminate "pain" wherever it occurs with an expression free of mentalistic terms.[19] We may then say this: Logical behaviorism does not entail ontological behaviorism.

Does ontological behaviorism entail logical behaviorism? Again, the answer has to be in the negative. From the fact that Xs are Ys, nothing interesting follows about the meanings of the expressions "X" and "Y"—in particular, nothing follows about their interdefinability. Consider some examples: We know that bolts of lightning are electric discharges in the atmosphere and that genes are DNA molecules. But the expressions "lightning" and "electric discharge in the atmosphere" are not conceptually related, much less synonymous; nor are the expressions "gene" and "DNA molecule."

In a similar vein, one could say, as some philosophers have said, that there are in this world no inner private episodes like pains, itches, and twinges but only observable behaviors or dispositions to exhibit such behaviors. One may say this because one holds a certain form of logical behaviorism or takes a dim view of supposedly private and subjective episodes in an inner theater. But one may be an ontological behaviorist on a methodological ground, affirming that there is *no need to posit* private inner events like pains and itches since, on account of their essentially subjective character, they can play no role in intersubjective communication and cannot be scientifically studied. A person holding such a position may well concede that the phenomenon purportedly designated by "pain" is an inner subjective state, but will insist that there is no reason to think that the word actually refers to anything real (compare with "witch," or "Big Foot").

The True Relationship Between Pain and Pain Behavior?

Our earlier discussion has revealed serious difficulties with any entailment claims about the relationship between pain and pain behavior, or more generally, between types of mental states and types of behavior. The considerations seemed to show that though our pains may cause our pain behaviors, this causal relation is a contingent, not a necessary, fact. But leaving the matter there is somehow unsatisfying: Surely pain behaviors—groans, winces, screams, writhings, attempts to get away, and all the rest—have something important to do with our notion of pain. How else could we learn, and teach, the concept of pain or the meaning of the word *pain*? Wouldn't we rightly deny the concept of pain to a person who does not at all appreciate the connection between pains and these characteristic pain behaviors? If a person observes someone writhing on the floor, clutching her broken leg, and screaming for help and yet refuses to acknowledge that she is experiencing pain, wouldn't it be correct to say that this person does not have the concept of pain, that he does not know what "pain" means? What we need is a positive account of the relationship between pain and pain behavior that explains their apparently intimate connection without making it into one of analytic entailment.

The following is one possible story. Let us begin with an analogy: How do we fix the meaning of "one meter long"—that is, the concept of a meter? We sketch an answer based on Saul Kripke's influential work on names and their references.[20] Consider the Standard Meter: a bar of platinum-iridium alloy kept in a vault near Paris.[21] Is the following statement necessarily, or analytically, true?

The Standard Meter is one meter long.

Does being the Standard Meter (or having the same length as the Standard Meter) entail being one meter long? The Standard Meter is a particular physical object, manufactured at a particular date and place and now located somewhere in France, and surely this metallic object might not have been the Standard Meter and might not have been one meter long. (It could have been fashioned into a bowl, or it could have been made into a longer rod of two meters.) In other words, it is a contingent fact that this particular platinum-iridium rod was selected as the Standard Meter, and it is a contingent fact that it is one meter long. No middle-sized physical object has the length it has necessarily; anything could be longer or shorter—or so it seems. We must conclude, then, that the statement that something has the same length as the Standard Meter does not logically entail that it is one meter long, and it is not analytically, or conceptually, true that if the length of an object coincides with that of the Standard Meter, it is one meter long.

But what, then, is the relationship between the Standard Meter and the concept of the meter? After all, the Standard Meter is not called that for nothing; there must be some intimate connection between the two. A plausible answer is that we specify the property of being one meter long (the meaning, if you wish, of the expression "one meter long") by the use of a contingent relationship in which the property stands. One meter is the length of this thing (namely, the Standard Meter) here and now. It is only contingently one meter long, but that is no barrier to our using it to specify what counts as one meter. This is just like when we point to a ripe tomato and say, "Red is the color of this tomato." It is only a contingent fact that this tomato is red (it could have been green), but we can use this contingent fact to specify what the color red is and what the word "red" means.

Let us see how a similar account might go for pain: We specify what pain is (or fix the meaning of "pain") by reference to a contingent fact about pain, namely, that pain causes winces and groans in humans. This is a contingent fact about this world. In worlds in which different laws hold, or worlds in which the central nervous systems of humans and those of other organisms are hooked up differently to peripheral sensory surfaces and motor output systems, the patterns of causal relations involving pain may be very different. But as things stand in this world, pain is the cause of winces and groans and certain other behaviors. In worlds in which pains do not cause winces and groans, different behaviors may count as pain behavior, in which case pain specifications in those worlds could advert to the behaviors caused by pains there. This is similar to the color case: If cucumbers but not ripe tomatoes were red, we would be specifying what "red" means by pointing to cucumbers instead.

The foregoing is only a sketch of an account but not an implausible one. It explains how (2) above, though only contingently true, can help specify what pain is and fix the reference of the term "pain." And it seems to show a good fit with the way we learn, and teach, the use of "pain" and other mental expressions denoting sensations. The approach brings mental expressions under the same rubric with many other expressions, as we have seen, such as "red" and "one meter long." It may well be that most terms for basic properties can be subsumed under this general Kripkean approach.

Scientific Behaviorism

So far we have been discussing behaviorism as a philosophical doctrine concerning the meanings of mental terms and the nature of mental states. But as we noted at the outset, "behaviorism" is also the name of an important and influential psychological movement initiated early in the twentieth century that came to dominate scientific psychology and the social sciences in North America and many other parts of the world for several decades. It held its position as the reigning methodology of the "behavioral sciences" until the latter half of the century, when "cognitivism" and "mentalism" began a strong and steady comeback.

Behaviorism in science can be viewed in two ways: First, as a precept on how psychology should be conducted as a science, it points to questions like what its proper domain should be, what conditions should be placed on admissible evidence, what its theories are supposed to accomplish, by what standards its explanations are to be evaluated, and so on. Second, behaviorism, especially B. F. Skinner's "radical behaviorism," is a specific behaviorist research paradigm seeking to construct psychological theories conforming to a fairly explicit and precisely formulated pattern (for example, Skinner's "operant conditioning"). Here we have room only for a brief and sketchy discussion of scientific behaviorism in the first sense. Discussion of Skinner's radical behaviorism is beyond the scope of this book.

We can begin with what may be called methodological behaviorism:

(I) The only admissible evidence for the science of psychology is observable behavioral data—that is, data concerning the observable physical behavior of organisms.

We can understand (I) somewhat more broadly than merely as a stricture on admissible "evidence" by focusing on the "data" it refers to. Data serve two closely related purposes in science: First, they constitute the domain of phenomena for which theories are constructed to provide explanations and predictions; second, they serve as the evidential basis that can support or undermine theories. What (I) says, therefore, is that psychological theories should attempt to explain and predict only data concerning observable behavior and that only such data should be used as evidence against which psychological theories are to be evaluated. These two points can be seen to collapse into one when we realize that explanatory and predictive successes and failures constitute, by and large, the only measure by which we evaluate how well theories are supported by evidence.

The main reason some psychologists and philosophers have insisted on the observability of psychological data is to ensure the *objective* or *intersubjective testability* of psychological theories. It is thought that introspective data—data obtained by a subject by inwardly inspecting her own inner mental theater—are essentially private and subjective and hence cannot serve as the basis for intersubjective validation of psychological theories. In short, the idea is that intersubjective access to data is required to ensure the possibility of intersubjective agreement in science and that the possibility of intersubjective agreement is required to ensure the scientific objectivity of psychology. Only behavioral (and more broadly, physical) data, it is thought, meet the condition of intersubjective observability. In short, (I) aims at securing the objectivity of psychology as a science.

What about a subject's verbal reports of her inner experiences? A subject in an experiment involving mental imagery might report: "I am now rotating the figure counterclockwise." What is wrong with taking the following as an item of our data: Subject S is rotating her mental image counterclockwise? Someone who holds (I) will say something like this: Strictly speaking, what we can properly consider an item of data here is S's utterance of the words "I am now rotating the figure counterclockwise." Counting S's actual mental operation of rotating her mental image as a datum involves the assumption that she is a competent speaker of English, that intersubjective meaning can be attached to reports of inner experience, and that she is reporting her experience correctly. These are all substantial psychological assumptions, and we cannot consider the subject's reports of her visual activity to meet the criterion of intersubjective verifiability. Therefore, unless these assumptions themselves can be behaviorally cashed out, the cognitive scientist is entitled only to the subject's utterance of the string of words, not the presumed content of those words, as part of her basic data.

Consciousness is usually thought to fall outside the province of psychological explanation for the behaviorist. Inner conscious states are not among the phenomena it is the business of psychological theory to explain or predict. In any case, many psychologists and cognitive scientists may find (I) by and large acceptable, although they are likely to disagree about just what is to count as *observable* behavior. (Some may, but others may not consider verbal reports, with their associated meanings, as observable behavior; some may regard verbal reports as admissible only as "noises.") A real disagreement arises, though, concerning the following stronger version of methodological behaviorism:

> (II) Psychological *theories* must not invoke the *internal states* of psychological subjects; that is, psychological explanations must not appeal to internal states of organisms, nor should references to such states occur in deriving predictions about behavior.

This appears to have been a tenet of Skinner's psychological program. On this principle, organisms are to be construed as veritable black boxes whose internal structure is forever closed to the psychological investigator. Psychological generalizations, therefore, must only correlate observable stimulus conditions as input, behavioral outputs, and subsequent reinforcements. But isn't it obvious that when the same stimulus is applied to two organisms, they can respond with different behavior output? How can we explain behavioral differences elicited by the same stimulus condition without invoking differences in their internal states?

The Skinnerian answer is that such behavioral differences can be explained by reference to the differences in the *history* of reinforcement for the two organisms; that is to say, the two organisms emit different behavior in response to the same stimulus because their *histories* involving external stimuli, elicited behaviors, and the reinforcements following the behaviors are different. But if such an explanation works, isn't that because the differences in the histories of the two organisms led to differences in their present internal states? Isn't it plausible to suppose that these differences *here and now* are what is directly implicated in the production of different behaviors *now*? To suppose otherwise would be to embrace "mnemic" causation—causal influence that leaps over a temporal gap with no intermediate links bridging cause and effect.

Apart from such metaphysical doubts, there appears to be an overwhelming consensus at this point that the stimulus-response-reinforcement model is simply inadequate to generate explanatory or predictive theories for vast areas of human and animal behaviors.

And why is it impermissible to invoke present internal differences as well as differences in histories to explain differences in behavior output? Notice how sweeping the constraint expressed by (II) really is: It outlaws references not only to inner mental states of the subject but also to its internal physical-biological states. Methodological concerns with the objectivity of psychology as a science provide an intelligible (if perhaps not sufficient) motivation for banishing the former, but it seems clearly insufficient to justify banning the latter from psychological theories and explanations. Even if it is true, as Skinner claims,[22] that invoking internal neurobiological states does not help psychological theorizing, that hardly constitutes a sufficient ground for prohibiting it as a matter of scientific methodology.

In view of this, we may consider a further version of behaviorism as a rule of psychological methodology:

(III) Psychological theories must make no reference to inner mental states in formulating psychological explanations.

Here, "mental" is tacitly understood to imply "nonphysical." This principle allows the introduction of internal biological states, including states of the central nervous system, into psychological theories and explanations, prohibiting only reference to inner mental states. But what is to count as such a state? Does this principle permit the use of such concepts as "drive," "information," "memory," "attention," "mental representation," and the like in psychological theories? To answer this question we would have to examine these concepts in the context of particular psychological theories making use of them; this is not a task for armchair philosophical conceptual analysis. We should keep in mind, though, that the chief rationale for (III)—in fact, the driving motivation for the entire behaviorist methodology—is the insistence on the objective testability of theories and public access to sharable data. This means that what (III) is intended to prohibit is the introduction of *private subjective* states for which objective access is thought to be problematic, not the use of theoretical constructs posited by psychological theories for explanatory and predictive purposes, as long as these meet the requirement of intersubjectivity. Unlike overt behavior, these constructs are not, as a rule, "directly observable," and they are not strictly definable or otherwise re-ducible in terms of observable behavior. However, they differ from the para-digmatic inner mental states in that they apparently do not show the first-person/third-person asymmetry of epistemic access. Scientific theories often introduce theoretical concepts for entities (electrons, magnetic fields, quarks) and properties (spin, polarization) that go far beyond the limits of human observation. Like any other science, psychological theory should be entitled to such theoretical constructs.

But in excluding private conscious states from psychological theory, (III) excludes them from playing any causal-explanatory role in relation to behav-ior. If it is true, as we ordinarily think, that some of our behavior is caused by inner mental states disallowed by (III), our psychological theory is likely to be incomplete: There may well be behavior for which no theory meeting (III) can provide full explanations. (Some of these issues are discussed further in chapters 7, 8, and 10.)

Are there other methodological constraints for psychological theory? How can we be sure that the states and entities posited by a psychological theory (for example, "intelligence," "mental representation," "drive reduc-tion") are "real"? If, in explaining the same data, one psychological theory posits one set of unobservable states and another theory posits an entirely different set, which theory, if any, should be believed? That is, which theory represents the *psychological reality* of the subjects? Does it make sense to raise such questions? If it does, should there be the further requirement that the entities and states posited by a psychological theory have a "biological real-ity"—that is, must they somehow be "realized" or "implemented" in the biological-physical structures and processes of the organism? These are im-portant questions about the science of psychology, and we deal with some of them later in our discussion of mind-body theories and the issue of re-ductionism (chapters 4, 5, 6, and 10).

Further Readings

The influential classic work representing logical behaviorism is Gilbert Ryle, *The Concept of Mind*. See also Rudolf Carnap, "Psychology in Physical Language." For an accessible Wittgen-steinian perspective on mentality and behavior, see Norman Malcolm's contributions in *Consciousness and Causality* by D. M. Armstrong and Norman Malcolm. For scientific behaviorism, see B. F. Skinner's *Science and Human Behavior* and *About Behaviorism*. Both are accessible to nonspecialists.

For a historically important critique of Skinnerian behaviorism, see Noam Chomsky's review of Skinner's *Verbal Behavior*. For criticism of logical behaviorism, see Roderick M. Chisholm, *Perceiving*, pp. 173–85; and Hilary Putnam, "Brains and Behavior."

Notes

1. William James, *The Principles of Psychology*, p. 15.

2. Ibid., p. 185.

3. J. B. Watson, "Psychology as the Behaviorist Views It," p. 158.

4. William James, *The Principles of Psychology*, p. 21 (emphasis in original).

5. Ludwig Wittgenstein, *Philosophical Investigations*, section 293. To make this story work, we must assume that there are no beetles around us, outside the little boxes.

6. For the notion of behavior as internally caused bodily motion, see Fred Dretske, *Explaining Behavior*, chs. 1 and 2.

7. Carl Hempel, "The Logical Analysis of Psychology," p. 91.

8. Positivists, including Hempel, customarily used a much looser sense of definition (and translatability); however, for logical behaviorism to be a significant thesis, we need to construe definition in a stronger sense.

9. Carl Hempel, "The Logical Analysis of Psychology," p. 17.

10. There is a long-standing controversy in moral theory as to whether certain beliefs (for example, the belief that you have a moral duty to help a friend) by themselves, without any associated desires, can motivate a person to act. The dispute, however, concerns only a small class of beliefs, chiefly evaluative and normative beliefs about what ought to be done, what is desirable, and the like.

11. For an early statement of this point, see Roderick M. Chisholm, *Perceiving*.

12. See Donald Davidson, "Mental Events," for some hints at this sort of indefinite defeasibility of the mental-behavioral relationship. This may be what is distinctive and interesting about "ceteris paribus laws" about mental phenomena; nothing similar seems present in such laws about physical phenomena.

13. The phenomena discussed in this paragraph and the next are noted in Berent Enç, "Redundancy, Degeneracy, and Deviance in Action."

14. We could use a somewhat weaker definition of entailment, thus: "M entails B" is true just in case "If M occurs, then *ceteris paribus* (or *under normal conditions*), B will occur" is true. The stronger definition used in the text simplifies discussion; however, the main points can be made with the weaker, perhaps more realistic, understanding of entailment.

15. Hilary Putnam, "Brains and Behavior."

16. Perhaps this can be called a "multiple realizability" thesis in regard to behavior. On multiple realizability, see chapters 4 and 10. Whether or not it has consequences for behaviorism that are similar to the supposed consequences of the multiple realizability of mental states is an interesting further question.

17. Species may be too wide here, given the fact that expressions of pain are, at least to some extent, culture-specific and even differ from person to person within the same culture.

18. See chapters 5 and 6 for discussion of the functionalist conception of pain as that of a "causal intermediary" between certain stimulus conditions (for example, tissue damage) and characteristic pain behaviors.

19. This does not mean that the original logical behaviorists, like Hempel and Gilbert Ryle, would have accepted (2) as a behavioral characterization of "pain." The point, however, is that it meets Hempel's translatability thesis—his form of logical behaviorism. Note that the "cause" is a topic-neutral term—it is neither mental nor behavioral-physical.

20. See Saul Kripke, *Naming and Necessity*.

21. The meter is no longer defined this way; the current definition, adopted in 1984 by the General Conference on Weights and Measures, is reportedly based on the distance traveled by light through a vacuum in a certain (very small) fraction of a second.

22. See B. F. Skinner, *Science and Human Behavior*.

4

Mind as the Brain

The Psychoneural Identity Theory

Some ancient Greeks thought that the heart was the organ responsible for thoughts and feelings—an idea that has survived, we are told, in the traditional symbolism of the heart as signifying love and romance. But the Greeks got it wrong; we now think, with good reason, that the brain is where the action is as far as our mental life is concerned. If you ask people where they think their minds or thoughts are located, they will point to their heads. But does this mean only that the mind and brain share the same location, or something stronger, namely, that the mind *is* the brain? We consider here a theory that makes this stronger claim—that the mind is identical with the brain and that for a creature to have mentality is for it to have a functioning brain with certain capacities and powers.

Mind-Brain Correlations

But why are we inclined to think that the brain is "the seat of our mental life," as Descartes might have put it? The answer seems clear: There are *pervasive and systematic psychoneural correlations*, that is, *correlations between mental phenomena and brain processes*. This is not something we know a priori; we know it from empirical evidence. For example, we observe that injuries to the brain often have a dramatic impact on mental life, affecting the

81

ability to reason, recall, and perceive, and that they can drastically impair a person's cognitive capacities and even alter her personality traits. Chemical changes in the brain brought on by ingestion of alcohol, antidepressants, and other psychoactive drugs can bring about changes in our moods, emotions, and cognitive functions. When a brain concussion knocks us out, our conscious life goes blank. We have various sophisticated medical imaging techniques that allow us to "see" just what is going on in our brains when we are engaged in certain mental activities, like seeing green or feeling agitated. All in all, it is safe to say that we now have overwhelming and incontrovertible evidence attesting to the centrality of the brain and its activities as determinants of our mental life.

A badly scraped elbow can cause you a searing pain, and a mild food poisoning is often accompanied by stomachaches and queasy feelings. Irradiations of your retinas causes visual sensations, which in turn cause beliefs about objects and events around you. Stimulations of your sensory surfaces lead to sensory and perceptual experiences of various kinds. However, peripheral neural events are only remote causes; we think that they bring about conscious experiences only because they cause appropriate states of the brain. This is how anesthesia works: If the nerve signals coming from sensory peripheries are blocked or the normal functions of the brain are interfered with so that the central neural processes that underlie conscious experience are prevented from occurring, there will be no experience of pain or no experience of anything. It is plausible that everything that occurs in mental life has a state of the brain (or the central nervous system) as its *proximate* physical basis. It would be difficult to deny that the very existence of our mentality depends on the existence of appropriate neural structures: If all the molecules that make up your brain were taken away, your whole mental life would be lost, just as surely as taking away all the molecules making up your body would result in your ceasing to exist. At least that is the way things seem. We may summarize all this in the following thesis:

Mind-Brain Correlation Thesis. For each type M of mental event that occurs to an organism *o*, there exists a brain state of kind B (M's "neural correlate" or "substrate") such that M occurs to *o* at time *t* if and only if B occurs to *o* at *t*.

According to this thesis, then, each type of mental event that can occur to an organism has a neural correlate that is both necessary and sufficient for its occurrence. So for each organism there is a set of mind-brain correlations covering every kind of mental state it is capable of having.

Two points may be noted about these brain-mind correlations:

1. They are "lawlike": The fact that pain is experienced when certain of your neural fibers (say, C-fibers and A-fibers) are activated is a matter of *lawful regularity*, not accidental co-occurrences.
2. Even the smallest change in your mental life cannot occur unless there is some specific (perhaps still unknown) change in your brain state; for example, where there is a difference between two conscious states, there must be a difference between the two corresponding neural substrates.[1]

Another way of putting these points, though this is not strictly equivalent, is to say that mentality *supervenes* on brain states and that this supervenience holds as a matter of law. Remember that this supervenience, if it indeed holds, is something we know from observation and experience, not a priori. Moreover, specific correlations—that is, correlations between specific types of mental states (say, pain) and specific types of brain states (say, the activation of certain neural fibers)—are again matters of empirical research and discovery, and we may assume that many of the details about these correlations are still largely unknown. However, it is knowledge of these specific correlations, rough and incomplete though it may be, that ultimately underlies our confidence in the general thesis of mind-brain correlation and mind-brain supervenience. If Aristotle had been correct (and he *might* have been correct) about the heart being the engine of our mentality, we would have a mind-heart correlation thesis and mind-heart supervenience rather than the mind-brain correlation thesis and mind-brain supervenience.

Making Sense of Mind-Brain Correlations

When a systematic correlation between two properties or event types has been observed, we want an explanation, or interpretation, of the correlation: Why do the properties F and G correlate? Why is it that an event of type F occurs just when an event of type G occurs? We do not want to countenance too many "brute," unexplained coincidences in nature. An explanatory demand of this kind becomes even more pressing when we observe systematic patterns of correlation between two large families of properties, like mental and neural properties. Let us first look at some examples of property correlations outside the mind-brain case:

a. Whenever the ambient temperature falls below 20 degrees Fahrenheit and stays there for several days, the local lakes and ponds freeze over. Why? The answer, of course, is that the low temperature *causes* the water in the ponds to freeze. The two events are *causally related*, and that is why the observed correlation occurs.

b. You enter a clock shop and find an astounding scene: Dozens and dozens of clocks of all shapes and sizes are busily ticking away, and they all show exactly the same time, 2:00. A while later, you see all of them showing exactly 2:30, and so on. What explains this marvelous correlation among these clocks? It could not be a coincidence, we think. One possible answer is that the shopkeeper synchronized all the clocks, which are all working properly, before the shop opened in the morning. Here, a *common past cause*, the shopkeeper's action in the morning, explains the correlations that are now observed; or, as we say, one clock showing 3:30 and another showing the same time are *collateral effects of a common cause*. There are no direct causal relationships between the clocks that are responsible for the correlations.

c. We can imagine a slightly different explanation of why the clocks are keeping the same time: These clocks actually are not very accurate, and some of them gain or lose time markedly every five minutes or so. But there is a little leprechaun whose job is to run around the shop, unseen by the customers, synchronizing the clocks every two or three minutes. That is why every time you look, the clocks show the same time. This again is a *common-cause* explanation of a correlation, but it is different from the story in (b) in the following respect: This explanation involves a continued intervention of a causal agent, whereas in (b) a single cause in the past is sufficient. In neither case, however, is there a direct cause-effect relationship between the correlated events.

d. Why do temperature and pressure covary for gases confined in a rigid container? The temperature and pressure of a gas are both dependent on the motions of the molecules that compose the gas: The temperature is the average kinetic energy of the molecules, and the pressure is the momentum imparted to the walls of the container (per unit area) by the molecules colliding with them. Thus, the rise in temperature and the rise in pressure can be viewed as *two aspects* of one and the same underlying microprocess.

e. Why does lightning occur just when there is an electric discharge between clouds or between clouds and the ground? Because lightning simply *is* an electric discharge involving clouds and the ground. There is here only one phenomenon, not two that are correlated with each other, and what we thought were distinct correlated phenomena turn out to be one and the same. Here the apparent correlation is understood as one of *identity*.

f. Why do the phases of the moon (full, half, quarter, and so on) covary with the tidal actions of the ocean (spring tides, neap tides, and so on)? Because the relative positions of the earth, the moon, and the sun determine both the phases of the moon and the combined strength of the gravitational forces of attraction exerted on the ocean water by the moon and the sun. So the changes in gravitational force are the proximate causes of tidal actions, and the relative positions of the three bodies can be thought of as their remote cause. The phases of the moon are merely collateral effects of the positions of the three bodies involved and serve only as an indication of what the positions are (full moon when the earth is between the sun and the moon on a straight line, and so on), having no causal role whatever on tidal actions.

What about explaining, or understanding, mind-brain correlations? Which of the models we have surveyed best fits the mind-body case? As we would expect, all of these models have been tried. We begin with some causal approaches to the mind-body relation:

Causal Interactionism. Descartes thought that causal interaction between the mind and the body occurred in the pineal gland (chapter 2). He speculated that "animal spirits"—fluids made up of extremely fine particles flowing around the pineal gland—cause it to move in various ways, and these motions of the gland in turn cause conscious states of the mind. Conversely, the mind could cause the gland to move in various ways, affecting the flow of the surrounding animal spirits. This in turn influenced the flow of these fluids to different parts of the body, ultimately issuing in various physiological changes and bodily movements.[2]

"Preestablished Harmony" Between Mind and Body. Leibniz, like many of his contemporaries, thought that no coherent sense could be made of

Descartes' idea that an immaterial mind, which is not even in physical space, could causally interact with a material body like the pineal gland, managing to move this not-so-insignificant lump of tissue hither and thither. On his view, the mind and the body are in a "preestablished harmony," rather like the clocks that were synchronized by the shopkeeper in the morning, with God having started off our minds and bodies in a harmonious relationship. Whether this is any less fantastical an idea than Descartes' idea of mind-body causation, however, is a debatable question.

Occasionalism.   According to Malebranche, another great Continental rationalist, whenever a mental event appears to cause a physical event or a physical event appears to cause a mental event, it is only an illusion. There is no direct causal relation between "finite minds" and bodies; when a mental event, say, your will to raise your arm, occurs, that only serves as an *occasion* for God to intervene and cause your arm to rise. Divine intervention is also responsible for the apparent causation of mental events by physical events: when your finger is cut, that again is an occasion for God to step in and cause you pain. This view is known as occasionalism. It was an outcome of the doctrine, accepted by Malebranche and many others at the time, that God is the only genuine causal agent in this world. The role of God, then, is rather like that of the little leprechaun in the clock shop whose job is to keep the clocks running synchronized at all times by continuous timely interventions.

The Double-Aspect Theory.   Spinoza claimed that mind and body are simply two correlated aspects of a single underlying substance that is in itself neither mental nor material. This theory, like the doctrine of preestablished harmony and occasionalism, denies direct causal relationships between the mental and the physical; however, unlike them, it does not invoke God's causal action to explain the mental-physical correlations. The observed correlations are there because they are two distinguishable aspects of one underlying reality. A modern form of this approach is known as neutral monism.

Epiphenomenalism.   According to T. H. Huxley, every mental event is caused by a physical event in the brain, but mental events have no causal power of their own, being the absolute terminal links of causal chains.[3] So all mental events are effects of the physiological processes going on in our nervous system, but they are powerless to cause anything else—not even other mental events. Thus, you "will" your arm to rise, and it rises. But to think that your volition is the cause of the rising of the arm is to commit the same error as thinking that the changes in the phases of the moon cause the changes in tidal motions. The real cause of the arm's rising is a certain neural event in your brain that also causes your volition to raise the arm, just as in the case of the moon and the tides the relative positions of the earth, the moon, and the sun are the true cause of both the tidal motions and the phases of the moon. (More on epiphenomenalism in chapter 7.)

Emergentism.   There is another interesting response to the question "Why are mental phenomena correlated with neural phenomena in the way they are?" It is this: The question is unanswerable—the correlations are "brute facts" that we must simply accept; they are not subject to further explanation. This is the position of emergentism. It holds that when biological processes attain a certain level of organizational complexity, a wholly new type of phenomenon, namely, consciousness, "emerges," and these "emergent" phenomena are not explainable in terms of the lower-level physical-biological phenomena. There is no explanation of why, say, pains rather than itches emerge from C-fiber activations or why pains emerge from C-fiber activations rather than another kind of neural state. Indeed, there is no explanation of why state conscious should emerge from neural-biological processes. That there are just these emergence relationships and not others must be accepted, in the words of Samuel Alexander, a leading theoretician of the emergence school, "with natural piety."[4] Thus, emergentism presents another possible response to the mind-body problem: Mental phenomena are brute emergent phenomena, and we should expect no further explanation of why they emerge. That they do must be recognized as a fundamental fact about the natural world. (More on emergentism in chapter 10.)

The Psychoneural (or Psychophysical, Mind-Body) Identity Theory.   This position, formulated and explicitly advanced as a solution to the mind-body problem in the late 1950s, advocates the *identification* of mental states and events with the physical processes in the brain. Just as there are no bolts of lightning as phenomena *over and above* atmospheric electric discharges, there are no mental events *over and above* the neural (ultimately physicochemical) processes in the brain. "Lightning" and "electric discharge" are not lexical synonyms, and the Greeks probably knew something about lightnings but nothing about electric discharges; nonetheless, lightnings are just electric discharges, and the two expressions "lightning" and "atmospheric electric discharge" refer to the same phenomenon. In the same way, the terms "pain" and "C-fiber activation" do not have the same meaning; Socrates knew a lot about pains but nothing about C-fiber activations. Still, the two terms may pick out the same phenomenon, and according to the identity theory, that is exactly the case: Pains turn out to be the activations of C-fibers, just as lightnings turned out to be electrical discharges. In many ways, mind-brain identity seems like a natural position to take; it is not just that we point to our heads when we are asked where our thoughts are. Unless you are willing to embrace Cartesian immaterial mental substances outside physical space, what could your mind be if not your brain?

*   *   *

But what are the arguments that favor the identification of mental events with brain events? Are there compelling, or at least plausible, arguments? There are three principal arguments for the mind-brain identity theory. These are the simplicity argument, the explanatory argument, and the causal argument. We will see how these arguments can be formulated and defended and what possible objections and difficulties arise for them. We will then turn to some arguments designed to show that the mind-brain identity theory is implausible and untenable.

The Argument from Simplicity

J. J. C. Smart, whose classic 1959 essay "Sensations and Brain Processes" played a major role in establishing the psychoneural identity theory as a major position on the mind-body problem, emphasizes the importance of *simplicity* as a ground for accepting the theory.[5] He writes:

> Why do I wish [to identify sensations with brain processes]? Mainly because of Occam's razor. . . . There does seem to be, so far as science is concerned, nothing in the world but increasingly complex arrangements of physical constituents. All except for one place: in consciousness. That is, for a full description of what is going on in a man you would have to mention not only the physical processes in his tissues, glands, nervous system, and so forth, but also his states of consciousness: his visual, auditory, and tactual sensations, his aches and pains. That these should be *correlated* with brain processes does not help, for to say that they are *correlated* is to say that they are something "over and above." . . . So sensations, states of consciousness, do seem to be the one sort of thing left outside the physicalist picture, and for various reasons I just cannot believe that this can be so. That everything

be explicable in terms of physics . . . except the occurrence of sensations seems to me frankly unbelievable.[6]

Occam's (or Ockham's) razor, named after the fourteenth-century philosopher William of Ockham, is a principle that advocates simplicity and parsimony as important virtues of theories and hypotheses. The following two formulations are among the standard ways of understanding this principle:[7]

I. Entities must not be multiplied beyond necessity.
II. What can be done with fewer assumptions should not be done with more.

Principle (I) urges us to adopt the simplest ontology possible, one that posits no unnecessary entities—that is, no entities that have no work to do. A crucial question in applying this principle, of course, is to determine what counts as going "beyond necessity," or what "work" needs to be done. The physicalist would hold that Cartesian immaterial minds are useless and unneeded posits; the Cartesian dualist, however, would disagree with the physicalist precisely on that point. Principle (II) can be taken as urging simplicity and economy in our theorizing: Choose the theory that gives the simplest, most parsimonious, descriptions and explanations of the phenomena in its domain—that is, the theory that does its descriptive and explanatory work with the fewest number of independent assumptions or hypotheses. When Napoleon asked the astronomer and mathematician Pierre de Laplace why God was absent from his theory of the planetary system, Laplace is reported to have replied, "Sir, I have no need of that hypothesis." To explain what needs to be explained (the stability of the planetary system in this instance), we can do well enough with physical laws alone; we do not *also* need, Laplace is saying, the assumption that God exists. Here, he is invoking version (II) of Ockham's razor.

There seem to be three lines of consideration that we might consider in attempting to argue for the mind-brain identity theory on the ground of simplicity.

First, identification in general reduces the number of entities and thereby enhances ontological simplicity. When you say X is the same thing as Y—or as Smart says, that X is not something "over and above" Y—you are saying that there is just one thing here, not two. So if pain as a mental kind is identified with its neural correlate, we simplify our ontology on two levels: First, there is no mental kind, being in pain, over and above C-fiber stimulation;

second—and this follows from the preceding point—there are no individual pain episodes over and above instances of C-fiber stimulation. In this rather obvious way, the mind-brain identity theory simplifies our ontology.

Second, it may also be argued that psychoneural identification is conducive to conceptual or linguistic simplicity as well. If all mental states are systematically identified with their neural correlates, there is a sense in which mentalistic language—language in which we speak of pains and thoughts—is *in principle* replaceable by a physical language in which we speak of neural processes. The mentalistic language certainly is practically indispensable and will almost certainly remain so; perhaps we will never have a full catalog of mental-neural correlations, and in any case, very few of us are going to be experts in brain science. On the identity theory, however, descriptions formulated in a mental vocabulary do not report facts or phenomena distinct from those reported by a comprehensive physical-biological language, and this makes them dispensable. There are no excess facts beyond physical facts to be described in some nonphysical language. In that sense, physical language is complete and universal.

Third, and this is what Smart seems to have in mind, suppose we stop short of identifying pain with C-fiber stimulation and stick with the correlation "Pain occurs if and only if (iff) Cfs occurs." As earlier noted, correlations cry out for explanation. How might such correlations be explained? In science, we standardly explain laws and correlations by deriving them from other, more fundamental laws and correlations. From what more basic correlations could we derive "Pain occurs iff Cfs occurs"? It seems quite certain that it cannot be derived from purely physical-biological correlations and laws alone. The reason is that these laws do not even speak of pain; the term, or concept, "pain" does not appear in physical-biological laws, for the simple reason that it is not part of the physical-biological language. So if the pain-Cfs correlation is to be explained, its explanatory premises (premises from which it is to be derived) will have to include at least one law correlating some mental phenomenon with a physical-biological phenomenon—that is, at least one psychoneural correlation. But this puts us back in square one: How do we explain this perhaps more fundamental mental-physical correlation? The upshot is that we are likely to be stuck with the pain-Cfs correlation and countless other such psychoneural correlations, one for each distinct type of mental state. (Think about how many mental states there are or could be, and in particular, consider this: For each declarative sentence *p*, such as "It will snow tomorrow," there is the belief that *p*—that is, the belief that it will snow tomorrow.) And all such correlations would have to be taken as "brute" basic laws of the world—"brute" in the sense that they are not further explainable and must be taken to be among the fundamental assumptions of our total theory of the world.

But such a theory of the world should strike us as intolerably complex and bloated—the antithesis of simplicity and elegance. For one thing, it includes a huge and motley crowd of psychoneural correlation laws—a potentially infinite number of them—among its basic laws. For another, each of these psychoneural laws is highly complex: Pain may be a "simple" sensory quality, but look at the physical side of the pain-Cfs correlation. It consists of an untold number of molecules, atoms, and particles. We expect our basic laws to be reasonably simple, and we expect to explain complex phenomena by combining and iteratively applying these simple laws. We do not expect basic laws to deal in physical structures consisting of zillions of particles in unimaginably complex configurations. This makes our total theory messy, inflated, and inelegant.

Compare this bloated picture with what we get if we move from psychoneural correlations to psychoneural identities—from "pain occurs iff Cfs occurs" to "pain = Cfs." Pain and Cfs are one and not two, and we are not faced by two distinct phenomena whose correlation needs to be explained. In this way, psychoneural identities permit us to transcend and eliminate psychoneural correlation laws—what Herbert Feigl aptly called "nomological danglers."[8] Moreover, as Smart emphasizes, the identification of the mental with the physical brings the mental within the purview of physical theory, and ultimately our basic physics constitutes a complete and comprehensive explanatory theory that covers the entire natural world. This picture is far simpler and more elegant than the earlier picture in which any complete theory of the world must include all those complex mind-brain laws in addition to the basic laws of physics. Anyway, that is the argument. It should be clear that this argument appeals to version (II) of Ockham's razor.

What should we think of the simplicity argument for psychoneural identification? We will forgo a detailed criticism and comments here. But the reader is invited to consider how a Cartesian, or a dualist of any stripe, might respond to it, keeping in mind that one person's "simple" theory may well be another person's "incomplete" theory. That is to say, what counts as "going beyond necessity" in a given situation can be a matter of dispute—in fact, it is often the very bone of contention between the disputants.

Two Explanatory Arguments for Psychoneural Identity

According to some philosophers, mind-brain identities can do important and indispensable explanatory work—that is, they help explain certain facts and phenomena that would otherwise remain unexplained, and this provides us with a sufficient warrant for their acceptance. Sometimes an appeal is made to the principle of "inference to the best explanation." This principle is usually taken as an inductive rule of inference, and there is widespread agreement that it is an important rule (if not the principal one, as some of its promoters claim) used in the empirical sciences to evaluate the merits of theories and hypotheses. The rule can be stated something like this:

> *Principle of Inference to the Best Explanation.* If hypothesis H gives the *best* explanation of phenomena in a given domain when compared with other rival hypotheses $H_1, \ldots, H_n$, we may accept H as true (or at least H should be preferred over $H_1, \ldots, H_n$).[9]

It is then argued that mind-brain identities, like "pain = Cfs," give the best explanations of certain facts, better than the explanations afforded by rival theories. The conclusion would then follow that the mind-body identity theory is the preferred perspective on the mind-body problem.

This argument comes in two versions, which diverge from each other in several significant ways. We consider them in turn.

Explanatory Argument 1

The two explanatory arguments differ on the question of what it is that is supposed to be explained by psychoneural identities—that is, on the question of the "explanandum." Explanatory argument 1 takes the explanandum to be psychoneural correlations, claiming that psychoneural identities give the best explanation of psychoneural correlations. Explanatory argument 2, in contrast, argues that the identities, rather than explaining the correlations, explain facts about mental phenomena that would otherwise remain unexplained. Let us now see how explanatory argument 1 is supposed to work.

In the first place, the claim is that specific psychoneural identities, like "pain = Cfs" and "consciousness = pyramidal cell activity," explain the corresponding correlations, like "pain occurs iff Cfs occurs" and "a person is conscious iff pyramidal cell activity is occurring in his or her brain." As an analogy, consider this: Someone might be curious why Clark Kent turns up whenever and wherever Superman turns up. What better, or simpler, explanation could be offered than the identity "Clark Kent *is* Superman"?[10] So the proponents of this form of explanatory argument claim that the following is an explanation of a psychoneural correlation and that it is the best available explanation of it:

(α) Pain = Cfs.
   Therefore, pain occurs iff Cfs occurs.

Similarly for consciousness and pyramidal cell activity, as well as countless other psychological and their correlated neural properties.

Second, the claim is also made that the psychoneural identity theory offers the best explanation of the pervasive fact of psychoneural correlations, like this:

(β) For every mental property M there is a physical property P such that M = P.
   Therefore, for every mental property M there is a physical property P such that M occurs iff P occurs.[11]

If we could show that psychoneural identities are the best explanations of psychoneural correlations, the principle of inference to the best explanation would sanction the conclusion that psychoneural identities are to be taken as true—or at least that the psychoneural identity theory is the preferred position on the mind-body problem. Anyway, that is the idea.

But does the argument work? Obviously, specific explanations like (α) are crucial; if they do not work as explanations, there is no chance that (β), the explanation of the general mind-correlation thesis, will work. So is (α) an explanation? And is it the best possible explanation of the correlation? A detailed discussion of the second question would be a complicated business: We would have to compare (α) with the explanations offered by epiphenomenalism, the double-aspect theory, the causal theory, and so on. But we can say this much in behalf of (α): It is ontologically the simplest. The reason is that all these other theories are dualist theories, and in consequence they have to countenance more entities—mental events in addition to brain events. But is (α) the *best* explanation? Fortunately, we can set aside this question because there are reasons to be skeptical about its being an explanation at all. If it is not an explanation, the question of whether it is the best explanation does not arise.

First consider this: If pain indeed is identical with Cfs, in what sense do they "correlate" with each other? For there is here only one thing, whether you call it "pain" or "Cfs," and as Smart says in the paragraph quoted earlier, you cannot correlate something with itself. For Smart, the very point of moving to the identity "pain = Cfs" is to transcend and cancel the correlation "pain occurs iff Cfs occurs." This is the "nomological dangler" to be eliminated. For it seduces us to ask wrongheaded and unanswerable questions like "Why does pain correlate with Cfs?" and "Why doesn't itch correlate with Cfs?" and "Why doesn't pain correlate with another neural state, say, the stimulation of A-fibers?" and "Why does any conscious experience correlate with Cfs?" and so on. By opting for the identity, we show that these questions have no answers, since the presupposition of the questions—namely, that pain *correlates* with Cfs—is false. The question "Why is it the case that *p*?" presupposes that *p* is true. When *p* is false, the question has no correct answer. Showing that a demand for an explanation rests on a false presupposition is one way to deal with the demand; providing an explanation is not the only way.

Second, although an appeal is made to the principle of inference to the best explanation as a scientific rule of induction, explanations of correlations in the sciences seem to work quite differently. There appear to be two principal ways of explaining correlations in science. First, scientists often explain a correlation by deducing it from more fundamental correlations and laws (as when the correlation between the length and the period of swing of a simple pendulum is explained in terms of more basic laws). Second, a correlation is explained by showing that the two correlated phenomena are collateral effects of a common cause. (Recall the earlier example in which is explained the correlation between the phases of the moon and tidal actions in terms of the astronomical configurations involving the sun, the moon, and the earth.) We do not often (if ever) see the scientist resorting to identities to explain correlations.

Finally, exactly how does (α) work as an explanation? How is the conclusion "pain occurs iff Cfs occurs" derived from "pain = Cfs"? In formal logic, there is no rule of inference that says "From 'X = Y' infer 'X occurs iff Y occurs'"—for good reason, since a nonlogical term like "occur" is not part of formal logic. Instead, what we find are the following two rules governing identity:

Axiom schema: X = X
Substitution rule: From "... X ...", and "X = Y", infer "... Y ..."

The first rule says that you can always write down as an axiom any sentence of the form "X = X," like "Socrates = Socrates" and "3 + 5 = 3 + 5." The second rule allows you to put "equals for equals." To put it another way, if X = Y and something is true of X, the same thing must be true of Y. This is the rule that is of the essence of identity. We can now see how "pain occurs iff Cfs occurs" may be derived from "pain = Cfs" as follows:

(γ) Pain occurs iff pain occurs.
    Pain = Cfs.
    Therefore, pain occurs iff Cfs occurs.

The first line is a tautology of sentential logic, an instance of "*p* iff *p*," where *p* is any sentence, and we may write down a tautology anywhere in a deduction. The third line, the desired correlation, is derived by substituting "Cfs" for the second occurrence of "pain" in this tautology, in accordance with the substitution rule. As you see, the single premise of this purported explanation is a contentless tautology, and the identity merely allows us to rewrite it by putting equals for equals. The conclusion "pain occurs iff Cfs occurs," on this derivation, is a mere *rewrite* of "pain occurs iff pain occurs" and is equally contentless. These considerations fit in well with Smart's view that identities cancel, or void, correlations rather than explain them.

The role of identities in explanations is not well understood; there has been little informative discussion of this issue in the literature. But it should be clear that there are reasons to be skeptical about the claim that psychoneural identities explain psychoneural correlations and that for that reason the identities should be accepted as true.

Explanatory Argument 2

According to this version of the explanation argument, mind-body identities do not explain mind-body correlations; rather, they enable us to explain certain facts about mentality that would otherwise go unexplained. How might we explain the fact that pain causes a feeling of distress? What is the causal mechanism involved? Suppose we have the following psychoneural identities available:

Pain = Cfs.
Distress = neural state N.

We might then be able to formulate the following neurophysiological explanation of why pain causes distress:

(θ) Neurophysiological laws
    Cfs causes neural state N.
    (I_1) Pain = Cfs.
    (I_2) Distress = neural state N.
    Therefore, pain causes distress.

Neurophysiological laws explain why Cfs causes N, and from this we derive our explanandum "Pain causes distress" with the help of the two psychoneural identities, (I_1) and (I_2). These identities help us explain a psychological regularity in terms of its underlying neural mechanism, and this seems just the kind of deeper scientific understanding we seek about higher-level psychological regularities.

Compare this with the situation in which we refuse to enhance correlations into identities. The best we could do with correlations would be something like this:

(λ) Neurophysiological laws
    Cfs   causes neural state N.
    (C_1) Pain occurs iff Cfs occurs.
    (C_2) Distress occurs iff neural state N occurs.
    Therefore, pain correlates with a phenomenon that causes a
       phenomenon with which distress correlates.

This hardly is an explanation of why pain causes distress. To explain it we need the identities (I_1) and (I_2); the correlations (C_1) and (C_2) are not enough. According to the proponents of this form of the explanatory arguments, an explanatory role of this kind played by mind-body identities yields sufficient warrant for their acceptance.

Ned Block and Robert Stalnaker, proponents of the explanatory argument of this form, are in agreement with J. J. C. Smart in regarding identities not as explaining their associated correlations but as helping us to get rid of them. They put the point this way:

If we believe that heat is correlated with but not identical to molecular kinetic energy, we should regard as legitimate the question why the correlation exists and what its mechanism is. But once we realize that heat is molecular kinetic energy, questions like this will be seen as wrongheaded.[12]

Similarly, for "pain occurs iff C-fiber stimulation occurs" and "pain = C-fiber stimulation." The latter helps us to avoid the awkward question "Why does pain correlate with Cfs, not with something else?" by ridding us of the correlation. We may summarize Block and Stalnaker's argument in favor of psychoneural identities as follows: These identities enable desirable psychological explanations while "disabling" improper demands for explanation.

What should we think of this argument? It is not difficult to see that the argument is highly problematic. We can accept the claim that derivation (θ) above is a neurophysiological explanation of why pain causes distress: Laws of neurophysiology directly explain why Cfs causes neural state N, and given the identities "pain = Cfs" and "distress = neural state N," we are justified in claiming that neurophysiological laws explain why pain causes distress. For there is here one fact described in two ways—in the scientific vocabulary and in the vernacular vocabulary. But there is a problem with the claim that the identities "pain = Cfs" and "distress = neural state N" play an *explanatory* role in this derivation. The fact is that the conclusion "pain causes distress" is a mere *rewrite* of the second line "Cfs causes neural state N" via the substitution rule governing identity; it only redescribes a fact that has already been explained. The explanatory activity is over and done with at the second line when "Cfs causes neural state N" has been derived from neurophysiological laws; we then go on to restate our explanatory accomplishment in a familiar "folk" vocabulary, and this is what the identities enable us to do. Since the identities have no explanatory role in all this, they are not eligible to be beneficiaries of the principle of inference to the best explanation.

Our conclusion, therefore, has to be that both forms of the explanatory argument are open to serious difficulties. Their fundamental weakness lies in a problematic understanding of the role of identities in explanation, an important topic that has not received much attention in the literature. The only clear (and also simple) view is that identities function simply as rewrite rules in explanatory derivations—or any derivation, for that matter. That is exactly what the substitution rule governing identity in formal logic tells us; there is nothing more and nothing less. We do not have to say that identities have no role to play *in* explanations. For they can help *justify* explanatory claims—the claim that we have explained something. As we just saw, (θ) justifies our claim that we have now explained why pain causes a sense of distress. It is only that identities do not generate explanations on their own.

An Argument from Mental Causation

By mental causation we mean any causal relation involving a mental event. A pin is stuck in your hand, causing you to experience a sharp pain; the pain causes your hand to withdraw in a jerky motion. The pain also causes a momentary sense of distress and a desire to be rid of it. Such causal relations are part of our everyday experience.

But pains do not occur without a physical basis; let us assume that pains are lawfully correlated with neural state N. So the sharp pain that caused the jerky withdrawal of your hand has an occurrence of N as its neural correlate. Is there any reason for not regarding the latter, a neural event, as a cause of your hand's jerky motion?

Consider this event's credentials as a cause of the motion of your hand: If the pain-hand withdrawal causal relation is covered by a law, then given the invariable correlation between pains and occurrences of N, there must also be a law relating occurrences of N with hand withdrawals. And it is plausible to assume that if we were to trace back the causal chain from the hand withdrawal, we would be tracing a series of physiological events back to the occurrence of N. The pain must somehow make use of this causal chain to be causally efficacious in the production of the movement of the hand; it is difficult to think that pain can act directly—that is, by telekinesis on the muscles—and cause them to contract, or that it can work through an independent causal path! All these considerations seem to favor the occurrence of N as the "real cause" of the hand movement; the pain's role as cause is in danger of being preempted. The simplest way to rescue the pain's causal role seems to be to identify it with the occurrence of N: If they are one and the same event, there is here one single cause of the hand withdrawal. It makes no difference to its causal status whether it is referred to as "pain" or "neural state N."

If in spite of these considerations you still want to insist on the pain as a separate cause of the hand movement, think of a new predicament in which you will find yourself. For the hand movement would now appear to have two distinct causes, the pain and the neural state N, each presumably sufficient to bring it about. Doesn't that make this (and every other case of mental-to-physical causation) a case of causal overdetermination? Given that the hand withdrawal has a sufficient physical cause, namely N, what *further* causal contribution can the pain make? There seems no leftover causal work that the pain has to be called on to perform. Again, the identification of the pain with its underlying neural event appears to dissolve all these puzzles. There is, of course, the epiphenomenalist solution: Both the hand withdrawal and the pain are caused by neural state N, and the pain itself has no further causal role in this situation. But unlike the identity solution, the epiphenomenalist move renders the pain causally inert and ends up simply denying our initial assumption that a sharp pain caused the hand's jerky motion. We should note, however, that although it may well be true that psychoneural identification will solve the mental causation problem, it may not be the only solution, or the best one. Moreover, what if these psychoneural identities are not available? If they are there, well and good. But if there is no reason to think that they are there, should we believe that they exist just because they would solve a problem for us? Shouldn't the availability of psychoneural identities be established on independent grounds? (Mental causation is discussed in greater detail in chapter 7.)

What Does "Identity" Mean?

The identity theory states that mental events are identical with brain processes. Sometimes such expressions as "state," "phenomenon," and "occurrence" are used interchangeably with "event" and "process." As a specific example of psychoneural identity, let us again consider the statement "pains are C fiber excitations." This is sometimes glossed as follows: "For a person (organism) to be in pain is for him to be in the C-fiber excitation state." For a proper understanding and evaluation of the identity theory we need to be clearer about the logic and ontology of such statements. Let us first consider the notion of "identity."

By expressions such as "the same" or "identical" we sometimes mean *equality* in some magnitude, or being *instances* or *tokens falling under the same kind* or *type*, and this sense must be sharply distinguished from *strict identity* or *identity proper*. When we say that the two base angles of an isosceles triangle are the same or identical, we only mean that their magnitude is the same, not that they are one and the same angle. (If that were the case, there would be only one angle here, not two!) And when we say, "I just bought the same book you bought yesterday," what we have in mind are two copies, or tokens, of the *same title*, not a single copy; whereas, when you say, "I have five books in my backpack," you are likely to have in mind five individual books, some, or even all, of which may be copies of the same title.

When X is identical with Y in the strict sense, we have one thing, not two. Socrates is identical with Xanthippe's husband. What we have two of are the names "Socrates" and "Xanthippe's husband." Two names and one object: The names pick out, or refer to, one and the same person.

Some identities are known a priori; for example, "5 + 7 = 12" and "2 = the smallest prime number." But the fact that water = H_2O or that the morning star = the evening star is something we have discovered from observation and experience; it is not something that could have been ascertained a priori or by merely investigating the meanings or concepts associated with the expressions "water," "H_2O," "the morning star," and "the evening star." So these identities are empirical, not a priori, truths.

The identity theorist would say that mind-body identities are empirical in the same way. The concept of pain and the concept of C-fiber excitations are distinct and independent, and this explains how it is possible for someone, say, Socrates, to know a lot about pains but nothing about C-fibers or their excitations. So this psychoneural identity is not certifiable conceptually or solely from the meanings of "pain" and "C-fiber activation." It is an empirical truth (assuming that it is a truth) that depends on sophisticated and laborious neurophysiological research. For this reason, mind-brain identities, it is claimed, are like "theoretical identities" in the sciences, like the following:

- Water is H_2O.
- Heat is molecular kinetic energy.
- The cause of AIDS is infection by the HIV virus.
- Light is electromagnetic radiation.

In each such case, a phenomenon or object is identified with something described in the theoretical vocabulary of science. Identities like these are a central part of our scientific knowledge of the world; each tells what something "really is"—its true *nature* as revealed by scientific investigation. As we saw earlier in connection with the second explanatory argument for psychoneural identities, such identities can have important explanatory roles. "Water = H_2O" can help us explain why water dissolves salt by allowing us to invoke the properties of H_2O in our explanation. Similarly, research in neurophysiology has revealed to us what pain really is—it is the excitation of C-fibers—and this identity may have a role in explaining psychological regularities involving pain.

Identity—or "strict" identity—is governed by the following law:

Indiscernibility of Identicals. If X is identical with Y, X and Y share all their properties in common—that is, for any property P, X has P if and only if Y has P.

This is sometimes called "Leibniz's law," although this term is also used to refer to the following, often disputed, principle, which is the converse of the first law:

Identity of Indiscernibles. If X and Y share all their properties in common, X is identical with Y.

The first law, the indiscernibility of identicals, is uncontroversial and manifestly true: If X *is* indeed identical with Y, there is one thing here and not two. So how could any property be had by X but not by Y? Saying that it could is to say that the property is both had and not had by one and the same thing, which obviously is a contradiction. In any case, this law tells us that all we need in order to refute an identity claim "X = Y" is a single property P, however trivial and inconsequential it may be, such that X has it and Y does not, or Y has it but X does not. We can call such a property a "differentiating property" for X and Y. As we shall soon see, that is the strategy employed by the foes of the identity theory: Various properties have been proposed as differentiating properties for the mental and the physical.

Token Physicalism and Type Physicalism

The identity theory standardly talks of "events," saying, as we have seen, that mental events are physical events in the brain. But what is an event? There are two alternative approaches to the metaphysics of events, and the choice between them makes a difference to the ways in which the identity theory can be understood. One view takes events as basic concrete particulars of the world, along with material objects.[13] Like material things, they have properties and fall under kinds. Thus, an event may be an explosion or the collapse of a bridge; it can be swift, violent, and unexpected. On this view, a particular occurrence of pain is an event that falls under the event kind pain; alternatively, we may say that that occurrence has the property of being a pain event. It can fall under other event kinds and have other properties as well: It is a dull, pounding pain, it is caused by a decayed tooth, it wakes you up in the middle of the night, and it lasts intermittently for more than three hours. And if the identity theory is correct, it is also a brain event, an event falling under the neural event kind C-fiber excitation.

On this view of events as basic particulars, therefore, the assertion that a given pain event, *e*, is a C-fiber excitation is to say that *e* falls under two event kinds, pain and C-fiber excitation—that is, *e* is both a pain and a C-fiber excitation. To put it another way, this event, *e*, has both the property of being a pain and the property of being a C-fiber excitation.

Consider now the standard statement of the identity theory:

(I) Every mental event is a physical event.

On the present construal of events, this comes to:

(Ia) *Token Physicalism*. Every event that falls under a mental event kind also falls under a physical event kind (or every event that has a mental property has also some physical property).[14]

We may consider talk of "event kinds" as equivalent to talk of "properties" of events, since every property of events can be thought of as defining a kind of events—namely, the kind comprising events with that property. (Ia) is also called "token-identity theory," since it identifies each mental "event token" with a physical "event token." An event token, or token event, is a dated individual occurrence, like the occurrence of pain to a particular person at a particular time. Event tokens are contrasted with event types, or event kinds, say, pains and itches. Token physicalists stress that their thesis, (Ia), does not entail a claim about the identity of mental types with physical types, a thesis called "type physicalism" or "type-identity theory":

(Ib) *Type Physicalism*. Mental kinds are physical kinds; alternatively, mental properties are physical properties.

Note that the terms "kind," "type," and "property" are used interchangeably in this context.

What is the relationship between token and type physicalism? Type physicalism obviously entails token physicalism; however, the converse is not the case, and this can be seen in terms of the following analogy. Consider:

(1) Every object that has a color has a shape.
(2) Colors are identical with shapes.

Statement (1) is obviously true; equally obviously, (2) is false. Colors and shapes do not even systematically correlate with each other; a red object can be a sphere or a cube or any other shape. In the same way, even if every event that has a mental property has a physical property (token physicalism), that does not even entail that mental properties are systematically correlated with physical properties, much less that they are identical with physical properties (type physicalism).

As you will recall, we have been using the statement "pains are C-fiber excitations" as a possible example of psychoneural identity. This statement identifies pain as a kind with C-fiber excitation as a kind; it is a type-identity statement and as such is part of type physicalism. As this example indicates, the psychoneural identity theory is standardly interpreted as type physicalism, not token physicalism.

There is another approach to events that makes type physicalism a natural way (in fact, the only way) of formulating the identity theory. On this view, an event is the exemplification (or instantiation) of a property by an object at a time. So my now being in pain (my instantiating the property of being in pain) is an event; your now being in pain and my being in pain yesterday are also events, but these events are all distinct. For event *e* and event *f* to be "the same event," on this account, they must be the instantiations of the same property by one and the same object at the same time; that is:

X's instantiation of property P at time t = Y's instantiation of property Q at time t^* if and only if X = Y, property P = property Q, and $t = t^*$.

Unlike the earlier view that takes events as basic and unanalyzed, the present view construes events as structured particulars consisting of properties, objects, and times. A mental event, then, is the instantiation of a mental property (by an object at a time), and similarly, a physical event is the instantiation of a physical property. Unless mental substances or souls are countenanced, the objects that do the instantiating in mental events as well as in physical events must be material things, like biological organisms and, possibly, certain complex electromechanical systems. This general account of events is called the "property exemplification theory."[15]

Take a particular mental event, say, George's being in pain at a time. If this event is identical with a physical event, George's being in a C-fiber excitation state, then the mental property of being in pain must be identical with the physical property of being in a C-fiber excitation state. So on the property exemplification account of events, the identity between a token mental event and a token physical event entails an identity between a mental property and a physical property. In general, then, there is no interesting distinction between token physicalism and type physicalism on the property exemplification approach to the nature of events.

As already noted, the classic identity theory due to Smart and Feigl is type physicalism—at least, this is the way it is usually understood. That is the main reason why we have presented the identity theory as a form of type physicalism here. Another reason is that token physicalism is a weak doctrine that does not say much; essentially, it says only that mental and physical properties are instantiated by the same entities. Any event or occurrence with a mental property has some physical property or other. But the theory says nothing about the relationship between mental properties and physical properties, the relation between pains, itches, thoughts, consciousness, and so on, on the one hand, and types of neural events, on the other. Token physicalism can be true even if there is nothing remotely resembling a systematic relationship between the mental and the physical (remember the example of colors and shapes). In a world in which token physicalism is true, there can be all sorts of mental properties and characteristics—the hurting sensation of pains, the bluish-gray of an afterimage, the bright red phenomenal color of a visual datum—and countless other sensory qualities, but there need be no dependencies, or even correlations, between these mental phenomena and neural processes. Notice that token physicalism, (Ia), does not entail

(II) Events (and objects) that are alike in physical respects must be alike in all mental respects

any more than "Every object that has a color has a shape" entails "Objects with the same color have the same shape."

You will have noticed that (II) is a form of mind-body supervenience. So the upshot is that token physicalism can be true even if mind-body supervenience fails. As far as token physicalism goes, the mental features of a given event are entirely unconstrained by what sort of biological-physical event it is; there could be a molecule-for-molecule physical duplicate of you who is wholly lacking in consciousness. This means that the theory says nothing about how the mental properties of an event might be physically based or explained. To put it another way, there could be another world just like the actual world in every physical detail except that mental properties are distributed over the events of that world in a drastically different way (say, rocks and trees are conscious but dogs and cats are not), or a world physically identical with our world but in which mentality and consciousness are totally absent. In view of all this, it is clear that token physicalism is not much of a physicalism. In fact, if mind-body supervenience is considered a minimum requirement of physicalism, token physicalism falls outside the scope of physicalism altogether.

A systematic property-to-property relationship between mentality and our bodily nature is of fundamental importance to a robust physicalist position. Moreover, that such a relationship exists seems to be a fundamental working assumption of brain science. This issue about properties arises also in debates concerning the possibility of "reducing" mentality to more basic physical-biological properties and processes. Token physicalism is a form of nonre-ductivism: It says nothing about property-to-property relationships between the mental and the physical, and such relationships are usually thought to be necessary for the reduction of the mental to the physical. It is not that token physicalism denies mind-body reduction; rather, it makes no commitment either way. However, philosophers who profess to be token physicalists embrace this position because they believe that mind-body reductionism is false (many of them do accept mind-body supervenience, however) and for them token physicalism is physicalism enough. We discuss questions concerning reduction and reductionism in greater detail later (chapter 10).

Type physicalism, in contrast, is a form of "reductive," or "reductionist," physicalism, since the thesis that mental properties are physical properties is simply the claim that there are no mental properties over and above physical properties. This arguably entails that there are no Cartesian mental substances, for if mental properties are just physical properties, either immaterial mental substances have physical properties, which is prima facie absurd, or they can have no properties of much interest, which only shows that they have no work to do, making them dispensable. It also entails that there are no mental facts over and above physical facts. This means that though we may continue to find mentalistic expressions useful and practically indispensable, their expulsion will not affect the total descriptive power of our language; physical language will in principle be adequate for the description of all the facts. Type physicalism is a strong and robust materialist doctrine. Perhaps it is too strong to be true.

Objections to the
Psychoneural Identity Theory

There are three main arguments against the mind-brain identity theory. They are the epistemological argument, the modal argument, and the multiple realization argument. We consider each in turn.

The Epistemological Argument

Epistemological Objection 1.   There is a group of objections based on the thought that the mental and the physical differ in their epistemological properties. One such objection may run as follows: Medieval peasants knew lots about pains but nothing about C-fibers, and in fact little about the brain. So how can pains be identical with C-fiber excitations?

This objection assumes that the two statements "S knows something about X" and "X = Y" together entail "S knows something about Y." But is this true? Perhaps there is a sense of "knows something about" in which the entailment holds. Little Billy knows something about lightning, and since lightning is an electric discharge, it follows, according to this pattern of reasoning, that Billy knows something about electric discharges. But then, in this sense, "S knows something about Y" does not entail that S has the concept of Y or can use the expression "Y" to make judgments, ask questions, and so on. The person S may not know, and have no idea, that X = Y; S may even lack the cognitive capacity to entertain the thought that X = Y, for this requires the possession of the concept of Y. Therefore, in this sense of "knowing something about," there is nothing incoherent about saying that the medieval peasants did know something about C-fiber excitations.

It is perhaps more plausible to argue that the entailment does not hold. To be sure, "S knows something about X" and "S knows that X = Y" plausibly entail "S knows something about Y." But it is false that the medieval peasants knew that pains are C-fiber excitations, and it seems perfectly coherent to assert that even though pain = C-fiber excitation, they knew nothing about C-fiber excitations, despite the fact that they knew lots about pains. Another way of putting this is to say that "being known by person S to be such and such" and other similar expressions, like "being believed by S to be such and such," do not express properties—or at least not properties that can serve as differentiating properties. If the present objection were sound, the same argument would show that water is not H_2O, that light is not electromagnetic radiation, and that genes are not DNA molecules.

Epistemological Objection 2. According to the identity theory, specific psychoneural identities (for example, "pains are C-fiber excitations") are empirical truths discovered through scientific observation and theoretical research. If "$D_1 = D_2$" is an empirical truth, the two names or descriptions, D_1 and D_2, must have *independent criteria of application.* Otherwise, the identity would be a priori knowable; consider, for example, identities like "bachelor = unmarried adult male" and "the husband of Xanthippe = Xanthippe's male spouse." When some occurrence is picked out by a subject as a pain rather than an itch or tingle, the subject must do so by *recognizing*, or *noticing*, a certain distinctive felt or experiential character, a phenomenal quality, of the occurrence—its experienced painfulness or hurtfulness. If pains were picked out by neurophysiological criteria (say, if we used C-fiber excitation as the criterion of pain), the identity of pain with a neural state could not be empirical; it would simply follow from the very criterion governing the concept of pain. This means, the objection goes, that to make sense of the supposed *empirical* character of psychoneural identities, we must acknowledge the existence of phenomenal properties distinct from neural properties.[16]

Sometimes the objection goes further, arguing that these phenomenal properties by which the subject is supposed to recognize her pains as pains must be *irreducibly psychic.* This claim seems implausible; intuitively, the hurtfulness by which we identify our own pains is nothing like a physical property. The token physicalist has nothing to fear here: She can cheerfully accept these phenomenal properties as irreducible mental properties. The type physicalist, on the other hand, must provide a more substantive answer: She must show that subjects do not identify mental states by noticing their irreducibly psychic features. Could the type physicalist argue that although a person does identify her experience by noticing its qualitative phenomenal features, they are not irreducible, since phenomenal properties as mental properties are identical, on her view, with physical-biological properties? But this reply is not likely to satisfy many people; it will invite the following response: "But surely when we notice our pains as pains, we do not do that by noticing biological or neural features of our brain states!" We immediately distinguish pains from itches and tickles; if we identified our experiences by their neurophysiological features, we should be able to tell which neurophysiological features represent pain, which represent itches, and so on. But is this credible?

Some philosophers have tried to respond to this question by analyzing away phenomenal properties. For example, Smart attempts to give phenomenal properties "topic-neutral translation."[17] According to him, when we say,

"Adam is experiencing an orangish-yellow afterimage," the content of our report may be conveyed by the following "topic-neutral" translation—topic-
neutral because it says nothing about whether what is being reported is
mental or physical:

> Something is going on in Adam that is like what goes on when he is
> looking at an orangish-yellow color patch illuminated in good light.

(We suppose "looking" is explained physically in terms of his being awake,
his eyes' being open and focused on the color patch, and so on). Smart
would add that this "something" that is going on in Adam is nothing but a
brain state.

But will this satisfy someone concerned with the problem of explaining
how someone manages to identify the kind of experience she is having?
There is perhaps something to be said for these translations if we approach
the matter strictly from the third-person point of view. But when you are reporting your own experience by saying, "I have a sharp pain in my left
thumb," are you saying something like what Smart says that you are? To
know that you are having an orangish-yellow afterimage, do you need to
know anything about what generally goes on whenever you look at orangish-
yellow color patches?

A more recent strategy that has become popular with latter-day-type physicalists is to press *concepts* into service and have them replace talk of properties in the foregoing objection. The main idea is to concede *conceptual*
differences between the mental and the neural but deny that these differences point to ontological differences, that is, differences in the properties to
which these concepts apply or refer.[18] When we say that a person notices a
pain by noticing its painfulness, this does not mean that the pain has the
property of painfulness; rather, it means that she is "conceptualizing" her experience under the phenomenal *concept* of being painful. This phenomenal
concept is not a neural or physical concept, and it is not identical with the
concept of C-fiber stimulation. But this is entirely consistent with there
being a single property, presumably a physical-neural property, that is picked
out by both a phenomenal and a neural concept. Thus, we have a dualism of
concepts, mental and physical, but a monism of properties, the entities referred to by these concepts. The advantage of framing the issues in terms of
phenomenal concepts rather than phenomenal properties consists, presumably, in the fact that properties, whether phenomenal or of other sorts,
are "out there" in the world, whereas concepts are part of our linguistic-

conceptual apparatus for representing and describing what is out there. So the trick is to take the phenomenal-neural differences out of the domain of facts of the world and bring them into the linguistic-conceptual domain. This, at any rate, is a move that has been made by the physicalist. Whether it really works as a way out is another question.

Epistemological Objection 3.   Your knowledge that you are thinking about an upcoming trip to East Asia is direct and private in the way that only first-person knowledge of one's own mental states can be. Others have to make inferences based on evidence and observation to find out what you are thinking, or even to know that you are thinking. But your knowledge is not based on evidence or inference; somehow you directly know. In contrast, you have no such privileged access to your brain states. Your neurologist and neurosurgeon probably have much better knowledge of your brain than you do. In brief, mental states are directly accessible by the subject; brain states—and physical states in general—are not so accessible. So how can mental states be brain states?

We should note that for this objection to work, it is not necessary to claim that the subject has *infallible* access to all her mental states. For one thing, infallibility or incorrigibility is not the issue; the issue is private direct access— that is, first-person access not based on inference from evidence or observation. For another, it is only necessary that the subject have direct and private access to at least *some* of her mental states. If that is the case, these mental states, according to this argument, cannot be identified with brain states, states for which public access is possible.

The identity theorist has to deny either the claim that we have direct private access to our own current mental states or the claim that we do not have such access to our brain states. She might say that when we know that we are in pain, we do have epistemic access to our Cfs, but our knowledge is under the description, or concept, "pain," not under the description "Cfs." Here there is one thing, Cfs (that is to say, pain), that can be known under two "modes of presentation"—pain and Cfs. Under one mode, the knowledge is private; under the other, it is public. It is like the same person is known both as "the husband of Xanthippe" and "the drinker of hemlock." You may know him under one description but not the other. So knowledge is relative to the mode of description or conceptualization. Certain brain states, like Cfs, can be known in two different modes or under two different sorts of concepts, mental and physical. Knowledge under one mode can be different from knowledge under the other, and they need not co-occur. So this reply is in line with the final physicalist reply to epistemological objection 2 discussed earlier. These replies, therefore, will stand or fall together.

The Modal Argument

Type physicalists used to say that mind-brain identities—for example, "pain = C-fiber activation"—are *contingent*, not necessary. That is, although pain is in fact C-fiber excitation, it could have been otherwise; there are possible worlds in which pain is not C-fiber excitation but some other brain state—perhaps not a brain state at all. The idea of contingent identity can be explained by an example such as this: "George W. Bush is the forty-third president of the United States." The identity is true, but it might have been false: There are possible worlds in which the identity does not hold—for example, one in which Al Gore was declared the winner of Florida in 2000, one in which Bush went into the ministry instead of politics, one in which Senator John McCain won the Republican nomination, and so on. In all these worlds someone other than George W. Bush would be the forty-third president of the United States.

But this is possible only because the expression "the forty-third president of the United States" can refer to different persons in different possible worlds; things might have gone in such a way that the expression designated someone other than Bush—for example, Gore or McCain. Expressions like "the forty-third president of the United States," "the winner of the 1994 Kentucky Derby," and "the tallest man in China," which can name different things in different possible worlds, are what Kripke calls "nonrigid designators."[19] In contrast, proper names like "George W. Bush" and "Socrates" are "rigid"—they designate the same object in all possible worlds in which they exist. It is true that the forty-third president of the United States might not have been the forty-third president of the United States (for example, if Bush had lost to Gore), but it is not true that George W. Bush might not have been George W. Bush. (George W. Bush might not have been called "George W. Bush," but that is another matter.) This shows that a contingent identity, "X = Y," is possible only if either of the two expressions, "X" or "Y," is a nonrigid designator, an expression that can refer to different things in different worlds.

Consider the term "C-fiber excitation": Could this designator be nonrigid? It would seem not: How could an event that in fact is the excitation of C-fibers not have been one? How could an event that is an instance of C-fiber excitation be, say, a volcano eruption or a collision of two stars in another possible world? A world in which no C-fiber excitation ever occurs is a world in which this event, which is a C-fiber excitation, does not occur. The term "pain" also seems rigid. If you are inclined to take the painfulness of pain as its essential defining property, you will say that "pain" rigidly designates an event or state with this quality of painfulness and that the expression designates an event of that sort across all possible worlds. A world in which nothing ever hurts is a world without pain.

It follows that if pain = Cfs, then this must be a necessary truth—that is, it must hold in every possible world. Descartes famously claims that it is possible for him to exist as a thinking and conscious thing even without a body. If that is possible, then pain could exist even if Cfs did not. Some philosophers have argued that "zombies"—creatures that are physically just like us but have no consciousness—are a possibility. If so, Cfs could exist without being accompanied by pain. If these are real possibilities, then "pain = Cfs" cannot be a necessary truth. Then, by the principle that if X and Y are rigid designators, the identity "X = Y" is necessarily true, if true, it follows that "pain = Cfs" is false—and, more generally, that psychophysical identities are all false.

Many mind-brain identity theorists would be likely to dispute the claim that it is possible that pain can exist even if Cfs does not, and they would question the claim that zombies are a real possibility. We can grant, they will argue, that in some sense these situations are "conceivable," that we can "imagine" such possibilities. But the fact that a situation is conceivable or imaginable does not entail that it is genuinely possible. For example, it is conceivable, they will say, that water is not H_2O, and that heat is not molecular kinetic energy; the concept of water and the concept of H_2O are logically independent of each other, and there is no conceptual incoherence or contradiction in the thought that water $\neq H_2O$. And we might even say that "water $\neq H_2O$" is *epistemically possible*: Relative to the state of knowledge not so long ago, it was possible that water could have turned out to be other than H_2O. That is, for all we knew a couple of hundred years ago, we might be living on a planet with XYZ, rather than H_2O, coming out of the tap, in our lakes and rivers, and so on, where XYZ is observationally indistinguishable from H_2O, although wholly different in molecular structure. Nonetheless, water = H_2O, and necessarily so. (See chapter 9 for more on water and XYZ.) The gist of the reply by the identity theorists then is that conceivability does not entail real possibility and that this is shown by a posteriori necessary truths like "water = H_2O" and "heat = molecular kinetic energy." For them, psychoneural identities—"pain = Cfs" and the rest—are necessary a posteriori truths just like these scientific identities. Issues about conceivability and possibility are highly complex and contentious, and they are being actively debated, without any resolution in sight.[20]

The Multiple Realization Argument

Type physicalism says that pain is C-fiber excitation. But that implies that unless an organism has C-fibers, it cannot have pain. But aren't there pain-capable organisms, like reptiles and mollusks, with nervous systems very different from the human nervous system? Perhaps in these species the neurons that work as nociceptive neurons—pain-receptor neurons—are not like human C-fibers at all; how can we be sure that all pain-capable animals have C-fibers? Can the type physicalist reply that it should be possible to come up with a more abstract and general physiological description of a brain state common to all organisms, across all species, that are in pain? This seems highly unlikely, and in any case, how about inorganic systems? Could there not be intelligent extraterrestrial creatures with a complex and rich mental life that is very much like ours but whose biology is not carbon-based? And is it not conceivable—in fact, nomologically possible if not practically feasible—to build intelligent electromechanical systems (that is, robots) to which we would be willing to attribute various mental states (especially perceptual and cognitive states)? Moreover, the neural substrates of certain mental functions can differ from person to person and may change over time even in a single person through maturation, learning, and brain injuries. Does it make sense to think that some single neural state is shared by all persons who believe that cats are smarter than dogs, or that $7 + 5 = 12$? Moreover, we should keep in mind that if pain is identical with some physical state C, this must hold not only in actual organisms and systems but in all possible organisms and systems. This is so because, as we argued earlier in our discussion of the modal argument, such identities, if true, must be necessarily true—that is, true in all possible worlds.

These considerations are widely thought to show that any given mental state is "multiply realizable"[21] in a large variety of physical-biological structures, with the consequence that it is not possible to identify mental states with physical states. If pain is identical with a physical state, it must be identical with some *particular* physical state, but there is no single neural correlate or substrate of pain. On the contrary, there are indefinitely many physical states that can "realize" (or "instantiate," or "implement") pain in all sorts of pain-capable organisms and systems. So pain, as a type of mental state, cannot be identified with a neural state type or with any other physical state type.

This is the influential "multiple realization" argument that Hilary Putnam and others advanced in the late 1960s and early 1970s. It has had a critical impact on the way philosophy of mind has developed since then. It was this argument, rather than any of the other objections to the identity theory, that was instrumental in bringing about an unexpected early retirement of type physicalism. Moreover, it helped to throw all forms of reductionist physicalism into disarray, ushering in the era of "nonreductive physicalism." What made the multiple realization argument distinctive, and different from other sundry objections to type physicalism, was the fact that it brought with it an attractive alternative conception of the mental, a fresh and well-motivated perspective on the mind-body problem. This is functionalism, which still is the most widely accepted position on the nature of mentality and the status of psychology and cognitive science. We turn to this influential approach to the problems of the mind in the next two chapters.

Further Readings

The classic sources of the identity theory are U. T. Place, "Is Consciousness a Brain Process?," Herbert Feigl, "The 'Mental' and the 'Physical,'" and J. J. C. Smart, "Sensations and Brain Processes," all of which are reprinted in *Philosophy of Mind: Classical and Contemporary Readings*, edited by David J. Chalmers. The Smart article is widely reprinted in anthologies on philosophy of mind. For more recent book-length treatments of physicalism and related issues, see Christopher S. Hill, *Sensations: A Defense of Type Physicalism*; Jeffrey Poland, *Physicalism: The Philosophical Foundation*; Andrew Melnyk, *A Physicalist Manifesto*; Thomas W. Polger, *Natural Minds*; and Jaegwon Kim, *Physicalism, or Something Near Enough*.

For criticisms and objections, you may browse the articles in *Objections to Physicalism*, edited by Howard Robinson. See also Saul Kripke, *Naming and Necessity*, lecture 3. John Heil's anthology, *Philosophy of Mind: A Guide and Anthology*, includes three essays (by John Foster, Peter Forrest, and E. J. Lowe) that are worth examining in a section with the title "Challenges to Contemporary Materialism."

For a defense of token physicalism and considerations against type physicalism, see Donald Davidson, "Mental Events." Also, Jerry A. Fodor's "Special Sciences, or the Disunity of Science as a Working Hypothesis" is relevant.

For the multiple realization argument against the identity theory, the original sources are Hilary Putnam, "Psychological Predicates," later retitled "The Nature of Mental States"; and Fodor's "Special Sciences." For more recent discussion, see Jaegwon Kim, "Multiple Realization and the Metaphysics of Reduction," and John Bickle, *Psychoneural Reduction: The New Wave*. There is an extensive discussion of realization and multiple realizability in Lawrence Shapiro, *The Mind Incarnate*. Also useful are Carl Gillett, "The Metaphysics of Realization, Multiple Realizability, and the Special Sciences," and Sydney Shoemaker, "Realization, Micro-realization, and Coincidence."

Notes

1. To be more precise, the difference here must be understood to be a difference in the two states' "intrinsic" properties—for example, how they feel or look—not a difference in their "extrinsic" or "relational" properties, such as one of the states occurring south of Boston and the other to its north.

2. See René Descartes, *The Passions of the Soul*.

3. See Thomas H. Huxley, "On the Hypothesis That Animals Are Automata, and Its History."

4. Samuel Alexander, *Space, Time, and Deity*. Vol. 2, p. 47.

5. J. J. C. Smart, "Sensations and Brain Processes." U. T. Place's "Is Consciousness a Brain Process?," published in 1956, predates Smart's article as perhaps the first modern statement of the identity theory.

6. Smart, "Sensations and Brain Processes," p. 117 (in the reprint version in *Philosophy of Mind: A Guide and Anthology*, ed. John Heil. Emphasis in original).

7. See the entry "William of Ockham" in the *Macmillan Encyclopedia of Philosophy*, 2nd ed.

8. Herbert Feigl, "The 'Mental' and the 'Physical,'" p. 428.

9. See Gilbert Harman, "The Inference to the Best Explanation." For a critique of the principle, see Bas Van Fraassen, *Laws and Symmetry*.

10. This example comes from Christopher S. Hill, *Sensations: A Defense of Type Materialism*, p. 24.

11. This is substantially the form in which Brian McLaughlin formulates his explanatory argument. See his "In Defense of New Wave Materialism: A Response to Horgan and Tienson." Hill (see note 10) and McLaughlin are two leading proponents of this form of the explanatory argument. See also Andrew Melnyck, *A Physicalist Manifesto*.

12. Ned Block and Robert Stalnaker, "Conceptual Analysis, Dualism, and the Explanatory Gap," p. 24.

13. This approach to events is usually associated with Donald Davidson; see Davidson, "The Individuation of Events."

14. A prime example of token physicalism is Donald Davidson's "anomalous monism." See Davidson, "Mental Events."

15. See Jaegwon Kim, "Events as Property Exemplifications."

16. This objection is worked out in detail in Jerome Shaffer, "Mental Events and the Brain."

17. See Smart, "Sensations and Brain Processes."

18. See, for example, Brian Loar, "Phenomenal States."

19. See Saul Kripke, *Naming and Necessity*, especially lecture 3, in which arguments against the identity theory are presented.

20. For further discussion of these issues, see the essays in *Conceivability and Possibility*, edited by Tamar Szabo Gendler and John Hawthorne.

21. The terms "variably realizable" and "variable realization" are commonly used by British writers.

5

Mind as a Computing Machine

Machine Functionalism

In 1967 Hilary Putnam published a paper of modest length titled "Psycho-logical Predicates."[1] This paper changed the debate in philosophy of mind in a fundamental way by doing three remarkable things: First, it quickly brought about the decline and fall of type physicalism, In particular, the psychoneural identity theory. Second, it ushered in functionalism, which has since been a highly influential—arguably the preeminent—position on the nature of mind. And third, it helped to install antireductionism as the received view on the nature of mental properties and other "higher-level" properties of the special sciences. Psychoneural type physicalism, which had been promoted as the only view of mentality properly informed by the best contemporary science, turned out to be unexpectedly short-lived, and by the mid-1970s most philosophers had abandoned reductionist physicalism not only as a view about psychology but as a doctrine about all special sciences.[2]

All this was the work of a single idea: *the multiple realizability of mental properties.* We have already discussed it as an argument against the psychoneural identity theory and, more generally, as a difficulty for type physicalism (chapter 4). What sets the multiple realization argument apart from numerous other objections to the psychoneural identity theory is the fact that it gave birth to a new conception of the mental that has played a key role in shaping a widely shared view of the nature and status of cognitive science and psychology.

Multiple Realizability and the Functional Conception of Mind

Perhaps not many of us now believe in angels—purely spiritual and immortal beings supposedly with a full mental life. Angels, as traditionally conceived, are wholly immaterial beings with knowledge and belief who can experience emotions and desires and are capable of performing actions. The idea of such a being may be a perfectly coherent one, like the idea of a unicorn or Bigfoot, but there is no evidence that there are beings fitting this description, just as there are no unicorns and probably no Bigfoot. So like unicorns but unlike married bachelors or four-sided triangles, there seems nothing conceptually impossible about angels. If the idea of an angel with beliefs, desires, and emotions is a consistent one, that would show that there is nothing in the idea of mentality as such that precludes purely nonphysical, wholly immaterial beings with psychological states.[3]

It seems, then, that we cannot set aside the possibility of immaterial realizations of mentality as a matter of an a priori conceptual fact.[4] Ruling out such a possibility requires commitment to a substantive metaphysical thesis, perhaps something like this:

Realization Physicalism. If something x has some mental property M (or is in mental state M) at time t, then x is a material thing and x has M at t in virtue of the fact that x has at t some physical property P that realizes M in x at t.

It is useful to think of this principle as a way of characterizing physicalism.[5] It says that anything that exhibits mentality must be a physical system—for example, a biological organism. Although the idea of mentality permits nonphysical entities to instantiate mental properties, the world is so constituted, according to this thesis, that only physical systems, in particular, biological organisms, turn out to realize mental properties—perhaps because they are the only things that exist in space-time (see chapter 2). Moreover, the principle requires that every mental property be physically based; each occurrence of a mental property is due to the occurrence of a physical "realizer" of the mental property. A simple way of putting the point would be this: Minds, if they exist, must be embodied.

Notice that this principle provides for the possibility of multiple realization of mental properties. Mental property M—say, being in pain—may be such that in humans C-fiber activation realizes it but in other species (say, octopuses and reptiles) physiological mechanisms that realize pain may be vastly different. Perhaps there might be non-carbon-based or non-protein-based biological organisms with mentality, and we cannot a priori preclude the possibility that nonbiological electromechanical systems, like the "intelligent" robots and androids in science fiction, might be capable of having beliefs, desires, and even sensations. All this suggests an interesting feature of mental concepts: They seem to carry no constraint on the actual physical-biological mechanisms that, in a given system, realize or implement them. In this sense, psychological concepts are like concepts of artifacts. For example, the idea of an "engine" is silent on the actual physical mechanism that realizes it—whether it uses gasoline or electricity or steam and, if it is a gasoline engine, whether it is a piston or rotary engine, how many cylinders it has, whether it uses a carburetor or fuel injection, and so on. As long as a physical device is capable of performing a certain specified job—namely, that of transforming various forms of energy into mechanical force or motion—it counts as an engine. The concept of an engine is given by a *job description*, or *causal role*, not a description of mechanisms that execute the job. Many biological concepts are similar in the same respect: What makes an organ a heart is the fact that it pumps blood. The human heart may be physically very unlike hearts in, say, reptiles or birds, but they all count as hearts because of the job they do in the organisms in which they are found.

What, then, is the job description of pain? The capacity for experiencing pain under appropriate conditions—for example, when an organism suffers tissue damage—is critical to its chances for adaptation and survival. There are unfortunate people who congenitally lack the capacity to sense pain, and few of them survive into adulthood.[6] In the course of coping with the hazards presented by their environment, animal species must have had to develop pain mechanisms, what we may call "tissue-damage detectors," and it is plausible that different species, interacting with different environmental conditions and evolving independently of one another, have developed different mechanisms for this purpose. It is natural to expect to find diverse evolutionary solutions to the problem of developing a tissue-damage detector. As a start, then, we can think of pain as specified by the job description "tissue-damage detector"—a mechanism that is activated by tissue damage and whose activation in turn causes appropriate behavioral responses such as withdrawal, avoidance, and escape.

Thinking of the workings of the mind in analogy with the operations of a computing machine is commonplace, both in the popular press and in serious philosophy and cognitive science, and we will soon begin looking into the mind-computer analogy in detail. A computational view of mentality also shows that we must expect mental states to be multiply realized. We know that any computational process can be implemented in a variety of physically diverse computing machines. Not only are there innumerable kinds of electronic digital computers (in addition to the semiconductor-based machines we are familiar with, think of the vacuum-tube computers of olden days), but also computers can be built with wheels and gears (as in Charles Babbage's original "Analytical Engine") or even with hydraulically operated systems of pipes and valves, although these would be unacceptably slow (not to say economically prohibitive) by our current standards. And all of these physically diverse computers can be performing "the same computation," say, solving a given differential equation. If minds are like computers and mental processes—in particular, cognitive processes—are, at bottom, computational processes, we should expect no prior constraint on just how minds and mental processes are physically implemented. Just as vastly different physical devices can execute the same computational program, so vastly different biological or physical structures should be able to subserve the same psychological processes. This is the core of the functionalist conception of the mind.

What these considerations point to, according to some, is the *abstractness* or *formality* of psychological properties in relation to physical or biological properties: Psychological kinds abstract from the physical and biological details of organisms so that states that are vastly different from a physicochemical point of view can fall under the same psychological kind, and organisms and systems that are widely diverse biologically and physically can instantiate the same psychological regularities. To put it another way, psychological kinds seem to concern *formal* patterns or structures of events and processes rather than their material constitutions or implementing physical mechanisms.[7] Conversely, the same physical structure, depending on the way it is causally embedded in a larger system, can subserve different psychological capacities and functions (just as the same computer chip can be used for different computational functions in various subsystems of a computer). After all, most neurons, it has been argued, are pretty much alike and largely interchangeable.[8]

What is it, then, that binds together all the physically diverse instances of a given mental kind? What do all pains—pains in humans, pains in canines, pains in octopuses, and pains in Martians—have in common in virtue of which they all fall under a single psychological kind, pain?[9] That is, what is the *principle of individuation* for mental kinds?

Let us first see how the type physicalist and the behaviorist answer this question. The psychoneural type physicalist says this: What all pains have in common that makes them instances of pain is a certain neurobiological property, namely, being an instance of C-fiber excitation (or some such state). That is, for the type physicalist, a mental kind is a physical kind (a neurobiological kind, for the psychoneural identity theorist). You could guess how the behaviorist answers the question: What all pains have in common is a certain behavioral property—or to put it another way, two organisms are both in pain at a time just in case at that time they exhibit, or are disposed to exhibit, the behavior patterns definitive of pain (for example, escape behavior, withdrawal behavior, and so on). For the behaviorist, then, a mental kind is a behavioral kind.

If you take the multiple realizability of mental states seriously, you will reject both these answers and opt for a "functionalist" conception. The main idea is that what is common to instances of a mental state must be sought at a higher level of abstraction. According to functionalism, a mental kind is a *functional kind*, or a *causal-functional kind*, since the "function" involved is to fill a certain causal role.[10] Let us go back to pain as a tissue-damage detector.[11] The concept of a tissue-damage detector is a *functional concept*, a concept specified by a job description, as we said: Any device is a tissue-damage detector for an organism just in case it can reliably respond to occurrences of tissue damage in the organism and transmit this information to other subsystems so that appropriate behavioral responses are produced. Functional concepts are ubiquitous: What makes something a mouse trap, a carburetor, or a thermometer is its ability to perform a certain function, not any specific physicochemical structure or mechanism. These concepts are specified by the functions that are to be performed, not by structural blueprints. Many concepts, in ordinary discourse and in the sciences, seem to be functional concepts in this sense; even many chemical and biological concepts (for example, catalyst, gene, heart) appear to have an essentially functional component.

To return to pain as a tissue-damage detector: Ideally, every instance of tissue damage, and nothing else, should activate this mechanism—turn it on—and this must further trigger other mechanisms with which it is hooked up, leading finally to behavior that will in normal circumstances spatially separate the damaged part, or the whole organism, from the external cause of the damage. Thus, the concept of pain is defined in terms of its function, and the function involved is to serve as a *causal intermediary* between typical pain inputs (tissue damage, trauma, and so on) and typical pain outputs (winces, groans, avoidance behavior, and so on). Moreover, functionalism makes two significant additions. First, among the causal conditions that activate the pain mechanism are other mental states (for example, you must be normally alert and not be absorbed in another activity, like intense competitive sports). Second, the outputs of the pain mechanism can include mental states as well (such as a sense of distress or a desire to be rid of the pain). The functionalist says that this is generally true of all mental kinds: Mental kinds are causal-functional kinds, and what all instances of a given mental kind have in common is the fact that they serve a certain *causal role* distinctive of that kind. As David Armstrong has put it, the concept of a mental state is that of an internal state apt to be caused by certain sensory inputs and apt to cause certain behavioral outputs.

Functional Properties and Their Realizers: Definitions

It will be useful to have explicit definitions of some of the terms we have been using more or less informally, relying on examples and intuitions. Let us begin with a formal characterization of a functional property:

F is a *functional property* (or kind) just in case F can be characterized by a definition of the following form:

For something x to have F (or to be an F) = $_{def}$ for x to have some property P such that C(P), where C(P) is a specification of the causal work that P is supposed to do in x.

We may call a definition having this form a "functional" definition. "C(P)," which specifies the causal role of F, is crucial. What makes a functional property the property it is, is the causal role associated with it; that is to say, F and G are the same functional property if and only if the causal role associated with F is the same as that associated with G. The term "causal work" in the above schema of functional definitions should be understood broadly to refer to "passive" as well as "active" work: For example, if tissue damage causes P to instantiate in an organism, that is part of P's causal work.

Thus, P's causal work refers to the *causal relations* involving the instances, or occurrences, of P in the organism or system in question.

Now we can define what it is for a property to "realize," or be a "realizer" of, a functional property:

> Let F be a functional property defined by a functional definition, as above. Property Q is said to *realize* F, or be a *realizer* or a *realization* of F, in system *x* if and only if C(Q), that is, Q fits the specification C in *x* (which is to say, Q in fact performs the specified causal work in system *x*).

Note that the definiens (the right-hand side) of a functional definition does not mention any particular property P that *x* has (when it has F); it only says that *x* has "some" property P fitting description C. In logical terminology, the definiens "quantifies over" properties (it in effect says, "There exists some property P such that *x* has P and C(P).") For this reason, functional properties are called "second-order" properties, with the properties quantified over (that is, properties eligible as instances of P) counting as "first-order" properties; they are second-order properties of a special kind—namely, those that are defined in terms of causal roles.

Let us see how this formal apparatus works. Consider the property of being a mousetrap. It is a functional property because it can be given the following functional definition:

> *x* is a mousetrap = $_{def}$ *x* has some property P such that P enables *x* to trap and hold or kill mice.

The definition does not specify any specific P that *x* must have; the causal work to be done obviously can be done in many different ways. There are the familiar spring-loaded traps, and there are wire cages with a door that slams shut when a mouse enters; we can imagine high-tech traps with an optical sensor and all sorts of other devices. This means that there are many—in fact, indefinitely many—"realizers" of the property of being a mousetrap; that is, all sorts of physical mechanisms can be mousetraps.

Functionalism and Behaviorism

Both functionalism and behaviorism speak of sensory input and behavioral output—or "stimulus" and "response"—as central to the concept of mentality. In this respect, functionalism is part of a broadly behavioral approach to mentality and can be considered a generalized and more sophisticated version of behaviorism. But there are also significant differences between them, of which the following two are the most important.

First, the functionalist takes mental states to be *real internal* states of an organism with causal powers; for an organism to be in pain is for it to be in an internal state (for example, a neurobiological state for humans) that is typically caused by tissue damage and that in turn typically causes winces, groans, and avoidance behavior. In contrast, the behaviorist eschews talk of internal states entirely, identifying mental states with actual or possible behavior. Thus, to be in pain, for the behaviorist, is to wince and groan or be disposed to wince and groan, but not, as the functionalist would have it, to be in some *internal state that causes* winces and groans.

Although both the behaviorist and the functionalist may refer to "behavioral dispositions" in speaking of mental states, what they mean by "disposition" can be quite different: The functionalist takes a "realist" approach to dispositions, whereas the behaviorist embraces an "instrumentalist" line. To see how realism and instrumentalism differ on this issue, consider how water solubility (that is, the disposition to dissolve in water) would be analyzed on each approach:

Instrumentalist analysis: x is soluble in water = $_{def}$ if x is immersed in water, x dissolves.

Realist analysis: x is soluble in water = $_{def}$ x is in a certain internal state S (that is, has a certain microstructure S) such that when x is immersed in water, S causes x to dissolve.

According to instrumentalism, therefore, the water solubility of a sugar cube is just the fact that a certain conditional ("if-then") statement holds for it; thus, on this view, water solubility is a "conditional" or "hypothetical" property of the sugar cube—that is, the property of *dissolving if immersed in water*. Realism, in contrast, takes solubility to be a categorical, presumably microstructural, internal state of the cube of sugar that is causally responsible for its dissolving when placed in water. (Further investigation might reveal the state to be that of having a certain crystalline molecular structure.) Neither analysis requires the sugar cube to be placed in water or actually to be dissolving in order to be water-soluble. However, we may note the following difference: If x dissolves in water and y does not, the realist will give a causal explanation of this difference in terms of a difference in their microstructure. For the instrumentalist, the difference may just be a brute fact: It is just that the conditional "if placed in water, it dissolves" holds true for *x* but not for *y*, a difference that need not be grounded in any further differences between *x* and *y*.

In speaking of mental states as behavioral dispositions, then, the functionalist takes them as actual inner states of persons and other organisms that in normal circumstances cause behavior of some specific type under certain specified input conditions. In contrast, the behaviorist takes them merely as input-output, or stimulus-response, correlations. Many behaviorists (especially methodological behaviorists) think that speaking of mental states as "inner causes" of behavior is scientifically unmotivated and philosophically unwarranted.[12]

The second significant difference between functionalism and behaviorism, one that gives the former a substantially greater theoretical power, is in the way "input" and "output" are construed for mental states. For the behaviorist, input and output consist entirely of observable physical stimulus conditions and observable behavioral responses. As briefly noted earlier, the functionalist allows reference to other *mental states* in the characterization of a given mental state. It is a crucial part of the functionalist conception of a mental state that its typical causes and effects can, and often do, include other mental states. Thus, for a ham sandwich to cause you to want to eat it, you must believe it to be a ham sandwich; a bad headache can cause you a feeling of distress and a desire to call your doctor.

The two points that have just been reviewed are related: If you think of mental states as actual inner states of psychological subjects, you would regard them as having real causal powers, powers to cause and be caused by other states and events, and there is no obvious reason to exclude mental states from figuring among the causes or effects of other mental states. In conceiving mentality this way, the functionalist is espousing *mental realism*—a position that considers mental states as having a genuine ontological status and counts them among the phenomena of the world with a place in its causal structure. Mental states are real for the behaviorist too, but only as behaviors or behavioral dispositions; for him, there is nothing mental over and above actual and possible behavior. For the functionalist, mental states are inner causes of behavior, and as such they are "over and above" behavior.

Including other mental events among the causes and effects of a given mental state is part of the functionalist's general conception of mental states as forming a complex causal network anchored to the external world at various points. At these points of contact, a psychological subject interacts with the outside world, receiving inputs and emitting outputs. And the identity of a given mental kind, whether it is a sensation like pain or a belief that it is going to rain or a desire for a ham sandwich, depends solely on the place it occupies in the causal network. That is, what makes a mental event the kind of mental event it is, is the way it is causally linked to other mental-event kinds and input-output conditions. Since each of these other mental-event kinds in turn has its identity determined by *its* causal relations to other mental events and to inputs and outputs, the identity of each mental kind depends ultimately on the whole system—its internal structure and the way it is causally linked to the external world via sensory inputs and behavior outputs. In this sense, functionalism gives us a *holistic* conception of mentality.

This holistic approach enables functionalism to sidestep one of the principal objections to behaviorism. This is the difficulty we saw earlier: A desire issues in overt behavior only when combined with an appropriate belief, and similarly, a belief leads to appropriate behavior only when a matching desire is present. For example, a person with a desire to eat an apple will eat an apple that is presented to her only if she believes it to be an apple (she would not eat it if she thought it was a fake wooden apple); a person who believes that it is going to rain will take an umbrella only if she has a desire not to get wet. As we saw, this apparently makes it impossible to define desire without reference to belief or define belief without reference to desire. The functionalist would say that this only points to the holistic character of mental states: It is an essential feature of a desire that it is the kind of internal state that in concert with an appropriate belief causes a certain behavior output, and similarly for belief and other mental states.

But doesn't this make the definitions circular? If the concept of desire cannot be defined without reference to belief, and the concept of belief in turn cannot be explained without reference to desire, how can either be understood at all? We will see below (chapter 6) how the holistic approach of functionalism deals with this question.

Turing Machines

Functionalism was originally formulated by Putnam in terms of "Turing machines," mathematically characterized computing machines due to the British mathematician-logician Alan M. Turing.[13] Although it is now customary to formulate functionalism in terms of causal-functional roles—as we have done and will do in more detail in the next chapter—it is instructive to begin our systematic treatment of functionalism by examining the Turing-machine version of functionalism, usually called machine functionalism. This also gives us the background needed to explore the idea that the workings of the mind are best understood in terms of the operations of a computing machine—that is, the computational view of the mind (or computationalism for short).

A Turing machine is made up of four components:

1. A *tape* divided into "squares" and unbounded in both directions
2. A *scanner-printer* ("head") positioned at one of the squares of the tape at any given time
3. A finite set of *internal states* (or *configurations*), $q_0, \ldots, q_n$
4. A finite *alphabet* consisting of symbols, $b_1, \ldots, b_m$

One and only one symbol appears on each square. (We may think of the blank as one of the symbols.)

The general operations of the machine are as follows:

A. At each time, the machine is in one of its internal states, q_i, and its head is scanning a particular square on the tape.
B. What the machine does at a given time *t* is completely determined by its internal state at *t* and the symbol its head is scanning at *t*.
C. Depending on its internal state and the symbol being scanned, the machine does three things:
(1) Its head replaces the symbol with another (possibly the same) symbol of the alphabet. (To put it another way, the head erases the symbol being scanned and prints a new one, which may be the same as the erased one.)
(2) Its head moves one square to the right or to the left (or halt, with the computation completed).
(3) The machine enters into a new internal state.

Let us consider a Turing machine that adds positive integers in the unary notation. (In this notation, number *n* is represented as a sequence of *n* strokes, each stroke occupying one square.) Consider the following picture in which the problem of adding 3 and 2 is presented to the machine, which is to be started off with its head in state q_0 and scanning the first digit:

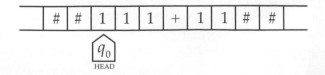

(The "scratch" symbol, #, marks the boundaries of the problem.) We want to "program" this Turing machine in such a way that when the computation is completed, the machine halts with a sequence of five consecutive strokes showing on the tape, like this:

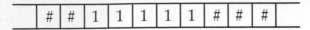

It is easy to see that there are various procedures by which the machine could accomplish this. One simple way is to have the machine (or its head) move to the right looking for the symbol +, replace it with a stroke, keep moving right until it finds the right-most stroke, and when it does, erase it (that is, replace it with the scratch symbol #) and then halt. The following simple "machine table" is a complete set of instructions that defines our adder (call it TM_1):

	q_0	q_1
1	$1Rq_0$	#Halt
+	$1Rq_0$	
#	$\#Lq_1$	

Here is how we read this table. On the left-most column you find the symbols of the machine alphabet listed vertically, and the top row lists the machine's internal states. Each entry in the interior matrix is an *instruction*: It tells the machine what to do when it is scanning the symbol shown in the left-most column of that row and is in the internal state listed at the top of the column. For example, the entry $1Rq_0$, at the intersection of q_0 and 1, tells the machine: "If you are scanning the symbol 1 and are in internal state q_0, replace 1 with 1 (that is, leave it unchanged), move to the right by one square, and go into internal state q_0 (that is, stay in the same state)." The entry immediately below, $1Rq_0$, tells the machine: "If you are in state q_0 and scanning the symbol +, replace + with 1, move to the right by one square, and go into state q_0." The L in the bottom entry, $\#Lq_1$, means "move left by one square"; the entry in the right-most column, #Halt, means "If you are scanning 1 and in state q_1, replace 1 with # and halt." It is easy to see (the reader is asked to figure this out on her own) the exact sequence of steps our Turing machine will follow to compute the sum 3 + 2.

The machine table of a Turing machine is a complete and exhaustive specification of the machine's operations. We may therefore identify a Turing machine with its machine table. Since a machine table is nothing but a set of instructions, this means that a Turing machine can be identified with a set of such instructions.

What sort of things are the "internal states" of a Turing machine? We talk about this general question later, but with our machine TM_1, it can be helpful to think of the specific machine states in the following intuitive way: q_0 is a + and # searching state—it is a state such that when TM_1 is in it, it keeps going right, looking for + and #, ignoring any 1s it encounters. Moreover, if the machine is in q_0 and finds a +, it replaces it with a 1 and keeps moving to the right, while staying in the same state; when it scans a # (thereby recognizing the right-most boundary of the given problem), it backs up to the left and goes into a new state q_1, the "print # over 1 and then halt" state. When TM_1 is in this state, it will replace any 1 it scans with a # and halt. Thus, each state "disposes" the machine to do a set of specific things depending on the symbol being scanned (which therefore can be likened to sensory input).

But this is not the only Turing machine that can add numbers in unary notation; there is another one that is simpler and works faster. It is clear that to add unary numbers it is not necessary for the machine to determine the right-most boundary of the given problem; all it needs to do is to erase the initial 1 being scanned when it is started off, and then move to the right to look for + and replace it with a 1. This is TM_2, with the following machine table:

	q_0	q_1
1	$\#Rq_1$	$1Rq_1$
+		1Halt
#		

We can readily build a third Turing machine, TM_3, that will do subtractions in the unary notation. Suppose the following subtraction problem is presented to the machine:

#	#	*b*	1	1	1	1	−	1	1	*b*	#	#

(Symbol *b* is used to mark the boundaries of the problem.) Starting the machine in state q_0 scanning the initial 1, we can write a machine table that computes $n - m$ by operating like this:

1. The machine starts off scanning the first 1 of n. It goes to the right until it locates m, the number being subtracted. (How does it recognize it has located m?) It then erases the first 1 of this number

(replacing it with a #), goes left, and erases the last 1 of n (again replacing it with a #).

2. The machine then goes right and repeats step 1 again and again, until it exhausts all the 1s in m. (How does the machine "know" that it has done this?) We then have the machine move right until it locates the subtraction sign −, which it erases (that is, replaces it with a #), and then halt. (If you like tidy output tapes, you may have the machine erase the *b*s before halting.)

3. If the machine runs out of the first set of strokes before it exhausts the second set (this means that $n < m$), we can have the machine print a certain symbol, say ?, to mean that the given problem is not well-defined. We must also provide for the case where $n = m$.

The reader is invited to write out a machine table that implements these operations.

We can also think of a "transcription machine," TM_4, that transcribes a given string of 1s to its right (or left). That is, if TM_4 is presented with the following tape to begin its computation,

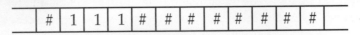

it ends with the following configuration of symbols on its tape:

#	1	1	1	#	1	1	1	#	#	#	#

The interest of the transcription machine lies in how it can be used to construct a multiplication machine, TM_5. The basic idea is simple: We can get $n \times m$ by transcribing the string of n 1s m times (that is, transcribing n repeatedly using m as a counter). The reader is encouraged to write a machine table for TM_5.

Since any arithmetical operation (squaring, taking the factorial, and so on) on natural numbers can be defined in terms of addition and multiplication, it follows that there is a Turing machine that computes any arithmetical operation. In fact, it can be shown that any computation performed by any computer can be done by a Turing machine. That is, being computable and being computable by a Turing machine turn out to be equivalent notions.

We can think of a Turing machine with two separate tapes (one for input, on which the problem to be computed is presented, and the other for actual computation and the final output) and two separate heads (one for scanning and one for printing). This helps us to think of a Turing machine as receiving "sensory stimuli" (the symbols on the input tape) through its scanner ("sense organ") and emitting specific behaviors in response (the symbols printed on the output tape by its printer head). It can be shown that any computation that can be done by a two-tape machine or a machine with any finite number of tapes can be done by a one-tape machine. So adding more tapes does not strengthen the computing power of Turing machines or substantively enrich the concept of a Turing machine.

Turing also showed how to build a "universal machine," which is like a general-purpose computer in that it is not dedicated to the computation of a specific function but can be programmed to compute any function you want. On the input tape of this machine, you specify two things: the machine table of the desired function in some standard notation that can be read by the universal machine and the values for which the function is to be computed. The universal machine is programmed to read any machine table and carry out the computation in accordance with the instructions of the machine table.

The notion of a Turing machine can be generalized to yield the notion of a *probabilistic automaton*. As you recall, each instruction of a Turing machine is *deterministic*: Given the internal state and the symbol being scanned, the immediate next operation is wholly and uniquely determined. An instruction of a probabilistic, or stochastic, automaton has the following general form: Given internal state q_i and scanned symbol b_j:

1. Print b_k with probability r_1, or print b_l with probability r_2, . . . , or print b_m with probability r_n (where the probabilities add up to 1).
2. Move R with probability r_1, or move L with probability r_2 (where the probabilities add up to 1).
3. Go into internal state q_j with probability r_1, or into q_k with probability r_2, . . . , or into q_m with probability r_n (again, the probabilities adding up to 1).

A machine can be made probabilistic in one or more of these three dimensions. The operations of a probabilistic automaton, therefore, are not deterministic; the current internal state of the machine and the symbol it is scanning do not together uniquely determine what the machine will do next. However, the behavior of such a machine is not random or arbitrary either: There are fixed and stable probabilities describing the machine's operations. If we are thinking of a machine that describes the behavior of an actual psychological subject, a probabilistic machine may be more realistic than a deterministic one; however, we may note the fact that it is generally possible to construct a deterministic machine that simulates the behavior of a probabilistic machine to any desired degree of accuracy, which makes probabilistic machines theoretically dispensable.

Physical Realizers of Turing Machines

Suppose that we give the machine table for our simple adding machine, TM_1, to an engineering class as an assignment: Each student is to build an actual physical device that will do the computations as specified by its machine table. What we are asking the students to build, therefore, are "physical realizers" of TM_1—real-life physical computing machines that will operate in accordance with the machine table of TM_1. We can safely predict that a huge, heterogeneous variety of machines will be turned in. Some of them may really look and work like the Turing machine as described: They will have a paper tape neatly divided into squares, with an actual physical "head" that can read, erase, and print symbols. Some will perhaps use magnetic tapes and heads that read, write, and erase electrically. Some machines will have no "tapes" or "heads" but instead use spaces on a computer disk or memory locations in its CPU to do the computation. A clever student with a sense of humor (and lots of time and other resources) might try to build a hydraulically operated device with pipes and valves instead of wires and switches. The possibilities are endless.

But what exactly is a physical realizer of a Turing machine? What makes a physical device a *realizer of* a given Turing machine? First, the symbols of the machine's alphabet must be given concrete physical embodiments; they could be blotches of ink on paper, patterns of magnetized iron particles on plastic tape, electric charges in capacitors, or what have you. Whatever they are, the physical device that does the "scanning" must be able to "read" them—that is, differentially respond to them—with a high degree of reliability. This means that the physical properties of the symbols place a set of constraints on the physical design of the scanner, but these constraints need not, and usually will not, determine a unique design; a great multitude of physical devices are likely to be adequate to serve as a scanner for the given set of physically embodied symbols. The same considerations apply to the machine's printer and outputs as well: The symbols the machine prints on its output tape (we are thinking of a two-tape machine) must be given physical shapes, and the printer must be designed to produce them on demand. The printer, of course, does not have to "print" anything in a literal sense; the operation could be wholly electronic, or the printer could be a speaker that vocalizes the output or an LCD monitor that visually displays it (then saves it for future computational purposes).

What about the "internal states" of the machine? How are they physically realized? Consider a particular instruction on the machine table of TM_1: If the machine is in state q_0 and scanning a +, replace that + with a 1, move right, and go into state q_1. Assume that Q_0 and Q_1 are the physical states realizing q_0 and q_1, respectively. Q_0 and Q_1, then, must satisfy the following condition: An occurrence of Q_0, together with the physical scanning of +, must *physically cause* three physical events: (1) The physical symbol + is replaced with the physical symbol 1; (2) the physical scanner-printer (head) moves one square to the right (on the physical tape) and scans it; and (3) the machine enters state Q_1. In general, then, what needs to be done is to *replace the functional or computational relations* among the various abstract parameters (symbols, states, and motions of the head) mentioned in the machine table *with appropriate causal relations among the physical embodiments* of these parameters.

From the logical point of view, the internal states are only "implicitly defined" in terms of their relations to other parameters: q_j is a state such that if the machine is in it and scanning symbol b_k, the machine replaces b_k with b_l, moves R (that is, to the right), and goes into state q_h; if the machine is scanning b_m, it does such and such; and so on. So q_j can be thought of as a function that maps symbols of the alphabet to the triples of the form $<b_k$, R (or L), $q_h>$. From the physical standpoint, Q_j, which realizes q_j, can be thought of as a *causal* intermediary between the physically realized symbols and the physical realizers of the triples—or equivalently, as a *disposition* to emit appropriate physical outputs (the triples) in response to different physical stimuli (the physical symbols scanned). This means that the intrinsic physical natures of the Qs that realize the qs are of no interest to us as long as they have the right causal properties; their intrinsic properties do not matter—or more accurately, they matter only to the extent that they affect the desired causal powers of the states and objects that have them. As long as these states perform their assigned causal work, they can be anything you please. Clearly, whether or not the Qs realize the qs depends crucially on how the tape, symbols, and so on, are physically realized; in fact, these are interdependent questions. It is plausible to suppose that, with some engineering ingenuity, a machine could be rewired so that physical states realizing distinct machine states could be interchanged without affecting the operation of the machine.

We see, then, a convergence of two ideas: the functionalist conception of a mental state as a state occupying a certain specific causal role and the idea of a physical state realizing an internal state of a Turing machine. Just as, on the functionalist view, what makes a given mental state the kind of mental state it is is its causal role with respect to sensory inputs, behavior outputs, and other mental states, so what makes a physical state the realizer of a given machine state is its causal relations to inputs, outputs, and other physical realizers of the machine's internal states. This is why it is natural for functionalists to look to Turing machines for a model of the mind.

Let S be a physical system (which may be an electromechanical device like a computer, a biological organism, a business organization, or anything else), and assume that we have adopted a vocabulary to describe its inputs and outputs. That is, we have a specification of what is to count as the inputs it receives from its surroundings and what is to count as its behavioral outputs. Assume, moreover, that we have specified what states of S are to count as its "internal states." We will say that a Turing machine M is a *machine description* of system S, relative to a given input-output specification and a specification of the internal states, just in case S realizes M relative to the input-output and internal state specifications. Thus, the relation of *being a machine description of* is the converse of the relation of *being a realizer (or realization) of*. We can also define a concept that is weaker than machine description: Let us say that a Turing machine M is a *behavioral description* of S (relative to an input-output specification) just in case M provides a correct description of S's input-output correlations. Thus, every machine description of S is also a behavioral description of S, but the converse does not in general hold. M can give a true description of the input-output correlations characterizing S, but its machine states may not be realized in S, and S's inner workings (that is, its computational processes) may not correctly mirror the functional-computational relationships given by M's machine table. In fact, there may be another Turing machine M*, distinct from M, that gives a correct machine description of S. It follows, then, that *two physical systems that are input-output equivalent may not be realizations of the same Turing machine*. (The pair of adding machines TM_1 and TM_2 illustrates such a situation.)

Machine Functionalism: Motivations and Claims

Machine functionalists claim that we can think of the mind as a Turing machine (or a probabilistic automaton). This of course needs to be filled out, but from the preceding discussion it should be pretty clear how the story will go. The central idea is that what it is for something to have mentality—that is, to have a psychology—is for it to be a physically realized Turing machine of appropriate complexity, with its mental states (that is, mental-state types) identified with the internal states of the machine table. Another way of explaining this idea is to use the notion of machine description: An organism has mentality just in case there is a Turing machine of appropriate complexity that is a machine description of it, and its mental-state kinds are to be identified with the internal states of that Turing machine. All this is, of course, relative to an appropriately chosen input-output specification, since you must know, or decide, what is to count as the organism's inputs and outputs before you can determine what Turing machine (or machines) it can be said to instantiate.

Let us consider the idea that *the psychology of an organism* can be represented by a Turing machine, an idea that is commonly held by machine functionalists.[14] Let V be a complete specification of all possible inputs and outputs of a psychological subject S, and let C be all actual and possible input-output correlations of S (that is, C is a complete specification of which input applied to S elicits which output, for all inputs and outputs listed in V). In constructing a *psychology* for S, we are trying to formulate a *theory* that gives a perspicuous systematization of C by positing a set of internal states in S. Such a theory *predicts* for any input applied to S what output will be emitted by S and also *explains* why that particular input will elicit that particular output. It is reasonable to suppose that for any behavioral system complex enough to have a psychology, this kind of systematization is not possible unless we advert to its internal states, for we must expect that the same input applied to S does not always prompt S to produce the same output. The actual output elicited by a given input depends, we must suppose, on the internal state of S at that time.

Before we proceed further, it is necessary to modify our notion of a Turing machine in one respect: The internal states, qs, of a Turing machine are *total* states of the machine at a given time, and the Qs that are their physical realizers are also *total* physical states at a time of the physically realized machine.

This means that the Turing machines we are talking about are not going to look very much like the psychological theories we are familiar with; the states posited by these theories are seldom, if ever, total states of a subject at a time. But this is a technical problem, something that we assume can be remedied with a finer-grained notion of an "internal state." We can then think of a total internal state as made up of these "partial" states, which combine in different ways to yield different total states. This modification should not change anything essential in the original conception of a Turing machine. In the discussion to follow, we use this modified notion of an internal state in most contexts.

To return to the question of representing the psychology of a subject S in terms of a Turing machine: What Turing machine, or machines, is adequate as a description of S's psychology? Evidently, any adequate Turing machine must be a behavioral description of S, in the sense defined earlier; that is, it must give a correct description of S's input-output correlations (relative to V). But as we have seen, there is bound to be more than one Turing machine—in fact, if there is one, there will be indefinitely more—that gives a correct representation of S's input-output correlations.

Since each of these machines is a correct behavioral description of our psychological subject S, they are all equally good as a *predictive instrument*. Although some of them may be easier to manipulate and computationally more efficient than others, they all predict the same behavior output for the same input conditions. This is a simple consequence of the notion of "behavioral description." In what sense, then, are they different Turing machines, and why do the differences matter?

It should be clear how behaviorally equivalent Turing machines, say, M_1 and M_2, can differ from each other. To say that they are different Turing machines is to say that their machine tables are different—that is how Turing machines are individuated. This means that when they are given the same input, M_1 and M_2 are likely to go through *different computational processes* to arrive at the same output. Each machine has a set of internal states—let us say $<q_0, q_1, \ldots, q_n>$ for M_1 and $<r_0, r_1, \ldots, r_m>$ for M_2. Let us suppose further that M_1 is a machine description of our psychological subject S, but M_2 is not. That is, S is a physical realizer of M_1 but not of M_2. This means that the computational relations represented in M_1, but not those represented in M_2, are mirrored in a set of causal relations among the physical-psychological states of S. So there are real physical (perhaps neurobiological) states in S, $<Q_0, Q_1, \ldots, Q_n>$, corresponding to M_1's internal states $<q_0, q_1, \ldots, q_n>$, and these Qs are causally hooked up to each other and to the physical scanner (sense organs) and the physical printer (motor mechanisms) in a way that ensures that for all computational processes generated by M_1, isomorphic causal processes occur in S. As we may say, S is a "causal isomorph" of M_1.

There is, then, a clear sense in which M_1 is, but M_2 is not, "psychologically real" for S, even though they are both accurate predictive theories of S's observable input-output behaviors. M_1 gives "the true psychology" of S in that, as we saw, S has a physical structure whose states constitute a causal system that mirrors the computational structure represented by the machine table of M_1 and in that the physical-causal operations of S form an isomorphic image of the computational operations of M_1. This makes a crucial difference when what we want is an *explanatory* theory, a theory that *explains why S does what it does under the given input conditions.* Suppose we say: When input i was applied to S, S emitted behavioral output o *because* it was in internal state Q. This can count as an explanation, it seems, only if the state appealed to—namely, Q—is a "real" state of the system. In particular, it can count as a *causal* explanation only if the state Q is what, in conjunction with i, caused o, and this cannot happen unless Q is actually a state of S. Now, it is clear that we can impute reality to Q only if it realizes an internal state of M_1, a Turing machine realized by S. In contrast, Turing machine M_2, which is not realized by S, has no "inner" psychological reality for S, even though it correctly captures all of S's input-output correlations. Although, like M_1, M_2 correlates input i with output o, the computational process whereby the correlation is effected does not reflect actual causal processes in S that lead from i to o (or physical embodiments thereof). The explanatory force of "S emitted o when it received input i because it was in state Q" derives from the causal relations involving Q and the physical embodiments of o and i.

The philosophical issues here depend, partly but critically, on the metaphysics of scientific theories you accept. If you think of scientific theories in general, or theories over some specific domain, merely as predictive instruments that enable us to infer or calculate further observations from the given data, you will not attach any existential significance to the posits of these theories—like the unobservable microparticles of theoretical physics and their (often quite strange) properties—and may regard them only as calculational aids in deriving predictions. A position like this is called "instrumentalism," or "antirealism," about scientific theory.[15] On such a view, the issue of "truth" does not arise for the theoretical principles, nor does the issue of "reality" for the entities and properties posited; the only thing that matters is the "empirical adequacy" of the theory—how accurately the theory works as a predictive device and how comprehensive its coverage is. If you accept an instrumentalist stance toward psychological theory, therefore, any Turing machine that is a behavioral description of a psychological subject is good enough, exactly as good as any other behaviorally adequate description of it, although you may prefer some over others on account of manipulative ease and computational cost. If this is your view of the nature of psychology, you will dismiss as meaningless the question which of the many behaviorally adequate psychologies is "really true" of the subject.

But if you adopt the perspective of "realism" on scientific theories, or at any rate about psychology, you will not think all behaviorally adequate descriptions are psychologically adequate. An adequate psychology for the realist must have "psychological reality": That is, the internal states it posits must be the real states of the organism with an active role as causal intermediaries between sensory inputs and behavior outputs, and this means that only a Turing machine that is a correct machine description of the organism is an acceptable psychological theory of it. The simplest and most elegant behavioral description may not be the one that correctly describes the inner processes that cause the subject's observable behavior; there is no a priori reason to suppose that our subject is put together according to the specifications of the simplest and most elegant theory (whatever your standards of simplicity and elegance might be).

Why should one want to go beyond the instrumentalist position and insist on psychological reality? There are two related reasons: (1) Psychological states, namely, the internal states of the psychological subject posited by a psychology, must be regarded as real, as we saw, if we expect the theory to generate explanations, especially causal explanations, of behavior. And this seems to be the attitude of working psychologists: It is their common, almost universal, practice to attribute to their subjects internal states, capacities, functions, and mechanisms (for example, information storage and retrieval, mental imagery, preference structure) and to refer to them in formulating what they regard as causal explanations of overt behavior. Further, (2) it seems natural to expect—this seems true of most psychologists and cognitive scientists—to find actual neural-biological mechanisms that underlie the psychological states, capacities, and functions posited by correct psychological theories. Research in the neural sciences has had impressive successes—and we expect this to continue—in identifying physiological mechanisms that implement psychological capacities and functions. It is a reflection of our realistic stance toward psychological theorizing that we generally expect, and perhaps insist on, physiological foundations for psychological theories. The requirement that the correct psychology of an organism be a machine description of it,[16] not merely a behaviorally adequate one, can be seen as an expression of a commitment to realism about psychological theory.

If the psychology of any organism can be represented as a Turing machine, it is natural to consider the possibility of using representability by a Turing machine to explicate, or define, what it is for something to have a psychology. As we saw, that precisely is what machine functionalism proposes: What it is for an organism, or system, to have a psychology—that is, what it is for an organism to have mentality—is for it to realize an appropriate Turing machine. It is not merely that anything with mentality has an appropriate machine description; machine functionalism makes the stronger claim that its having a machine description of an appropriate kind is *constitutive of* its mentality. This is a philosophical thesis about the nature of mentality: Mentality, or having a mind, consists in realizing an appropriate Turing machine. What makes us creatures with mentality, therefore, is the fact that we are Turing machines. Functionalism acknowledges that having a brain of a certain structural complexity is important to mentality, but the importance of the brain lies exactly in its being a physical Turing machine. It is our brain's computational powers, not its biological properties, that constitute our mentality. In short, our brain is our mind because it is a computing machine, not because it is composed of the kind of protein-based biological stuff it is composed of.

Machine Functionalism: Further Issues

Suppose that two systems, S_1 and S_2, are *in the same mental state* (at the same time or different times). What does this mean on the machine-functionalist conception of a mental kind? A mental kind, as you will remember, is supposed to be an internal state of a Turing machine (of an "appropriate kind"); so for S_1 and S_2 to be in the same state, there must be some Turing machine state q such that S_1 is in q and S_2 is also in q. But what does this mean?

S_1 and S_2 are both physical systems, and we know that they could be systems of very different sorts (recall multiple realizability). As physical systems, they have physical states (that is, they instantiate certain physical properties); to say that they are both in machine state q at time t is to say this: There are physical states Q_1 and Q_2 such that Q_1 realizes q in S_1, and Q_2 realizes q in S_2, and, at t, S_1 is in Q_1 and S_2 in Q_2. Multiple realizability tells us that Q_1 and Q_2 probably have not much in common qua physical states; one could be a biological state and the other an electromagnetic one. What binds the two states together is only the fact that in their respective systems they implement the same internal machine state. That is to say, the two states play the same computational role in their respective systems.

But talk of "the same internal machine state q" makes sense only in relation to a given machine table. That is to say, internal states of a Turing machine are identifiable only relative to a given machine table: In terms of the layout of machine tables we used earlier, an internal state q is wholly characterized by the vertical column of instructions appearing under it. But these instructions refer to other internal states, say, q_i, q_j, and q_k, and if you look up the instructions falling under these, you are likely to find references back to state q. So these states are interdefined. What all this means is that *the sameness or difference of an internal state across different machine tables—that is, across different Turing machines—has no meaning*. It makes no sense to say of an internal state q_i of one Turing machine and a state q_k of another that q_i is, or that it is not, the same state as q_k; nor does it make sense to say of a physical state Q_i of a physically realized Turing machine that it realizes, or does not realize, the same internal machine state q as does a physical state Q_k of another physical machine, *unless the two physical machines are realizations of the same Turing machine*.

Evidently, then, the machine-functionalist conception of mental kinds has the following consequence: For any two subjects to be in the same mental state, they must realize the same Turing machine. But if they realize the same Turing machine, their total psychology must be identical. That is, on machine functionalism, two subjects' total psychology must be identical if they are to share even a single psychological state—or even to give meaning to the talk of their being, or not being, in the same psychological state. This sounds absurd: It does not seem reasonable to require that for two persons to share a mental state—say, the belief that snow is white—the total set of psychological regularities governing their behavior must be exactly identical. Before we discuss this issue further, we must attend to another matter, and this is the problem of how the inputs and outputs of a system are to be specified.

Suppose that two systems, S_1 and S_2, realize the same Turing machine; that is, the same Turing machine gives a correct machine description for each. We know that realization is relative to a particular input-output specification; that is, we must know what is to count as input conditions and what is to count as behavior outputs of the system before we can tell whether it realizes a given Turing machine. Let V_1 and V_2 be the input-output specifications for S_1 and S_2, respectively, relative to which they share the same machine description. Since the same machine table is involved, V_1 and V_2 must be isomorphic: The elements of V_1 can be correlated, one to one, with the elements of V_2 in a way that preserves their roles in the machine table. And we are assuming, of course, that our Turing machine has the appropriate complexity to qualify as a psychological system.

But suppose that S_1 is a real psychological system, perhaps a human (call him Larry), whereas S_2 is a computer, an electromechanical device (call it MAX). So the inputs and outputs specified by V_2 are the usual inputs and outputs appropriate for a computing machine, perhaps strings of symbols entered on the keyboard and strings of symbols on the monitor or its print-out. Now, whether MAX can be considered a psychological system at all is a question we take up later, but granting it the full psychological status that we grant Larry should strike us as in effect *conflating a psychological subject with a computer simulation of it*. It is to refuse to acknowledge a distinction between a real thing and a computer simulation of a real thing. No one is likely to confuse the operation of a jet engine or the spread of rabies in wildlife with their computer simulations. It is difficult to believe that this distinction suddenly vanishes when we perform a computer simulation of the psychology of a person.

One thing that obviously seems wrong about our computer, MAX, as a psychological system when we compare it with Larry is its inputs and outputs: Although its input-output specification is isomorphic to Larry's, it seems entirely inappropriate for psychology. It may not be easy to characterize the differences precisely, but we would not consider inputs and outputs consisting merely of strings of symbols as appropriate for something with true mentality. Grinding out strings of symbols is not like the full-blown behavior that we see in Larry. For one thing, MAX's outputs have nothing to do with its survival or continued proper functioning, and its inputs do not have the function of providing MAX with information about its surroundings. As a result, MAX's outputs lack what may be called "teleological aptness" as a response to its inputs. All this makes it difficult to think of MAX's outputs as constituting real behavior or action, something that is necessary if we are to regard it as a genuine psychological system.

Qua realizations of a Turing machine, MAX and Larry are symmetrically related. If, however, we see here an asymmetry in point of mentality, it is clear that the nature of inputs and outputs is an important factor, and our considerations seem to show that for a system realizing a Turing machine to count as a psychological system, its input-output specification (relative to which it realizes the machine) must be *psychologically appropriate*. Exactly what this appropriateness consists in is an interesting and complex question that requires further exploration. In any case, the machine functionalist must confront this question: Is it possible to give a characterization of this input-output appropriateness that is consistent with functionalism—in particular, without using mentalistic terms or concepts? Recall a similar point we discussed in connection with behaviorism: Not to beg the question, the behavior that the behaviorist is allowed to talk about in giving behavioristic definitions of mental concepts must be "physical behavior," not intentional action with an explicit or implicit mental component (such as reading the morning paper, being impolite to a waiter, or going to a concert). If your project is to get mentality out of behavior, your notion of behavior must not presuppose mentality.

The same restriction applies to the machine functionalist: Her project is to define mentality in terms of Turing machines and input-output relations. The additional tool she can make use of, something not available to the behaviorist, is the concept of a Turing machine with its "internal" states, but her input and output are subject to the same constraint—her input-output, like the behaviorist's, must be physical input-output. If this is right, it seems no easy task for the machine functionalist to distinguish, in a principled way, Larry's inputs-outputs from MAX's, and hence genuine psychological systems from their simulations. We pointed out earlier that Larry's outputs, given his inputs, seem *teleologically apt*, whereas MAX's do not. They have something to do with his proper functioning in his environment—coping with environmental conditions and changes and satisfying his needs and desires. But can this notion of teleology—purposiveness or goal-directedness—be explained in a psychologically neutral way, without begging the question? Perhaps, some biological-evolutionary story could be attempted, but it remains an open question whether such a bioteleological attempt will succeed. In any case, that would take us beyond machine functionalism proper. These considerations give credence to the idea that in order to have genuine mentality, a system must be embedded in a natural environment (ideally including other systems like it), interacting and coping with it and behaving appropriately in response to the ever-changing stimulus conditions it encounters.

Let us now return to the question of whether machine functionalism is committed to the consequence that two psychological subjects can be in the same psychological state only if they have an identical total psychology. As we saw, the implication appears to follow from the fact that, on machine functionalism, being in the same psychological state is being in the same internal machine state and that the sameness of a machine state makes sense only in relation to the same Turing machine. What is perhaps worse, it seems to follow that it makes no sense to say that two psychological subjects are *not* in the same psychological state unless they have an identical total psychology! But this conclusion must be slightly weakened in consideration of the fact that the input-output specifications of the two subjects realizing the same Turing machine may be different and that the individuation of psychologies may have to be made sensitive to input-output specifications (we return shortly to this point). So let us speak of "isomorphic" psychologies for psychologies that are instances of the same Turing machine *modulo* input-output specification. We then have the following result: On machine functionalism, for two psychological subjects to share even a single mental state, their total psychologies must be isomorphic to each other. Recall Putnam's complaint against the psychoneural identity theory: This theory makes it impossible for both humans and octopuses to be in the same pain state unless they share the same brain state, an unlikely possibility. But it would seem that machine functionalism runs into an exactly identical predicament: For an octopus and a human to be in the same pain state, they must share an isomorphic psychology—an unlikely possibility, to say the least! And for two humans to share a single mental state, they must have an exactly identical total psychology (since the same input-output specification presumably must hold for all or most humans). No analogous consequence follows from the psychoneural identity theory; in this respect, therefore, machine functionalism seems to fare worse than the theory it hopes to replace. All this is a consequence of a fact mentioned earlier, namely, that on functionalism, the individuation of mental kinds is essentially holistic.

Things are perhaps not as bleak for machine functionalism, however, as they might appear, for the following line of response seems available: For both humans and octopuses to be in pain, it is not necessary that *total* octopus psychology coincide with, or be isomorphic to, *total* human psychology. It is only necessary that there be *some* Turing machine that is a correct machine description of both and in which pain figures as an internal machine state; it does not matter if this shared Turing machine falls short of the maximally detailed Turing machines that describe them (these machines represent their "total psychologies"). So what is necessary is that humans and octopuses share a partial, or abbreviated, psychology that encompasses pains. Whether or not pain psychology can so readily be isolated, or abstracted, from the total psychology is a question worth pondering, especially in the context of the functionalist conception of mentality, but there is another potential difficulty here that we should briefly consider.

Recall the point that all this talk of humans' and octopuses' realizing a Turing machine is relative to an input-output specification. Doesn't this mean, in view of our earlier discussion of a real psychological subject and a computer simulation of one, that the input and output conditions characteristic of humans when they are in pain must be appropriately similar, if not identical, to those characteristic of octopuses' pains, if both humans and octopuses can be said to be in pain? Consider the output side: Do octopuses wince and groan in reaction to pain? They perhaps can wince, but they surely cannot groan or scream and yell "Ouch!" How similar is octopuses' escape behavior, from the purely physical point of view, to the escape behavior of, say, middle-aged, middle-class American males? Is there an abstract enough *nonmental* description of pain behavior that is appropriate for humans and octopuses and all other pain-capable organisms and systems? If there is not, machine functionalism seems to succumb again to the same difficulty that the functionalist has charged against the brain-state theory: An octopus and a human cannot be in the same pain state. Again, the best bet for the functionalist seems to be to appeal to the "teleological appropriateness" of an octopus's and a person's escape behaviors—that is, the fact that the behaviors are biologically appropriate responses to the stimulus conditions in enhancing their chances of survival and their well-being in their respective environments.

There is a further "appropriateness" condition for Turing machines that we must now consider. You will remember our saying that for a machine functionalist, a system has mentality just in case it realizes an "appropriately complex" Turing machine. This proviso is necessary because there are all sorts of simple Turing machines (recall our sample machines) that clearly do not suffice to generate mentality. But how complex is complex enough? What is complexity anyway, and how is it measured? And what kind of complexity is "appropriate" for mentality? These are important but difficult questions, and machine functionalism, unsurprisingly, has not produced detailed general answers to them. What we have, though, is an intriguing proposal, from Turing himself, of a test to determine whether a computing machine can "think." This is the celebrated "Turing test," and we now turn to this proposal.

The Turing Test

Turing's innovative proposal is to bypass these general theoretical questions about appropriateness in favor of a concrete operational test that can evaluate the performance capabilities of computing machines vis-à-vis average humans who, as all sides would agree, are fully mental.[17] The idea is that if machines can do as well as humans on certain appropriate intellectual tasks, then they must be judged no less psychological ("intelligent") than humans.

What, then, are these tasks? Obviously, they must be those that, intuitively, require intelligence and mentality to perform; Turing describes a game, the "imitation game," to test for the presence of these capacities.

The imitation game is played as follows. There are three players: the interrogator, a man, and a woman, with the interrogator segregated from the other two in another room. The man and woman are known only as "X" and "Y" to the interrogator, whose object is to identify which is the man and which is the woman by asking questions via keyboard terminals and monitors. The man's object is to mislead the interrogator into an erroneous identification, whereas the woman's job is to help the interrogator. There are no restrictions on the topics of the questions asked.

Suppose, Turing says, we now replace the man with a computing machine. Now the aim of the interrogator is to find out which is human and which is a machine. The machine is programmed to fool the interrogator into thinking that it is a human. Will the machine do as well as the man in the first game in fooling the interrogator into making wrong guesses? Turing's proposal is that if the machine does as well as the man, then we must credit it with all the intelligence that we would normally confer on a human; it must be judged to possess the full mentality that humans possess.

The gist of Turing's idea can be captured in a simpler test: By asking questions (or just holding a conversation) via keyboard terminals, can we find out whether we are talking to a human or a computing machine? (This is the way the Turing test is now being performed.) If there is a computer that can consistently fool us so that our success in guessing its identity is no better than what could be achieved by random guesses, we must concede, it seems, that this machine has the kind of mentality that we grant to humans. There already are chess-playing computers that would fool most people this way, but only in playing chess: Average chess players would not be able to tell if they are playing a human opponent or a computer. But the Turing test covers all possible areas of human concern: music and poetry, politics and sports, how to fix a leaking faucet or make a soufflé—no holds are barred.

The Turing test is designed to isolate the questions of intelligence and mentality from irrelevant considerations, such as the appearance of the machine (as Turing points out, it does not have to win beauty contests to qualify as a thinker), details of its composition and structure, whether it speaks and moves about like a human, and so on. The test is to focus on a broad range of rational, intellectual capacities and functions. But how good is the test?

Some have pointed out that the test is both too tough and too narrow. Too tough because something does not have to be smart enough to outwit a human to have mentality or intelligence; in particular, the possession of a language should not be a prerequisite for mentality (think of mute animals). Human intelligence itself encompasses a pretty broad range, and there appears to be no compelling reason to set the minimal threshold of mentality at the level of performance required by the Turing test. The test is perhaps also too narrow in that it seems at best to be a test for the presence of *humanlike* mentality, the kind of intelligence that characterizes humans. Why couldn't there be creatures, or machines, that are intelligent and have a psychology but would fail the Turing test, which, after all, is designed to test whether the computer can fool a *human* interrogator into thinking it is a *human*? Furthermore, it is difficult to see it as a test for the presence of mental states like sensations and perceptions, although it may be an excellent test of broadly intellectual and cognitive capacities (reasoning, memory, and so on). To see something as a full psychological system we must see it in a real-life context, we might argue; we must see it coping with its environment, receiving sensory information from its surroundings, and behaving appropriately in response to it.

Various replies can be attempted to counter these criticisms, but can we say, as Turing himself did, that the Turing test at least provides us with a *sufficient* condition for mentality, although, for the reasons just given, it cannot be considered a necessary condition? If something passes the test, it is at least as smart as we are, and since we have intelligence and mentality, it would be only fair to grant it the same status—or so we might argue. This reasoning seems to presuppose the following thesis:

> *Turing's Thesis.* If two systems are input-output equivalent, they have the same psychological status; in particular, one is mental just in case the other is.

We call it Turing's Thesis because Turing seems to be committed to it. Why is Turing committed to it? Because the Turing test looks only at inputs and outputs: If two computers produce the same output for the same input, for all possible inputs—that is, if they are input-output equivalent—their performance on the Turing test will be exactly identical, and one will be judged to have mentality if and only if the other is. This means that if two Turing machines are correct behavioral descriptions of some system (relative to the same input-output specification), then they satisfy the "appropriateness" condition to the same degree. (Remember that "appropriateness" here refers to appropriateness for mentality.) In this way the general philosophical stance implicit in Turing's Thesis is more behavioristic than machine-functionalist. For machine functionalism is consistent with the denial of Turing's thesis: It says that input-output equivalence, or behavioral equivalence, is not sufficient to guarantee the same degree of mentality. What arguably follows from machine functionalism is only that systems that realize the same Turing machine—that is, systems for which an identical Turing machine is a correct machine description—enjoy the same degree of mentality.

It appears, then, that Turing's Thesis is mistaken: Internal processing ought to make a difference to mentality. Imagine two machines, each of which does basic arithmetic operations for integers up to 100. Both give correct answers for any input of the form $n + m$, $n \times m$, $n - m$, and $n \div m$ for whole numbers n and m less than or equal to 100. But one of the machines calculates ("figures out") the answer by applying the usual algorithms we use for these operations, whereas the other has a file in which answers are stored for all possible problems of addition, multiplication, subtraction, and division for integers up to 100, and its computation consists in "looking up" the answer for any problem given to it. The second machine is really more like a filing cabinet than a computing machine; it does nothing that we would normally describe as "calculation" or "computation." Neither machine is nearly complex enough to be considered for possible mentality; however, the example should convince us that we need to consider the structure of internal processing, as well as input-output correlations, in deciding whether a given system has mentality.[18] If this is correct, it shows the inadequacy of a purely behavioral test, such as the Turing test, as a criterion of mentality.

So Turing's Thesis seems incorrect: Input-output equivalence does not imply equal mentality. But this does not necessarily invalidate the Turing test, for it may well be that given the inherent richness and complexity of the imitation game, any computing machine that can consistently fool humans—in fact, any machine that is in the ballpark for the competition—has to be running a highly sophisticated, unquestionably "intelligent" program, and there is no real chance that this machine could be operating like a gigantic filing system with a superfast retrieval mechanism.[19]

The "Chinese Room"

John Searle has constructed an intriguing thought-experiment to show that mentality cannot be equated with a computing machine running a program, no matter how complex, "intelligent," and sophisticated it is.[20] Searle invites us to imagine a room—the "Chinese room"—in which someone (say, Searle himself) who understands no Chinese is confined. He has a set of rules (the "rule book") for systematically transforming strings of symbols to yield further symbol strings. These symbol strings are in fact Chinese expressions, and the transformation rules are purely *formal* in the sense that their application depends solely on the shapes of the symbols involved, not their meanings. So you can apply these rules without knowing any Chinese; all that is required is that you recognize Chinese characters by their shapes. Searle becomes very adept at manipulating Chinese expressions in accordance with the rules given to him (we may suppose that Searle has memorized the whole rule book) so that every time a string of Chinese characters is sent in, Searle goes to work and promptly sends out an appropriate string of Chinese characters. From the perspective of someone outside the room who understands Chinese, the input strings are questions in Chinese and the output strings sent out by Searle are appropriate responses to these questions. The input-output relationships are what we would expect if someone with a genuine understanding of Chinese, instead of Searle, were locked inside the room. And yet Searle does not understand any Chinese, and there is no understanding of Chinese going on anywhere inside the Chinese room. What goes on in the room is only manipulation of symbols on the basis of their shapes, or "syntax," but real understanding involves "semantics," knowing what these symbols represent, or mean. Although Searle's behavior is input-output equivalent to that of a speaker of Chinese, Searle understands no Chinese.

Now, replace Searle with a computer running Searle's rule book as its program. This changes nothing: Both Searle and the computer are syntax-driven machines manipulating strings of symbols according to their syntax. In general, what goes on inside a computer is exactly like what goes on in the Chinese room (with Searle in it): rule-governed manipulations of symbols based on their syntactic shapes. There is no more understanding of Chinese in the computer than there is in the Chinese room. The conclusion to be drawn, Searle argues, is that mentality is more than rule-governed syntactic manipulation of symbols and that there is no way to get semantics—or what the symbols mean or represent—from their syntax. And this means that understanding and other intelligent mental states and activities cannot arise from mere syntactic processes. Computational processes are essentially and exclusively syntactic; they do not depend at all on what the symbols being manipulated might mean or represent, or whether they mean anything at all.

Searle's argument has elicited a large number of critical responses, and just what the argument succeeds in showing remains highly controversial. Although its intuitive appeal and power cannot be denied, we have to be careful in assessing its significance. The appeal of Searle's example may be due, some have argued, to certain misleading assumptions tacitly made in the way he describes what is going on in the Chinese room. We can agree with Searle that input-output equivalence does not constitute psychological equivalence, and that the fact that the Chinese room is input-output equivalent with a speaker of Chinese does not show that the Chinese room, or Searle with his rule book, is a system with a genuine understanding of Chinese. As has already been pointed out, we must attend to internal processing—the kind of program being run—when considering the question of mentality for the system. And here it may be seriously misleading to represent the man locked inside the room as merely "manipulating symbols." Given the sophisticated linguistic processing that has to be performed, we must expect that an extremely sophisticated and highly complex program, something that may far exceed any computer program that has yet been written, will be necessary. It is by no means clear that any human could manage to do what Searle imagines himself to be doing in the Chinese room—that is, short of throwing away the rule book and learning some real Chinese.

Searle has a reply, however: Make the program as complex and intricate as you want, but no amount of syntactic symbol-pushing will generate meaning and understanding. Computation is syntax-driven: As long as the computer is given the same strings of 0s and 1s, it will generate certain further strings of 0s and 1s, no matter what these strings stand for—the prices of bags of potato chips or the addresses of a group of employees or the temperatures of the major cities in New England. The computer would move through exactly the same computational process even if the 0s and 1s meant nothing at all. However, our intentional states, like beliefs and desires, are what they are because they mean, or represent, something. My belief that it is raining outside has the content "it is raining outside," and in virtue of having this content the belief represents, or purports to represent, a specific weather condition in my environment. Suppose this belief causes in me a desire to take an umbrella to work. This causal relation holds in part because the belief and the desire have the particular contents that they have; my belief does not cause a desire to wear my best suit to work, and the belief that it is sunny outside does not cause me to want to take an umbrella with me. Mental processes are driven by representational contents, or meanings. Hence, they cannot be syntax-driven computational processes, and the mind cannot just be a computer running a program, no matter how complex and sophisticated the program may be. The mind is a "semantic engine"; the computer, in contrast, is only a "syntactic engine."

If this is the general argument underlying the Chinese room thought-experiment, it clearly raises a legitimate and perplexing issue about meaning and mental causation. However, this is a general problem that arises for any materialist conception of mentality, quite apart from the specific issue of the computational account of mentality. Consider the position that Searle himself favors: Mentality can arise only in complex biological systems, like the human brain. It seems that the same neurobiological causal processes will go on no matter what the neural states involved represent about the world or whether they represent anything at all. Neural processes seem no more responsive to meaning and representational content than are computational processes. Local physical-biological conditions in the brain, not the distal states of affairs represented by them, are what drive neural processes. If so, isn't Searle in the same boat as Turing and other computationalists?

There is also an important prior question: How do neural states get to represent anything? That is, how do they come to have representational content, and moreover, how do they get to have the particular content that they have? An influential view is that content or meaning arises from our complex interaction with the world around us—in particular, perception and action. So why not make our computer into a robot with a capacity for perception, inference, and action and embed it in the world, like the android Commander Data in one of the *Star Trek* series? (This is what Searle calls the "robot reply"; he rejects it, however.) Wouldn't this also help solve the question of the "teleological aptness" of input-output correlations that we discussed earlier? Our later discussion (in chapter 9) of the general question of how mental states come to have the content they have will be relevant to an assessment of the Chinese room argument.

Further Readings

The classic source of machine functionalism is Hilary Putnam's "Psychological Predicates" (later reprinted as "The Nature of Mental States"). See also his "Robots: Machines or Artificially Created Life?" and "The Mental Life of Some Machines"; all three papers are reprinted in his *Mind, Language, and Reality: Philosophical Papers*, volume 2. The first of these is widely reprinted elsewhere, including *Philosophy of Mind: Classical and Contemporary Readings*, edited by David J. Chalmers, and *Philosophy of Mind: A Guide and Anthology*, edited by John Heil. Ned Block's "What Is Functionalism?" is a clear and concise introduction to functionalism.

For a teleological approach to functionalism, see William G. Lycan, *Consciousness*, chapter 4. For a general biological-evolutionary perspective on mentality, see Ruth G. Millikan, *Language, Thought, and Other Biological Categories*.

For issues involving the Turing test and the Chinese room argument, see Alan M. Turing, "Computing Machinery and Intelligence"; John R. Searle, "Minds, Brains, and Programs"; and Ned Block, "The Mind as Software in the Brain." These articles are reprinted in Heil's *Philosophy of Mind*. Also recommended are Block, "Psychologism and Behaviorism," and Daniel C. Dennett, *Consciousness Explained*, chapter 14. Entries on "Turing Test" and "Chinese Room Argument" in the *Stanford Online Encyclopedia of Philosophy* are useful resources.

For criticisms of machine functionalism (and functionalism in general), see Ned Block, "Troubles with Functionalism," and John R. Searle, *The Rediscovery of the Mind*.

Notes

1. Later retitled "The Nature of Mental States" (1979).

2. Donald Davidson's argument for mental anomalism, as we shall see in chapter 10, also played a part in the decline of reductionism.

3. At least some of them, for it could be argued that certain psychological states can be had only by materially embodied subjects—for example, feelings of hunger and thirst, bodily sensations like pain and itch, and sexual desire.

4. The terms "realize" and "realizer" are given explicit explanations in a later section. In the meantime, you will not go far astray if you read "P realizes M" as "P is a neural substrate, or base, of M."

5. This principle entails mind-body supervenience, which we characterized as minimal physicalism in chapter 1. Further, it arguably entails the thesis of ontological physicalism, as stated in that chapter.

6. See Ronald Melzack, *The Puzzle of Pain*, pp. 15–16.

7. Some have argued that this function-versus-mechanism dichotomy is pervasive at all levels, not restricted to the mental-physical case; see, for example, William G. Lycan, *Consciousness*.

8. As I take it, something like this is the point of Karl Lashley's principle of "equipotentiality"; see his *Brain Mechanisms and Intelligence*, p. 25.

9. To borrow Ned Block's formulation of the question in "What Is Functionalism?" pp. 178–179.

10. As we shall see in connection with machine functionalism, there is another sense of "function," the mathematical sense, involved in "functionalism."

11. Strictly speaking, it is more accurate to say that having *the capacity to sense pain* is being equipped with a tissue-damage detector, and that pain, as an occurrence, is the activation of such a detector.

12. See, for example, B. F. Skinner, "Selections from *Science and Human Behavior*."

13. A treatment of the mathematical theory of computability in terms of Turing machines can be found in Martin Davis, *Computability and Unsolvability*, and in George S. Boolos, John P. Burgess, and Richard C. Jeffrey, *Computability and Logic*.

14. See, for example, Putnam, "Psychological Predicates."

15. For a statement and defense of a position of this kind, see Bas Van Fraassen, *The Scientific Image*.

16. Is there, for any given psychological subject, a *unique* Turing machine that is a machine description (relative to a specification of input and output conditions), or can there be (perhaps there always must be) multiple, nontrivially different machine descriptions? Does realism

about psychology require that there be a unique one? The reader is invited to reflect on these questions.

17. Alan M. Turing, "Computing Machinery and Intelligence."

18. For an elaboration of this point, see Ned Block, "Psychologism and Behaviorism."

19. Daniel C. Dennett, *Consciousness Explained*, pp. 435–440.

20. John R. Searle, "Minds, Brains, and Programs."

6

Mind as a Causal System

Causal-Theoretical Functionalism

In the preceding chapter, we discussed the functionalist attempt to use the concept of a Turing machine to explicate the nature of mentality and its relationship to the physical. Here we examine another formulation of functionalism in terms of "causal role." Central to any version of functionalism is the idea that a mental state can be characterized in terms of the input-output relations it mediates, where the inputs and outputs may include other mental states as well as sensory stimuli and physical behaviors. Mental phenomena are conceived as nodes in a complex causal network that engages in causal transactions with the outside world by receiving sensory inputs and emitting behavioral outputs.

What, according to functionalism, distinguishes one mental kind (say, pain) from another (say, itch) is the distinctive input-output relationship associated with each kind. Causal-theoretical functionalism conceives of this input-output relationship as a causal relation, one that is mediated by mental states. Different mental states are different because they are implicated in different input-output causal relationships. Pain differs from itch in that each has its own distinctive causal role: Pains typically are caused by tissue damage and cause winces, groans, and escape behavior; in contrast, itches typically are caused by skin irritation and cause scratching. But tissue damage causes pain only if certain other conditions are present, some of which are mental in their own right; not only must you have a properly functioning nervous system, but you must also be normally alert and not engrossed in another task. Moreover, among the typical effects of pain are further mental events, such as a feeling of distress and a desire to be relieved of it. But this seems to involve us in a regress or circularity: To explain what a given mental state is, we need to refer to other mental states, and explaining these can only be expected to require reference to further mental states, and so on—a process that can go on in an unending regress or loop back in a circle. Circularity threatens to arise at a more general level as well, in the functionalist conception of mentality itself: To be a mental state is to be an internal state serving as a causal intermediary between sensory inputs and mental states as causes, on the one hand, and behaviors and other mental states as effects, on the other. Viewed as a definition of what it is to be a mental state, this is obviously circular. To circumvent the threatened circularity, machine functionalism exploits the concept of a Turing machine in characterizing mentality (chapter 5). To achieve the same end, causal-theoretical functionalism attempts to use the entire network of causal relations involving all psychological states—in effect, a comprehensive psychological theory—to anchor the physical-behavioral definitions of individual mental properties.

The Ramsey-Lewis Method

Consider the following "pain theory":

(T) For any x, if x *suffers tissue damage* and **is normally alert**, x **is in pain**; if x *is awake*, x tends to be **normally alert**; if x **is in pain**, x *winces* and *groans* and **goes into a state of distress**; and if x **is not normally alert** or x **is in a state of distress**, x *tends to make more typing errors*.

We assume that the statements constituting T describe lawful regularities (or causal relations). The italicized expressions are nonmental predicates designating observable physical, biological, and behavioral properties; the expressions in boldface are psychological expressions designating mental properties. T is, of course, much less than what we know about pain and its relationship to other events and states, but let us assume that T encapsulates what is important about our knowledge of pain. What kind of "theory" T must be if T is to serve as a basis of functional definitions of "pain" and other mental expressions is a question taken up in a later section. Here T serves only as an example to illustrate the formal technique originally due to Frank Ramsey and adapted by David Lewis for formulating functional definitions of mental kinds.[1]

We first "Ramseify" T by "existentially generalizing" over each mental expression occurring in it, which yields this:

(T_R) There exist states M_1, M_2, and M_3 such that for any x, if x *suffers tissue damage* and is in M_1, x is in M_2; if *x is awake*, x tends to be in M_1; if x is in M_2, x *winces* and *groans* and goes into M_3; and if x is either not in M_1 or is in M_3, x *tends to make more typing errors*.

The main thing to notice about T_R vis-à-vis T is that instead of referring (as T does) to specific mental states, T_R speaks only of *there being some states or other*, M_1, M_2, and M_3, which are related to each other and to observable physical-behavioral states in the way specified by T. Evidently, T logically implies T_R (essentially in the manner in which "x is in pain" logically implies "There is some state M such that x is in M"). Note that in contrast to T, its Ramseification T_R contains no psychological expressions but only physical-behavioral expressions such as "suffers tissue damage," "winces," and so on. Terms like "M_1," "M_2," and "M_3" are called predicate variables (they are like the xs and ys in mathematics, though these are "individual" variables)—they are "topic-neutral" logical terms, neither physical nor psychological. Expressions like "is normally alert" and "is in pain" are predicate constants, that is, actual predicates.

Ramsey, who invented the procedure now called "Ramseification," showed that although T_R is weaker than T (since it is implied by, but does not imply, T), T_R is just as powerful as T as far as physical-behavioral prediction goes; the two theories make exactly the same inferential connections between nonpsychological statements.[2] For example, both theories entail that if someone is awake and suffers tissue damage, she will wince, and that if she does not groan, either she has not suffered tissue damage or she is not awake. Since T_R is free of psychological expressions, it can serve as a basis for defining psychological expressions without circularity.

To make our sample definitions manageable, we abbreviate T_R as "$\exists M_1$, M_2, $M_3[T(M_1, M_2, M_3)]$." (The symbol $\exists$, called the "existential quantifier," is read: "there exist.") Consider, then:[3]

x is in pain $=_{\text{def}} \exists M_1, M_2, M_3[T(M_1, M_2, M_3)$ and x is in $M_2]$

Note that "M_2" is the predicate variable that replaced "is in pain" in T. Similarly, we can define "is alert" and "is in distress" (although our little theory T was made up mainly to give us a reasonable definition of "pain"):

x is normally alert = $_{def}\exists M_1, M_2, M_3$ [T(M_1, M_2, M_3) and x is in M_1]

x is in distress = $_{def}\exists M_1, M_2, M_3$ [T(M_1, M_2, M_3) and x is in M_3]

Let us see what these definitions say. Consider the definition of "being in pain": It says that you are in pain just in case there are certain states, M_1, M_2, and M_3, that are related among themselves and with such physical-behavioral states like tissue damage, wincing and groaning, and typing performance as specified in T_R *and* you are in M_2. It is clear that this definition gives us a concept of pain in terms of its causal-nomological relations and that among its causes and effects are other "mental" states (although these are not specified as such but referred to only as "some" states of the psychological subject) as well as physical and behavioral events and states. Notice also that there is a sense in which the three mental concepts are interdefined but without circularity; each of the defined expressions is completely eliminable by its definiens (the right-hand side of the definition), which is completely free of psychological expressions. Whether or not these definitions are adequate in all respects, it is evident that the circularity problem has been solved.

So the trick is to define psychological concepts en masse. Our T is a fragment of a theory, something made up to show how the method works; to generate more realistic functional definitions of psychological concepts by the Ramsey-Lewis method, we need a much more comprehensive underlying psychological theory encompassing many more psychological kinds and richer and more complex causal-nomological relationships to inputs and outputs. Such a theory will be analogous to a Turing machine that models a full psychology, and the resemblance of the present method with the approach of machine functionalism should be clear, at least in broad outlines. In fact, we can think of the Turing machine approach as a special case of the Ramsey-Lewis method in which the psychological theory is presented in the form of a Turing machine table with the internal machine states, the *q*s, corresponding to the predicate variables, the Ms. We discuss the relationship between the two approaches in more detail later.

The Choice of an
Underlying Psychological Theory

So what should the underlying psychological theory T be like if it is to yield, by the Ramsey-Lewis technique, appropriate functional definitions of psychological properties? If we are to recover a psychological property from T_R by the Ramsey-Lewis method, the property must appear in T to begin with. So T must refer to all psychological properties. Moreover, T must carry enough information about each psychological property—about how it is nomologically connected with input conditions, behavior outputs, and other psychological properties—to circumscribe it closely enough to identify it as one that is distinct from other psychological properties. Given all this, there are two major possibilities to consider.

We might, with Lewis, consider using the platitudes of our shared *commonsense psychology* to form the underlying theory. The statements making up our "pain theory" T are examples of such platitudes, and there are countless others about, for instance, what makes people angry and how angry people behave, how wants and beliefs combine to generate further wants, how perceptions cause beliefs and memories, and how beliefs lead to further beliefs. Few people are able to articulate these principles of "folk psychology," but most mature people use them constantly in attributing mental states to people, making predictions about how people will behave, and understanding why people do what they do. We know these psychological regularities "tacitly," perhaps in much the way we "know" the grammar of the language we speak—without being able to state any explicit rules. Without a suitably internalized commonsense psychology in this sense, we would hardly be able to manage our daily transactions with other people and enjoy the kind of communal life that we take for granted.[4] It is important that the vernacular psychology that serves as the underlying theory for functional definitions consists of *commonly known* generalizations. This is essential if we are to ensure that functional definitions yield the psychological concepts that all of us share. It is the shared funds of vernacular psychological knowledge that collectively define our commonsense mental concepts; there is no other conceivable source from which our mental concepts could magically spring.

We must remember that commonsense psychology is, well, only commonsensical: It may be incomplete and partial or contain serious errors. If mental concepts are to be defined in terms of causal-nomological relations, shouldn't we use our best theory about how mental events and states are involved in causal-nomological relations among themselves and with physical and be-havioral events and processes? *Scientific psychology*, after all, is in the business of investigating these regularities, and the best scientific psychology we can muster *is* the best overall theory about the causal-nomological facts of mental events and states.

There are problems and difficulties with each of these choices. Let us first note one important fact: If the underlying theory T is false, we cannot count on any mental concepts defined on its basis to have nonempty extensions—that is, on there being any instances to which the concepts apply. For if T is false, its Ramseification, T_R, may also be false; in fact, if T has false nonmen-tal consequences (for example, T makes wrong behavioral predictions), T_R will be false as well. (Recall that T and T_R have the same physical-behavioral content.) If T_R is false, every concept defined on its basis by the Ramsey-Lewis method will be vacuous—that is, it will not apply to anything. This is easy to see for our sample "pain theory" T. Suppose this theory is false—in particular, suppose that what T says about the state of distress is false and that in fact there is no state that is related, in the way specified by T, with the other internal states and inputs and outputs. This makes our sample T_R false as well, since there is nothing that can fill in for M_3. This would mean that "pain" as defined on the basis of T_R cannot be true of anything: Nothing sat-isfies the defining condition of "pain." The same goes for "normally alert" and "the state of distress." So if T, the underlying theory, is false, all mental concepts defined on its basis by the Ramsey-Lewis method will turn out to have the same extension, namely, the null extension!

This means that we had better make sure that the underlying theory is true. If our T is to yield our psychological concepts all at once, it is going to be a long conjunction of myriad psychological generalizations, and even a single false component will render the whole conjunction false. So we must face these questions: What is going to be included in our T, and how certain can we be that T is true? Consider the case of scientific psychology: It is surely going to be a difficult, perhaps impossible, task to decide what parts of current scientific psychology are well enough established to be considered uncontroversially true. Psychology has been flourishing as a science for many decades now, but it is comparatively young as a science, with its methodolog-ical foundations still in dispute, and it is fair to say that it has yet to produce a robust enough common core of generally accepted laws and theories. In this respect, psychology has a long way to go before it reaches the status of, say, physics, chemistry, or even biology.

These reflections lead to the following thought: On the Ramsey-Lewis method of defining psychological concepts, every dispute about the underlying theory T is going to be a dispute about psychological concepts. This creates a seemingly paradoxical situation: If two psychologists should disagree about some psychological generalization that is part of theory T, which we should expect to be a common occurrence, this would mean that they are using different sets of psychological concepts. But this seems to imply that they cannot really disagree, since the very possibility of disagreement presupposes that the same concepts are shared. How could I accept and you reject a given proposition unless we shared the concepts in terms of which the proposition is formulated?

Consider now the option of using commonsense psychology to anchor psychological concepts. Can we be sure that all of our psychological platitudes, or even any of them, are true—that is, that they hold up as systematic scientific psychology makes progress? Some have even argued that advances in scientific psychology have already shown commonsense psychology to be massively false and that, considered as a theory, it must be abandoned.⁾ Consider the generalization, used as part of our pain theory, that tissue damage causes pain in a normally alert person. It is clear that there are many exceptions to this regularity: A normally alert person who is totally absorbed in another task may not feel pain when she suffers minor tissue damage. Truly massive tissue damage may well cause a person to go into a coma. And what is to count as "normally alert" in any case? Alert enough to experience pain when one is hurt? The platitudes of commonsense psychology may serve us competently enough in our daily life in anticipating behaviors of our fellow humans and making sense of them. But are we prepared to say that they are literally true? One way to alleviate these worries is to point out that we should think of our folk-psychological generalizations as hedged by generous escape clauses ("all other things being equal," "under normal conditions," "in the absence of interfering forces," and so on). Whether such weakened, noncommittal generalizations can introduce sufficiently restrictive constraints to yield well-defined psychological concepts is something to think about.

In one respect, though, commonsense psychology seems to have an advantage over scientific psychology: its apparently greater stability. Theories and concepts of systematic psychology come and go; given what we know about the rise and fall of scientific theories, especially in the social and human domains, it is reasonable to expect that most of what we now consider our best theories in psychology will be abandoned and replaced sooner or later—

probably sooner rather than later. The rough regularities codified in commonsense psychology appear considerably more stable (perhaps because they are rough); can we really imagine giving up the virtual truism that a person's desire for something and her belief that doing a certain thing will secure it tends to cause her to do it? This basic principle, which links belief and desire to action, is a central principle of commonsense psychology that underwrites the very possibility of making sense of why people do what they do. It is plausible to think that it was as central to the way the ancient Greeks or Chinese made sense of themselves and their fellows as it is to our own folk-psychological explanatory practices. Our shared folk-psychological heritage is what enables us to understand, and empathize with, the actions and emotions of the heroes and heroines in Greek tragedies and historical Chinese fiction. Indeed, if there were a culture, past or present, for whose members the central principles of our folk psychology, such as the one that relates belief and desire to action, did not hold true, its institutions and practices would hardly be intelligible to us, and its language might not even be translatable into our own. The source and nature of this relative permanence and commonality of folk-psychological platitudes are in need of explanation, but it seems clear that folk psychology enjoys a degree of stability and universality that eludes scientific psychology.

We should note, though, that vernacular psychology and scientific psychology need not necessarily be thought to be in competition with each other. We could say that vernacular psychology is the appropriate underlying theory for the functional definition of vernacular psychological concepts, while scientific psychology is the appropriate one for scientific psychological concepts. If we believe, however, that scientific psychology shows, or has shown, vernacular psychology to be seriously flawed (for example, showing that many of its central generalizations are in fact false[6]), we would have to reject the utility of the concepts generated from it by the Ramsey-Lewis method, for as we saw, these concepts would then apply to nothing. We could insist that even so, the Ramsey-Lewis method does yield appropriate definitions of these concepts, noting that it is a fact about the concepts of a seriously flawed theory (for example, the concepts of phlogiston, magnetic effluvium, and caloric fluid) that they have no applications in the real world. The difficulty with the Ramsey-Lewis method, however, is that vernacular psychology does not have to be seriously flawed to render its concepts empty; a single false psychological platitude is enough to bankrupt the whole system, by making all of our psychological concepts inapplicable to anything real.

There is one final point about our sample functionalist definitions: They can accommodate the phenomenon of multiple realization of mental states. This is easily seen. Suppose that the original psychology, T, is true of both humans and Martians, whose physiology, let us assume, is very different from ours (it is inorganic, say). Then T_R, too, would be true for both humans and Martians: It is only that the triple of physical-biological states $<H_1, H_2, H_3>$, which realizes the three mental states <pain, normal alertness, distress> and therefore satisfies T_R for humans, is different from the triple of physical states $<I_1, I_2, I_3>$, which realizes the mental triple in Martians. But in either case there exists a triple of states that are connected in the specified ways, as T_R demands. So when you are in H_1, you are in pain, and when Mork the Martian is in I_1, he is in pain, since each of you satisfies the functionalist definition of pain as stated.

Functionalism as Physicalism

Let us return to scientific psychology as the underlying theory to be Ramseified. As we noted, we want this theory to be a true theory. Now, there is another question about the truth of psychological theories that we need to discuss. Let us assume that psychological theories posit internal states to systematize correlations between sensory inputs and behavioral outputs. These internal states are the putative psychological states of the organism. Suppose now that each of two theories, T_1 and T_2, gives a correct systematization of inputs and outputs for a given psychological subject S, but that each posits a different set of internal states. That is, T_1 and T_2 are both *behaviorally adequate* psychologies for S, but each attributes to S a different internal psychological mechanism that connects S's inputs to its outputs. Is there some further fact about these theories, or about S, that determines which (if any) is the correct psychology of S and hence the theory to be Ramseified to yield causal-functional definitions of mental states?

If psychology is a truly autonomous special science, under no methodological, theoretical, or ontological constraints from any other science, we would have to say that the only ground for preferring one or the other of two behaviorally adequate theories consists in broad formal considerations of notational simplicity, ease of deriving predictions, and the like. There could be no further hard, fact-based grounds favoring one theory over the other. As you will recall, behaviorally adequate psychologies for subject S are analogous to Turing machines that are "behavioral descriptions" of S (see chapter 5). You will also recall that according to machine functionalism, not every behavioral description of S is a correct psychology of S and that a correct psychology is one that is a machine description of S—namely, a Turing machine that is physically realized by S. This means that there are internal physical states of S that realize the internal machine states of the Turing machine in question—that is, there are in S "real" internal physical states that are (causally) related to each other and to sensory inputs and behavioral outputs as specified by the machine table of the Turing machine.

It is clear, then, that causal-theoretical functionalism, formulated on the Ramsey-Lewis model, does not as yet have a physical requirement built into it. According to machine functionalism as formulated in the preceding chapter, for subject S to be in any mental state, S must be a *physical realization* of an appropriate Turing machine; in contrast, causal-theoretical functionalism as developed thus far in this chapter requires only that there be "internal states" of S that are connected among themselves and to inputs and outputs as specified by S's psychology, without saying anything about the nature of these internal states. What we saw in connection with machine functionalism was that it is the further physical requirement—to the effect that the states of S that realize the machine's internal states be physical states—that makes it possible to pick out S's correct psychology. In the same way, the only way to discriminate between behaviorally adequate psychologies is to explicitly introduce a similar physicalist requirement, perhaps something like this:

(P) The states that the Ramseified psychological theory, T_R, affirms to exist are physical-neural states; that is, the variables, M_1, M_2, . . . of T_R and in the definitions of specific mental states (see our sample definitions of "pain," and so on) range over physical-neural states.

A functionalist who accepts (P)—that is, a physicalist functionalist—will interpret the ontology of our original, un-Ramseified psychological theory in an analogous way: The internal states posited by a correct psychological theory are physical-neural states. These considerations have the following implications for psychology: Unless these physicalist constraints are introduced, there is no way of discriminating between behaviorally adequate psychologies; conversely, the fact that we do not think all behaviorally adequate psychologies are "correct" or "true" signifies our commitment to the reality of the internal, theoretical states posited by our psychologies, and the only way this psychological realism is cashed out is to regard these states as internal *physical* states of the organism involved. This is equivalent in substance to the thesis of realization physicalism discussed in the preceding chapter—the thesis that all psychological states must be physically realized.

This appears to reflect the actual research strategies in psychology and the methodological assumptions that undergird them: The correct psychological theory must, in addition to being behaviorally adequate, have "physical reality" in the sense that the psychological capacities, dispositions, and mechanisms it posits have a physical (presumably neurobiological) basis. The psychology that gives the most elegant and simplest systematization of human behavior may not be the true psychology, any more than the simplest artificial intelligence program (or Turing machine) that accomplishes a certain intelligent task (for instance, proving logic theorems) accurately reflects the way we humans perform it. The psychological theory that is formally the most elegant may not describe the way humans (or other organisms or systems under consideration) actually process their sensory inputs and produce behavioral outputs. There is no reason, either a priori or empirical, to believe that the mechanism that underlies our psychology, something that has evolved over many millions of years in the midst of myriad unpredictable natural forces, must be in accord with our notion of what is simple and elegant in a scientific theory. The psychological capacities and mechanisms posited by a true psychological theory must be real, and the only reality to which we can appeal in this context seems to be physical reality. These considerations, quite apart from the arguments pro and con concerning the physical reducibility of psychology, cast serious doubts on the claim that psychology is an autonomous science not answerable to lower-level physical-biological sciences.

The antiphysicalist might argue that psychological capacities and mechanisms have their own separate, nonphysical reality. But it is difficult to imagine what they could be when divorced from any physical underpinnings; perhaps they are some ghostly mechanisms in Cartesian mental substances. This may be a logically possible position, but hardly a plausible one (see chapter 2). In any case, as noted earlier, physicalism is the default position for discussions in contemporary philosophy of mind.

Objections and Difficulties

In this section, we review several points that are often thought to present major obstacles to the functionalist program. Some of the problematic features of machine functionalism discussed in the preceding chapter apply to functionalism generally, and these will not be taken up again here.

Qualia

Consider the question: What do all instances of pain have in common in virtue of which they are pains? You will recognize the functionalist answer: their characteristic causal role—their typical causes (tissue damage, trauma) and effects (pain behavior). But isn't there a more obvious answer? What all instances of pain have in common in virtue of which they are all cases of pain is that they *hurt*. Pains hurt, itches itch, tickles tickle. Can there be anything more obvious than that?

Sensations have characteristic *qualitative* features; these are called "phenomenal" or "phenomenological" or "sensory" qualities—"qualia" is now the standard term. Seeing a ripe tomato has a certain distinctive sensory quality that is unmistakably different from the sensory quality involved in seeing a bunch of spinach leaves. We are familiar with the smells of roses and ammonia; we can tell the sound of a drum from that of a gong; the feel of a cool, smooth granite countertop as we run our fingers over it is distinctively different from the feel of sandpaper. Our waking life is a continuous feast of qualia—colors, smells, sounds, and all the rest. When we are temporarily unable to taste or smell properly because of a bad cold, eating a favorite food can be like chewing cardboard and we are made acutely aware of what is missing from our experience.

By identifying sensory events with causal roles, however, functionalism appears to miss their qualitative aspects altogether. For it seems quite possible that causal roles and phenomenal qualities come apart, and the possibility of "qualia inversion" seems to prove it. It would seem that the following situation is perfectly conceivable: When you look at a ripe tomato, your color experience is like the color I experience when I look at a bunch of spinach, and vice versa. That is, your experience of red might be qualitatively like my experience of green, and your experience of green is like my experience of red. These differences need not show up in any observable behavioral differences: We both say "red" when we are asked what color ripe tomatoes are, and we both describe the color of spinach as "green"; we are equally good at picking tomatoes out of mounds of lettuce leaves. In fact, you and I both seem to be able to imagine that your color spectrum is systematically inverted with respect to mine, without this being manifested in any behavioral difference. Moreover, it seems possible to think of a system, like an electromechanical robot, that is functionally—that is, in terms of inputs and outputs—equivalent to us but to which we have no good reason to attribute any qualitative experiences (again, think of Commander Data). This is called the "absent qualia" problem.[7] If inverted qualia, or absent qualia, are possible in functionally equivalent systems, qualia cannot be captured by functional definitions, and functionalism cannot be an account of all psychological states and properties. This is the qualia argument against functionalism.

Can the functionalist offer the following reply? On the functionalist account, mental states are realized by the internal physical states of the psychological subject; so for humans, the experience of red, as a mental state, is realized by a specific neural state. This means that you and I cannot differ in respect of the qualia we experience as long as we are in the same neural state; given that both you and I are in the same neural state, something that is in principle ascertainable by observation, either both of us experience red or neither does.

But this reply falls short for two reasons. First, even if it is correct as far as it goes, it does not address the qualia issue for physically different systems (say, you and the Martian) that realize the same psychology. Nothing it says makes qualia inversion impossible for you and the Martian; nor does it rule out the possibility that qualia are absent from the Martian experience. Second, the reply assumes that qualia supervene on physical-neural states, but this supervenience assumption is what is at issue. However, the issue about qualia supervenience concerns the broader issues about physicalism; it is not specifically a problem with functionalism.

This issue concerning qualia has been controversial, with some philosophers doubting the coherence of the very idea of inverted or absent qualia.[8] We return to the issue of qualia in connection with the more general question of consciousness and its reducibility (chapters 8 and 10).

The Cross-Wired Brain

Let us consider the following very simple, idealized model of how pain and itch mechanisms work: Each of us has a "pain box" and an "itch box" in our brains. We can think of the pain box as consisting of a bundle of neural fibers ("nociceptive neurons") somewhere in the brain that gets activated when we experience pain, and similarly for the itch box. When pain sensors in our tissues are stimulated, they send neural signals up the pain input channel to the pain box, which then gets activated and sends signals down its output channel to our motor systems to cause appropriate pain behavior (winces and groans). The itch mechanism works similarly: When a mosquito bites you, your itch receptors send signals up the itch input channel to your itch box, and so on, finally culminating in your itch behavior (scratching).

Suppose that a mad neurosurgeon rewires your brain by crisscrossing both the input and output channels of your pain and itch centers. That is, the signals from your pain receptors now go to your (former) itch box and the signals from this box now trigger your motor system to emit winces and groans; similarly, the signals from your itch receptors are now routed to your (former) pain box, which sends its signals to the motor system, causing scratching behavior. Even though your brain is cross-wired with respect to mine, we both realize the same functional psychology: We both scratch when bitten by mosquitoes, and wince and groan when our fingers are burned. From the functionalist point of view, we instantiate the same pain-itch psychology.

Suppose that we both step barefoot on an upright thumbtack; both of us give out a sharp shriek of pain and hobble to the nearest chair. I am in pain. But what about you? The functionalist says that you are in pain also. What makes a neural mechanism inside the brain a pain box is exactly the fact that it receives input from pain receptors and sends output to cause pain behavior. With the cross-wiring of your brain, your former itch box has now become your pain box, and when it is activated, you are in pain. At least that is what the functionalist conception of pain implies. But is this an acceptable consequence?

This obviously is a version of the inverted qualia problem: Here the qualia that are inverted are pain and itch (or the painfulness of pains and the itchiness of itches), where the supposed inversion is made to happen through anatomical intervention. Many will feel a strong pull toward the thought that if your brain has been cross-wired as described, what you experience when you step on an upright thumbtack is an itch, not a pain, in spite of the fact that the input-output relation that you exhibit is one that is appropriate for pain. The appeal of this hypothesis is, at bottom, the appeal of the brain-state theory of mentality. Most of us have a strong, if not overwhelming, inclination to think that types of conscious experience, such as pain and itch, supervene on the *local* states and processes of the brain no matter how they are hooked up with the rest of the body or the external world, and that the qualitative character of our mental states is conceptually and causally independent of their causal roles in relation to sensory inputs and behavioral outputs. Such an assumption is implicit, for example, in the popular philosophical thought-experiment with "the brain in a vat," in which a disembodied brain kept alive in a vat of liquid is maintained in a normal state of consciousness by being fed appropriate electric signals generated by a supercomputer. The qualia we experience are causally dependent on the inputs: As our neural system is presently wired, cuts and pinpricks cause pains, not itches. But this is a contingent fact about our neural mechanism: It seems perfectly conceivable (even technically feasible at some point in the future) to reroute the causal chains involved so that cuts and pinpricks cause itches, not pains, and skin irritations cause pains, not itches, without disturbing the overall functional organization of our behavior.

Functional Properties, Disjunctive Properties, and Causal Powers

The functionalist claim is often expressed by assertions like, "Mental states are causal roles," and, "Mental properties (kinds) are functional properties (kinds)." We should get clear about the logic and ontology of such claims. The concept of a functional property and related concepts were introduced in the preceding chapter, but let us briefly review them before we go on with some difficulties and puzzles for functionalism. Begin with the example of pain: For something, S, to be in pain (that is, for S to have, or instantiate, the property of being in pain) is, according to functionalism, for S to be in some state (or to instantiate some property) with causal connections to appropriate inputs (for example, tissue damage, trauma) and outputs (pain behavior). For simplicity, let us talk uniformly in terms of *properties* rather than *states*. We may then say: The property of being in pain is the property of having some property with a certain causal specification (that is, in terms of its causal relations to certain inputs and outputs). Thus, in general, we have the following canonical expression for all mental properties:

Mental property M is the property of having a property with causal specification H.

As a rule, the functionalist believes in the multiple realizability of mental properties: For every mental property M, there will in general be many (in fact, indefinitely many) properties, Q_1, Q_2, . . . , each meeting the causal specification H, and an object will count as instantiating M just in case it instantiates one or another of these Qs. As you may recall, a property defined the way M is defined is often called a "second-order" property; in contrast, the Qs, their realizers, are "first-order" properties. (No special meaning needs to be attached to the terms "first-order" and "second-order"; these are relative terms—the Qs might themselves be second-order relative to another set of properties.) If M is pain, then, its first-order realizers are neural properties, at least for organisms, and we expect them to vary from one species to another.

This construal of mental properties as second-order properties seems to create some puzzles. If M is the property of having some property meeting specification H, where Q_1, Q_2, . . . , are the properties satisfying H—that is, the Qs are the realizers of M—it would seem to follow that M is identical with the *disjunctive* property of having Q_1 or Q_2 or . . . . Isn't it evident that to have M just *is* to have either Q_1 or Q_2 or . . . ? (For example, red, green, and blue are primary colors. Suppose something has a primary color; doesn't that amount simply to having red or green or blue?) Most philosophers who believe in the multiple realizability of mental properties deny that mental properties are disjunctive properties—disjunctions of their realizers—for the reason that the first-order realizing properties are extremely diverse and heterogeneous, so much so that their disjunction cannot be considered a well-behaved property with the kind of systematic unity required for propertyhood. As you may recall, the rejection of such disjunctions as legitimate properties was at the heart of the multiple realization argument against psychoneural-type physicalism. Functionalists have often touted the phenomenon of multiple realization as a basis for the claim that the properties studied by cognitive science are formal and abstract—abstracted from the material compositional details of the cognitive systems. What our considerations appear to show is that cognitive science properties so conceived threaten to turn out to be heterogeneous disjunctions of properties after all. And these disjunctions seem not to be suitable as nomological properties—properties in terms of which laws and causal explanations can be formulated. If this is right, it would disqualify mental properties, construed as second-order properties, as serious scientific properties.

But the functionalist may stand her ground, refusing to identify second-order properties with the disjunctions of their realizers, and she may reject disjunctive properties in general as bona-fide properties, on the ground that from the fact that both P and Q are properties, it does not follow that there is a disjunctive property, that of having P or Q. From the fact that being round and being green are properties, it does not follow, some have argued, that there is such a property as being round or green; some things that have this "property" (say, a red, round table and a green, square doormat) have nothing in common in virtue of having it. However, we need not embroil ourselves in this dispute about disjunctive properties, for the issue here is independent of the question about disjunctive properties.

For there is another line of argument, based on broad causal considerations, that seems to lead to the same conclusion. It is a widely accepted assumption, or at least a desideratum, that mental properties have causal powers: Instantiating a mental property can, and does, cause other events to occur (that is, cause other properties to be instantiated). In fact, this is the founding premise of causal-theoretical functionalism. Unless mental properties have causal powers, there would be little point in worrying about them. The possibility of invoking mental events in explaining behavior, or any other events, would be lost if mental properties should turn out to be causally impotent. But on the functionalist account of mental properties, just where does a mental property get its causal powers? In particular, what is the relationship between mental property M's causal powers and the causal powers of its realizers, the Qs?

It is difficult to imagine that M's causal powers could magically materialize on their own; it is much more plausible to think—it probably is the only plausible thing to think—that M's causal powers arise out of those of its realizers, the Qs. In fact, not only do they "arise out" of them, but the causal powers of any given instance of M must be the same as those of the particular Q_i that realizes M on that occasion. Carburetors can have no causal powers beyond those of the physical structures that perform the specified function of carburetors, and an individual carburetor's causal powers must be exactly those of the particular physical device in which it is realized (if for no other reason than the simple fact that this physical device is the carburetor).[9] To believe that it could have excess causal powers beyond those of the physical realizer is to believe in magic: Where *could* they possibly come from?

Let us consider this issue in some detail by reference to machine functionalism. A psychological subject, on this version of functionalism, is a physical-biological system that realizes an appropriate Turing machine (relative to some input-output specification). And for it to be in mental state M is for it to be in a physical state P where P realizes M—that is, P is a physical state that is causally connected in appropriate ways with other internal physical states and physical inputs and outputs. In this situation, all that there is, when the system is in mental state M, is its physical state P; being in M has no excess reality over and beyond being in P, and whatever causal powers that accrue to the system in virtue of being in M must be those of state P. It seems evident that this instance of M can have no causal powers over and beyond those of P.

But we must remember that M is multiply realized—say, by P_1, P_2, and P_3 (the finitude assumption will make no difference). If multiplicity has any meaning here, these Ps must be importantly different, and the differences that matter must be *causal* differences. To put it another way, the physical realizers of M count as different because they have different, perhaps extremely diverse, causal powers. For this reason, it is not possible to associate a unique set of causal powers with M; each instance of M, of course, is an instance of P_1 or an instance of P_2 or an instance of P_3 and as such represents a unique set of causal powers. However, M taken as a kind or property does not. That is to say, two arbitrary M-instances cannot be counted on to have much in common in their causal powers beyond the functional causal role associated with M. In view of this, it is difficult to regard M as a property with any causal-nomological unity, and we are led to think that M has little chance of entering into significant lawful relationships with other properties. All this makes the scientific usefulness of M highly problematic. Moreover, it has been suggested that kinds in science are individuated on the basis of causal powers; that is, to be recognized as a useful property in a scientific theory, a property must possess (or be) a determinate set of causal powers.[10] In other words, the resemblance that defines kinds in science is primarily *causal-nomological resemblance*: Things that are similar in causal powers and play similar roles in laws are classified as falling under the same kind. Such a principle of individuation for scientific kinds disqualifies M and other multiply realizable properties as scientific kinds. This surely makes the science of the Ms, namely, the psychological and cognitive sciences, a dubious prospect.

These are somewhat surprising conclusions, not the least because most functionalists are ardent champions of psychology and cognitive science—in fact, of all the special sciences—as forming irreducible and autonomous domains in relation to the underlying physical-biological sciences, and this arguably is the received view concerning the nature and status of psychology. But if our reasoning here is at all in the right direction, the conjunction of functionalism and the multiple realizability of the mental apparently leads to the conclusion that psychology is in danger of losing its unity and integrity as a science. On functionalism, then, mental kinds are in danger of fragmenting into their multiply diverse physical realizers and ending up without the kind of causal-nomological unity and integrity required of scientific kinds.[11]

Roles Versus Realizers:
The Status of Cognitive Science

Some will object to the considerations that have led to these deflationary conclusions about the scientific status of psychological and cognitive properties and kinds as functionally conceived. Most functionalists, including many practicing cognitive and behavioral scientists, will find them unwelcome. For they believe, or want to believe, all of the following four theses:

(1) psychological-cognitive properties are multiply realizable; hence, (2) they are irreducible to physical properties; however, (3) this does not affect their status as legitimate scientific kinds; from all this it follows that (4) cognitive and behavioral science is an autonomous science irreducible to more basic, "lower-level" sciences like biology and physics. The fragmentation of psychological-cognitive properties as scientific properties was made plausible, they will argue, by our single-minded focus on their lower-level realizers. It is this narrow focus on the diversity of the possible realizers of mental properties that makes us lose sight of their unity as properties—the kind of unity that is invisible "bottom up." Instead, our focus should be on the "roles" that these properties represent, and we should never forget that psychological-cognitive properties are "role" properties. So we might want to distinguish between "role functionalism" and "realizer functionalism."[12] Role functionalism identifies each mental property with being in a state that plays a specified causal role (we can call such properties "role" properties) and keeps them clearly distinct from the physical mechanisms that fill the role, that is, the mechanisms that enable systems with the mental property to do what they are supposed to do. In contrast, realizer functionalism associates mental properties more closely with their realizers and identifies each specific *instance* of a mental property with an *instance* of its physical realizer. So the different outlooks of the two functionalisms may be stated like this:

Realizer Functionalism. My experiencing pain at time t is identical with my C-fibers being activated at t (where C-fiber activation is the pain realizer in me); the octopus's experiencing pain at t is identical with its X-fibers being activated at t (where X-fiber activation is the octopus's pain realizer); and so on.

Role Functionalism. My experiencing pain at time t is identical with my being at t in a state that plays causal role R (that is, the role of detecting bodily damage and triggering appropriate behavioral responses); the octopus's experiencing pain at t is identical with its being, at t, in a state that plays the same causal role R; and so on.

So where the realizer functionalist sees differences and disunity among instances of pain with different realizers, the role functionalist sees similarities and unity. The role property associated with being in pain is what all pains have in common, and the role functionalist claims that these role properties are thought to constitute the subject matter of psychology and cognitive science; the aim of these sciences is to discover laws and regularities holding for these properties, and this can be done without attending to the physical and compositional details of their realizing mechanisms. In this sense, these sciences operate with entities and properties that are abstracted from the details of the lower-level sciences. Going back to the four theses (1) through (4), it will be claimed that they should be understood as concerning mental properties as conceived in accordance with role functionalism.

Evidently, for role properties to serve these purposes, they must be robustly causal and nomological properties. Here is what Don Ross and David Spurrett, advocates of role functionalism, say:

> The foundational assumptions of cognitive science, along with those of other special sciences, deeply depend on role functionalism. Such functionalism is crucially supposed to deliver a kind of causal understanding. Indeed, the very point of functionalism (on role *or* realizer versions) is to capture what is salient about what systems actually do, and how they interact, *without* having to get bogged down in micro-scale physical details.[13]

These remarks on behalf of role functionalism challenge the considerations reviewed in the preceding section pointing to the conclusion that the conjunction of functionalism (in fact, role functionalism) and the multiple realizability of mental states would undermine the scientific usefulness of mental properties. The reader is urged to think about whether the remarks by Ross and Spurrett constitute an adequate rebuttal to our earlier considerations.

Perhaps it might be argued that the actual practices and accomplishments of cognitive science and other special sciences go to show the emptiness of the essentially philosophical and a priori arguments of the preceding section. In spite of the heterogeneity of their underlying implementing mechanisms, functional role properties enter into laws and regularities that hold across diverse physical realizers. Ned Block, for example, has given some examples of psychological laws—in particular, those regarding stimulus generalization (due to the psychologist Roger Shepard)—that evidently seem to hold for all sorts of organisms and systems.[14] How these empirical results are to be correctly interpreted and understood, however, is an open question. A more detailed discussion of these issues takes us beyond core philosophy of mind and into the philosophy of psychology and cognitive science in a serious way. Readers who have a background in these sciences are invited to reflect on the issues further.

Further Readings

For statements of causal-theoretical functionalism, see David Lewis, "Psychophysical and Theoretical Identifications," and David Armstrong, "The Nature of Mind." Recommended also are Sydney Shoemaker, "Some Varieties of Functionalism," and Ned Block, "What Is Functionalism?"

Hilary Putnam, who was the first to articulate functionalism, has become one of its most severe critics; see his *Representation and Reality*, especially chapters 5 and 6. For other criticisms of functionalism, see Ned Block, "Troubles with Functionalism"; Christopher S. Hill, *Sensations: A Defense of Type Materialism*, chapter 3; and John R. Searle, *The Rediscovery of the Mind*. On the problem of qualia, see chapter 8 and the suggested readings therein. On the causal powers of functional properties, see Ned Block, "Can the Mind Change the World?"

The most influential statement of the multiple realization argument is Jerry Fodor, "Special Sciences, or the Disunity of Science as a Working Hypothesis." For discussion and analysis, see Jaegwon Kim, "Multiple Realization and the Metaphysics of Reduction." Replying to Kim are Ned Block, "Anti-Reductionism Slaps Back," and Jerry Fodor, "Special Sciences: Still Autonomous After All These Years." For a comprehensive defense of the possibility of cognitive science, see Don Ross and David Spurrett, "What to Say to a Skeptical Metaphysician: A Defense Manual for Cognitive and Behavioral Scientists."

Notes

1. See David Lewis, "How to Define Theoretical Terms," and "Psychophysical and Theoretical Identifications."

2. Ramsey's original construction was in a more general setting of "theoretical" and "observational" terms rather than "psychological" and "physical-behavioral" terms. For details, see Lewis, "Psychophysical and Theoretical Identifications."

3. Here we follow Ned Block's method (rather than Lewis's) in his "What Is Functionalism?"

4. These remarks are generally in line with the "theory theory" of commonsense psychology. There is a competing account, the "simulation theory," according to which our use of commonsense psychology is not a matter of possessing a theory and applying its laws and generalizations but of "simulating" the behavior of others, using ourselves as models. See Robert M. Gordon, "Folk Psychology as Simulation," and Alvin I. Goldman, "Interpretation Psychologized." Prima facie, the simulation approach to folk psychology creates difficulties for the Ramsey-Lewis functionalization of mental terms. However, the precise implications of the theory need to be determined in greater detail.

5. For such a view, see Paul Churchland, "Eliminative Materialism and the Propositional Attitudes."

6. But it is difficult to imagine how the belief-desire-action principle *could* be shown to be empirically false. It has been argued that this principle is a priori true and hence resists empirical falsification. However, not all principles of vernacular psychology need to have the same status. It may be possible, however, that there is a core set of principles of vernacular psychology that can be considered a priori true and that suffice as a basis of the application of the Ramsey-Lewis method.

7. See Ned Block, "Troubles with Functionalism."

8. On the possibility of qualia inversion, see Sydney Shoemaker, "Inverted Spectrum"; Ned Block, "Are Absent Qualia Impossible?"; C. L. Hardin, *Color for Philosophers*; and Martine Nida-Rümelin, "Pseudo-Normal Vision: An Actual Case of Qualia Inversion?"

9. Being a carburetor is a functional property defined by a job description ("mixer of air and gasoline vapors" or some such), and a variety of physical devices can serve this purpose.

10. See, for example, Jerry Fodor, *Psychosemantics*, ch. 2.

11. For further discussion, see Jaegwon Kim, "Multiple Realization and the Metaphysics of Reduction."

12. These terms are borrowed from Don Ross and David Spurrett, "What to Say to a Skeptical Metaphysician: A Defense Manual for Cognitive and Behavioral Scientists." The discussion here is indebted to this article. The distinction between role and realizer functionalism closely parallels Ned Block's distinction between the functional-state identity theory and the functional specification theory in his "What Is Functionalism?"

13. Ross and Spurrett, "What to Say to a Skeptical Metaphysician."

14. Ned Block, "Anti-Reductionism Slaps Back."

7

Mental Causation

Causal relations involving mental events are among the familiar facts of everyday experience. My fingers are busily dancing about on the computer keyboard because I want to write about mental causation. The word "because" connecting my want and the movements of my fingers is naturally taken to express a causal connection: My want causes my fingers to move. And we can causally explain the movements of my fingers—for example, why they hit the keys *m, e, n, t, a*, and *l* in succession—by reference to my desire to type the word "mental". This is a case of *mental-to-physical* causation. There are two other kinds of causal relations in which mental events figure: *physical-to-mental* and *mental-to-mental* causation. Sensations are among the familiar examples involving causal relations of the physical-to-mental kind: Burns cause pains, irradiations of the retina cause visual sensations, and food poisoning can cause nauseous feelings. Instances of mental-to-mental causation are equally familiar. We often believe one thing (say, that we had better take an umbrella to work) because we believe another thing (say, that it is going to rain later today). This is a case in which a belief causes another belief. Your belief that you have won a fellowship to graduate school causes a feeling of pride and satisfaction, which in turn causes you to want to call your parents. On a grander scale, it is human knowledge, desires, dreams, greed, and ambitions that led our forebears to build the ancient pyramids of Egypt and the Great Wall of China and to produce glorious music, literature, and other artworks; these mental events have also been responsible for the detonation of atom bombs, global warming, and the destruction of the rain forests. Mental events are intricately woven into the complex mosaic of causal relations of the world. At least that is the way things seem to us.

If your mind is going to cause your limbs to move, it presumably must first cause an appropriate neural event in your brain. But how is that possible? How can a mind, or a mental phenomenon, cause a bundle of neurons to fire? Through what mechanisms does a mental event, like a thought or a feeling, manage to initiate, or insert itself into, a causal chain of physical-neural events? And how is it possible that a chain of physical and biological events and processes terminates, suddenly and magically, in a full-blown conscious experience, with all its vivid colors, shapes, and sounds? Think of your total sensory experience right now—visual, tactual, auditory, olfactory, and the rest: How is it possible for all this to arise out of the electrochemical processes in the gray matter of your brain?

Agency and Mental Causation

An agent is someone with the capacity to *perform actions for reasons*, and most actions involve bodily movements. In this sense, we are all agents: We do such things as turning on the stove, heating water in a kettle, making coffee, and entertaining friends. An action is something we "do"; it is unlike a "mere happening," like sweating, shuddering, or being awakened by the noise of a jackhammer.

What do actions involve? Consider Susan's heating water in a kettle. This must at least include her *causing* the water in the kettle to rise in temperature. Why did Susan heat the water? When someone performs an action, it always makes sense to ask why, even if the correct answer might be, "For no particular reason." Susan, let us suppose, heated water to make coffee. That is, she *wanted* to make coffee and *believed* that she needed hot water to make coffee—and to be boringly detailed, she *believed* that by heating water in the kettle she could get the hot water she needed. When we know all this, we know why Susan heated water; we understand her action. Beliefs and desires guide actions, and by citing appropriate beliefs and desires, we are able to explain and make sense of why people do what they do.[1]

We may consider the following schema as the fundamental principle that connects desire, belief, and action:

Desire-Belief-Action Principle. (DBA): If agent S desires something and believes that doing A is an optimal way of securing it, S will do A.

As stated, DBA is too strong. For one thing, we often choose not to act on our desires, and sometimes we change them, or try to get rid of them, when we realize that pursuing them is too costly and may lead to consequences that we want to avoid. For example, you wake up in the middle of the night and want a glass of milk, but the thought of getting out of bed in the chilly winter night keeps you from doing it. Further, even when we try to act on our desires and beliefs about the means needed to realize them, we may find ourselves physically incapable of performing the action: It may be that when you have finally overcome your aversion to getting out of the bed, you find yourself chained to your bed! To save DBA, we can tinker with it in various ways; for example, we can add further conditions to the antecedent of DBA (such as the condition that there are no other conflicting desires) or weaken the consequent (for example, by turning it into a probability or tendency statement, or adding the all-purpose hedge "other things being equal" or "under normal conditions"). In any event, there seems little question that a principle like DBA is fundamental to the way we explain and understand actions, both our own and those of our fellow human beings, in terms of reasons. DBA is the fundamental schema that anchors reason-based explanations of actions, or "rationalizations." In saying this, we need not imply that beliefs and desires are the only possible reasons for actions; for example, emotions and feelings are often invoked as reasons, as witness, "I hit him because he insulted my wife and that made me angry," or, "He jumped up and down for joy."[2]

What the exceptions to DBA we have considered show is that an agent may have a reason—a "good" reason—to do something but fail to do it. Sometimes there may be more than one belief-desire pair that is related to a given action, as specified by DBA: In addition to your desire for a glass of milk, you heard a suspicious noise from downstairs and wanted to check it out. Let us suppose that you finally did get out of bed to venture down the stairway. Why did you do that? What explains it? It is possible that you went downstairs because you thought you really ought to check out the noise, not out of your desire for milk. If so, it is your desire to check the noise, not your desire for milk, that explains why you went downstairs in the middle of the night. It would be correct for you to say, "I went downstairs because I wanted to check out the noise," but incorrect to say, "I went downstairs because I wanted a glass of milk," although you did get your milk too. We can also put the point this way: Your desire to check out the noise and your desire for milk were both *reasons*—in fact, *good reasons*—for going downstairs, but the first, not the second, was the *reason for which* you did what you did; it is the *motivating reason*. And it is "reason for which," not mere "reason for," that explains the action. But what precisely is the difference between them? That is, what distinguishes explanatory reasons from reasons that do no explanatory work?

A widely accepted—though by no means undisputed—answer defended by Donald Davidson is the simple thesis that a reason for which an action is done is one that *causes* it.[3] That is, what makes a reason for an action an explanatory reason is its role in the causation of that action. Thus, on Davidson's view, the crucial difference between my desire to check out the noise and my desire for a glass of milk lies in the fact that the former, not the latter, caused me to go downstairs. This makes explanation of action by reasons, or "rationalizing" explanation, a species of causal explanation: Reasons explain actions in virtue of being their causes.

If this is correct, it follows that agency is possible only if mental causation is possible. For an agent is someone who is able to act for reasons and whose actions can be explained and evaluated in terms of the reasons for which she acted. And this entails that reasons—that is, mental states like beliefs, desires, and emotions—must be able to cause us to do what we do. Since what we do almost always involves movements of our limbs and other bodily parts, this means that agency—at least human agency—presupposes the possibility of mental-to-physical causation. Somehow your beliefs and desires must cause your limbs to move in appropriate ways so that in about ten seconds you find your whole body displaced from your bedroom to downstairs. A world in which agents exist is one in which mental causation is possible.

Mental Causation, Mental Realism, and Epiphenomenalism

Perception involves the causation of mental events—perceptual experiences—by physical processes. In fact, the very idea of perceiving something—say, seeing a tree—involves the idea that the object seen is a cause of an appropriate perceptual experience. Suppose that there is a tree in front of you and that you are having a visual experience of the sort you would be having if your retinas were stimulated by the light rays reflected by the tree. But you would not be seeing the tree if a holographic image of a tree that is visually indistinguishable from the tree were interposed between you and the tree. You would be seeing the holographic image of a tree, not the real tree, even though your perceptual experience in the two cases would have been exactly alike. This difference too seems to be a causal one: Your perceptual experience is caused by a tree holograph, not by the tree.

Perception is our sole window on the world; without it, we could learn nothing about what goes on around us. If, therefore, perception necessarily involves mental causation, there could be no knowledge of the world without mental causation. Moreover, a significant part of our knowledge of the world is based on experimentation, not mere observation. Experimentation differs from passive observation in that it requires our active intervention in the course of natural events; we design and deliberately set up the experimental conditions and then observe the outcome. This means that experimentation presupposes mental-to-physical causation and is impossible without it. Much of our knowledge of causal relations—in general, knowledge of what happens under what conditions—is based on experimentation, and such knowledge is essential not only to our theoretical knowledge of the world but also to our ability to predict and control the course of natural events. We must conclude, then, that if minds were not able to causally connect with physical events and processes, we could have neither the practical knowledge required to inform our decisions and actions nor the theoretical knowledge that gives us an understanding of the world around us.

Mental-to-mental causation also seems essential to human knowledge. Consider the process of inferring one proposition from another. Suppose someone asks you, "Is the number of planets odd or even?" If you are like most people, you would probably proceed as follows: "Well, how many planets are there? Nine, of course, and nine is an odd number because it isn't a multiple of two. So there are an odd number of planets." You have just inferred the proposition that there are an odd number of planets from the proposition that there are nine planets, and you have formed a new belief on the basis of this inference. This process evidently involves mental causation: Your belief that the number of planets is odd was caused, through a chain of inference, by your belief that there are nine planets. Inference is one way in which beliefs can generate other beliefs. A brief reflection makes it evident that most of our beliefs are generated by other beliefs we hold, and "generation" here could only mean causal generation. It follows, then, that all three types of mental causation—mental-to-physical, physical-to-mental, and mental-to-mental—are implicated in the possibility of human knowledge.

Epiphenomenalism is the view that although all mental events are caused by physical events, mental events are only "epiphenomena"—that is, events without powers to cause any other event. Mental events are effects of physical (presumably neural) processes, but they do not in turn cause anything else, being powerless to affect physical events or even other mental events; they are the absolute termini of causal chains. The noted nineteenth-century biologist T. H. Huxley has this to say about the consciousness of animals:

> The consciousness of brutes would appear to be related to the mechanism of their body simply as a collateral product of its working and to be as completely without any power of modifying that working as the steam-whistle which accompanies the work of a locomotive engine is without influence upon its machinery. Their volition, if they have any, is an emotion indicative of physical changes, not a cause of such changes.

What about human consciousness? Huxley goes on:

> It is quite true that, to the best of my judgment, the argumentation which applies to brutes holds equally good of men; and, therefore, that all states of consciousness in us, as in them, are immediately caused by molecular changes of the brain-substance. It seems to me that in men, as in brutes, there is no proof that any state of consciousness is the cause of change in the motion of the matter of organism. . . . We are conscious automata.[4]

What was Huxley's argument that convinced him that the consciousness of animals is causally inert? Huxley's reasoning appears to have been something like this: In animal experiments (Huxley mentions experiments with frogs), it can be shown that animals are able to perform complex bodily operations when we have compelling neuroanatomical evidence that they cannot be conscious, and this shows that consciousness is not needed as a cause of these bodily behaviors. Moreover, the same phenomenon is observed in the case of humans: As an example, Huxley cites the case of a brain-injured French sergeant who was reduced to a condition comparable to that of a frog with the anterior part of its brain removed—that is, we have every reason to believe that the unfortunate war veteran had no capacity for consciousness—but who could perform complex actions that we normally take to require consciousness, like avoiding obstacles when walking around in a familiar place, eating and drinking, dressing and undressing, and going to bed at the accustomed time. Huxley takes cases of this kind to show that consciousness is a cause of behavior production in neither humans nor animals. Whether Huxley's reasoning here is sound is something the reader is invited to think about.

Consider a moving car and the series of shadows it casts as it races along the highway: The shadows are caused by the moving car but have no effect on the car's motion. Nor are the shadows at different times causally connected: The shadow at a given instant *t* is caused not by the shadow an instant earlier but by the car itself at *t*. A person who observes the moving shadows but not the car may very well be led to attribute causal relations between the shadows, the earlier ones causing the later ones, but he would be mistaken. Similarly, you may think that your headache has caused your desire to take aspirin, but that, according to the epiphenomenalist, would be a similar mistake: The headache and the desire for aspirin are both caused by two successive (causally related) brain states, but they are not related as cause to effect any more than two successive shadows of the moving car. The apparent regularities that we observe in mental events, the epiphenomenalist argues, do not represent genuine causal connections; like the regularities characterizing the car's moving shadows or the successive symptoms of a disease, they are merely reflections of the real causal processes at a more fundamental level.

These are the claims of epiphenomenalism. Few philosophers have been self-professed epiphenomenalists, although there are those whose views appear to lead to such a position (as we will see below). We are more likely to find epiphenomenalist thinking among scientists in brain science. They are apt to treat mentality, especially consciousness, as a mere shadow or afterglow thrown off by the complex neural processes going on in the brain; these physical-biological processes are what at bottom do all the pushing and pulling to keep the human organism functioning. If conscious events really had causal powers to influence neural events, there could be no complete neural-physical explanations of neural events unless consciousness was explicitly brought into neuroscience as an independent causal agent in its own right. That is, there could be no complete physical-biological theory of neural phenomena. Very few neuroscientists would countenance such a possibility.

How should we respond to the epiphenomenalist stance on the status of mind? Samuel Alexander, a leading emergentist during the early twentieth century, comments on epiphenomenalism with the following pithy remark:

[Epiphenomenalism] supposes something to exist in nature which has nothing to do, no purpose to serve, a species of noblesse which depends on the work of its inferiors, but is kept for show and might as well, and undoubtedly would in time, be abolished.[5]

Alexander is saying that if epiphenomenalism is true, mentality has no work to do and hence is entirely useless, and that this renders it pointless to recognize it as something real. Our beliefs and desires would have no role in causing our decisions and actions and would be entirely useless in their explanations; our perception and knowledge would have nothing to do with our artistic creations or technological inventions. *Being real and having causal powers go hand in hand; to deprive the mental of causal potency is in effect to deprive it of its reality.*

It is important to see that what Alexander has said is not an *argument* against epiphenomenalism: His comment only points out, in a stark and forceful way, what accepting epiphenomenalism would entail. We should also remind ourselves that the typical epiphenomenalist does not reject the reality of mental causation altogether; she only denies mind-to-body and mind-to-mind causation, not body-to-mind causation. In this sense, she gives the mental a well-defined place in the causal structure of the world; mental events are integrated into that structure as effects of neural processes. This means that there is a stronger form of epiphenomenalism, according to which the mental is both causeless and effectless—that is, the mental is simply acausal. To a person holding such a view, mental events are in total causal isolation from the rest of the world, even from other mental events; each mental event is a solitary island, with no connection to anything else. (Recall the discussion in chapter 2 of mental causation in substance dualism.) Its existence would be entirely inexplicable since it has no cause, and it would make no difference to anything else since it has no effect. It would be a mystery how the existence of such things could be known to us. As Alexander declares, they could just as well be "abolished"—that is, regarded as nonexistent. No philosopher appears to have explicitly held or argued for this stronger form of epiphenomenalism; however, as we will see, there are views on the mind-body problem that seem to lead to "strong" epiphenomenalism (as we may call it).

So why not grant the mind full causal powers, among them the power to influence bodily processes? This would give the mental a full measure of reality and recognize what after all is so manifestly evident to common sense. That is just what Descartes tried to do with his thesis that minds and bodies, even though they are substances of very different sorts, are in intimate causal commerce with each other. But we saw the impossible difficulties besetting his program (chapter 2). Everyone will acknowledge that mental causation is a desideratum—something important, or even essential, to save. Jerry Fodor is not jesting when he writes:

> I'm not really convinced that it matters very much whether the mental is physical; still less that it matters very much whether we can prove that it is. Whereas, if it isn't literally true that my wanting is causally responsible for my reaching, and my itching is causally responsible for my scratching, and my believing is causally responsible for my saying . . . , if none of that is literally true, then practically everything I believe about anything is false and it's the end of the world.[6]

For Fodor, then, mental causation is absolutely nonnegotiable. And it is understandable why anyone should feel this way: Giving up mental causation amounts to giving up our conception of ourselves as agents and cognizers. Is it even *possible* for us to give up the idea that we are agents, that we perceive and know certain things about the world?

In his first sentence in the foregoing quoted passage, Fodor is saying that being able to defend a theory of the mind-body relation is far less important than safeguarding mental causation. That is not an implausible perspective to take: Whether or not a stance on the mind-body problem is acceptable depends importantly, if not solely, on how successful it is in giving an account of mental causation. On this criterion, Descartes' substance dualism, in the opinion of many, must be deemed a failure. So the main question is this: Which positions on the mind-body problem allow full-fledged mental causation and provide an explanation of how it is possible? We consider this question in the sections to follow.

Psychophysical Laws and "Anomalous Monism"

The expulsion of Cartesian immaterial minds perhaps brightens the prospect of understanding how mental causation is possible. For we no longer have to contend with a seemingly hopeless question: How could immaterial souls with no physical characteristics—no bulk, no mass, no energy, no charge, and no location in space—causally influence, and be influenced by, physical objects and processes? Today few philosophers or scientists regard minds as substances of a special nonphysical sort; mental events and processes are now viewed as occurring in complex physical systems like biological organisms, not in immaterial minds. The problem of mental causation, therefore, is now formulated in terms of two kinds of events, mental and physical, not in terms of two kinds of substances: How is it possible for a mental event (such as a pain or a thought) to cause a physical event (a limb withdrawal, an utterance)? Or in terms of properties: How is it possible for an instantiation of a mental property (for example, that of experiencing pain) to cause a physical property to be instantiated?

But why is this supposed to be a "problem"? We do not usually think that there is a special philosophical problem about, say, chemical events causally influencing biological processes or a nation's economic and political conditions causally affecting each other. So what is it about mentality and physicality that make causal relations between them a philosophical problem? For substance dualism, it is, at bottom, the extreme heterogeneity of minds and bodies, in particular, the nonspatiality of minds and the spatiality of bodies (as argued in chapter 2), that makes causal relations between them problematic. Given that mental substances have now been expunged, aren't we home free with mental causation? The answer is that certain other assumptions and doctrines that demand our respect appear to present obstacles to mental causation.

One such doctrine centers on the question of whether there are *laws connecting mental phenomena with physical phenomena*—that is, psychophysical laws—that are needed to underwrite causal connections between them. Donald Davidson's well-known "anomalism of the mental" states that there can be no such laws.[7] A principle connecting laws and causation that is widely, if not universally, accepted, is this: *Causally connected events must instantiate, or be subsumed under, a law.* If heating a metallic rod causes its length to increase, there must be a general law connecting events of the first type and events of the second type; that is, there must be a law stating that the heating of a metallic rod is generally followed by an increase in its length. But if causal connections require laws and there are no laws connecting mental events with physical events, it would seem to follow that there could be no mental-physical causation. This line of reasoning is examined in more detail later in the chapter. But is there any reason to doubt the existence of laws connecting mental and physical phenomena?

In earlier chapters, we often assumed that there are lawful connections between mental and physical events; you surely recall the stock example of pain and C-fiber excitation. The psychoneural identity theory, as we saw, assumes that each type of mental event is lawfully correlated with a type of physical event. Talk of "physical realization" of mental events also presupposes that there are lawlike connections between a mental event of a given kind and its diverse physical realizers, for a physical realizer of a mental event must at least be sufficient, as a matter of law, for the occurrence of that mental event. However, Davidson explicitly restricts his claim about the nonexistence of psychophysical laws to intentional mental events and states ("propositional attitudes")—that is, states with propositional content, like beliefs, desires, hopes, and intentions. He explicitly excludes from consideration sensory events and states, like pains, itches, and mental images. Why does Davidson think that there exist no laws connecting, say, beliefs with physical-neural events? Doesn't—in fact, shouldn't—every mental event have a neural substrate, that is, a neural state that, as a matter of law, suffices for its occurrence?

Before we take a look at Davidson's argument, let us consider some examples. Take the belief that it is inappropriate for the president of the United States to get a $500 haircut. How reasonable is it to expect to find a neural substrate for this belief? Is it at all plausible to think that all and only people who have this belief share a certain specific neural state? It makes perfectly good sense to try to find neural correlates for pains, sensations of thirst and hunger, visual images, and the like, but somehow it does not seem to make much sense to look for the neural correlates of mental states like our sample belief or for such things as your sudden realization that you have a philosophy paper due tomorrow at noon, your hope that airfares to California will come down after Christmas, and the like. Is it just that these mental states are so complex that it is very difficult, perhaps impossible, for us to discover their neural bases? Or is it the case that they are simply not the sort of state for which neural correlates could exist and that it makes no sense to look for them?

There is another line of consideration for being skeptical about psychophysical laws, and this has to do with the way we individuate mental states. If you are like most people, you do not know the difference between birches and beeches—that is, when you are confronted by a birch (or a beech), you cannot reliably tell whether it is a birch or a beech. But you have heard your gardener talk about the birches in your backyard, and you believe what he says. And you are apt to utter sentences like, "The birches in my yard have pretty foliage in the fall," "Birches are nice trees to have if you have a large yard," and the like. On the basis of these utterances, we may attribute to you the belief that there are birches in your backyard, that the birches have nice foliage in the fall, and so on. Now imagine the following counterfactual situation: Everything is identical with the story that was just told except that in this contrary-to-fact situation the words "birch" and "beech" have exchanged their meanings. That is, in the counterfactual situation, "birch" means beech, and "beech" means birch; and when your gardener, in the counterfactual situation, talks to you about the trees he calls "birches," he is talking about beeches. Now, when you utter sentences like, "The birches in my yard are pretty in the fall," in this counterfactual situation, we must attribute to you not the belief that the birches in your yard are pretty in the fall but the belief that the beeches in your yard are pretty in the fall. That is so not because you in the counterfactual world are different from you in the actual world in any intrinsic respect (in the counterfactual world your neural processes are exactly the same as your neural processes in the actual world), but because in that other world, the linguistic practice in your speech community is different. Since "birch" means beech in that world, when you utter the word "birch" in that world, we must take you to be talking about beeches, even though nothing about you is different. (Remember that you learned to use the word "birch" from your gardener.) What all this means is that what content a given belief has—for example, whether your belief is about beeches or birches—depends, at least in part but crucially, on external factors, conditions outside your skin, such as the linguistic practices of the community. That is, belief content is individuated externally, not purely internally. It follows, then, that whether a given belief is a birch-belief or a beech-belief is not a distinction capturable at the neural-brain level. If so, it will not be possible to find regular, lawlike relationships between your brain states, which are entirely internal to your body, on the one hand, and beliefs as individuated by their content, on the other. Consequently, it would be fruitless to try to discover neural correlates for beliefs and other propositional attitudes (for more on mental content, see chapter 9).

These considerations are not intended to be conclusive arguments for the impossibility of psychophysical laws but only to dispel, or at least weaken, the strong presumption many of us are apt to hold that there must "obviously" be such laws since mentality depends on what goes on in the brain. (What the considerations in the preceding paragraph show is that mentality does not wholly depend on what goes on inside the brain.) It is now time to turn to Davidson's famous but notoriously difficult argument against psychophysical laws, which will be presented here only in outline; for a full appreciation of the argument, you are urged to consult the original sources.[8]

A crucial premise of Davidson's argument is the thesis that the ascription of intentional states, like beliefs and desires, is regulated by certain *principles of rationality* that ensure that the total set of such states attributed to a person will be as rational and coherent as possible. This is why, for example, we refrain from attributing to a person manifestly contradictory beliefs, even when the sentences uttered have the surface logical form of a contradiction. When someone replies, "Well, I do and I don't," when asked, "Do you like Ralph Nader?" we do not take her to be expressing a literally contradictory belief—the belief that she both likes and does not like Nader. Rather, we take her to be saying something like, "I like some aspects of Nader (say, his concerns for social and economic justice), but I don't like other aspects (say, his presidential ambitions)." If she were to insist, "No, I don't mean that; I really both do and don't like Nader, period," we would not know what to make of her; perhaps her "and" does not mean what the English "and" means, or perhaps she does not have a full grasp of "not." We cast about for some consistent interpretation of her meaning because an interpreter of a person's speech and mental states is under the mandate that an acceptable interpretation must make her come out with a consistent and reasonably coherent set of beliefs—as coherent and rational as evidence permits When we fail to come up with a consistent interpretation, we are apt to blame our own interpretive efforts rather than accuse our subject of harboring explicitly inconsistent beliefs. We also attribute to a subject beliefs that are obvious logical consequences of beliefs already attributed to him. For example, if we have ascribed to a person the belief that Boston is less than sixty miles from Providence, we would, and should, ascribe to him the belief that Boston is less than seventy miles from Providence, the belief that Boston is less than one hundred miles from Providence, and countless others. We do not need independent evidence for these further belief attributions; if we are not prepared to attribute any one of these further beliefs, we should reconsider our original belief attribution and be prepared to withdraw it. Our concept of belief does not allow us to say that someone believes that Boston is within sixty miles of Providence but does not believe that it is within seventy miles—unless we are able to give an intelligible explanation of how this could happen in this particular case. This principle, which requires that the set of beliefs be "closed" under obvious logical entailment, goes beyond the simple requirement of consistency in a person's belief system; it requires that the belief system be coherent as a whole—it must in some sense hang together, without unexplained gaps. In any case, Davidson's thesis is that the requirement of rationality and coherence[9] is of the essence of the mental—that is, it is *constitutive* of the mental in the sense that it is exactly what makes the mental mental. Keep in mind that Davidson is speaking only of intentional states, like belief and desire, not sensory states and events like pains and afterimages.

But it is clear that the physical domain is subject to no such requirement; as Davidson says, the principle of rationality and coherence has "no echo" in physical theory. Suppose now that we have laws connecting beliefs with brain states; in particular, suppose we have laws that specify a neural substrate for each of our beliefs—a series of laws of the form "N occurs to a person at t if and only if B occurs to that person at t," where N is a neural state and B is a belief with a particular content (for example, the belief that there are birches in your yard). If such laws were available, we could attribute beliefs to a subject, *one by one*, independently of the constraints of the rationality principle. For in order to determine whether she has a certain belief B, all we would need to do is ascertain whether B's neural substrate N is present in her; there would be no need to check whether this belief makes sense in the context of her other beliefs or even what other beliefs she has. In short, we could read her mind by reading her brain. The upshot is that the practice of belief attribution would no longer need to be regulated by the rationality principle. By being connected by law with neural state N, belief B becomes hostage to the constraints of physical theory. On Davidson's view, as we saw, the rationality principle is constitutive of mentality, and beliefs that have escaped its jurisdiction can no longer be considered mental states. If, therefore, belief is to retain its identity and integrity as a mental phenomenon, its attribution must be regulated by the rationality principle and hence cannot be connected by law to a physical substrate.

Let us assume that Davidson has made a plausible case for the impossibility of psychophysical laws (we may call his thesis "psychophysical anomalism") so that it is worthwhile to explore its consequences. One question that was raised earlier is whether it might make mental causation impossible. Here the argument could go like this: Causal relations require laws, and this means that causal relations between mental events and physical events require psychophysical laws, laws connecting mental and physical events. But Davidson's psychophysical anomalism holds that there can be no such laws, whence it follows that there can be no causal relations between mental and physical phenomena. Davidson, however, is a believer in mental causation; he explicitly holds that mental events sometimes cause, and are caused by, physical events. This means that Davidson must reject the argument just sketched that attempts to derive the nonexistence of mental causation from the impossibility of psychophysical laws. How does he do that?

What Davidson disputes in this argument is its first step, namely, the inference from the premise that *causation requires laws* to the conclusion that *psychophysical causation requires psychophysical laws*. Let us look into this in some detail. To begin, what is it for one individual event *c* to cause another individual event *e*? This holds, on Davidson's view, only if the two events instantiate a law, in the following sense: *c* falls under a certain event kind (or description) F, *e* falls under an event kind G, and there is a law connecting events of kind F with events of kind G (as cause to effect). This is a form of the widely accepted nomological model of causation: Causal connections must instantiate, or be subsumed under, general laws. Suppose, then, that a particular mental event, *m*, causes a physical event, *p*. This means, according to the nomological conception of causation, that for some event kinds, C and E, *m* falls under C and *p* falls under E, and there is a law that connects events of kind C with events of kind E. This makes it evident that laws connect individual events only as they fall under kinds. Thus, when psychophysical anomalism says that there are no psychophysical laws, what it says is that there are no laws connecting mental kinds with physical kinds. So what follows is only that *if mental event* m *causes physical event* p, *kinds C and E, under which* m *and* p, *respectively, fall and which are connected by law, must both be physical kinds.* In particular, C, under which mental event *m* falls, cannot be a mental kind; it must be a physical one. This means that *m* is a physical event! For an event is mental or physical according to whether it falls under a mental kind or a physical kind. Note that this "or" is not exclusive; *m*, being a mental event, must fall under a mental kind, but that does not prevent it from falling under a physical kind as well. This argument applies to all mental events that are causally related to physical events, and there appears to be no reason not to think that every mental event has some causal connection, directly or via a chain of other events, with a physical event. All such events, on Davidson's argument, are physical events.[10]

That is Davidson's "anomalous monism." It is a monism because it claims that all individual events, mental events included, are physical events (you will recall this as "token physicalism"; see chapter 1). Moreover, it is physical monism that does not require psychophysical laws; in fact, as we just saw, it is based on the nonexistence of such laws, whence the term "anomalous" monism. Davidson's world, then, looks like this: It consists exclusively of physical objects and physical events, but some physical events fall under mental kinds (or have mental properties) and therefore are mental events. Laws connect physical kinds and properties with other physical kinds and properties, and these laws generate causal relations between individual events. Thus, all causal relations of this world are exclusively grounded in physical laws.

Is Anomalous Monism a Form of Epiphenomenalism?

One of the premises from which Davidson derives anomalous monism is the claim that mental events can be, and sometimes are, causes and effects of physical events. On anomalous monism, however, to say that a mental event *m* is a cause of an event *p* (*p* may be mental or physical) amounts only to this: *m* has a physical property Q (or falls under a physical kind Q) such that an appropriate law connects Q (or events with property Q) with some physical property P of *p*. Since no laws exist that connect mental and physical properties, purely physical laws must do all the causal work, and this means that individual events can enter into causal relations only because they possess physical properties that figure in laws. Consider an example: Your desire for a drink of water causes you to turn on the tap. On Davidson's nomological conception of causation, this requires a law that subsumes the two events, your desiring a drink of water and your turning on the tap. However, psychophysical anomalism says that this law must be a physical law, since there are no laws connecting mental-event kinds with physical-event kinds. Hence, your desire for a drink of water must be redescribed physically—that is, an appropriate physical property of your desire must be identified—before it can be brought under a law. In the absence of psychophysical laws, therefore, it is the physical properties of mental events that determine, wholly and exclusively, what causal relations they enter into. In particular, the fact that your desire for a drink of water is a desire for a drink of water—that is, the fact that it is an event of this mental kind—apparently has no bearing on its causation of your turning on the tap. What is causally relevant is its physical properties—presumably the fact that it is a neural event of a certain kind.

It seems, then, that under anomalous monism, mental properties are causal idlers with no work to do. To be sure, anomalous monism is not epiphenomenalism in the classic sense, since individual mental events are allowed to be causes of other events. The point, though, is that it is an epiphenomenalism of *mental properties*—we may call it "mental property epiphenomenalism"[11]—in that it renders mental properties and kinds causally irrelevant. Moreover, it is a form of "strong" epiphenomenalism described earlier: Mental properties play no role in making mental events either causes or effects. To make this vivid: If you were to redistribute mental properties over the events of this world any way you please—you might even remove them entirely from all events, making all of them purely physical—that would not alter, in the slightest way, the network of causal relations of this world; it would not add or subtract a single causal relation anywhere in the world!

This shows the importance of properties in the debate over mental causation: It is the causal efficacy of mental properties that we need to vindicate and give an account of. With mental substances out of the picture, there are only mental properties left to play any causal role, whether these are construed as properties of events or of objects. If mentality is to do any causal work, it must be the case that having a given mental property rather than another, or having it rather than not having it, must make a causal difference; it must be the case that an event, because it has a certain mental property (for example, being a desire for a drink of water), enters into a causal relation (it causes you to look for a water fountain) that it would otherwise not have entered into. We must therefore conclude that Davidson's anomalous monism fails to pass the test of mental causation; by failing to account for the causal efficacy and relevance of mental properties, it fails to explain the possibility of mental causation.

The challenge posed by Davidson's psychophysical anomalism, therefore, is to answer the following question: How can anomalous mental properties, properties that are not fit for laws, be causally efficacious properties? It would seem that there are only two ways of responding to this challenge: First, we may try to reject its principal premise, namely, psychophysical anomalism, by finding faults with Davidson's argument and then offering plausible reasons for thinking that there are indeed laws connecting mental and physical properties. Second, we may try to show that the nomological conception of causality—in particular, as it is understood by Davidson—is not the only way to understand causality and that there are alternative conceptions of causation on which mental properties, though anomalous, could still be causally efficacious. Let us explore the second possibility.

Counterfactuals and Mental Causation

There indeed is an alternative approach to causation that on the face of it does not seem to require laws, and this is the counterfactual account of causation. According to this approach, to say that event c caused event e is to say that if c had not occurred, e would not have occurred.[12] The basic idea that a cause is the *sine qua non* condition, or *necessary* condition, of its effect is a similar idea. This approach has much intuitive plausibility. The overturned space heater caused the house fire. Why do we say that? Because if the space heater had not overturned, the fire would not have occurred. What is the basis of saying that the accident was caused by a sudden braking on a rain-slick road? Because if the driver had not suddenly stepped on his brake pedal on the wet road, the accident would not have occurred. In such cases we seem to depend on counterfactual ("what if") considerations rather than laws. Especially if you insist on exceptionless "strict laws," as Davidson does, we obviously are not in possession of such laws to support these perfectly ordinary and familiar causal claims. The situation seems the same when mental events are involved: There is no mystery about why I think that my desire for a drink of water caused me to step into the dark kitchen last night and stumble over the sleeping dog. I think that because I believe the evidently true counterfactual "If I had not wanted a drink of water last night, I would not have gone into the kitchen and stumbled over the dog." In confidently making these ordinary causal or counterfactual claims, we seem entirely unconcerned about the question whether there are laws about wanting a glass of water and stumbling over a sleeping dog. Even if we were to reflect on such questions, we would be undeterred by the unlikely possibility that such laws exist or can be found. To summarize, then, the idea is this: We know that mental events, in virtue of their mental properties, can, and sometimes do, cause physical events because we can, and sometimes do, know appropriate psychophysical counterfactuals to be true. Mental causation is possible because such counterfactuals are sometimes true.

Does this solve the problem of mental causation? Before you embrace it as a solution, you should consider the following line of response. If "*c* caused *e*" just *means* "If *c* had not occurred, *e* would not have occurred," neither could "ground" the other; that is, neither could be offered as an explanation of how the other can be true. That George is an unmarried adult male cannot in any sense be a ground for, or explain, George's being a bachelor. Here there is a single fact expressed in two trivially equivalent ways. The same goes for "My desire for a drink of water caused my walking into the kitchen" and "If I had not wanted a drink of water, I would not have walked into the kitchen." If we are concerned about how the first could be true, then we should be equally concerned about how the second could be true. For the two sentences express the same fact. So, at this stage, the counterfactual approach itself amounts to nothing more than a reaffirmation of faith in the reality of mental causation.

The counterfactualist is likely to reply as follows: The counterfactual account goes beyond a mere reaffirmation of mental causation, for it opens up the possibility of accounting for mental causation in terms of an account of how mental-physical counterfactuals can be true. To show that there is a special problem about mental causation, you must show that there is a special problem about the truth of these counterfactuals. Moreover, by adopting the counterfactual strategy, we divorce mental causation from contentious questions about psychophysical laws.

This reply is fair enough. So are there special problems about these psychophysical counterfactuals? Do we have an understanding of how such counterfactuals can be true? There are many philosophical puzzles and difficulties surrounding counterfactuals, especially about their "semantics"—that is, conditions under which counterfactuals can be evaluated as true or false. There are two main approaches to counterfactuals: (1) the nomic-derivational approach, and (2) the possible-world approach. On the nomic-derivational approach, the counterfactual conditional "If P were the case, Q would be the case" (where P and Q are propositions) is true just in case the consequent, Q, of the conditional can be logically derived from its antecedent, P, when taken together with laws and statements of conditions holding on the occasion.[13] Consider an example: "If this match had been struck, it would have lighted." This counterfactual is true since its consequent, "The match lighted," can be derived from its antecedent, "The match was struck," in conjunction with the law "Whenever a dry match is struck in the presence of oxygen it lights," taken together with the auxiliary premises "The match was dry" and "There was oxygen present."

It should be immediately obvious that on this analysis of counterfactuals, the counterfactual account of mental causation does not make the problem of mental causation go away. For the truth of the psychophysical counterfactuals—like "If I had not wanted to check out the strange noise, I would not have gone downstairs," and, "If Jones's C-fibers had been activated, she would have felt pain"—would require laws that would enable the derivation of the physical consequents from their psychological antecedents (or vice versa), and it is difficult to see how any laws could serve this purpose unless they were psychophysical laws, laws connecting mental with physical phenomena. On the nomic-derivational approach, therefore, Davidson's problem of psychophysical laws arises all over again.

So let us consider the possible-world approach to the truth conditions of counterfactuals. In a simplified form, it says this: The counterfactual "If P were the case, Q would be the case" is true just in case Q is true in the world in which P is true and that, apart from P's being true there, is as much like the actual world as possible. (To put it another way: Q is true in the closest P-world.)[14] In other words, to see whether or not this counterfactual is true, we go through the following steps: Since this is a counterfactual, its antecedent, P, is false in the actual world. We must go to a possible world ("world" for short) in which P is true and see whether Q is also true there. But there are many worlds in which P is true—that is, there are many P-worlds—and in some of these Q is true and in others false. So which P-world should we pick in which to check on Q? The answer: Pick the P-world that is the most similar, or the closest, to the actual world. The counterfactual "If P were true, Q would be true" is true if Q is true in the closest P-world; it is false otherwise.

Let us see how this works with the counterfactual "If this match had been struck, it would have lighted." In the actual world, the match was not struck; so suppose that the match was struck (this means, go to a world in which the match was struck), but keep other conditions the same as much as possible. Certain other conditions must also be altered under the counterfactual supposition that the match was struck: For example, in the actual world the match lay motionless in the matchbox and there was no disturbance in the air in its vicinity, so these conditions have to be changed to keep the world consistent as a whole. However, we need not, and should not, change the fact that the match was dry and the fact that sufficient oxygen was present in the ambient air. So in the world we have picked, the following conditions, among others, obtain: The match was struck, it was dry, and oxygen was present in the vicinity. The counterfactual is true if and only if the match lighted in that world. Did the match light in that world? In asking this question, we are asking which of the following two worlds is closer to the actual world:[15]

W_1: The match was struck; it was dry; oxygen was present; the match lighted.

W_2: The match was struck; it was dry; oxygen was present; the match did not light.

We would judge, it seems, that of the two, W_1 is closer to the actual world, thereby making the counterfactual true. But why do we judge this way? Because we believe that in the actual world there is a lawful regularity to the effect that when a dry match is struck in the presence of oxygen it ignites, and W_1, but not W_2, respects this regularity. So in judging that this match, which in fact was dry and bathed in oxygen, would have lighted if it had been struck, we seem to be making crucial use of the law just mentioned. If in the actual world dry matches, when struck in the presence of oxygen, seldom or never light, there seems little question that we would go for W_2 as the closer world and judge the counterfactual "If this match had been struck, it would have lighted" to be false. It is difficult to see what else could be involved in our judgment that W_1, not W_2, is the world that is closer to the actual world other than considerations of lawful regularities.

Now consider a psychophysical counterfactual: "If Brian had not wanted to check out the noise, he wouldn't have gone downstairs." Suppose that we take this counterfactual to be true, and on that basis we judge that Brian's desire to check out the noise caused him to go downstairs. Consider the following two worlds:

W_3: Brian didn't want to check out the noise; he didn't go downstairs.

W_4: Brian didn't want to check out the noise; he went downstairs anyway.

If W_4 is closer to the actual world than W_3 is, that would falsify our counterfactual. So why should we think that W_3 is closer than W_4? In the actual world, Brian wanted to check out the noise and went downstairs. As far as these two particular facts are concerned, W_4 evidently is closer to the actual world than W_3 is. So why would we hold W_3 to be closer and hence the counterfactual to be true? The only plausible answer, again, seems to be something like this: We know, or believe, that there are certain lawful regularities and propensities governing Brian's wants, beliefs, and so on, on the one hand, and his behavior patterns, on the other, and that, given the absence of something like a desire to check out a suspicious noise, along with other conditions prevailing at the time, his not going downstairs at that particular time fits these regularities and propensities better than the supposition that he would have gone downstairs at that time. We consider such regularities and propensities to be reliable and lawlike and commonly appeal to them in assessing counterfactuals of this kind (and also in making predictions and guesses as to how a person will behave), even though we may have only the vaguest idea about the details and lack the ability to articulate them in a precise way.

Again, the centrality of psychophysical laws to mental causation is apparent. Although there is room for further discussion on this point, it seems plausible that considerations of lawful regularities governing mental and physical phenomena are often involved in the evaluation of psychophysical counterfactuals of the sort that can ground causal relations. We need not know the details of such regularities, but we must believe that they exist and know their rough content and shape to be able to evaluate these counterfactuals as true or false. So are we back where we started, with Davidson and his argument for the impossibility of psychophysical laws?

Not exactly, fortunately. Because the laws involved need not be laws of the kind Davidson has in mind—what he calls "strict" laws. These are exceptionless, explicitly articulated laws that form a closed and comprehensive theory, like the fundamental laws of physics. Rather, the laws involved in evaluating these quotidian counterfactuals—indeed, laws on the basis of which we make causal judgments in much of science—are rough-and-ready generalizations tacitly qualified by generous escape clauses ("ceteris paribus," "under normal conditions," "in the absence of interfering forces," and so on) and apparently immune to falsification by isolated negative instances. Laws of this type, sometimes called "ceteris paribus laws," seem to satisfy the usual criteria of lawlikeness: As we saw, they seem to have the power to ground counterfactuals, and our credence in them is enhanced as we observe more and more positive instances. Their logical form, their verification conditions, and their efficacy in explanations and predictions are not well understood, but it seems beyond question that they are the essential staple that sustains and nourishes our counterfactuals and causal discourse.[16]

Does the recognition that causal relations involving mental events are supported by these "nonstrict," ceteris paribus laws solve the problem of mental causation? It does enable us to get around the anomalist difficulty raised by Davidsonian considerations—at least for now. We can see, however, that even this difficulty has not been fully resolved. For it may well be that these nonstrict laws are possible only if strict laws are possible and that where there are no underlying strict laws that can explain them or otherwise ground them, they remain only rough, fortuitous correlations. It may well be that their lawlike appearance is illusory and that this makes them incapable of grounding causal relations.

Physical Causal Closure and the "Exclusion Argument"

Suppose, then, that we have somehow overcome the difficulties arising from the possibility that there are no precise and exceptionless (or "strict") laws connecting mental with physical phenomena. We are still not home free: There is another challenge to mental causation that we must confront, one that arises from the principle, embraced by most physicalists, that the physical domain is *causally closed*. What does this mean? Pick any physical event— say, the decay of a uranium atom or the collision of two stars in distant space—and trace its causal ancestry or posterity as far as you would like; the principle of causal closure of the physical domain says that this will never take you outside the physical domain. Thus, no causal chain involving a physical event ever crosses the boundary of the physical into the nonphysical: If x is a physical event and y is a cause or effect of x, then y too must be a physical event. For our purposes, it is convenient to use a somewhat weaker form of causal closure stated in this form:

Causal Closure of the Physical Domain. If a physical event has a cause (occurring) at time t, it has a sufficient physical cause at t.

Notice a few things about this principle. First, it does not flat out say that a physical event can have no nonphysical cause; all it says is that in our search for its cause, we never need to look outside the physical domain. In that sense, the physical domain is causally, and hence explanatorily, self-sufficient and self-contained. Second, it does not say that every physical event has a cause or a causal explanation; in this regard, it differs from physical determinism, the thesis that every physical event has a sufficient physical cause. Third, the closure principle is consistent with mind-body dualism: As far as it goes, there might be a separate domain of Cartesian immaterial minds. All it requires is that there be no injection of causal influence into the physical domain from outside.

Most philosophers, including anyone who considers himself or herself a physicalist of any kind, accepts physical causal closure. If the closure should not hold, there would be physical events for whose explanation we would have to look to nonphysical causal agents, like spirits or divine forces outside spacetime. That is exactly the situation depicted in Descartes' interactionist dualism (chapter 2). If closure should fail, theoretical physics would be in principle incompletable, and it is fair to say that research programs in physics, and the rest of the physical sciences, presuppose something like the closure principle. It is worth noting that neither the biological domain nor the psychological domain is causally closed: There are nonbiological events that cause biological events (for example, radiation causing cells to mutate), and we are familiar with cases in which nonpsychological events (such as purely physical events) cause psychological events (for instance, in perception).

It is easy to see that this closure principle brings about difficulties for mental causation, in particular mental-to-physical causation. Suppose that a mental event, m, causes a physical event, p. The closure principle says that there must also be a physical cause of p—an event, p^*, occurring at the same time as m, that is a sufficient cause of p. This puts us in a dilemma: Either we have to say that $m = p^*$—namely, identify the mental cause with the physical cause as a single event—or else we have to say that p has two distinct causes, m and p^*, that is, it is causally overdetermined. The first horn turns what was supposed to be a case of mental-to-physical causation into an instance of physical-to-physical causation, a result only a reductionist physicalist would welcome. Grasping the second horn of the dilemma would force us to admit that every case of mental-to-physical causation is a case of causal overdetermination, one in which a physical cause, even if the mental cause had not occurred, would have brought about the physical effect. This seems like a bizarre thing to say, but quite apart from that, it appears to weaken the status of the mental event as a cause of the physical effect. To vindicate m as a genuine cause of p, m should be able to bring about p without there being a synchronous physical event that also serves as a sufficient cause of p. According to our foregoing reasoning, however, every mental event has a physical causal partner that would have brought about the effect anyway, even if the mental event had been taken out of the picture entirely.

This thought can be developed along the following lines. Consider the following constraint:

> *Exclusion Principle*. No event can have more than two or more sufficient causes, all occurring at the same time, unless it is a genuine case of overdetermination.

Genuine overdetermination occurs in the following sorts of examples: Two bullets hit a person at the same time, and this kills the person, where each bullet would have sufficed to cause the death; a house fire is caused by a short circuit and at the same time by a lightning strike. In these cases, two independent causal chains converge at a single effect. Given this, the exclusion principle should look obviously, almost trivially, true.

Return now to our case of mental-to-physical causation. We begin with the assumption that there is a case in which a mental event causes a physical event:

(1) m is a cause of p.

As we saw, it follows from (1) and physical causal closure that there is also a physical event p^* such that:

(2) p^* is a cause of p.

Let us suppose that we want to reject both horns of the dilemma; that is, we want to claim:

(3) $m \neq p^*$.

Suppose we assume further:

(4) This is not a case of overdetermination.

Given the closure and the exclusion principles, these four propositions put us in trouble: According to (1), (2), and (3), p has two distinct causes, m and p^*; since (4) says that this is not a case of overdetermination, the exclusion principle kicks in, saying that either m or p^* must be disqualified as a cause of p. Which one? The answer: p^* stays, m must go. The reason is simple: If we try to retain m, the closure principle applies again and says that there must also be a physical cause of p—and what could this be if not p^*? Obviously, we are back at the same situation: Unless we eliminate m and keep p^*, we would be off to an infinite regress, or treading water forever in the same place.

The foregoing argument is the so-called "exclusion argument," since it aims to show that a mental cause of a physical event is always excluded by a distinct physical cause.[17] The apparent moral of the argument is that mental-to-physical causation is illusory; it never happens. That, anyway, is the way the implications of the argument are usually understood. However, it should be clear that that is not the only way to read the lesson of the argument: If we are prepared to reject the antiphysicalist assumption (3) by embracing the mind-body identity "$m = p^*$," we can escape the epiphenomenalist consequence of the argument. If $m = p^*$, here there is only one event and hence only one cause of p, so the exclusion principle has no application and no conclusion follows to the effect that the initial supposition "m causes p" is false. The real moral of the argument, therefore, is this: Either choose serious physicalism (some call this reductionist physicalism) or face the specter of epiphenomenalism. Note that the epiphenomenalism involved here concerns only the efficacy of mental events in the causation of physical events, not the causal power of mentality in general. However, a more serious epiphenomenalism rears its head in the next section.

The "Supervenience Argument" and Epiphenomenalism

When you throw mind-body supervenience into the mix, an even more serious threat of epiphenomenalism arises. (The following line of consideration can be carried on in terms of the idea that mental properties are "realized" by physical-neural properties rather than the idea that the former supervene on the latter.) Let us understand mind-body supervenience in the following form:

Mind-Body Supervenience. When a mental property, M, is instantiated by something x at t, that is in virtue of the fact that x instantiates, at t, a physical property, P (that is, a physical "supervenience base"), such that anything that has P at any time necessarily has M at the same time.

So whenever you experience a headache, that is in virtue of the fact that you are in some neural state N at the time, where N is a supervenience base of headaches in the sense that anyone who is in N must be having a headache. There are no free-floating mental states; every mental state is anchored in a physical-neural base on which it supervenes.

Given mind-body supervenience, a line of argument can be developed that appears to have serious epiphenomenalist consequences. Suppose that a mental event, an instantiation of mental property M, causes another mental property, M*, to instantiate. According to mind-body supervenience, M* is instantiated on this occasion in virtue of the fact that a physical property—one of its supervenience bases—is instantiated on this occasion. Call this physical base P*. Why is M* instantiated on this occasion? What is responsible for the fact that M* occurs on this occasion? There appear to be two presumptive answers: (i) because an instance of M caused M* to instantiate (our original supposition), and (ii) because a supervenience base, P*, of M*, was instantiated on this occasion. Now, there appears to be strong reason to think that (ii) trumps (i): If its supervenience base P* occurs, M* must occur (and M cannot occur unless one of its supervenience bases is present), no matter what preceded M*'s occurrence—that is, *as long as P* is there, M* is guaranteed to be there even if its supposed cause M did not occur.* This undermines M's claim to have brought about this instance of M*; it seems that P* must take the primary credit for giving rise to M* on this occasion.

Is there a way of reconciling M's claim to have caused M* to instantiate and P*'s claim to be M*'s supervenience base on this occasion? The only way

of harmonizing the two claims seems to be this: M caused M* to instantiate
by causing M's supervenience base P* to instantiate.* In general, it seems like a
plausible principle to say that to cause, or causally affect, a supervenient
property, you must cause, or tinker with, its supervenience base properties. If
you are not happy with a painting you have just finished and want to improve it, there is no way you could alter the aesthetic qualities of the painting
(for example, make it more expressive, more dramatic, or less sentimental)
except by altering the physical properties on which the aesthetic properties
supervene. You must bring out your brushes and oils and do physical work
on the canvas. And you take aspirin to relieve your headache because you
hope that the ingestion of aspirin will bring about physicochemical changes
in the neural states on which headaches supervene.

If this argument is correct, it shows that, given mind-body supervenience,
mental-to-mental causation (an instance of M causing M* to instantiate)
leads inevitably to mental-to-physical causation (an instance of M causing
P*, M*'s supervenience base, to instantiate). This argument, which we may
call the "supervenience argument," shows that mental-to-mental causation is
possible only if mental-to-physical causation is possible. (More generally, we
may say that "same-level" causation entails "downward" causation.)

But see where the two arguments, the exclusion argument and the supervenience argument, lead us. According to the supervenience argument,
mental-to-mental causation is possible only if mental-to-physical causation is
possible. But the exclusion argument says that mental-to-physical causation
is not possible. So it follows that neither mental-to-mental nor mental-to-
physical causation is possible. This goes beyond the epiphenomenalism of
mental-to-physical causation; the two arguments together show that mental
events have no causal efficacy at all—that is, no power to cause any event,
mental or physical. It is important to keep in mind that all this holds on the
assumption that we do not choose the option of reductionist physicalism,
that is, we choose not to reject the premise "m ≠ p*" of the exclusion argument. (A similar premise is implicitly invoked in the supervenience argument.) So the upshot of these two arguments is this: If you want to avoid
general epiphenomenalism, you must be prepared to embrace reductionist
physicalism—to put it another way, you must choose between epiphenomenalism and reductionism.

Neither option is palatable. To most of us, epiphenomenalism seems just
false, or even incoherent (recall Fodor's lament quoted earlier). And reductionist physicalism does not seem much better: If we save mental causation by
reducing mentality to mere patterns of electrochemical activity in the brain,

have we really saved mentality as something special and distinctive? Moreover, what if the mental is not reducible to the physical? Aren't we then stuck with epiphenomenalism whether we like it or not? This is the conundrum of mental causation. (We continue discussion of these issues in chapter 10.)

Further Issues: The Extrinsicness of Mental States

Computers compute with 0s and 1s. Suppose you have a computer running a certain program, say, a program that monitors the inventory of a supermarket. Given a string of 0s and 1s as input (a can of Campbell's tomato soup has just been scanned at a checkout station), the computer goes through a series of computations and emits an output (the count of Campbell's tomato soup in stock has been adjusted, and so on). Thus, the input string of 0s and 1s represents a can of Campbell's tomato soup being sold, and the output string of 0s and 1s represents the amount of Campbell's tomato soup still in stock. When the manager checks the computer for a report on the available stock of Campbell's tomato soup, the computer "reports" that the present stock is such and such, and it does so *because* "it has been told" (by the checkout scanners) that twenty-five cans have been sold so far today. And this "because" is naturally understood as signifying a causal relation.

But we also know that it makes no difference to the computer what the strings of 0s and 1s *mean* or *represent*. If the input string had meant the direction and speed of wind at the local airport or the identification code of an employee, or even if it had meant nothing at all, the computer would have gone through exactly the same computational process and produced the same output string. In this case, the output string too would have meant something else, but what is clear is that the "meanings," or "representational contents," of these 0s and 1s are in the eye of the computer programmer or user, not something that is involved in the computational process. Give the computer the same string of 0s and 1s as input, and it will go through the same computation every time and give you the same output. The "semantics" of these strings is irrelevant to computation; what matters is their shape—that is, their syntax. The computer is a "syntactic engine," not a "semantic engine"; it is driven by the shapes of symbols, not their meanings.

According to an influential view of psychology known as the "computational theory of mind" (or "computationalism"), cognitive mental processes are best viewed as computational processes on mental representations (chapter 5). On this view, constructing a psychological theory is like writing a computer program; such a theory will specify, for each input (say, a sensory stimulus), the computational process that a cognizer will undergo to produce an output (say, the visual detection of an edge). But what the considerations of the preceding paragraph seem to show is that, on the computational view of psychology, the meanings, or contents, of internal representations make no difference to psychological processes. Suppose a certain internal representation, i, represents the state of affairs S (say, that there are horses in the field); having S as its representational content, or meaning, is the semantics of i. But if we suppose, as is often done on the computational model, that internal representations form a languagelike system, i must also have a syntax, or formal grammatical structure. So if our considerations are right, it is the syntax of i, not its semantics, that determines the course of the computational process involving i. The fact that i means that there are horses in the field rather than, say, that there are lions in the field is of no causal relevance to what other representations issue from i. The computational process that i initiates will be wholly determined by i's syntactic shape. But this is to say that the *contents* of our beliefs and desires and of other propositional attitudes have no causal relevance for psychology; it is only their syntax that makes a difference to what they cause.

The point actually is independent of computationalism and can be seen to arise for any broadly physicalist view of mentality. Assume that beliefs and desires and other intentional states are neural states. Each such state, in addition to being a neural state with biological-physical properties, has a specific content (for example, that water is wet, or that George W. Bush is from Texas). That a given state has the content it has is a *relational*, or *extrinsic*, *property* of that state, for the fact that your belief is about water, or about Bush, is in part determined by your causal-historical associations with water and Bush (chapter 9). Let us consider what this means and why it is so.

Suppose there is in some remote region of this universe another planet, "Twin Earth," that is exactly like our Earth, except for the following fact: On Twin Earth, there is no water, that is, no H_2O, but an observably indistinguishable chemical substance, XYZ, fills the lakes and oceans there, comes out of the tap in Twin Earth homes, and so on. Each of us has a doppelganger there who is an exact molecular duplicate of us. (Let us ignore the fact that your twin has XYZ molecules in her body where you have H_2O molecules in your body.) On Twin Earth, people speak Twin English, which is just like English, except for the fact that their word "water" refers to XYZ, not water, and when they utter sentences containing the expression "water," they are talking about XYZ, not water. Thus, Twin Earth people have thoughts about XYZ, where we have thoughts about water, and when you believe that water is wet, your doppelganger on Twin Earth has the belief that XYZ is wet, even though you and she are molecule-for-molecule duplicates. And when you think that George Bush is from Texas, your twin thinks that the Twin Earth Bush (he is the president of the Twin Earth United States) is from Twin Earth Texas. And so on. The differences in Earth and Twin Earth belief contents (and contents of other intentional states) are due not to internal physical or mental differences in the believers but to the differences in the environments in which the believers are embedded (see the discussion of "wide content" in chapter 9). Contents, therefore, are extrinsic, not intrinsic; they depend on your causal history and your relationships to the objects and events in your surroundings. States that have the same intrinsic properties— the same neural-physical properties—may have different contents if they are embedded in different environments. Further, an identical internal state that lacks an appropriate relationship to the external world may have no representational content at all.

But isn't it plausible to suppose that behavior causation is "local" and depends only on the intrinsic neural-physical properties of these states, not their extrinsic relational properties? Isn't it plausible to suppose that someone whose momentary neural-physical state is exactly identical with yours will behave just the way you do—say, raise the right arm—whether or not her brain state has the same content as yours? This raises doubts about the causal relevance of contents because the properties of our mental states implicated in behavior causation are plausibly expected to be intrinsic. What causes your behavior, we feel, must be *local—in* you, *here and now*; after all, the behavior it is supposed to cause is here and now. But contents of mental states are relational and extrinsic; they depend on what is out there in the world outside you, or on what occurred in the past and is no longer here. To summarize, contents do not supervene on the intrinsic properties of the states that carry them; on the other hand, we expect behavior causation to be local and depend only on intrinsic properties of the behaving organism. This, then, is yet another problem of mental causation. It challenges us to answer the following question: How can intentional mental states be efficacious in behavior causation in virtue of their contents?

Various attempts have been made to reconcile the extrinsicness of contents with their causal efficacy, but it is fair to say that we do not as yet have a fully satisfactory account (see "Further Readings"). The problem has turned out to be a highly complex one involving many issues in metaphysics, philosophy of language, and philosophy of science.[18]

Further Readings

Donald Davidson's "Mental Events" is the primary source of anomalous monism. On the problem of mental causation associated with anomalous monism, see Ernest Sosa, "Mind-Body Interaction and Supervenient Causation," and Louise Antony, "Anomalous Monism and the Problem of Explanatory Force." Davidson responds in "Thinking Causes," which appears in *Mental Causation*, edited by John Heil and Alfred Mele. This volume also contains rejoinders to Davidson by Kim, Sosa, and Brian McLaughlin, as well as a number of other papers on mental causation.

For counterfactual-based accounts of mental causation, see Ernest LePore and Barry Loewer, "Mind Matters," and Terence Horgan, "Mental Quausation."

For issues related to the causal role of extrinsic mental states, see Fred Dretske, "Minds, Machines, and Money: What Really Explains Behavior," and Tim Crane, "The Causal Efficacy of Content: A Functionalist Theory." Many of the issues arising in this area are discussed in Lynne Rudder Baker, *Explaining Attitudes*; Dretske, *Explaining Behavior*; and Pierre Jacob, *What Minds Can Do*.

On the exclusion and supervenience arguments, see Jaegwon Kim, *Mind in a Physical World* and *Physicalism, or Something Near Enough*. Interesting papers on this topic can be found in *Physicalism and Mental Causation*, edited by Sven Walter and Heinz-Dieter Heckmann. Recommended also are Stephen Yablo, "Mental Causation," and Karen Bennett, "Why the Exclusion Problem Seems Intractable, and How, Just Maybe, to Tract It."

Notes

1. Some philosophers insert another step between beliefs-desires and actions, by taking beliefs/desires to lead to the formation of *intentions* and *decisions*, which in turn lead to actions. Whether or not an intermediate stage of this sort is necessary may very well depend on the kind of action at issue. Details concerning action, agency, and action explanation are discussed in a subfield of philosophy called action theory, or the philosophy of action.

2. Whether or not explanations appealing to emotions presuppose belief-desire explanations is a controversial issue. For discussion, see Michael Smith, "The Possibility of Philosophy of Action," and Frederick Stoutland, "Real Reasons."

3. Donald Davidson, "Actions, Reasons, and Causes." For noncausal approaches, see Carl Ginet, *On Action*, and Frederick Stoutland, "Real Reasons."

4. Thomas H. Huxley, "On the Hypothesis That Animals Are Automata, and Its History," *Philosophy of Mind: Classical and Contemporary Readings*, ed. David J. Chalmers, pp. 29–30.

5. Samuel Alexander, *Space, Time, and Deity*, vol. 2, p. 8.

6. Jerry A. Fodor, "Making Mind Matter More," in Fodor, *A Theory of Content and Other Essays*, p. 156.

7. More precisely, Davidson's claim is that there are no "strict" laws connecting psychological and physical phenomena. See his "Mental Events."

8. See Davidson's "Mental Events." For an interpretive reconstruction of Davidson's argument, see Jaegwon Kim, "Psychophysical Laws."

9. This is a form of what is called "the principle of charity"; Davidson also requires that an interpretation of a person's belief system make her beliefs come out largely *true*. See the discussion of interpretation theory in chapter 9.

10. In "Mental Events," Davidson defends the stronger thesis that there are no laws at all about mental phenomena, whether psychophysical or purely psychological; his view is that laws (or "strict laws") can be found only in basic physics (see "Thinking Causes"). A sharp-eyed reader will have noticed that Davidson's argument requires this stronger thesis, since the argument as it stands leaves open the possibility that the two causally connected events, m and p, instantiate a purely psychological law, from which it would follow that p is a mental event. Given that laws are found only in physics, Davidson's conclusion can be strengthened: Any event (of any kind) that causes, or is caused by, another event (of any kind) is a physical event.

11. Brian McLaughlin calls it "type epiphenomenalism" in his "Type Epiphenomenalism, Type Dualism, and the Causal Priority of the Physical." Several philosophers independently raised these epiphenomenalist difficulties for anomalous monism; Frederick Stoutland was probably the first to do so, in his "Oblique Causation and Reasons for Action."

12. This is not quite correct. The counterfactual analysis of causation only requires that there be a chain of these "counterfactual dependencies" connecting cause and effect. But this and other refinements do not affect the discussion to follow. For the first full analysis of causation based on this idea, see David Lewis, "Causation."

13. See Ernest Nagel, *The Structure of Science*, ch. 4.

14. For a detailed development of this approach, see David Lewis, *Counterfactuals*.

15. These worlds are very much underdescribed, of course; we are assuming that the worlds are roughly the same in other respects.

16. Later in his career, Davidson too came to accept nonstrict laws as capable of grounding causal relations; see his "Thinking Causes." But this may very well undermine his argument for anomalous monism.

17. For more detail, see Jaegwon Kim, *Physicalism, or Something Near Enough*, ch. 2.

18. The inability to reach a satisfactory solution to this problem can add fuel to the eliminativist argument on content-carrying mental states, along the lines urged by Paul Churchland in "Eliminative Materialism and the Propositional Attitudes." If contents are causally inefficacious, how can they play a role in causal-explanatory accounts of human behavior? And if they can have no such role, why should we posit them, whether in commonsense psychology or in the science of human behavior?

8

Consciousness

Nothing could be more ordinary and familiar to us than the phenomenon of consciousness. We are conscious at every moment of our waking lives; it is a ubiquitous and unsurprising feature of everyday existence—except when we are in deep sleep, in a coma, or otherwise, well, unconscious. In one of its senses, *conscious* is just another word for "awake" or "aware," and we know what it is to be awake and aware—to awaken from sleep, general anesthesia, or a temporary loss of consciousness caused by a trauma to the head and regain an awareness of what goes on in and around us.

Moreover, consciousness is, presumptively, a central and crucial feature of mentality—or at any rate the kind of mentality that we possess and value; without consciousness, we would no longer be creatures with mentality, or the kind of being that we think we are. A brain-dead person has suffered an irreversible loss of consciousness (as well as many other neural-mental functions), and that seems the reason why brain death should matter to us personally and ethically. Most of us would be inclined to feel that for all human intents and purposes, a person who has permanently lost the capacity for consciousness is no longer with us. For Descartes, being conscious (or "thinking," in his broad usage of this term) is of the essence of mentality. It is self-evident, according to him, that "there can be nothing in the mind, in so far as it is a thinking thing, of which it is not aware" and that "we cannot have any thought of which we are not aware at the very moment when it is in us."[1] On the Cartesian conception, our mental life is exhausted by the contents of our awareness—that is, things of which we are conscious. So why has consciousness baffled so many thinkers throughout history, leading them to despair of ever reaching a solution to the "mystery of consciousness"? Why was consciousness shunned by both psychologists and philosophers during much of the twentieth century? Why are there still respected philosophers who argue that consciousness, at least in one of its forms, does not really exist, that it is only a fiction of philosophical confusion?

Before we take up substantive issues, it will be useful to clarify our terminology. "Conscious," as an adjective, applies both to persons and organisms and to their states. We are conscious creatures, but cabbages, amoebas, and flowerpots are not. This, of course, does not mean that we are conscious at every moment of our existence; we are conscious when we are awake and alert and not conscious while in a deep sleep or coma. We are also conscious, or aware, *of* things, states, or facts (for example, the blinking red traffic lights, a nagging pain in the back, being tailed by a highway patrol car). In cases of this sort, "conscious" and "aware" have roughly the same meaning. Moreover, we also apply the term "conscious" to events, states, and processes. Familiar sensory states and events, such as pains, itches, and mental images, are conscious states and events. Emotions, like anger, joy, and sadness, are usually conscious, although some may well not be; many of our beliefs, desires, hopes, and memories are also conscious, though here again, there may be beliefs and desires of which we are not aware. I have a conscious belief that it is about time to finish up the day's work and head home and a conscious hope that I can finish writing this section before I have to go. And so on.

What is the relationship between these two uses of "conscious," as applied to persons ("subject consciousness," as we might call it) and as applied to their states ("state consciousness")? Can we say something like this: "A state of a person is a conscious state just in case that person is aware, or conscious, of it?" It seems true that if a given state is a conscious state, the person whose state it is must be aware of it. The converse, however, seems false: It is not the case that if you are aware of a state, then that state is a conscious state. You are aware of your age and weight and conscious of the flickering of a fluorescent lightbulb that is about to burn out, but that is not to say that your age and weight or the flickering light are conscious states. More to the point, you are normally conscious of your posture and orientation (whether you are standing or lying down, for instance, or whether your legs are crossed), and this kind of proprioceptive awareness is direct and immediate, but surely these bodily states are not conscious states. The suggested relationship between state consciousness and subject consciousness makes better sense when restricted to mental states: A mental state is a conscious state just in case the subject whose state it is is conscious of it.

Aspects of Consciousness

In philosophical and psychological discussions of consciousness, we can discern several related but distinguishable aspects of consciousness, one or another of which may be the focus of attention in a given discussion. Thus, it sometimes happens—it used to happen much more frequently—that when someone claims to have an "account" or "theory" of consciousness, what is being offered concerns only one of the several distinguishable aspects, or kinds, of consciousness and is completely silent on the rest. As a result, those who profess to be debating "the problem of consciousness" sometimes do not even appear to be talking about the same thing. It is useful, therefore, to begin with a survey of some prominent aspects of the phenomena that collectively go by the name "consciousness."

Phenomenal Consciousness: "Qualia"

When you look at a ripe tomato, you sense its color in a certain way, a way that is different from the way you sense the color of a mound of lettuce leaves. If you crush the tomato and bring it close to your nose, it smells in a distinctive way that is different from the way a crushed lemon smells. Across sense modalities, smelling gasoline is very different from tasting it (or so we may assume!). Sensory mental events and states, like seeing a ripe red tomato, smelling gasoline, experiencing a shooting pain up and down your leg, and the like, have distinctive qualitative characters, that is, felt or sensed qualities, by means of which they are identified as sensations of a certain type. It is now customary to refer to these sensory qualities of mental states as "phenomenal" (or "phenomenological") properties, "raw feels," or "qualia."[2]

Sometimes the notion of a quale is explained by saying that when you are in a mental state with a qualitative character, there is *something that it is like to be in that state*. You know what it is like to see a golden yellow patch against a dark green background (say, when you are looking at a Van Gogh landscape), but a person who is yellow-green color-blind presumably does not know what it is like *for you* to have this experience. Conversely, normally sighted persons do not know, at least firsthand, what it is like for the color-blind person to see yellow against green. Moreover, it is also said that for any conscious creature—say, a bat (an example made famous by Thomas Nagel)—there is *something that it is like to be that creature*, whereas there is nothing it is like to be, say, a table or a tree. Nagel has famously argued that we cannot know what it is like to be a bat; nor can we know, according to him, what it is like to echolocate a flying moth by using sonar—what the sensory presentation involved in such an activity is like.[3]

Qualitative sensory characters are present in mental states not usually classified as sensations. Anger, remorse, envy, pride, and other emotions appear to have distinctive qualitative feels to them; after all, emotions are "experienced." Unlike sensory experiences, however, they do not seem to be type-classified (as, for example, anger or envy) solely, or even primarily, on the basis of how they feel. For example, it may be difficult, perhaps impossible, to categorize an emotion as one of resentment, envy, or jealousy on the basis of its felt qualities alone. Nor does every instance of an emotion need to be accompanied by a distinctive felt character. Suppose you are unhappy, even upset, about the deep budget deficits of the federal government. Must your unhappiness be accompanied by some special felt quality? Probably not. Even if it is, must the same quality be present in all other cases in which you are upset or unhappy about something? Being in such a state seems more a matter of having certain beliefs, attitudes, and dispositions (such as the belief that large and continuing budget deficits are bad for the economy, or your eagerness to work for the opposition in the next election) than having an experience with a distinctive experiential quality. Moreover, it is now commonplace to acknowledge emotions of which the subject is not aware, and such unconscious states cannot be constituted, even in part, by phenomenal qualities.

Might it be the case that all beliefs share a special distinctive phenomenal feel? The answer must be no—for the rather uninteresting reason that the existence of unconscious mental states, including beliefs, is now widely recognized. Freudian depth psychology, parts of which have by now been assimilated by our commonsense psychology, has told us about the psychological mechanism by which we repress beliefs, desires, and emotions that are unacceptable to our conscious minds. Nowadays we routinely hear news of people whose repressed memories of childhood abuse are recovered through therapy. But these are controversial cases, and we do not need them as examples of beliefs of which the subject is unaware. If I ask you, "Do you believe that some neurosurgeons wear hats?" you would probably say yes; you do believe that some neurosurgeons wear hats. This is a belief you have always had (you would have said yes if I had asked you the question two years ago); it is not a new belief that you have just acquired, although you have become aware of this belief just now. My question made an unconscious belief an "occurrent" one. Obviously, there are countless other such beliefs that you hold. Beliefs that are not occurrent are sometimes called "dispositional" beliefs. It is clear that dispositional beliefs cannot have any phenomenal character, for the simple reason that their subjects are not aware of them.

So the question about the phenomenal character of mental states becomes interesting only if it is restricted to conscious mental states—states of which their subjects are aware. Take beliefs as a start: Are all conscious instances of the belief that George Washington was the first president of the United States, in different persons or for the same person at different times, characterized by a special qualitative character unique to beliefs with this content? The answer must be no: One person with this belief might have a mental image of George Washington (as on the dollar bill), another may simply have the words "George Washington" hovering in her mind, and still another may have no particular mental image or any other sort of phenomenal occurrence. But there is also a more general question: Do all occurrent beliefs—beliefs we are actively entertaining—share some specific belieflike phenomenal character? Some have claimed that when we are aware of a thought as a belief, there is a certain feel of assertoric or affirmative judging, a sort of "Oh, yes!" feeling. Similarly, we might claim that an occurrent disbelief is accompanied by a directly experienced feel of denial and that remembering is accompanied by a certain feeling of déjà vu. Perhaps desiring, hoping, and wishing are always accompanied by a felt feeling of yearning or longing combined with a sense of present privation. (If so, how could we distinguish desiring from hoping or wishing on the basis of their accompanying qualia?)

But such claims are difficult to assess. The "Oh, yes!" feeling may be nothing more than our coming to be aware that we believe a certain proposition. Such awareness does not seem to be accompanied by a particular kind of sensory quality. When you want to find out how your bruised elbow is coming along, you can focus your attention on the elbow and try to see whether the pain is still there. Here there clearly is a special kind of sensory feel, a quale, that you are looking for and can identify in your experience. However, when you are unsure whether you really believe some proposition—say, that euthanasia is morally permissible, that you think Mozart is a greater composer than Bach, or that the Republicans will be in power for the next decade—you do not look for a quale of a special type. It seems absurd to suggest that there is some sensed quality Q such that if you find Q attached to your thought that euthanasia is morally permissible, then you say, "Aha! Now I know I believe that euthanasia is morally permissible," and if you don't find Q, you say, "Now I know—I don't have that belief!"

If there are no distinctive phenomenal qualities associated with types of intentional mental states—beliefs, desires, intentions, and the rest—we face the following interesting question: How do you find out that you *believe*, rather than, say, merely *hope*, that it will rain tomorrow? Such knowledge, at least in normal circumstances, seems direct and immediate in the sense that it is not based on evidence or observation and that the only possible answer to the question "How do you know?" is "I just do." One thing that is certain is that we do not find out whether we believe or hope by looking inward to detect specific qualia. Nor is it obvious that we know that we are angry, or that we are embarrassed, by detecting a special phenomenal quality. How, then, do we know that we are angry rather than embarrassed? Or embarrassed rather than ashamed? Sometimes we find that it is not possible to classify our feeling as one of embarrassment or shame—perhaps it is both. But then how do we know *that*? There do not appear to be simple answers to such questions. It is possible that these questions are scientific ones and are amenable to research in psychology and cognitive science. (There apparently is a psychological theory according to which the physiological changes, such as increases in blood pressure and pulse rates, that we may be inclined to take to be caused by an emotion, say, anger, in fact *constitute* anger rather than being its *effects*; these physiological states collectively are what anger *is*. Such a theory may well have implications for how we come to know we are angry.)

In any case, it seems plausible that there are conscious mental states with no special phenomenal character. In general, mental occurrences that we call "experiences" appear to be those that possess phenomenal properties. Sensing and perceiving are experiences, but we do not think of believing and thinking as experiences. If this is so, the idea of phenomenal character and the idea of there being something it is like may come apart, though only slightly. For it certainly seems that there is something it is like to believe something, to suspend judgment about something, to wonder about something, or to hope for something. But as we saw, at least many instances of these states do not seem to have any phenomenal character.

To sum up, mental states come in two groups—those of which the subject is conscious or aware and those of which the subject is not aware or conscious. The first group in turn can be divided into two subgroups—those that have, or are accompanied by, qualitative characters, or qualia, and those that do not. Conscious states with qualia can again be subdivided: those that are type-classified or -individuated on the basis of their qualitative character (for example, pain, smell of ammonia, visual sensing of green) and those, even though they are accompanied by qualia, that are not type-classified in terms of, or primarily in terms of, their qualitative character (such as emotions). Perhaps we can mark this last division by saying that conscious states in the first group are wholly *constituted* by qualia and that those in the second group, though they possess qualitative characters, are not constituted by them, perhaps not even partially.[4]

Epistemic Subjectivity: Privacy and Special Epistemic Access

Subjectivity is often claimed to be of the essence of consciousness.[5] However, subjectivity has no fixed, unambiguous meaning. One sense of subjectivity is epistemological, having to do with the supposed special nature of knowledge of conscious states. The main idea is that a subject has a special epistemic access to her own current conscious states; we seem to be "immediately aware," as Descartes said, of our own feelings, thoughts, and perceptions and enjoy a special sort of first-person authority with regard to them.

A precise explanation of just what this "immediate" or "direct" access consists in is a controversial question.[6] For our purposes, it suffices to note the following three features: (1) Such knowledge is not based on evidence about other things—observation of what we say or do, what others tell us, physical or physiological cues, and the like. Your knowledge that you are having a toothache, that you are thinking about what to do this weekend, and such, is *direct* and *immediate* in that it is not based on, or mediated by, other things you know. (2) Your knowledge of your own current mental states carries special authority—"first-person authority"—in the sense that your claim to have such knowledge cannot, except in special circumstances, be overridden by third-person testimony. Concerning the queasy feelings you are experiencing in your stomach, your afterimages, the itchy spot on your shoulder, what you are thinking about, and other such matters, *what you say goes, at least in normal circumstances*, and others must defer to your avowals. As the qualifying proviso implies, first-person authority need not be thought to be absolute and unconditional; under special circumstances, your claim to know might be overridden. What might such special circumstances be? One obvious and uninteresting case is one in which you misdescribe your sensation. (Suppose that there is independent evidence that your grasp of the language in which you make the report is less than perfect and that behavioral and physiological evidence indicates that you are almost certainly experiencing another kind of sensation.) Or we might argue that our neurophysiological knowledge could at some point reach a state where it becomes possible to check, and correct, first-person avowals against physiological data (say, data obtained through sophisticated neural imaging techniques). In any case, whatever the degree or firmness of first-person authority, it is evident that the subject does occupy a specially privileged position in regard to her own mind. Note, though, that points (1) and (2) hold only for a subject's *current* mental states, not her past or future ones. (3) As these remarks indicate, there is an asymmetry between first- and third-person knowledge of conscious states. Neither of the foregoing two points applies to third-person knowledge, that is, knowledge of another person's conscious states. The subject alone enjoys immediate and specially authoritative access to her conscious states (and only to hers); the rest of us have to listen to what she has to say or observe her behavior or examine her brain. The idea that minds are "private" or "subjective" reflects this epistemic asymmetry between first- and third-person access to mental states.

In recognizing the subject's special epistemic position in relation to her own current conscious states, we need not adopt the model of complete and perfect "transparency"—nor the stronger claim that the subject's mind, while wholly transparent to herself, is totally opaque and impenetrable to others. In particular, the thesis does not include the claim that the subject is either infallible or omniscient in regard to her present conscious states. Infallibility would mean that whatever she believes about such states must be true. Point (1) says only that her knowledge, or belief, concerning such states is not based on, or inferred from, evidence. That does not mean that what she believes is necessarily true. Point (2) says that whatever she believes and says about her present conscious states stands as presumptively true—that is, it enjoys a kind of immunity against third-person challenges; it is not overturned or overridden by an observer's contrary testimony unless there are special reasons (and it is not easy to think up realistic cases in which these special reasons obtain). Nor do these points add up to the claim that she has omniscient knowledge about her conscious mind—that is, she knows every aspect of her conscious states. So the recognition of first-person authority does not necessarily lead to the extreme Cartesian thesis[7] of the complete transparency to the subject of her own mind. Such a position may well be false; however, that should not blind us to the very important epistemic properties of conscious states—in particular, the asymmetry between first- and third-person knowledge of such states.

A related but different sense of "access" used in connection with consciousness is currently on the scene, and we should at least briefly note it
here. The access we have been discussing is epistemic access in the sense of
the subject's *being aware of,* or *coming to know,* something. The second sense
of access, introduced by Ned Block, who contrasts it with phenomenal consciousness (in the sense discussed earlier), concerns the *availability* of the
content of a conscious state for the subject's verbal reports and for her "exec-
utive module" for inference and rational guidance of behavior and action.[8]
Suppose your sensory-perceptual system registers a piece of information with
content p (say, that there is a green couch in front of you). The state with this
information is "access-conscious" in case information p is available for verbal
reports (for example, when appropriately prompted, you respond, "I see a
green couch in front of me," or, "There is a green couch over there"). Moreover, this information can be used by you to guide your action (say, you walk
around the couch on the way to the door rather than bumping into it) or to
make further inferences ("There is something in the room that weighs more
than fifty pounds"). This is a rough characterization of a concept intended
to do explanatory-theoretical work in psychology, but it is not without ties to
the commonsense psychological framework in which our discussion is
couched. We can see some ways in which this idea of access is related to our
notion of epistemic access: If the content, or information, carried in a mental
state is epistemically accessible to us, we can, in normal circumstances, report
that we are in such a state and this knowledge can enter our belief system and
guide our actions. Is the converse also true—that is, if a state is access-
conscious, does it follow that the subject has the kind of special epistemic access we have discussed? How is consciousness of qualia related to access consciousness in Block's sense? These are interesting questions but we must set
them aside.

Perspectival Subjectivity:
The First-Person Point of View

Some philosophers have closely associated subjectivity of consciousness with
the notion of a first-person *point of view,* or *perspective.* Nagel writes:

> If physicalism is to be defended, the phenomenological features must them-
> selves be given a physical account. But when we examine their subjective
> character it seems that such a result is impossible. The reason is that *every
> subjective phenomenon is essentially connected with a single point of view,* and

it seems inevitable that an objective, physical theory will abandon that point of view.[9]

And in a later essay:

Yet subjective aspects of the mental can be apprehended only from the point of view of the creature itself . . . , whereas what is physical is simply there, and can be externally apprehended from more than one point of view.[10]

Nagel is saying that the subjectivity of mental phenomena is essentially connected with—perhaps consists in—there being "a single point of view" from which these phenomena are apprehended. This fits in with the claim discussed earlier that conscious states have phenomenal (or phenomenological) features in the sense that there is something it is like to be in such states. For there can be no impersonal "what it is like"; it is always what it is like *for a given subject* (for you, for humans, for bats) to see yellow, to taste pineapple, to echolocate a moth in flight. Things do not look, or appear, this way or that way, period; they look a certain way to one perceiving subject and perhaps a different way to another. There can be no "looks" or "appearances" in a world devoid of subjects capable of having experiences.

Understood this way, the talk about "points of view" appears to have two parts. First, there is the idea that for any conscious state there is a conscious subject whose state it is and that the content of consciousness consists in how things look or appear to that subject. Second, there is the idea that for each conscious state there is a *unique* subject, a single person, whose consciousness it is or, as Nagel puts it, who "apprehends" it. But these points are not new to us. That any "state" must be a state *of* some thing is a truism about all states, mental or otherwise. That a conscious state must be a state of some subject whose experience it constitutes is a point presupposed in our earlier discussion concerning phenomenal characters and direct awareness. And we have already discussed the idea of a "single subject" involved in consciousness, namely, the supposed privacy of consciousness and the first- and third-person asymmetry.

There is, however, another way in which "the first-person point of view" has been associated with the notion of subjectivity. Consider the following sentences:

(S) The shortest spy believes that he (himself) is clever.
(P) The shortest spy believes that the shortest spy is clever.

In (S), a person, the shortest spy, is referring to himself *qua himself* in attributing to himself the property of being clever. In contrast, in (P), that person is attributing cleverness to himself, not qua himself but qua third person—that is, as conceived from the third-person point of view. For we can imagine that the person who in fact is the shortest spy has been told by a source he trusts that the shortest spy is clever but he has no idea who the shortest spy is.

We can see, then, that (S) and (P) are logically independent of each other—that is, neither implies the other. For even if (S) is true, (P) can be false if the shortest spy does not know, or believe, that he is the shortest spy and does not believe that there are clever spies. Conversely, (P) can be true and yet (S) false if the person who is the shortest spy thinks that someone else is the shortest spy and has a low self-esteem about his own intelligence. So we see that the following two general locutions are not equivalent:

(S*) x believes himself or herself to be F.
(P*) x believes x to be F.

These points remain true when other intentional mental verbs are substituted for "believes"; you may want to verify this with verbs such as "doubts," "hopes," "wants," and the like.

But apparently this phenomenon is unique to psychological cases, for consider the following sentences that do not involve psychological verbs:

(1) x causes himself or herself to be F.
(1a) x causes x to be F.

(2) By mistake x kicked himself or herself.
(2a) By mistake x kicked x.

The two sentences in each pair are equivalent. The difference introduced by the use of a reflexive pronoun ("himself," "herself"), or reflexive reference to the subject, seems unique to first-person mental ascriptions to the self. For this reason, some have proposed that the subjectivity of the mental—at least one essential aspect of it—consists in this special kind of reflexivity of first-person reference to the self.[11]

In our discussion of consciousness, however, we set aside this aspect of subjectivity, for the phenomenon, while it raises some deeply interesting philosophical issues, arises for intentional mental states in general and does not specifically concern *conscious* mental states as such, although of course this does not necessarily rule out the existence of interesting connections at a deeper level.

Does Consciousness Involve Higher-Order Perceptions and Thoughts?

One idea that often turns up in philosophical accounts of consciousness is that consciousness is a kind of inner awareness—that is, awareness of one's own mental states. The model is that of a kind of internal scanner or monitor that keeps tabs on the internal goings-on of a system. When you are driving alone on an uncrowded, monotonous highway, you sometimes go on "automatic pilot": You perceive the conditions of the road and make necessary adjustments to the steering wheel and accelerator to keep the car moving at a steady speed in your lane, but there is a sense in which your perceptions are not fully conscious. That is, you are not actively aware of what you see and hear, although you do see and hear (otherwise you would crash!), and you may be unable to recall much about the conditions of the traffic for several minutes at a time. Or consider pains: We are told that in the heat of competition or combat, an injured athlete or wounded soldier can be entirely unaware of his pain. His attention is wholly occupied with other tasks, and he is not conscious of his pain. In such a case we may have an instance of pain that is not a conscious pain, and the reason may be that there is no active internal scanning, or monitoring, of the pain.

David Armstrong has proposed an account of this kind. According to Armstrong, consciousness can be thought of as "perception or awareness of the state of our own mind."[12] When you go on automatic pilot while driving, you perceive the conditions around you, but you do not perceive your perceptions. The injured athlete does not perceive his pain, and this is exactly what makes his pain nonconscious. When he comes to notice the pain, it becomes a conscious pain. So there are "first-order" perceptions and sensations (for example, you seeing another car moving past you, your pain), and there are perceptions of these first-order perceptions and sensations—that is, "second-order" or "higher-order" perceptions of them. We can then say something like this: A mental state is a conscious state just in case there is a higher-order perception of it—or perception that one is in that state. And a creature is conscious just in case it is capable of having these higher-order perceptions. An approach like this is called a "higher-order perception" theory (or HOP) of consciousness.

In a similar vein, David Rosenthal has suggested that "a mental state's being conscious consists in one's having a *thought* that one is in that very mental state."[13] On this account, then, a mental state is a conscious state just in case there is a higher-order thought, or awareness, that one is in that state. As you would expect, this approach is called the "higher-order thought" theory (or HOT). So consciousness involves a sort of "metapsychological" state, that is, a psychological state about another psychological state. A view like this typically allows the existence of mental states, even sensory states, that are not conscious—that is, those not accompanied by higher-order thoughts. And this for good reason—otherwise there would be an infinite progression of higher and still higher mental states, without end.

How plausible is this view of consciousness? There is no question that it has a certain initial plausibility and that it nicely fits some typical cases of mental states that we recognize as conscious. And the Armstrong-style view may open the door to a functionalist explanation of consciousness: On the functionalist view, first-order perceptions receive an account in terms of their causal roles or functions—in terms of their typical stimulus conditions and behavioral-psychological outputs—and if this is right, we might plausibly attempt a similar functional account of consciousness as an internal monitoring activity directed at these first-order perceptions and other mental states. Perhaps such an account could explain the role of consciousness in organizing and coordinating disparate perceptions—say, perceptions coming through different sensory channels—and even yield a functionalist account of "the unity of consciousness." At every moment of our waking lives we are bombarded by sensory stimuli of all sorts. The role of consciousness in the proper coordination and integration of an organism's myriad sensations and perceptions and the selection of some of them for special attention may be crucial to its ability to cope with the constantly changing forces of its environment, and this means that an approach such as Armstrong's may fit well with an evolutionary explanation of the emergence of consciousness in higher organisms.

But a functional account like this can seem implausible when examined from the subjective point of view. It may be plausible enough to say that a pain is a conscious pain just when you perceive it or are aware of it. But what is it that you are aware of when you are aware of a pain? According to the functionalist story, pain is a causal-functional role: To be in pain is to be in a state apt to be caused by tissue damage and apt to cause pain behaviors. To be aware of your pain, then, would be to be aware that you are in such a functional state. But this seems plainly wrong: When you are aware of pain, you are aware of its hurtfulness—you are aware that your knee hurts. At least, what you are aware of, when you are aware of the pain in your knee, is not being in a functional state. For one thing, your awareness of being in such a state cannot be direct or immediate in the way your awareness of a pain is; rather, it is the kind of awareness, or belief, that we would expect to be based on evidence and observation. Note, however, that if this is a difficulty, it is a difficulty for the functionalist version of the higher-order approach to consciousness, not necessarily for the general approach in terms of higher-order states.

What of the higher-order thought account of consciousness? We immediately notice that according to this approach, only creatures with the capacity for higher-order thoughts can be conscious; this may rule out most of the animal kingdom, including human infants, from the realm of consciousness. Higher-order thoughts supposedly implicated in consciousness have the form "I am aware that I am in state M," where "M" refers to a type of mental state (for example, pain, the belief that your car is running out of gas). Having such a thought would require, at minimum, an ability to refer to oneself, and this in turn seems to entail the possession of some notion of self, the idea of oneself as distinct from other things and subjects. Admittedly, all this is a complex and speculative affair: It is not clear what sorts of general conceptual, cognitive, and other sorts of psychological capacities are involved in having self-referential thoughts. Moreover, doesn't such a thought (the thought that you are in a state of kind M) require the possession of the concept of M? (If you have the thought that you see a tree, don't you have to have the concept of a tree—what a tree is?) Unless you have the concepts of belief, how can you have the thought that you believe it is raining, something that is required for this belief to be a conscious belief? The possession of the concept of belief seems to represent a very high and sophisticated level of cognitive and conceptual development. It is highly plausible that some lower forms of animals, perhaps reptiles and fish, have sensations and perceptions and that the contents of their sensations and perceptions are phenomenally represented to them. (As Nagel says, there must be something it is like for the bat to echolocate a fluttering moth.) But how plausible is it to suppose that these animals have the cognitive capacity to form self-regarding thoughts of the sort required by the higher-order thought account of consciousness? In fact, it is not clear that we would want to attribute any intentional states, like beliefs and thoughts, to such creatures.[14] Would we for that reason deny consciousness to such animals? Don't infants not yet capable of self-referential thought experience pain when they have colic? It may be one thing to have *conscious* sensations and quite another to have *thoughts about* such sensations. On the face of it, the latter would seem to require a higher and more complex set of cognitive capacities than the former. The gist of the difficulty, then, is this: The higher-order thought account of consciousness makes the capacity for intentional states—of a fairly sophisticated sort—a prerequisite for having conscious states. To put it another way, in order to have a conscious X, where X is a type of conscious state (like pain), the higher-order thought theory requires the subject to have the concept of X. This seems like an excessive requirement.

When we reflect on these and related issues, the higher-order thought model seems to fare better as an account of *self-consciousness* than of consciousness itself.[15] It seems clear that self-consciousness requires an ability to form thoughts involving oneself and to take the first-person point of view and attribute properties to oneself qua oneself. In this sense, the view of consciousness under discussion seems better suited for the second and third aspects of consciousness delineated earlier, namely, direct and unmediated awareness of one's own mental states and the idea of first-person perspective; it appears to have little to say about the phenomenal aspects of consciousness. Moreover, not every mental state of which we are aware— of which we have a second-order thought—needs to be a conscious state. For example, if after several sessions with your therapist you become aware of your hidden hostile feelings toward your roommate, that need not make your hostility a conscious state. You now believe, and perhaps know, that you harbor hostile feelings toward him, but this need not turn your feelings into conscious feelings. For this to happen, you must begin to *experience*, or *feel*, these feelings, and that does not seem like the same thing as merely believing that you have them. Consciousness of a mental state includes an awareness of it, but a special kind of awareness seems required if the awareness is to count as an instance of conscious awareness.

Various organisms and artificial systems have sensory receptors or scanners through which they acquire information about their environment, process and store the information in various ways, and use it to guide their behavior. Birds, bees, and even the lowliest insects do it, as do electromechanical robots and even simple burglar alarm systems. And some of the more sophisticated systems of this kind may, as Armstrong says, incorporate an internal monitoring device that keeps an eye on the flow and processing of information through the system and uses this meta-information for a more efficient processing and utilization of information. What is not obvious, however, is why such a system has to be a conscious system. How and why must consciousness, in its genuine and literal sense, emerge from a capacity to monitor first-order information processing? Is it incoherent to suppose that all monitoring of that sort could go on in an electromechanical system totally lacking in consciousness? Consciousness in humans may be a way of monitoring certain internal goings-on; that may be its biological function. But that is not to say that the essence of consciousness is such monitoring, or that whenever there is such monitoring, there must be consciousness.

Phenomenal Consciousness: The "Explanatory Gap" and the "Hard Problem"

As we saw earlier (chapter 1), most philosophers accept mind-body supervenience in something like the following form:

> If an organism is in some mental state M at *t*, then there must be a neural-physical state P such that the organism is in P at *t*, and any organism that is in P at any time is necessarily in mental state M at the same time.

We may call P a "supervenience base" of M. Consider pain as our M. According to mind-body supervenience, whenever you are in pain, there is a neural-physical supervenience base of your pain. Call this neural state N. Whenever N occurs, you experience pain, and we may suppose that unless N occurs, you do not experience pain. We also say things like, pain "arises out" of N, or "emerges" from N.

But why is it that pain, not itch or tickle, occurs when neural state N occurs? What is it about the neural-biological-physical properties of N that make it the case that pain, not another kind of sensory experience, arises when N occurs? Further, why does pain not arise from a different neural state? Why does any conscious experience arise from N? Here we are asking for an explanation of why the pain-N supervenience relation holds. The problem of the explanatory gap is that of providing such an explanation— that is, the problem of closing the apparent "gap" between phenomenal consciousness and the brain.[16]

If there is indeed an explanatory gap here, its existence does not depend on using the idiom of supervenience. Even if you want to limit yourself to the talk of psychophysical correlations, the problem still arises. Suppose pain correlates with neural state N. Why does pain correlate with N rather than another neural state? Why doesn't itch or tickle correlate with N? If pain correlates with N and itch with a different neural state N*, there must be an explanation of this fact, we feel, in terms of the neural-physical differences between N and N* and the qualitative differences between pain and itch. What would such an explanation look like? How would anyone go about finding such an explanation? Could neurobiological research ever discover explanations of these and other psychoneural correlations? What *further* scientific research could meet these apparent explanatory needs? These questions, among others, constitute the explanatory gap problem.

Although the term "explanatory gap" is relatively new, the problem is not. Well over one hundred years ago William James wrote:

> According to the assumptions of this book, thoughts accompany the brain's workings, and those thoughts are cognitive of realities. The whole relation is one which we can only write down empirically, confessing that no glimmer of explanation of it is yet in sight. That brains should give rise to a knowing consciousness at all, this is the one mystery which returns, no matter of what sort the consciousness and of what sort the knowledge may be. Sensations, aware of mere qualities, involve the mystery as much as thoughts, aware of complex systems, involve it.[17]

James recognizes that thoughts and sensations correlate with ("accompany") brain processes, but we can only make a list of these correlations ("write down empirically," as he puts it). Making up a running list of observed psychoneural correlations does not amount to having an explanatory insight into why these particular correlations hold—or why there are psychoneural correlations at all. According to James, it is one "mystery" for which there is no "glimmer of explanation." And James was not alone; even earlier, the noted British biologist T. H. Huxley had written:

> But what consciousness is, we know not; and how it is that anything so remarkable as a state of consciousness comes about as the result of irritating nervous tissue is just as unaccountable as any other ultimate fact of Nature.[18]

You will recognize that the deep puzzle that Huxley saw in consciousness is essentially the mystery that James despaired of penetrating.

More recently, the problem of phenomenal consciousness has also been called the "hard problem" of consciousness. According to ontological physicalism, a position that rejects immaterial minds as bearers of mental properties, it is physical systems, like biological organisms, that have mental properties—that is, have beliefs and desires, learn and remember, experience pains and remorse, are upset and fearful, and all the rest. Now consider this question posed by David Chalmers: "How could a physical system be the sort of thing that could *learn*, or that could *remember?*"[19] Chalmers calls this an "easy" problem—a tractable component of the mind-body problem. As he acknowledges, the scientific problem of uncovering the details of the neural mechanisms of memory may present the brain scientist with formidably difficult challenges. And yet there is here a well-defined research project: Identify the underlying neural systems—say, in humans and higher mammals—that do the job of processing information received from perceptual systems, store it, and retrieve it as needed. The problem, although not easy from a scientific point of view, does not seem to pose any special puzzles or mysteries from the philosophical point of view; conceptually and philosophically, it is an "easy" problem. The reason for all this is that memory is a "functional" concept, a concept defined in terms of the job that memory performs in the cognitive-psychological economy of an organism (chapter 5). So the question "How could a physical system manage to remember?" seems to have answers of the following straightforward form: A physical system with neural mechanism N can remember because to remember is to perform a certain task T, and neural mechanism N enables a system to perform T; moreover, we can explain exactly how N performs T in this system and others like it. Identifying mechanism N is a scientific research project, and the functional characterization of remembering in terms of task T is what makes it possible to define the research program. There is no special philosophical mystery here, or so it seems.

Compare this situation with one that involves qualitative states of consciousness. That is, instead of asking, "How could a physical system be the sort of thing that could *remember?*" ask, "How could a physical system be the sort of thing that could *experience pain?*" This is what Chalmers calls the "hard" problem—the hard, and possibly intractable, part of the mind-body problem. The problem is hard because pain apparently resists a functional characterization. Granted, pains have typical input conditions (tissue damage and trauma) and typical behavioral outputs (winces, groans, avoidance behavior). But many of us are inclined to believe that what makes pain pain is the fact that it is experienced as painful—that is, it hurts. This phenomenal, qualitative aspect of pain seems not capturable in terms of any particular task associated with pain. Uncovering the neural mechanism of pain—that is, the neural mechanism that responds to tissue damage and triggers characteristic pain responses—is the "easy" part, although, of course, it probably is a challenging problem for the brain scientist. What is "hard" is the philosophical problem of answering the questions "Why is pain experienced when this neural mechanism is activated? What is it about this mechanism that explains why pain rather than itch, or anything at all, is experienced when it is activated?"

The "hardness" of the hard problem can be glimpsed from the following fact: The question "How can neural mechanism N enable a system to perform task C?" where C is the task associated with remembering, seems answerable *within* neurophysiology and associated physical-behavioral sciences. In contrast, "How can neural mechanism N enable a system to experience pain?" does not seem answerable within neurophysiology and its associated sciences, because "pain," or the concept of pain, does not even occur in neurophysiology or other physical-behavioral sciences. Pain, as the term is being used here, is an inner conscious event; what it is like to experience pain as opposed to, say, what it is like to experience an itch or see yellow is of the essence of pain in this sense. Pain as a type of phenomenal consciousness therefore lies outside the scope of brain science. Given this, it is difficult to see how there could be a scientific solution to our problem within brain science. If neuroscience does not have the expressive resources even to talk about pain (as a quale), how can it explain why pain correlates with a neural state with which it in fact correlates?

That the explanatory gap cannot be filled, or that the hard problem cannot be solved, is the central doctrine of emergentism. Psychoneural correlations are among the ultimate unexplainable brute facts, and Samuel Alexander and C. Lloyd Morgan, leading emergentists of the early twentieth century, counseled us to accept them with "natural piety"—stop asking why and just be grateful that consciousness has emerged!

But should we give up the hope for explanations of psychoneural correlations for good and accept the explanatory gap as unclosable and the hard problem as unsolvable? What exactly would it take to give a physical-neural account of phenomenal consciousness, an account that meets the demand for an explanation of why a particular sensory quality correlates with, or supervenes on, a specific neural substrate? And what would it take to deal with the explanatory gap? These questions are now often posed in terms of *reduction* and *reductive explanation*. The thought is that to achieve a solution to the hard problem and close the explanatory gap, we must be able to *reduce* consciousness to neural states, or *reductively explain* consciousness in terms of neural processes. To pursue our problem along these lines, we need a workable general conception of what it is to reduce, or reductively explain, a set of phenomena (say, consciousness) on the basis of another set of phenomena (for example, neural states).

It is no accident that so many thinkers, both philosophers and scientists, have spoken of the "mystery" of consciousness. It is not an exaggeration to say that the mystery of the mind is, in essence, the mystery of consciousness. Other aspects of mentality, like belief, emotion, and action, may well have explanations along the line of the functional-neural account of memory sketched earlier. However, phenomenal experiences, or qualia, apparently present us with an entirely new problem not easily amenable to such a model. To make further progress with these issues, we need to set them in a more general context of reduction, reductive explanation, and related issues. We resume this discussion later in the book (chapter 10).

Qualia Representationalism and Externalism

Suppose you are looking at a ripe tomato, in good light. You have a visual experience with certain qualitative characters, or qualia—say, redness and roundness. Focus your attention on these qualities of your experience and try to determine the exact hue of the color, the precise shape you see, and so on—that is, try to closely introspect the qualities characterizing your experience. When you do this, some philosophers argue, you will find yourself focusing on and examining the qualities of the tomato out there in front of you. Your visual experience of the tomato is "diaphanous" in that when you try to introspectively examine its qualitative character, you seem to look right through it to the properties of the object seen, namely, the tomato. This phenomenon is called the "diaphanousness" or "transparency" of experience.[20]

Phenomena like the supposed diaphanousness of conscious experiences have led some philosophers to explore the thesis that qualia are just the representational contents of experiences and that these represented contents are the properties of the external objects represented. The view that qualia are essentially representational is called *representationalism*; it is of their essence that they represent things, properties, and states of affairs (other than themselves). The red quale of your visual experience of the tomato is nothing but what your experience represents the color of the tomato as being, and when the representation is veridical, the quale is the actual red color of the tomato. So the kind of approach being described is also an *externalism* about qualia—qualia *are* the properties that external objects are represented as having. This position, which locates qualia out there in the world, would enable us to reject qualia as privately introspectible qualities of inner experiences, making the approach particularly welcome to a robust physicalism about consciousness.

But how can this be? Aren't qualia, by definition, the qualities of your conscious experiences? How could these qualities be found in the external things around you? Hasn't Nagel convincingly argued that you and I can have no cognitive access to what it is like to be a bat and that qualia characterizing bats' experiences are beyond our conceptual and cognitive reach? But according to the qualia externalist-representationalist, we have been misled into looking in the wrong place—we are trying to peek into a bat's mind and see what qualia are lurking in it. The idea is not just hopeless but incoherent.

So where should we look? The qualia externalist tells us to look at the external environment of the bats and try to see what objects the bats are representing and what properties these objects have. Speaking of a marine parasite that attaches itself to a host only if the host's temperature is 18°C, Fred Dretske, an able proponent of the position, writes:

> If you know what it is to be 18° C, you know how the host feels to the parasite. You know what the parasite's experience is like as it "senses" the host. If knowing what it is like to be such a parasite is knowing how things seem to it, how it represents the objects it perceives, you do not have to be a parasite to know what it is like to be one. All you have to know is what temperature is. . . . To know what it is like for this parasite, one looks, not in the parasite, but at what the parasite is "looking" at—the host [to whom the parasite has attached itself].[21]

But why? How would looking at the host the creature is "looking" at, or representing, help us to find out what it is like for it to experience the temperature of 18°C? It seems that a line of consideration like the following has been influential in motivating the externalist-representationalist approach. We begin with a conception of what "qualia" are supposed to be:

(1) Qualia are, by definition, the way things *seem, look,* or *appear* to a conscious creature.

So if a tomato looks red and round to me (that is, my visual experience represents the tomato as being red and round), redness and roundness are the qualia of my visual experience of the tomato. This is a representationalist interpretation of qualia. In the following, we will see how this representational view leads to qualia externalism.[22]

(2) If things ever are the way they look or appear, qualia are exactly the properties that the perceived or represented object has. If a perceptual experience represents an object to be F (for example, the object looks F to you), and if this experience is veridical (true to the facts), then the object *is* F.

This seems reasonable: If things really are the way they are represented in perception, they must have the properties that they are represented to have. If the tomato is the way it is represented in your visual experience, and if it is represented as being red and round, it must really be red and round. This sounds like a tautology. What about the parasite that attaches itself to a host only when the host's temperature is 18°C? When the parasite's temperature-sensing organ is working properly and its temperature perception is veridical, the host's temperature is 18°C. The way the host's temperature is represented by the parasite to be is the way the temperature actually is, namely, 18°C. This means that the quale of the parasite's temperature representation is nothing other than the temperature 18°C. We have, therefore, the following conclusion:

(3) Qualia, or phenomenal properties of experience, are among the objective properties of external objects represented in conscious experience.

To find out what it is like to be a bat in flight, zeroing in on a moth, we must shift our attention from the bat to the moth and track its fluttery trajectory through the darkness of the night.

An externalist approach like this is often motivated at a deeper level by a desire to accommodate qualia within a physicalist-materialist scheme. The grapes look green to you. That is, your visual experience has the quale green. So green is instantiated. But then some *object* must instantiate it; *something must be green*. But what could this thing be? If we look inside your brain, we find nothing green there. To invoke a nonphysical mental item, like a "sense-datum" or "percept," that has the quale green goes against physicalist ontology, which tolerates no nonphysical particular in the spacetime world. Moreover, there is no inner private theater for such objects to inhabit. The contents of our spacetime world are exhausted by physical-material particulars and their aggregates. Return to the question: Where is the green quale of your visual experience of the grapes instantiated? In the grapes, of course!

This answer has the virtues of boldness and simplicity, if not intuitive plausibility. Qualia representationalism-externalism has gained the support of a number of philosophers, but philosophical opinions remain sharply divided. The representationalist group considers qualia to be wholly representational—that is, qualia are fully explicable in terms of, or reducible to, their representational contents, and in line with general content externalism (chapter 9), these contents are taken as external—that is, external to the perceiving and conscious subjects. Those who disagree need not deny that qualia are representational; they can accept the view that almost all qualia, even all of them, serve a representational role. What they deny is that representational contents are all there is to qualia. There are things about the qualitative features of conscious experience that are not a matter of their representing something.

What are the reasons for doubting representationalism? We will briefly describe two. The first could go like this: Spectrum inversion is at least a metaphysical possibility. That is, where you see red, I see green, and vice versa. We both say that tomatoes are red and lettuce is green; our verbal usage coincides exactly. But the color quale of your visual experience when you look at a tomato is the same as the color quale I experience when I look at lettuce, and vice versa. We both represent tomatoes as red and lettuce as green when we assert, "Tomatoes are red and lettuce is green." But the qualia we experience are different, so representational contents cannot be all there is to qualia.[23] Second, even if within a sense modality, like vision, qualia differences and similarities amount to no more than differences and similarities in representational contents, surely there are intermodal qualia differences that are not merely differences in representational contents—for example, the qualitative differences between visual experiences and tactual experiences. We can form a belief—a representation of an external state of affairs, say, "My cat has just jumped on my lap"—on the basis of both a visual experience and a tactual experience. Isn't it obvious that there is a qualitative difference between these experiences even though the representation to which each of them leads is identical? Such examples do not silence qualia representationalists; they try to find further representational differences between these experiences that might account for their qualitative differences.

What of the series of considerations—(1), (2), and (3)—that appears to lead to qualia externalism? Philosophers have distinguished between two senses of "appear," "seem," and "look"—the "epistemic" (or "doxastic") sense and the "phenomenal" sense. These expressions are used in the epistemic sense when we say things like, "It appears that (seems that, looks like) the Republicans will control Washington politics for years to come," and, "Prospects for a compromise seem (appear, look) quite bleak." In this usage, "appears," "seems," and "looks" have roughly the sense of "there is reason to believe," "there is evidence indicating," or "I am inclined to believe." We are already familiar with the phenomenal sense of these expressions: When the tomato appears or looks red to you, your visual experience is characterized by a certain qualitative property, the quale red. Red indicates the way in which the tomato visually appears or looks. When you say, in a typical situation, "This tomato looks red," you are talking about an aspect of your visual experience of the tomato; you do not mean to say, "There is reason to believe that this tomato is red," or, "The evidence indicates that the tomato is red." If it is a green tomato bathed in red light and you know that this is the case, you can still report, "The tomato looks red."[24]

With this distinction in mind, let us return to (1), (2), and (3). A plausible case can be made for the objection that "appear" and "seem" are used equivocally in (1) and (2). More specifically, (1) is acceptable as a definition of qualia only if "appear" and "seem" are used in their phenomenal, or sensuous, sense. Qualia are the ways in which objects and events around me, and in me, present themselves in my experience; they are how the yellow of Van Gogh's sunflowers appears to me, how the pain in my knee feels (it hurts!), how the air permeated with burning sulfur smells. But it is a disputable question whether these qualia can also be the properties of objects around us— that is, whether sunflowers are yellow in the same sense in which my visual experience is of yellow, or whether there is an event in my knee, or in my brain, that actually is painful in the way my pains are painful to me. Now consider the antecedent of (2): "If things ever are the way they appear to be." This supposition makes sense only if "appear" is interpreted in its epistemic, or doxastic, sense—that is, to mean something like "If things are the way our perceptual experience indicates them to be." And under this supposition, it would follow that things do, at least sometimes, have the properties we believe them to have on the basis of our perceptual experience. But then the consequent would not follow: There is no reason to think qualia as defined in (1), in terms of the phenomenal sense of "appear," can be properties of an external object. It would seem that in order to make (2) plausible, we must understand "seem" and "appear" in (1)—the supposed definition of qualia— in the doxastic sense; (1) would then say something like, "Qualia are the properties that things seem or appear to have—that is, the properties that we have reason to think that things have on the basis of visual experience." The trouble obviously is that if (1) is interpreted this way, there is no reason to accept it as true of qualia, much less a definition of what qualia are.

Here we have only skimmed the continuing debates between representationalists and externalists on the one hand and those opposed to their approach on the other. The division between the two camps seems deep and well entrenched. The debates have been intense and are likely to continue. This is one of the more important current issues about consciousness.

Does Consciousness Supervene on Physical Properties?

The subjectivity of consciousness, in the sense of awareness of our own psychological states, seems, as we have seen, explicable in principle in terms of some internal monitoring mechanism, and this provides us with a basis for a possible physical-neural explanation of self-awareness. Moreover, the "directness" and "immediacy" of such awareness perhaps can be explained in terms of a direct coupling of such a scanning device to a speech center, a mechanism responsible for verbal reports. The first- and third-person asymmetry of access seems no particular mystery: It arises from the simple fact that my scanning device (and its associated speech center), not yours, is directly monitoring my internal states. These ideas are rough and may ultimately fail. However, what they show is the possibility of understanding the subjectivity of consciousness in the sense of direct first-person access to one's own mental states, because at least we can imagine a possible mechanism that can implement it at the physical-physiological level. That is, we can see what it would be like to have an explanation of the subjectivity of consciousness. That shows that at least we understand the problem.

On this view of consciousness as direct awareness of internal states, consciousness would be supervenient on the basic physical-biological structure and functioning of the organism. The fact that an organism is equipped with the capacity directly to monitor its current internal states is a fact about its physical-biological organization and must be manifested through the patterns of its behavior in response to input conditions. This means that if two organisms are identical in their physical-biological makeup, they cannot differ in their capacity for self-monitoring. In that sense, consciousness as special first-person epistemic authority may well be supervenient on physical and biological facts (on supervenience, see chapter 1).

What, then, of the phenomenal aspect of consciousness? Do qualia supervene on the physical-biological constitution of organisms? You feel pain when

your C-fibers are stimulated; is it necessarily the case that your *physical* duplicate feels pain when her C-fibers are stimulated? In our world, pains and
other qualitative states exist, and we suppose them to depend, in regular lawlike ways, on what goes on in the physical-biological domain. Is there a possible world that is a total physical duplicate of this world but in which there are
no phenomenal mental states? Many philosophers think that qualia do not
supervene on physical-biological facts. For example, Saul Kripke writes:

> What about the case of the stimulation of C-fibers? To create this phenome-
> non, it would seem that God need only create beings with C-fibers capable of
> the appropriate type of physical stimulation; whether the beings are conscious
> or not is irrelevant here. It would seem, though, that to make the C-fiber
> stimulation correspond to pain, or be felt as pain, God must do something in
> addition to the mere creation of the C-fiber stimulation; He must let the
> creatures feel the C-fibers as pain, and not as a tickle, or as warmth, or as
> nothing, as apparently would also have been within His powers.[25]

Kripke contrasts this situation with one involving molecular motion and
heat: After God created molecular motion, he did not have to perform an additional act to create heat. When molecular motion came into being, heat
came along with it.

If Kripke is right, there are two kinds of possible worlds that, though identical with our world in all physical respects, are different in mental respects: First,
there are worlds with different physical-phenomenal correlations (for example,
C-fiber stimulation correlates with itches rather than pains), and second, there
are those in which there are no phenomenal mental events at all—"zombie
worlds." In the latter, there are people exactly like you and me, behaving just as
we do (including making noises like "That toothache kept me awake all night,
and I am too tired to work on the paper right now"), but they are zombies with
no experience of pain, fatigue, sensing green, or any of the rest.

But is Kripke right? How is it possible for God to create C-fiber stimulation but not pain? Let us look at various considerations against qualia
supervenience:

1. There is no conceptual connection between the concept of pain and
   that of C-fiber stimulation (that is, no connection of meaning between the terms "pain" and "C-fiber stimulation"), and therefore
   there is no contradiction in the supposition that an organism has its
   C-fibers stimulated without experiencing pain or any other sensation.

This argument, however, is not entirely persuasive, for there is no conceptual connection between heat and molecular motion either, nor between water and H_2O, and yet there is no possible world in which molecular motion exists but heat does not, or a world that contains H_2O but no water. In considering this reply, we must ask whether the case of pain and C-fiber excitation is relevantly similar to cases like heat–molecular motion and water-H_2O.

2. "Inverted spectra" are possible: It is perfectly conceivable that there are worlds that are just like ours in all physical respects but in which people, when looking at the things we look at, experience colors that are complementary to the colors we experience.[26] In such worlds, cabbages are green and tomatoes are red, just as they are in the actual world; however, people there experience red when they look at cabbages and green when they look at tomatoes, although they call cabbages "green" and tomatoes "red." Such worlds seem perfectly conceivable, with no hidden contradictions. In fact, why isn't it conceivable that there could be a world in which colors are sensed the way sounds are sensed by us and vice versa—worlds with inverted sense modalities? (Arthur Rimbaud, the French poet, saw colors in vowels, like this: "A black, E white, I red, U green, and O blue."[27])

3. In fact, why couldn't there be people in the actual world, perhaps among our friends and relatives, whose color spectra are inverted with respect to ours, although their relevant neural states are the same? As just noted, they call tomatoes "red" and cabbages "green," as we do, and all our observable behaviors coincide perfectly. However, their color experiences are different from ours.[28] We normally do not imagine such possibilities; we think that when you and I are in relevantly similar neurophysiological states, we experience the same sensation. But such an assumption is precisely the assumption that sensory states supervene on physical conditions, which is what is at issue. What matters to our shared knowledge of the world and our ability to coordinate our actions is the fact that we can discriminate the same range of colors, not how these colors appear to us (see chapter 10).

4. Implicit in these remarks is the point that qualia also do not supervene on functional properties of organisms.[29] A functional property

is, roughly, a property in virtue of which an organism responds to a given sensory input by emitting some specific behavior output. You and your physical duplicate must share the same functional properties—that is, functional properties supervene on physical properties (think about why this must be so). So if qualia should supervene on functional properties, they would supervene on physical properties. This means that to question the supervenience of qualia on physical properties is ipso facto to question their supervenience on functional properties.[30]

The main argument for the failure of the physical supervenience of qualia, then, is the apparent conceivability of zombies and qualia inversions in organisms physically indistinguishable from us.[31] Conceivability may not in itself imply real possibility, and the exact relationship between conceivability and possibility is a difficult issue. Moreover, we could make errors in judging what is conceivable and what is not, and our judgments may depend on available empirical information. Knowing what we now know, we may not be able to conceive a world in which water is not H_2O, but people who did not have the same information might have judged differently. In the case of qualitative characters of mental states, however, is there anything about them that, should we come to know it, would convince us that zombies and qualia inversions are not really possible? Don't we already know all we need to know, or can know, about these subjective phenomenal characters of our experience? Is there anything about them that we can learn from objective, empirical science? Research in neuropsychology will perhaps tell us more about the biological basis of phenomenal experiences, but it is difficult to see how that could be relevant as evidence for qualia supervenience. Such discoveries will tell us more about lawful correlations between qualia and underlying neural states, but the question has to do with whether these correlations are *metaphysically necessary*— whether there are possible worlds in which the correlations fail. What is more, it is not so obvious that neurophysiological research could even establish correlations between qualia and neural states. For the claimed correlations, we might point out, only correlate neural states with *verbal reports* of qualia, not with qualia themselves, from which it follows that these correlations may be consistent with qualia inversions. At best, it might be argued, scientific research could only correlate neural states with the color similarities and differences a subject can discriminate, not with the intrinsic qualities of his color experiences.

The case against qualia supervenience therefore is not conclusive, though it is quite substantial. Are there, then, considerations in favor of qualia supervenience? It would seem that the only positive considerations are broad metaphysical ones that might very well be accused of begging the question. Say you are already committed to physicalism: You then have two choices about qualia—either to deny their existence or to try to accommodate them somehow within a physicalist framework. Given the choice between accommodation and rejection, you opt for accommodation, since a flat denial of the existence of qualia, you may feel, makes your physicalism fly in the face of common sense. You may then find supervenience an appealing way for bringing qualia into the physicalist fold—close enough to it, at any rate. For qualia supervenience at least guarantees that once all the physical details of an organism, or a world, are fixed, that fixes all the facts concerning the organism or world—including, of course, facts about qualia. If this does not make qualia full-fledged physical items, it at least makes them dependent on physical facts, and that protects the primacy and priority of the physical. That, you may feel, is good enough. Furthermore, qualia supervenience seems to open a way of accounting for the causal relevance of qualia. If qualia are genuine existents, their existence must make a causal difference. But any reasonable version of physicalism must consider the physical world to be causally closed (see chapter 7), and it would seem that if qualia are to be brought into the causal structure of the world, they must at least be supervenient on physical facts of the world. Supervenience by itself may not be enough to confer *causal efficacy* on qualia, but it may suffice to make them *causally relevant* in some broad sense. In any case, without qualia supervenience, there may well be no hope of providing qualia with a place in the network of causal relations of this world.[32] But this is not an argument for qualia supervenience; it only means that qualia supervenience is on our wish list. For all we know, qualia might be epiphenomenal. This cannot be ruled out a priori, and it would not be proper to use its denial as a premise in a philosophical argument.

Who Needs Qualia?

We thus find ourselves in a dilemma: If qualia supervene on physical-biological processes, why they supervene—why they supervene on, or arise from, the specific neural substrates from which they in fact arise—remains a mystery, something that seems entirely inexplicable from the physical point of view. (This does not mean that this would be any easier to explain from a nonphysicalist perspective.) Yet if they do not supervene, they must be taken as phenomena entirely outside the physical domain. At this point, some may feel that the basic physicalist approach to mentality is in deep trouble and that it is time to begin exploring nonphysicalist alternatives. But to many philosophers, serious dualism is not a viable option (chapter 2); at least, it is not obvious how positing immaterial souls helps us with our problems. Some have taken the heroic route of denying the existence of qualia. This we may call "qualia nihilism" (or "qualia eliminativism").

Qualia nihilism comes in two varieties. The first is the claim that qualia, whether or not they really exist, have no place, no role to play, in psychology or cognitive science in generating law-based explanations and predictions of human behavior. This form of qualia nihilism is to be distinguished from behaviorism; unlike the latter, it does not oppose the positing of inner states, whether these are physiological or psychological, in framing theories of behavior. And it need not shrink from mentioning consciousness: It can allow consciousness in the sense of awareness (or inner monitoring) an active psychological role. It says only that the purely qualitative aspects of our consciousness have no role in explaining and predicting behavior. We can call this "methodological" qualia nihilism, or "methodological" qualia epiphenomenalism.

You may be led to this version of qualia nihilism by considerations along the following lines. Qualia are subjective and not intersubjectively accessible, and this makes their direct scientific study impossible. Moreover, unlike the unobservable theoretical posits of physical sciences, the intrinsic features of qualia do not seem to have any observably testable consequences, for as far as behavior goes, just what qualia a subject is experiencing seems to make no difference. What does make a difference is that the subject can distinguish, say, red from green—for example, she can tell reliably when the traffic light says "Go!" or "Stop!"[33] However, whether she has inner experiences of color qualia, or just what the intrinsic qualities of her color qualia are, has no role in explaining why she brakes when the red light goes on and starts up again when the light turns green. What matters is only that there is a sensory neural mechanism that enables her to respond differentially to red, green, and yellow. What has behavioral consequences and hence does explanatory work is the subject's discriminative ability, not the qualitative character of her inner experience. This means that qualia have nothing to contribute to the explanatory-predictive theory of human behavior; the subject's discriminative abilities with respect to physical stimuli and the neural mechanism underlying them can do all the needed work. Or so we might reason.

Let us now briefly turn to what may be called "philosophical" qualia nihilism. Proponents of this position argue that there "really" are no such things as qualia and that a close analysis of the concept of a quale shows qualia to be merely a piece of philosophical invention. Arguments for qualia nihilism of this sort typically begin with an enumeration of the properties traditionally associated with qualia, such as the subject's infallible and incorrigible first-person access to them, their ineffability and inaccessibility to the third person, and their intrinsicness. These arguments then attempt to show that either one or more of these concepts are incoherent or hopelessly obscure or that they are empty, applying to nothing recognizable in our mental life.[34] One problem with many of these arguments is that they try to force qualia to bear the burden of all the exaggerated claims ever made about their special features, with the unsurprising result that nothing *can* qualify as qualia. To believe in qualia, it is not necessary, for example, to insist on absolute first-person infallibility or third-person inaccessibility. And then there are the analogies advanced by qualiaphobes[35] who liken belief in qualia to the discredited belief in witches, phlogiston, and magnetic effluvia. The idea is that belief in qualia will be discredited when neuroscience reaches the stage where it can explain human behavior without recourse to an inner mental life, just as belief in phlogiston was abandoned when the oxidation theory of combustion took hold. (This harks back to the argument for methodological qualia nihilism considered earlier.) But the reasoning here appears to involve the premise that qualia, like phlogiston and magnetic effluvia, are only theoretical constructs posited to explain a range of observable data in a given domain, an assumption that is rejected by those who take qualia seriously.

And then there is Wittgenstein's parable of "the beetle in the box" (first introduced in chapter 3):

> Suppose everyone had a box with something in it; we call it a "beetle." No one can look into anyone else's box, and everyone says he knows what a beetle is only by looking at *his* beetle. Here it would be quite possible for everyone to have something different in his box.[36]

As Wittgenstein says, the box might even be empty, and it is not clear how the word "beetle" could have a role in public language, in communicating intersubjective information. The point is, of course, that our talk of private, directly accessible qualia, in our little private boxes (we call them "minds"), is just like this beetle talk.

It is difficult to know just how to respond to this and other arguments against qualia and the intelligibility of qualia talk—except to say that when I look inside my box, I find something there with just *these* characteristics. I can also add further explanations: I usually find something with similar characteristics when someone steps on my toes or a pin is stuck in my hand, but not when someone massages my back. If this does not help, probably nothing will. It is indeed a mystery how we could use words for qualia for intersubjective communication—at least what we normally assume to be intersubjective communication. There is the story that when Louis Armstrong was asked to explain what jazz is, he replied, "If you got to ask, you ain't never gonna get to know."[37] If there should be people who seriously and sincerely want to find out what qualia are, that might show not only that zombies are metaphysically possible but that some actually exist in this world!

Further Readings

There has been a consciousness boom in both philosophy and science and a corresponding surge in publications. The following paragraphs cite only a handful of what is available.

Owen Flanagan's *Consciousness Reconsidered* includes a clear and balanced survey of the contemporary debate on consciousness, even though it is a bit dated.

In *Consciousness Explained*, Daniel C. Dennett offers a lively and original account ("the multiple draft theory")—at the cognitive level—of consciousness but defends a nihilist-eliminativist stance on qualia.

For representationalist-externalist accounts of consciousness and qualia, see Fred Dretske, *Naturalizing the Mind*; Michael Tye, *Ten Problems of Consciousness*; and William Lycan, *Consciousness and Experience*. For discussion, see Ned Block, "Mental Paint."

John R. Searle, *The Rediscovery of the Mind*, mounts a sustained critique of the functionalist-computationalist approach to consciousness and intentionality.

On phenomenal consciousness and the explanatory gap, see David Chalmers, *The Conscious Mind*; Joseph Levine, *Purple Haze*; Ned Block and Robert Stalnaker, "Conceptual Analysis, Dualism, and the Explanatory Gap"; and Jaegwon Kim, *Physicalism, or Something Near Enough*, chapters 4 and 6.

The Nature of Consciousness: Philosophical Debates, edited by Ned Block, Owen Flanagan, and Güven Güzeldere, is a comprehensive and indispensable anthology of articles on consciousness. A collection of new essays, many of them touching on issues discussed in this chapter, is *Consciousness: New Philosophical Perspectives*, edited by Quentin Smith and Aleksandar Jokic.

Notes

1. Rene Descartes, "Author's Replies to the Fourth Set of Objections," p. 171.
2. "Qualia" is now the standard term. Note that sometimes it is also used to refer to states with such qualitative characters.

3. Thomas Nagel, "What Is It Like to Be a Bat?" Nagel popularized the expression "what it is like" in connection with the phenomenal, or qualitative, aspects of consciousness.

4. If anger, say, is *partially constituted* by a quale ("anger quale"), then all instances of anger must exhibit this anger quale; this quale is part of what makes it an instance of anger. But it may well be that though each instance of anger has a certain quale, there is no single anger quale present in all instances of anger.

5. See, for example, John R. Searle, *The Rediscovery of the Mind*, especially ch. 4.

6. This was discussed in some detail in chapter 1.

7. "Cartesian" since it is often associated with Descartes. We leave open the question whether Descartes himself unambiguously advocated such a thesis.

8. Ned Block, "On a Confusion About a Function of Consciousness."

9. Nagel, "What Is It Like to Be a Bat?," p. 437 (emphasis added).

10. Thomas Nagel, "Subjective and Objective," p. 201 (emphasis added).

11. See, for example, Roderick M. Chisholm, *The First Person*, ch. 3, and Hector-Neri Castaneda, "On the Phenomeno-Logic of the I."

12. David Armstrong, "The Nature of Mind," p. 198.

13. David Rosenthal, "The Independence of Consciousness and Sensory Quality," p. 31. See also Rosenthal, "Explaining Consciousness."

14. For an argument, see Donald Davidson, "Rational Animals."

15. David Chalmers makes this point in *The Conscious Mind*.

16. The term "explanatory gap" was introduced by Joseph Levine in his "Materialism and Qualia: The Explanatory Gap."

17. William James, *The Principles of Psychology*, p. 647 in the 1981 reprint edition.

18. T. H. Huxley, *Lessons in Elementary Physiology*, p. 202.

19. David Chalmers, *The Conscious Mind*, p. 24.

20. See Gilbert Harman, "The Intrinsic Quality of Experience," and Michael Tye, *Ten Problems of Consciousness*, pp. 30–31 (on the "problem of transparency").

21. Fred Dretske, *Naturalizing the Mind*, p. 83.

22. Can there be an internalist form of representationalism? The answer is not clear. For discussion, see Ned Block, "Mental Paint."

23. If you think interpersonal spectrum inversion makes no sense, we can imagine spectrum inversion in the same person over time. See Sydney Shoemaker, "Inverted Spectrum." See also Martine Nida-Rümelin, "Pseudo-Normal Vision: An Actual Case of Qualia Inversion?"

24. There is yet another sense of "appear" meaning "make an appearance," as in, "Following the senator's speech, the president and the first lady appeared on the stage." Obviously, we need not be concerned with this sense of "appear."

25. Saul Kripke, *Naming and Necessity*, pp. 153–154. The target of Kripke's argument is the identification of pain with C-fiber stimulation; however, his argument applies with equal force against the supervenience of pain on C-fiber stimulation.

26. This is based on Ned Block's "Inverted Earth."

27. Arthur Rimbaud, "Voyelles."

28. For complexities and complications in the supposition of inverted spectra, see C. L. Hardin, *Color for Philosophers*. See also Sydney Shoemaker, "Absent Qualia Are Impossible: A Reply to Block" and "The Inverted Spectrum"; and Michael Tye, "Qualia, Content, and the Inverted Spectrum."

29. This point is discussed in connection with functionalism; see chapter 5.

30. It is consistent to hold the supervenience of qualia on physical properties but deny their supervenience on functional properties. We might, for example, hold that qualia arise out of biological processes and that an electromechanical system (say, a robot) that is functionally indistinguishable from us can be without consciousness. John Searle, in *The Rediscovery of the Mind*, appears to hold a view of this kind.

31. There has been an active and wide-ranging debate over the relationship between conceivability and real possibility. The collection *Conceivability and Possibility*, edited by Tamar Szabo Gendler and John Hawthorne, includes a number of interesting papers on the topic (including a comprehensive introduction).

32. For further discussion, see chapters 7 and 10; see also Terence Horgan, "Supervenient Qualia," for a causal argument for qualia supervenience.

33. Assume that this holds true even when the positions of green, yellow, and red lights are randomized. (I understand that color-blind people use the relative positions of these lights as cues.)

34. For arguments along these lines, see Daniel C. Dennett, "Quining Qualia." See also Paul Churchland's arguments in "Eliminative Materialism and the Propositional Attitudes." Even though Churchland's target is intentional mental states, not qualia, some may be willing to apply the same lines of consideration against qualia.

35. Who call the believers in qualia "qualia-freaks."

36. Ludwig Wittgenstein, *Philosophical Investigations*, section 293.

37. This anecdote is taken from Ned Block, who uses it to make the same point in his "Troubles with Functionalism."

9

Mental Content

You hope that it will be warmer tomorrow, and I believe that it will. But Mary doubts it and hopes that she is right. Here we have various "intentional" (or "content-bearing" or "content-carrying") states: your *hoping* that it will be warmer tomorrow, my *believing*, and Mary's *doubting*, that it will be so. All of these states, though they are states of different persons and involve different *attitudes* (believing, hoping, and doubting), have the same *content*: the proposition that it will be warmer tomorrow, expressed by the embedded sentence "it will be warmer tomorrow." This content *represents* a certain state of affairs, its being warmer tomorrow. Different subjects can adopt the same intentional attitude toward it, and the same subject can have different attitudes toward it (for example, you believe it and are pleased about it; later you come to disbelieve it). But in virtue of what do these intentional states, or propositional attitudes, have the content they have and represent the state of affairs they represent? More specifically, what makes it the case that your hope and my belief have the same content? There is a simple, and not wholly uninformative, answer: because they each have the content expressed by the same content sentence "it will be warmer tomorrow." But then the substantive question is this: What is it about your hope and my belief that makes it the case that the same sentence can capture their content? We do not expect it to be a brute fact about these mental states that they have the content they have or that they share the same content; there must be an explanation. These are the basic questions about mental content.

The questions can be raised another way. It is not just persons who have mental states with content. All sorts of animals perceive their surroundings through their sensory systems, process information gained thereby, and use it in coping with things and events around them. We humans do this in our own distinctive ways, though perhaps not in ways that are fundamentally different from those of other higher species of animals. It seems, then, that certain physical-biological states of organisms, presumably states of their brains or nervous systems, can carry information about their surroundings, representing them as being this way or that way (for example, here is a red apple, or a large, brown, bear-shaped hulk is approaching me from the left), and that processing and using these representations in appropriate ways is highly important to them in surviving and flourishing in their environments. These physical-biological states have representational content—they are *about* things, inside or outside an organism, and *represent them as being such and such*. In a word, these states have *meanings*: A neural state that represents a bear as approaching *means* that a bear is approaching. But how do neural-physical states come to have meanings—and come to have the particular meanings that they have? Just what is it about a configuration of nerve fibers or a pattern of their activation that makes it carry the content "there is a red apple on the table" rather than, say, "there are cows in Canada," or perhaps nothing at all?

This question about the nature of mental content has a companion question, a question about how contents are *attributed* to the mental states of persons and other intentional systems. We routinely ascribe states with content to persons, animals, and even some nonbiological systems. If we had no such practice—if we were to stop attributing to our fellow human beings beliefs, desires, emotions, and the like—our communal life would surely suffer a massive collapse. There would be little understanding or anticipating of what other people will do, and this would severely undermine interpersonal transactions. Moreover, it is by attributing these states to ourselves that we come to understand ourselves as cognizers and agents. A capacity for self-attribution of beliefs, desires, intentions, and the rest is arguably a precondition of personhood. Moreover, we often attribute such states to nonhuman animals and sometimes even to purely mechanical or electronic systems. (Even such humble mechanisms as supermarket doors are said to "see that a customer is approaching.") What makes it possible for us to attribute content-carrying states to persons and other organisms? What procedures and principles do we follow when we do this? According to some philosophers, the two questions, one about the nature of mental content and the other about its attribution, are intimately connected.

Interpretation Theory

Suppose you are a field anthropologist-linguist visiting a tribe of people never before visited by an outsider. Your job is to find out what these people believe, remember, desire, fear, hope, and so on, and to be able to understand their speech. That is, your project is to map their "mental world" and develop a grammar and dictionary for their language. So your job involves two tasks: interpreting their minds, to find out what they believe, desire, and so on; and interpreting their speech, to determine what their utterances mean. This is the project of "radical interpretation"· You are to construct an interpretation of the natives' speech and their minds from scratch, on the basis of your observation of their behavior and their environment, without the aid of a native translator-informant or a dictionary. (This is what makes it "radical" interpretation.)[1]

Brief reflection shows that the twin tasks are interconnected and interdependent. In particular, belief, among all mental states, can be seen to hold the key to radical interpretation: It is the crucial link between a speaker's utterances and their meanings. If a native speaker sincerely asserts sentence S (or more broadly, "holds S true," in Davidson's terminology) and S means that there goes a rabbit, then the speaker believes that there goes a rabbit, and in asserting S she expresses her belief that there goes a rabbit. Conversely, if the speaker believes that there goes a rabbit and uses sentence S to express this belief, S means that there goes a rabbit. If you knew how to interpret the native's speech, it would be relatively easy to find out what she believes by observing her speech behavior. (All you need to know is what sentences she holds true.) If you had knowledge of what belief she is expressing by uttering S on a given occasion, you know what S, as part of her language, means. When you begin, you have knowledge of neither her beliefs nor her meanings, and your project is to secure them both through your observation of how she behaves in the context of her environment. There are, then, three variables involved: behavior, belief, and meaning. One of the three, behavior, is accessible to you, since you can observe it, and you have to solve for the two unknown variables, belief and meaning. Where do you start?

Suppose you find that Karl, one of your subjects, affirmatively utters, or holds true,[2] the sentence "Es regnet" when, and only when, it is raining in his vicinity. (This is highly idealized, but the main point should apply, with suitable provisos, to real-life situations.) You observe a similar behavior pattern in many others in Karl's speech community, and you project the following hypothesis:

(R) Speakers of language L (that is, Karl's language) utter "Es regnet" at time *t* if and only if it is raining at *t* in their vicinity.

So we are taking (R) to be something we can empirically establish by observing the behavior, in particular, speech behavior, of our subjects in the context of what is happening in their environment. Assuming, then, that we have (R) in hand, it would be natural to entertain the following two hypotheses:

(S) In language L, "Es regnet" means that it is raining (in the speaker's vicinity).

(M) When speakers of L utter (or are disposed to utter) "Es regnet," this indicates that they believe that it is raining (in their vicinity) and they use "Es regnet" to express this belief.

In this way you get your first toehold in the language and minds of the natives, and something like this seems like the only way.

These hypotheses, (S) and (M), are natural and plausible. But what makes them so? What sanctions the inferential move from (R) to (S) and (M)? When you observe Karl uttering the words "Es regnet," you see yourself that it is raining out there (that is how you confirm [R]). You have determined observationally that Karl is expressing a belief about the current condition of the weather. This assumption is reinforced when you observe him, and others in his speech community, do this time after time. But what belief is Karl expressing when he makes this utterance? What is the content of the belief that Karl expresses when he affirms "Es regnet"? Answering this question is the crux of our interpretive project. The obvious answer seems to be that Karl's belief has the content "it is raining." But why? Why not the belief with the content "it is a sunny day" or "it is snowing"? What are the tacit principles that help to rule out these possibilities?

You attribute the content "it is raining" to Karl's belief *because you assume that his belief is true*. You know that his belief is about the weather outside, and you see that it is raining. What you need, and all you need, to get to the conclusion that his belief has the content "it is raining" is the further premise that his belief is true. In general, then, the following principle gives you what you need:

Principle of Charity. Speakers' beliefs are by and large true. (Moreover, they are largely correct in making inferences and rational in forming expectations and making decisions.[3])

With this principle in hand, we can make sense of the transition from (R) to (S) and (M) in the following way:

In uttering "Es regnet," Karl is expressing a belief about the current weather condition in his vicinity, and we may assume, by the charity principle, that this belief is true. The current weather condition is that it is raining. So Karl's belief has the content that it is raining, and he is using the sentence "Es regnet" to express this belief (M), whence it further follows that "Es regnet" means that it is raining (S).

We do not attribute the content "it is not raining" or "it is snowing" because that would make Karl's and his friends' beliefs about whether or not it is raining around them almost invariably false. That is a bare logical possibility; there is no logical contradiction in the idea that a group of speakers are almost always wrong about rains in their vicinity, but it is not something that can be taken seriously. Such possibilities must be excluded if we are to have any chance at constructing a workable interpretive scheme.

Clearly, the same points apply to interpreting utterances about colors, shapes, and other observable properties of middle-sized things around Karl. When Karl and his friends invariably respond with "Rot" when we show them cherries, ripe tomatoes, and McIntosh apples and withhold it when they are shown lemons, eggplants, and snowballs, it would make no sense to speculate that "rot" might mean *green*, that Karl and his friends systematically misperceive colors, and that in consequence they have massively erroneous beliefs about the colors of objects around them. The only plausible thing to say is that "rot" means *red* in Karl's language and that Karl is expressing the (true) belief that the apple held in front of him is red. All this is not to say that our speakers never have false beliefs about colors or about anything else; they may have them in huge numbers. But unless we assume that their beliefs, especially those about the manifestly observable properties of things and events around them, are largely correct, we have no hope of gaining entry into their cognitive world.

So what happens is that we interpret the speakers in such a way as to credit them with beliefs that are by and large true and coherent. But since *we* are doing the interpreting, this in effect means *true and coherent by our light.* Under our interpretation, therefore, our subjects come out with *beliefs that are largely in agreement with our own.* The attribution of a system of beliefs and other intentional states is essential to the understanding of other people, of what they say and do. From all this an interesting conclusion follows: We can interpret and understand only those people whose belief systems are largely like our own.

The charity principle therefore rules out, a priori, interpretations that attribute to our subjects beliefs that are mostly false or incoherent; any interpretive scheme according to which our subjects' beliefs are massively false or manifestly inconsistent (for example, they come out believing that there are round squares) cannot, for that very reason, be a correct interpretation. Further, we can think of a generalized charity principle that enjoins us to interpret all of our subjects' intentional states, including desires, aversions, intentions, and the rest, in a way that renders them maximally coherent among themselves and enables us to make the best sense of their observed behavior. In any case, we should note the following important point: There is no reason to think that in any interpretive project there is a single unique interpretation that best meets this requirement. This is evident when we reflect on the fact that the charity principle requires only that the entire *system* of beliefs attributed to a subject be by and large true but it does not tell us which ones of her beliefs must come out true. In practice as well as in theory, there are likely to be ties, or indeterminate and unstable near-ties, among possible interpretations: That is, we are likely to end up with more than one maximally true, coherent, and rational scheme of interpretation that can explain all the observational data. (This phenomenon is called "indeterminacy of interpretation.") We can see that this is almost certainly the case when we note the fact that our criteria of coherence and rationality are bound to be somewhat vague and imprecise (in fact, this may be necessary to ensure their flexible application to a wide and unpredictable range of situations) and that their applications to specific situations are likely to be fraught with ambiguities. At any rate, it is easy to see how interpretational indeterminacy can arise by considering a simple example.

We see Karl eating raw spinach leaves. Why is he doing that? We can see that there are indefinitely many belief-desire pairs that we could attribute to Karl that would explain why he is doing what he is doing. For example:

Karl believes that eating raw spinach will improve his stamina, and he very much wants to improve his stamina.

Karl believes that eating raw spinach will help him get rid of his bad breath, and he has been very self-conscious about his bad breath.

Karl believes that eating raw spinach will please his mother, and he will do anything to make her happy.

Karl believes that eating raw spinach will annoy his mother, and he will go to any length to annoy her.

You get the idea: This can go on without end. We can expect many of these potential explanations to be excluded by further observation of Karl's behavior and by consideration of coherence with other beliefs and desires that we want to attribute to him. But it is difficult to imagine that this will eliminate all but one of the indefinitely many possible belief-desire pairs that can explain Karl's spinach eating. Moreover, it is likely that any one of these pairs could be protected no matter what if we were willing to make drastic enough adjustments elsewhere in Karl's total system of beliefs, desires, and other mental states.

Suppose, then, that there are two interpretive schemes of Karl's mental states that, as far as we can determine, satisfy the charity principle to the same degree and work equally well in explaining his behavior. Suppose further that one of these systems attributes to Karl the belief that eating raw spinach is good for one's stamina, and the second instead attributes to him the belief that eating spinach will please his mother. As far as interpretation theory goes, the schemes are tied, and neither could be pronounced to be superior to the other. But what is the fact of the matter concerning Karl's belief system? Does he or doesn't he believe that eating raw spinach improves stamina?

There are two possible approaches we could take in response to these questions. The first is to take interpretation as the rock-bottom foundation of content-carrying mental states by embracing a principle perhaps like this:

For S to have the belief that p is for the belief that p to be part of the best (most coherent, maximally true, and so on) interpretive scheme of S's total system of propositional attitudes (including beliefs, desires, and the rest). There is no further fact of the matter about whether or not S believes that p.

It will be natural to generalize this principle so that it applies to all propositional attitudes, not just beliefs. On this principle, then, interpretation is *constitutive* of intentionality; it is what ultimately determines whether any supposed belief exists.[4] Interpretation is not merely an epistemological procedure for finding out what Karl believes. This constitutive view of interpretation, when combined with the indeterminacy of interpretation, can be seen to lead to apparent problems. Suppose that several interpretive schemes are tied for first and the belief that *p* is an element of some but not all of these schemes. In such a case we would have to conclude that there is no fact of the matter about whether or not Karl has this belief. Whether Karl believes that *p* therefore is a question without a determinate answer. To be sure, the question about this particular bit of belief may be settled by further observation of Karl; however, indeterminacies are almost certain to remain even when all the observations are in. (Surely, at some point after Karl's death, there is nothing further to observe that will be relevant!) Some will see in this kind of position a form of *content irrealism*. If beliefs are among the objectively existing entities of the world, either Karl believes that raw spinach is good for his stamina or he does not. There must be a fact about the existence of this belief, independent of any interpretive scheme that someone might construct for Karl. So if the existence of beliefs is genuinely indeterminate, we would have to conclude, it seems, that beliefs are not part of objective reality. Evidently, the same conclusion would apply to all intentional states.[5]

An alternative line of consideration can lead to *content relativism* rather than content irrealism: Instead of accepting the indeterminacy of belief, we might hold that whether or not a given belief exists is *relative to a scheme of interpretation*. It is not a question that can be answered absolutely, independently of a choice of an interpretive scheme. Whether or not Karl has that particular belief depends on the interpretive theory relative to which we view Karl's belief system. But a relativism of this kind creates a host of difficult and puzzling metaphysical questions. What is it for a belief to "exist relative to a scheme" to begin with? Is it anything more than "the scheme attributes the belief to Karl"? If so, shouldn't we ask the further question whether what the scheme says is *correct*? But this takes us right back to the nonrelativized notion of belief existence. Moreover, is all existence relative to some scheme or other, or is it just the existence of belief and other propositional attitudes that is relative in this way? Either way, many further questions and puzzles await us.

There is a further point to consider: Interpretation involves an interpreter, and the interpreter herself is an intentional system, a person with beliefs, desires, and so forth. How do we account for *her* beliefs and desires—*how do her intentional states get their contents*? And when she tries to maximize agreement between her beliefs and her subject's beliefs, how does she know what she believes? That is, *how is self-interpretation possible*? Don't we need an account of how we can know the contents of our own beliefs and desires? Do we just look inward, and are they just there for us to see? It is clear that the interpretation approach to mental content must, on pain of circularity, confront the issue of self-interpretation.

All this may lead you to reject the constitutive view of interpretation and pull you toward a realist position about intentional states, which insists that there is a fact of the matter about the existence of Karl's belief about spinach that is independent of any interpretive schemes. If Karl is a real and genuine intentional system, there must be a determinate answer to the question whether or not he has this belief; whether or not someone is interpreting Karl, or what any interpretive scheme says about Karl's belief system, should be entirely irrelevant to that question. This is content realism, a position that views interpretation only as a way of finding out something about Karl's belief system, not as constitutive of it. Interpretation therefore is given only an epistemological function, that of ascertaining what intentional states a given subject has; it does not have the ontological role of grounding their existence.

You may find content realism appealing. If so, there is more work to do; you must provide an alternative realist account of what constitutes the content of intentional states—what it is about a belief that gives it the content it has. It is only if you take the constitutive view of interpretation that interpretation theory gives you a solution to the problem of mental content—that is, an answer to the question "How does a belief get to have the content it has?"

The Causal-Correlational Approach: Informational Semantics

A fly flits across a frog's visual field, and the frog's tongue darts out, snaring the fly. The content of the frog's visual perception is a moving fly (which is only a complicated way of saying that the frog sees a fly). Or so we would say. Suppose now that in a world pretty much like our own (this could be some remote region of this world) frogs that are like our frogs exist but there are no flies. Instead there are "schmies," very small reptiles roughly the size, shape, and color of earthly flies, and they fly around just the way our flies do and are found in the kind of habitat that our flies inhabit. In that world frogs feed on schmies, not flies. Now, in this other world, a schmy flits across a frog's visual field, and the frog flicks out its tongue and catches it. What is the content of this frog's visual perception? What does the frog's visual percept represent? The answer: a moving schmy.

From the frogs' "internal" perspectives, there is no difference, we may suppose, between our frog's perceptual state and the other-worldly frog's perceptual state: Both register a black speck flitting across the visual field. However, we attribute different contents to them, and the difference here lies outside the frogs' perceptual systems; it is a difference in the kind of object that stands in a certain relationship to the perceptual states of the frogs. It is not only that in these particular instances a fly caused the perceptual state of our frog and a schmy caused a corresponding state in the other-worldly frog; there is also a more general fact, namely, that the habitat of earthly frogs includes flies, not schmies, and it is flies, not schmies, with which they are in daily perceptual and other causal contact. The converse is the case with other-worldly frogs and schmies. Our frogs' perceptual episodes involving a flitting black speck *indicate*, or *mean*, the presence of a fly; similar perceptual episodes in other-worldly frogs *indicate* the presence of a schmy. (Think about how we should describe the situation if in this world there were both flies and schmies, in roughly equal proportions, and our frogs fed on them indiscriminately.)

Consider a mercury thermometer: The height of the column of mercury indicates, and carries information about, the ambient temperature. When the thermometer registers 32°C, we can say, "The thermometer says that the temperature is 32°C"; we may even say that the state of the thermometer has the content "32°C." Why? Because there is a lawful correlation between the height of the mercury and the outside temperature. It is for that reason that the device is a thermometer, something that carries *information* about ambient temperature.

Suppose that under normal conditions a certain state of an organism covaries regularly and reliably with the presence of a horse. That is, this state occurs in you when, and only when, a horse is present in your vicinity (and you are awake and alert, sufficient illumination is present, you are appropriately oriented in relation to the horse, and so on). The occurrence of this state, then, can serve as an *indicator*[6] of the presence of a horse; it carries the information "horse" (or "a horse is out there"). And it seems appropriate to say that this state, which covaries with the presence of horses, *represents* the presence of a horse and has it as its content. The suggestion is that something like this account works for intentional content in general, and this is the causal-correlational approach. (The term "causal" is used because on some accounts making use of this approach, the presence of horses is supposed to cause the internal "horse-indicator" state.) This approach seems to work well with contents of perceptual states, as we just saw in the fly-schmy case. I perceive red, and my perceptual state has "red" as its content because I am having the kind of perceptual experience typically correlated with—in fact, caused by—the presence of a red object. Whether I perceive red or green has little to do with the intrinsic qualities of my internal states; rather, it depends essentially on the properties of the objects with which I am in causal-correlational relations. Those internal states that are typically caused by red objects, or that lawfully correlate with the presence of red objects nearby, have the content "red" for that very reason, not because of any of their intrinsic properties. Two thermometers of very different construction—say, a mercury thermometer and a gas thermometer—both represent the temperature to be 30°C in spite of the fact that the internal states of the two thermometers that covary with temperature—the height of a column of mercury in the first and the pressure of a gas in the second—are different. In a similar way, two intentional systems, one biological and the other electromechanical, can share the belief that it is getting warmer outside. The causal-correlational approach to content, also called informational semantics, has been very influential; it explains mental content in a naturalistic way and seems considerably simpler than the interpretational approach considered earlier.

How well does this approach work with intentional states in general? We may consider a simple version of this approach, perhaps something like this:[7]

(C) Subject S has the belief with content p (that is, S believes that p) just in case, under optimal conditions, S has this belief if and only if p obtains.

And we can state a more generic version:

(C*) A representation of kind R represents S (or R has S as its content) if and only if whenever (and only whenever) R is instantiated (or "tokened") S is instantiated.

To make (C) at all viable, we should restrict it to cases of "observational beliefs"—beliefs about matters that are perceptually observable to S. For (C) is obviously implausible when applied to beliefs like the belief that God exists or that light travels at a finite velocity and beliefs about abstract matters (say, the belief that there is no largest prime number). It is much more plausible for observational beliefs like the belief that there are red flowers on my desk or that there are horses in the field. The proviso "under optimal conditions" is included since for the state of affairs p (for example, the presence of horses) to correlate with, or cause, subject S's belief that p, favorable perceptual conditions must obtain, such as that S's visual organs are functioning properly, the illumination is adequate, S's attention is not seriously distracted, and so on. Similar comments apply to (C*).

Although there seem to be some serious difficulties that (C) has to overcome, remember that (C) is only a rough-and-ready first pass, and none of the objections to be enumerated here need be taken as a disabling blow to the general approach.

1. The belief that there are horses in the field correlates reliably, let us suppose, with the presence of horses in the field. But it also correlates reliably with the presence of horse genes in the field (since the latter correlate reliably with the presence of horses). According to (C), someone observing horses in the field should have the belief that there are horse genes in the field. But this surely is wrong. Moreover, the belief that there are horses in the field also correlates with the array of light rays, reflected by the horses, traveling from the field to the observer, but again, the observer does not have the belief that these light rays are traveling toward him. The general problem, then, is that an account like (C) cannot differentiate between belief with p as its content and belief with q as its content if p and q reliably correlate with each other. For any two correlated states of affairs p and q, (C) entails that one believes that p if and only if one believes that q, which seems prima facie incorrect.

2. Someone is looking at the horses in the field. Does she have the belief that there are horses in the field? Not necessarily, for it may be that her ontology does not include whole objects like horses but only things like undetached horse parts, time-slices of horses, and the like. If so, the content of her belief is not that there are horses in the field but that there are (undetached) horse parts in the field.

3. Belief is *holistic* in the sense that what you believe is shaped, often crucially, by what else you believe. When you observe horselike shapes in the field, you are not likely to believe that there are horses in the field if you have read in the papers that many cardboard horses have

been put up there for a children's fair, or if you believe you are hallucinating, and so on. Correlational accounts make beliefs basically atomistic, at least for observational beliefs, but even our observational beliefs are constrained by other beliefs we hold, and the correlational approach needs to be made much more complex and elaborate to take this aspect of belief content into account.

4. The belief that there are horses in the field is caused not only by horses in the field but also by cows and moose at dusk, cardboard horses at a distance, robot horses, and so on. In fact, this belief correlates more reliably with the disjunction "horses or cows and moose at dusk or cardboard horses or. . . ." If so, why should we not say that when you are looking at the horses in the field, your belief has the *disjunctive* content "there are horses *or* cows *or* moose at dusk *or* cardboard horses *or* robot horses in the field"? This so-called disjunction problem has turned out to be a recalcitrant difficulty for the causal-correlational approach; it has been actively discussed, but no solution that is likely to command a consensus is in sight.[8]

5. We seem to have direct and immediate knowledge of what we believe, desire, and so on. I know, directly and without having to depend on evidence, that I believe it will rain tomorrow. That is, I seem to have direct knowledge of the content of my beliefs. There may be exceptions, but that does not overturn the general point. According to the correlational approach, my belief that there are horses in the field has the content it has because it correlates, or co-varies, with the presence of horses in my vicinity. But this correlation is not something that I know directly, without evidence or observation. So the correlational approach appears inconsistent with the special privileged status of our knowledge of the contents of our own mental states. (We discuss this issue further later, in connection with content externalism.)

These are some of the initial difficulties that face the correlational approach; whether, or to what extent, these difficulties can be overcome without compromising the naturalistic-reductive spirit of the correlational approach remains an open question. Quite possibly, most of the difficulties are not really serious and can be resolved by further elaborations and supplementations. It may well be that this approach is the most promising one—in fact, the only viable one that promises to give a non-question-begging, naturalistic account of mental content.

Misrepresentation and the Teleological Approach

One important fact about representation is the possibility of *misrepresentation*. Misrepresentation does occur; you, or a mental-neural state of yours, may represent that there are horses in the field when there are no horses in sight. Or your perception may represent a red tomato in front of you when there is none (think about Macbeth and his bloody dagger). In such cases, misrepresentation occurs: The representational state misrepresents, and the representation is false. Representations have contents, and contents are "evaluable" in respect of truth, veracity, fidelity, and related criteria of representational "success." It seems clear, then, that any account of representation must allow for the possibility of misrepresentation as well of course as correct, or successful, representation, just as any account of belief must allow for the possibility of false belief. One way of seeing how this could be a problem with the correlational approach is to go back to the disjunction problem discussed earlier. Suppose you form a representation with the content "there are horses over there" when there are no horses but only cows seen in the dusk. In such a case it would be natural to regard your purported representation as a misrepresentation—namely, as an instance of your representing something that does not exist, or representing something to be such and such when it is not such and such. But if we follow (C), or (C*), literally, this seems impossible. If your representation was occasioned by cows seen in the dusk as well as horses, we would have to say that the representation has the content "horses or cows seen in the dusk" and that as such the representation is "correct" or "veridical." It would seem that (C) does not allow false beliefs or misrepresentations. But there surely are cases of misrepresentation; our cognitive systems are liable to produce false representations, even though they may be generally reliable.

This is where the teleological approach comes in to help out.[9] The basic concept employed in the teleological approach is that of a "function." For representation R to indicate (and thus represent) C, it is neither sufficient—nor necessary—that "whenever R occurs C occurs" holds. Rather, what must hold is that R has the *function* of indicating C—to put it more intuitively, R *is supposed* to indicate C and it is R's *job* to indicate C. Your representation has the content "there are horses over there" and not "there are horses or cows in the dusk over there" because it has the function of indicating the presence of horses, not horses or cows in the dusk. But things can go wrong, and systems do not always perform as they are supposed to. You form a representation of horses in the absence of horses; such a representation is *supposed* to be formed only when horses are present. That is exactly what makes it a case of misrepresentation. So it seems that the correlational-causal approach suitably supplemented with reference to function could solve the problem of misrepresentation.

But how does a state of a person or organism come to have this kind of "function"? It is easy enough to understand function talk in connection with artifacts because we can invoke the purposes and intentions of their designers and users. A thermometer registers 100°C, when the temperature is 80°C. So the reading of the thermometer misrepresents the temperature, because that reading is supposed to—it is its job to—represent 100°C. That is the way the thermometer was designed to work and the way we expect it to work. It is the purposes and expectations external to the thermometer that give sense to the talk of functions. But this is precisely something that we cannot say about representations of natural systems, like us and higher animals. What gives a mental state (or a neural state) the function of representing some particular object or state of affairs? What gives a representation the job of representing "horses" rather than "horses or cows in the dusk"?

Most philosophers who take the teleological approach attempt to explain function in terms of evolution and natural selection. To say that representation R has the function of indicating C is to say that R has been selected, in the course of the evolution of the species to which the organism belongs, for the job of indicating C. This is like the fact that the heart has the function of pumping blood, or that the pineal gland has the function of secreting the hormone melatonin, because these organs have been evolutionarily selected for their performance of these tasks. Proper performance of these tasks presumably conferred adaptive advantages to our ancestors. Similarly, we may presume that if R's function is to indicate C, performance of this job has given our ancestors biological advantages and, as some philosophers put it, R has been "recruited" by the evolutionary process to perform this function.

However, exactly how the notion of function is to be explained is a further question that appears relatively independent of the core idea of the teleological approach. There are various and diverse biological-evolutionary accounts of function in the literature (see "Further Readings" at the end of this chapter). Even if the theory of evolution were false and all biological organisms, including us, were created by God (so that we were God's "artifacts"), something like the teleological approach could still be right. It is God who gave our representations the indicating functions they have. But almost all contemporary philosophers of mind and of biology are naturalists, and it is important to them that function talk does not need to involve references to supernatural or transcendental plans, purposes, or designs. That is why they appeal to biology, or to learning and adaptation, and evolution for an account of function. But the overall plausibility of the teleological approach should be evaluable independently of particular explications of the concept of function.

Narrow Content and Wide Content: Content Externalism

One thing that the correlational account of mental content highlights is this: Content has a lot to do with what is going on in the world, outside the physical boundaries of the subject. As far as what goes on inside is concerned, the frog in our world and the other-worldly frog are indistinguishable—they are in the same neural-sensory state, both registering a moving black dot. But in describing the representational content of their states, or what they "see," we advert to the conditions in the environments of the frogs: One frog sees a fly and the other sees a schmy. Or consider a simpler case: Peter is looking at a tomato, and Mary is also looking at one (a different tomato, but we suppose that it looks pretty much the same as the one Peter is looking at). Mary thinks to herself, "This tomato has gone bad," and Peter too thinks, "This tomato has gone bad." From the internal point of view, Mary's perceptual experience is indistinguishable from Peter's (we may suppose their neural states too are relevantly similar), and they would express their thoughts using the same words. But it is clear that the contents of their beliefs are different. For they involve different objects: Mary's belief is about the tomato she is looking at, and Peter's belief is about a different object altogether. Moreover, Mary's belief may be true and Peter's false, or vice versa. On the standard understanding of the notion of "content," beliefs with the same content must be true together or false together (that is, contents are "truth conditions"). Obviously, the fact that Peter's and Mary's beliefs have different content is due to facts external to them; the difference in content cannot be explained in terms of what is going on inside the perceivers. It seems, then, that at least in this and other similar cases belief contents are differentiated, or "individuated," by reference to conditions external to the believer.

Beliefs whose content is individuated in this way are said to have "wide" or "broad" content. In contrast, beliefs whose content is individuated solely on the basis of what goes on inside the persons holding them are said to have "narrow" content. Alternatively, we may say that the content of an intentional state is narrow just in case it supervenes on the internal-intrinsic properties of the subject who is in that state, and that it is wide otherwise. This means that two individuals who are exactly alike in all intrinsic-internal respects must have the same narrow content beliefs but may well diverge in their wide content beliefs. Thus, our two frogs are exactly alike in internal-intrinsic respects but unlike in what their perceptual states represent. So the contents of these states do not supervene internally and are therefore wide.

Several well-known thought-experiments have been instrumental in persuading most philosophers that most, perhaps all, of our ordinary beliefs (and other intentional states) have wide content, that the beliefs and desires we hold are not simply a matter of what is going on inside our minds or heads. This is the doctrine of *content externalism*. Among these thought-experiments, the following two, the first due to Hilary Putnam and the second to Tyler Burge,[10] have been particularly influential.

Thought-Experiment 1: Earth and Twin Earth

Imagine a planet, "Twin Earth," somewhere in the remote region of space, which is just like the earth we inhabit, except in one respect: On Twin Earth, a certain chemical substance with the molecular structure XYZ, which has all the observable characteristics of water (it is transparent, dissolves salt and sugar, quenches thirst, puts out fire, freezes at $0°C$, and so on), replaces water everywhere. So lakes and oceans on Twin Earth are filled with XYZ, not H_2O (that is, water), and Twin Earth people drink XYZ when they are thirsty, bathe and swim in XYZ, do their laundry in XYZ, and so on. Some Twin Earth people speak English, which is indistinguishable from our English, and their use of the expression "water" is indistinguishable from its use on Earth.

But there is a difference: The Twin Earth "water" and our "water" refer to different things. (They have different "extensions," as logicians say). When a Twin Earth inhabitant says, "Water is transparent," what she means to say is that XYZ is transparent. When you utter the same words, what you mean is that water is transparent. "Water" from a Twin Earth mouth means XYZ, not water, and the same word as spoken by you means water, not XYZ. If you are the first visitor to Twin Earth and find out the truth about their "water," you may report back to your friends on Earth as follows: "At first I thought that the stuff that fills the oceans and lakes around here, and the stuff people here drink and bathe in, was water, and it really looks and tastes just like our water. But I just found out that it isn't water at all, although people around here call it 'water.' It's really XYZ, not water." You will not translate the Twin Earth word "water" into the English word "water"; you will need to invent a new word, perhaps "twater." There is a robust sense of meaning, then, in which the Twin Earth "water" and our "water" have different meanings, although what goes on inside the minds, or heads, of Twin Earth people may be exactly the same as what goes in ours, and their speech behavior involving their word "water" is indistinguishable from ours with our word "water." This semantic difference between our "water" and Twin Earth "water" is reflected in the way we describe and individuate mental states of people on Earth and people on Twin Earth. When a Twin Earth person says to the waiter, "Please bring me a glass of water!" she is expressing her desire for twater, and we will report, in *oratio obliqua*, that she wants some twater, not that she wants some water. When you say the same thing, you are expressing a desire for water, and we will say that you want water. You believe that water is wet, and your Twin Earth doppelganger believes that twater is wet. And so on. To summarize, then, people on Earth have water-thoughts and water-desires, whereas Twin Earth people have twater-thoughts and twater-desires; this difference is due to differences in the environmental factors external to the subjects, not to any differences in what goes on "inside" them.

Suppose we send an astronaut, Jones, to Twin Earth. She does not realize at first that the liquid she sees in the lakes and coming out of the tap is not water. She is offered a glass of this transparent liquid by her Twin Earth host and thinks to herself, "That's a nice, cool glass of water—just what I needed." Consider Jones's belief that the glass contains cold water. This belief is false, since the glass contains not water but XYZ, or twater. Although she is now on Twin Earth, in an environment full of twater and devoid of water, she is still subject to the standards current on Earth: Her words mean, and her thoughts are individuated, in accordance with the criteria that prevail on Earth. What this shows is that a person's *past associations* with her environment play a role in determining her present meanings and thought contents. If Jones stays on Twin Earth long enough—say, a dozen years—we will likely interpret her word "water" to mean twater, not water, and attribute to her twater-thoughts rather than water-thoughts—that is, eventually she will come under the linguistic conventions and constraints of Twin Earth.

If these considerations are by and large correct, they show that two supervenience theses fail: First, the meanings of our expressions do not in general supervene on our *internal*, or *intrinsic*, physical-psychological states. I and my molecule-for-molecule-identical Twin Earth doppelganger are indistinguishable as far as our internal lives, both physical and mental, are concerned, and yet our words have different meanings—my "water" means water and his "water" means XYZ. Second, and this is what is of immediate interest to us, the contents of beliefs and other intentional states also fail to supervene on internal physical-psychological states. You have water-thoughts and your doppelganger has twater-thoughts. And there is strong reason for thinking that beliefs are individuated by content—that is, that we regard beliefs with the same content as the same belief, and beliefs with different content count as different. What beliefs you hold depends on your relationship, both past and present, to the things and events in your surroundings, as well as on what goes on inside you. The same goes for other content-bearing intentional states. If this is right, the thought-experiment establishes the existence of intentional states with wide content.

Thought-Experiment 2: Arthritis and "Tharthritis"

Consider a person, call him Peter, in two situations. (1) *The actual situation*: Peter thinks "arthritis" means inflammation of the bones. (It actually means inflammation of the bone joints.) Feeling pain and swelling in his thigh, Peter complains to his doctor, "I have arthritis in my thigh." His doctor tells him that people can have arthritis only in their joints. Two points should be noted: First, Peter believed, before he talked to his doctor, that he had arthritis in his thigh; and second, this belief was false.

(2) *A counterfactual situation*: Nothing has changed with our Peter. Experiencing swelling and pain in his thigh, he complains to his doctor, "I have arthritis in my thigh." What is different about the counterfactual situation concerns the use of the word "arthritis" in Peter's speech community: In the situation we are imagining, the word is used to refer to inflammation of bones, not just bone joints. That is, in the counterfactual situation Peter has a correct understanding of the word "arthritis," unlike in the actual situation. In the counterfactual situation, then, Peter is expressing a true belief when he utters "I have arthritis in my thigh." But how should we report Peter's belief concerning the condition of his thigh in the counterfactual situation—that is, report in *our* language (in this world)? We cannot say that Peter believes that he has arthritis in his thigh, because in our language "arthritis" means inflammation of joints and he clearly does not have that, making his counterfactual belief false. We might coin a new expression (to

be part of our language), "tharthritis," to mean inflammation of bones as well as of joints, and say that Peter, in the counterfactual situation, believes that he has tharthritis in his thigh. Again, note two points: First, in the counterfactual situation, Peter believes not that he has arthritis in his thigh but that he has tharthritis in his thigh; and second, this belief is true.

What this thought-experiment shows is that the content of belief depends, at least in part but crucially, on the speech practices of the linguistic community in which we situate the subject. Peter in the actual situation and Peter in the counterfactual situation are exactly alike when taken as an individual person (that is, when we consider his internal-intrinsic properties alone), including his speech habits (he speaks the same idiolect in both situations) and inner mental life. Yet he has different beliefs in the two situations: Peter in the actual world has the belief that he has arthritis in his thigh, which is false, but in the counterfactual situation he has the belief that he has tharthritis in his thigh, which is true. If this is right, beliefs and other intentional states do not supervene on the internal physical-psychological states of persons; if supervenience is wanted, we must also include in the supervenience base the linguistic practices of the community to which persons belong.

Burge argues plausibly that the example can be generalized to show that almost all contents are wide—that is, externally individuated. Take the word "brisket" (another of his examples): Some of us mistakenly think that brisket comes only from beef, and it is easy to see how a case analogous to the arthritis example can be set up. (The reader is invited to try it.) According to Burge, the same situation arises for any word whose meaning is incompletely understood—in fact, any word whose meaning *could* be incompletely understood, which includes pretty much every word. When we profess our beliefs using such words, our beliefs are identified and individuated by the socially determined meanings of these words (recall Peter and his "arthritis" in the actual situation), and a Burge-style counterfactual situation can be set up for each such word. Moreover, we seem to identify our own beliefs by reflecting on the words we would use to express them, even if we are aware that our understanding of these words is incomplete or even defective. (How many of us know the correct meaning of, say, "mortgage," "justice of the peace," or "galaxy"?) This shows, it has been argued, that almost all of our ordinary belief attributions involve wide content.

If this is right, the question naturally arises: Are there beliefs whose content is not determined by external factors? That is, are there beliefs with narrow content? There appear to be beliefs, and other intentional states, that do not imply the existence of anything, or do not refer to anything, outside the subject who has them. For example, Peter's belief that he is in pain or that he exists or that there are no unicorns does not require that anything other than Peter exist, and it would seem that the content of these beliefs is independent of conditions external to Peter. If so, the narrowness of these beliefs is not threatened by considerations of the sort that emerged from thought-experiment 1. But what of thought-experiment 2? Consider Peter's belief that he is in pain. Could we run on the word "pain" Burge's argument on "arthritis"? Surely it is possible for someone to misunderstand the word "pain" or any other sensation term. Suppose Peter thinks that "pain" applies to both pains and severe itches and that on experiencing a bad itch on his shoulder, he complains to his wife about an annoying "pain" in the shoulder. If the Burge-style considerations apply here, we have to say that Peter is expressing his belief that he is experiencing pain in his shoulder and that this is a false belief.

The question is whether that is indeed what we would, or should, say. It would not seem unreasonable that knowing what we know about Peter's misunderstanding of the word "pain" and the sensation he is actually experiencing, the correct thing to say is that he believes, and in fact knows, that he is experiencing itches on his shoulder. It is only that in saying, "I am having pains in my shoulder," he is misdescribing his sensation and hence misreporting his belief. Now, consider the following counterfactual situation: In the linguistic community to which Peter belongs, "pain" is in fact used to refer to pains and severe itches. How would we report, in our own words, the content of Peter's belief in the counterfactual situation when he utters "I have pains in my shoulder"? There are these possibilities: (i) We say "He believes that he is experiencing pains in his shoulder"; (ii) we say "He believes that he is experiencing severe itches in his shoulder"; and (iii) we do not have a word in English that can be used for expressing the content of his belief (but we could introduce a neologism, "painitch," and say "Peter believes that he is experiencing painitches in his shoulder"). Obviously, (i) has to be ruled out; if (iii) is what we should say, the arthritis argument applies to the present case as well, since this would show that a change in the social environment of the subject can change the belief content attributed to him. But it is not obvious that this, rather than (ii), is the correct option. It seems to be an open question, then, whether the arthritis argument applies to cases involving beliefs about one's own sensations, and there seems to be a reason for the inclination to say of Peter in the actual world that he believes he is having severe itches rather than that he believes he is having pains. The reason is that if we were to opt for the latter, it would make his belief false, and this is a belief about his own current sensations. But we assume that under normal circumstances people do not make mistakes in identifying their current sensory experiences. This assumption need not be taken as a contentious philosophical doctrine; arguably, recognition of first-person authority on such matters also reflects our common social-linguistic practices, and this may very well override the kinds of considerations advanced by Burge in the case of arthritis and the rest.

Another point to consider is beliefs of animals without speech. Do cats and dogs have beliefs and other intentional states whose contents can be reported in the form: "Fido believes that p," where p stands in for a declarative sentence? Clearly, the arthritis-style arguments cannot be applied to such beliefs since animals do not belong to any speech community and the only language that is involved is our own, namely, the language of the person who makes such belief attributions. In what sense, then, could animal beliefs be externally individuated? There may or may not be an obvious answer to this question. In any event, this example can cut both ways as far as Burge's argument is concerned, for we might argue, as some philosophers have,[11] that nonlinguistic animals are not capable of having intentional states (in particular, beliefs) and that this is connected with the inapplicability of the arthritis argument. This appears to have an interesting—and to some, implausible—implication: Only animals that use language for social communication are capable of having beliefs and other intentional states.

The Metaphysics of Wide Content States

Considerations involved in the two thought-experiments show that many, if not all, of our ordinary beliefs and other intentional states have wide content. Their contents are "external": They are determined, at least in part, by factors outside the subject—factors in her physical and social environment and in her history of interaction with it. Before these externalist considerations were brought to our attention, philosophers used to think that beliefs, desires, and the like are "in the mind," or at least "in the head." Putnam, the inventor of the Twin Earth parable, declared: "Cut the pie any way you like, 'meanings' just ain't in the head."[12] Should we believe that beliefs and desires are not in the head, or in the mind, either? If so, where are they? *Outside* the head? Let us consider some possibilities.

1. We might say that the belief that water and oil do not mix is constituted in part by water and oil—that the belief itself, in some sense, involves the actual stuff, water and oil, in addition to the person (or

her "head") having the belief. A similar response in the case of arthritis would be that Peter's belief that he has arthritis is in part constituted by his linguistic community. The general idea is that all the factors that play a role in the determination of the content of a belief *ontologically constitute* that belief; the belief is a state that comprises these items within itself. Thus, we have a simple explanation for just how your belief that water is wet differs from your Twin Earth doppelganger's belief that twater is wet: Yours includes water as a constituent, and hers includes twater as a constituent. On this approach, then, beliefs extrude from the subject's head into the world, and there are no bounds to how far they can reach. The whole universe would, on this approach, be a constituent of your beliefs about the universe! Moreover, all beliefs about the universe would appear to have exactly the same constituent, namely, the universe. This sounds absurd, and it is absurd. We can also see that this general approach would make causation of beliefs difficult to explain.

2. We might consider the belief that water and oil do not mix as a *relation* holding between the subject, on the one hand, and water and oil, on the other. Or alternatively, we take the belief as a *relational property* of the subject involving water and oil. (That Socrates is married to Xanthippe is a relational fact; Socrates also has the relational property of being married to Xanthippe, and conversely, Xanthippe has the relational property of being married to Socrates.) This approach makes causation of beliefs more tractable: We can ask, and will sometimes be able to answer, how a subject came to bear this belief relation to water and oil, just as we can ask how Xanthippe came to have the relational property of being married to Socrates. But what of other determinants of content? As we saw, belief content is determined in part by the history of one's interaction with one's environment. And what of the social-linguistic determinants, as in Burge's examples? It seems at least awkward to consider beliefs as relations with respect to these factors.

3. The third possibility is to consider beliefs to be wholly internal to the subjects who have them but consider their contents, when they are wide, as giving *relational specifications*, or *descriptions*, of these contents. On this view, beliefs may be neural states or other types of physical states of organisms to which they are attributed, and as

such they are "in" the believer's head, or mind. Contents, then, are construed as ways of specifying, or describing, the contents of these states; wide contents are thus specifications in terms that involve factors and conditions external to the subject, both physical and social, both current and historical. We can refer to, or pick out, Socrates by relational descriptions, that is, in terms of his relational properties—for example, "the husband of Xanthippe," "the Greek philosopher who drank hemlock," "Plato's mentor," and so on. But this does not mean that Xanthippe, hemlock, or Plato is a constituent part of Socrates, nor does it mean that Socrates is some kind of a "relational entity." Similarly, when we specify Jones's belief as the belief that water and oil do not mix, we are specifying this belief relationally, in terms of water and oil, but this does not mean that water and oil are constituents of the belief or that the belief itself is a relation to water and oil.

Let us look at this last approach in a bit more detail. Consider physical magnitudes such as mass and length, which are standardly considered to be paradigm examples of intrinsic properties of material objects. How do we *specify*, *represent*, or *measure* the mass or length of an object? The answer: relationally. To say that this metal rod has a mass of three kilograms is to say that it bears a certain relationship to the International Prototype Kilogram. (It would balance, on an equal-arm balance, three objects each of which balances the Standard Kilogram.) Likewise, to say that the rod has a length of two meters is to say that it is twice the length of the Standard Meter (or twice the distance traveled by light in a vacuum in a certain specified fraction of a second). These properties, mass and length, are intrinsic, but their specifications or representations are extrinsic and relational, involving relationships to other things and properties in the world. Moreover, the availability of such extrinsic representations may be essential to the utility of these properties in the formulation of scientific laws and explanations. They make it possible to relate a given intrinsic property to other significant properties in theoretically interesting and fruitful ways. Similar considerations might explain the usefulness of wide contents, or relational descriptions of beliefs, in vernacular explanations of human behavior.

In physical measurements, we use numbers to specify properties of objects, and these numbers involve relationships to other objects. In attributing to persons beliefs, we use propositions, or content sentences, to specify them, and these propositions often involve relations to things outside the persons. When we say that Jones believes that water is wet, we are using the content sentence "water is wet" to specify this belief, and the appropriateness of this sentence as a specification of the belief depends on Jones's relationship, past and present, to her environment. What Burge's examples show is that the choice of a content sentence depends also on the social-linguistic facts about the person holding the belief. In a sense, we are "measuring" people's mental states using sentences, just as we measure physical magnitudes using numbers.[13] Just as the assignment of numbers in measurement depends on relationships to things other than the things whose magnitudes are being measured, the use of content sentences in the specification of intentional states makes use of, and depends on, factors outside the subject. In both cases the informativeness and utility of the specifications—the assigned numbers or sentences—depend crucially on the involvement of external factors and conditions.[14]

This approach seems to have much to recommend itself over the other two. It locates beliefs and other intentional states squarely within the subjects; ontologically, they are states of the persons holding them, not something that somehow extrudes from them. This is a more elegant metaphysical picture than its alternatives. What is "wide" about these states is their specifications or descriptions, not the states themselves. And there are good reasons for using wide content specifications. For one, we want them to indicate the representational contents of beliefs (and other intentional states)—what states of affairs are represented by them—and it is no surprise that this involves reference to external conditions. After all, the whole point of beliefs is to represent states of affairs in the world, outside the believer. For another, the sorts of social-linguistic constraints involved in Burge's examples seem crucial to the uniformity, stability, and intersubjectivity of content attributions. The upshot is that it is important not to conflate the ontological status of intentional states with the modes of their specification.

The Possibility of Narrow Content

You believe that water extinguishes fires, and your twin on Twin Earth believes that twater extinguishes fires. The two beliefs have different contents: What you believe is not the same as what your twin believes. But leaving the matter here is unsatisfying; it misses something important—something *psychologically* important—that you and your twin share in holding these beliefs. "Narrow content" is supposed to capture this something you and your twin share.

First, we seem to have a strong sense that both you and your twin conceptualize the same state of affairs in holding the beliefs about water and twater, respectively; the way things seem to you when you think that fresh water fills the Great Lakes must be the same, we feel, as the way things seem to your twin when she thinks that fresh twater fills the Twin Earth Great Lakes. From an internal psychological perspective, your thought and her thought seem to have the same significance. In thinking of water, you perhaps have the idea of a substance that is transparent, flows a certain way, tastes a certain way, and so on; in thinking of twater, your twin has the same associations. Or take the frog case: Isn't it plausible to suppose that the frog in our world that detects a fly and the other-worldly frog that detects a schmy are in the same perceptual state—a state whose content consists in a black dot flitting across the visual field? There is a strong intuitive pull toward the view that there is something important that is common to your psychological life and your twin's, and to our frog's perceptual state and the other-worldly frog's, that could reasonably be called "content."

Second, consider your behavior and your twin's behavior: They show a lot in common. For example, when you find your couch on fire, you pour water on it; when your twin finds her couch on fire, she pours twater on it. If you were visiting Twin Earth and found a couch on fire there, you would pour twater on it too (and conversely, if your twin is visiting Earth). In ordinary situations your behavior involving water is the same as her behavior involving twater; moreover, your behavior would remain the same if twater were substituted for water everywhere, and this goes for your twin as well *mutatis mutandis*. It seems then that the water-twater difference is psychologically irrelevant—irrelevant for behavior causation and explanation. That is, the difference between water-thoughts and twater-thoughts cancels itself out, so to speak. What is important for psychological explanation seems to be what you and your twin share, namely, thoughts with narrow content. So the question arises: Does psychological theory need wide content? Can it get by with narrow content alone (assuming there is such a thing)?

We have seen some examples of beliefs that plausibly do not depend on the existence of anything outside the subject holding them: your beliefs that you exist, that you are in pain, that unicorns do not exist, and the like. Although we have left open the question of whether the arthritis argument applies to them, they are at least "internal" or "intrinsic" to the subject in the sense that for these beliefs to exist, nothing outside the subject needs to exist. It appears, then, that these beliefs do not involve anything external to the believer and therefore that these beliefs supervene solely on the factors internal to him (again barring the possibility that the Burge-style considerations generalize to all expressions without exceptions).

However, a closer look reveals that some of these beliefs are not supervenient only on internal states of the believer. For we need to consider the involvement of the subject herself in the belief. Consider Mary's belief that she is in pain. The content of this belief is that she—that is, Mary—is in pain. This is the state of affairs represented by the belief, and this belief is true just in case that state of affairs obtains—that is, just in case Mary is in pain. Now, put Mary's twin on Twin Earth (or a perfect physical replica of Mary on Earth) in the same internal physical state that Mary is in when she has this belief. If mind-body supervenience, as *intuitively understood*, holds, it would seem that Mary's twin too will have the belief that she is in pain. However, her belief has the content that *she* (Twin Earth Mary) is in pain, not that *Mary* is in pain. The belief is true if and only if Mary's twin is in pain. It seems to follow, then, that belief contents in cases of this kind do not supervene on the internal-intrinsic physical properties of persons. This means that the following two ideas that are normally taken to lie at the core of the notion of "narrow content" fail to coincide: (1) Narrow content is internal and intrinsic to the believer and does not involve anything outside her current state; and (2) narrow content, unlike wide content, supervenes on the current internal physical state of the believer. Mary's belief that she is in pain, and all other beliefs whose content sentence includes reflexive self-reference (for example, your belief that you exist, or that you are tall) satisfy (1) but not (2).

One possible tack to take is this: What examples of this kind show is not that these beliefs do not supervene on the internal physical states of the believer, but rather that we should revise the notion of "same belief"—that is, we need to revise the criteria of belief individuation. In our discussion thus far, individual beliefs (or "belief tokens") have been considered to be "the same belief" (or the same "belief type") just in case they have the same content; on this view, two beliefs have the same content only if their truth condition is the same (that is, necessarily they are true together or false together). As we saw, Mary's belief that she, Mary, is in pain and her twin's belief that she, the twin Mary, is in pain do not have the same truth condition and hence must count as belonging to different belief types. That is why supervenience fails for these beliefs. However, there is an obvious and natural sense in which Mary and her twin have "the same belief"—even beliefs with "the same content"—when each believes that she is in pain. More work, however, needs to be done to capture this notion of content or sameness of belief,[15] and that is part of the project of explicating the notion of narrow content.

As noted, it is widely accepted that most of our ordinary belief attributions, as well as attributions of other intentional states, involve wide content. Some hold not only that all contents are wide but that the very notion of narrow content makes no sense. One point often made against narrow content is its alleged ineffability: How do we capture the shared content of Jones's belief that water is wet and her twin's belief that twater is wet? And if there is something shared, why is it a kind of "content"?

One way the friends of narrow content have tried to deal with such questions is to treat narrow content as an abstract technical notion, roughly in the following sense. The thing that Mary and her twin share plays the following role: If anyone has it and has acquired her language on Earth (or in an environment containing water), her word "water" refers to water and she has water-thoughts; if anyone has it and has acquired her language on Twin Earth (or in an environment containing twater), her word "water" refers to twater and she has twater-thoughts; for anyone who has it and has acquired her language in an environment in which a substance with molecular structure PQR replaces water (or XYZ) everywhere, her word "water" refers to PQR; and so on. The same idea applies to the frog case: What the two frogs, one in this world and the other in a world with schmies but no flies, have in common is this: If a frog has it and inhabits an environment with flies, it has the capacity to have flies as part of its perceptual content, and similarly for frogs in a schmy-inclusive environment. Technically, narrow content is taken as a function from environmental contexts (including contexts of language acquisition) to wide contents (or truth conditions).[16] One question that has to be answered is why narrow content in that sense is a kind of content. For isn't it true, by definition, that content is "semantically evaluable"—that is, that it is something that can be true or false? Narrow content, conceived as a function from environment to wide content, does not seem to meet this conception of content; it does not seem like the sort of thing that can be said to be true or false. Here various strategies for meeting this point seem possible; however, whether any of them will work is an open question.

Two Problems with Content Externalism

We briefly survey here two outstanding issues confronting the thesis that most, perhaps all, of our intentional mental states have wide content. (The first was briefly alluded to earlier.)

The Causal-Explanatory Efficacy of Wide Content

Even if we acknowledge that commonsense psychology individuates intentional states widely and formulates causal explanations of behavior in terms of wide content states, we might well ask whether this is an ineliminable feature of such explanations. Several considerations can be advanced to cast doubt on the causal-explanatory efficacy of wide content states. First, we have already noted the similarity between the behaviors of people on Earth and those of their Twin Earth counterparts in relation to water and twater, respectively. We saw that in formulating causal explanations of behaviors, the difference between water-thoughts and twater-thoughts somehow cancels itself out by failing to manifest itself in a difference in the generation of behavior. Second, to put the point another way, if you are a psychologist who has already developed a working psychological theory of people on Earth, formulated in terms of content-bearing intentional states, you obviously would not start all over again from scratch when you want to develop a psychological theory for Twin Earth people. In fact, you are likely to say that people on Earth and those on Twin Earth have "the same psychology"—that is, the same psychological theory holds for both groups. In view of this, isn't it more appropriate to take the difference between water-thoughts and twater-thoughts, or water-desires and twater-desires, merely as a difference in the values of a contextual parameter to be fixed to suit the situations to which the theory is applied rather than as an integral element of the theory itself? If this is correct, doesn't wide content drop out as part of the theoretical apparatus of psychological theory?

Moreover, there is a metaphysical point to consider: The proximate cause of my physical behavior (say, my bodily motions), we feel, must be "local"— it must be a series of neural events originating in my central nervous system that causes the contraction of appropriate muscles, which in turn moves my limbs. This means that what these neural events represent in the outside world is irrelevant to behavior causation: If the same neural events occur in a different environment so that they have different representational (wide) content, they would still cause the same physical behavior. That is, we have reason to think that proximate causes of behavior are *locally* supervenient on the internal physical states of an organism, but that wide content states are not so supervenient. Hence, the wideness of wide content states is not relevant to causal explanations of physical behavior.

One way in which the friends of wide content have tried to counter these considerations goes as follows. What we typically attempt to explain in commonsense psychology is not physical behavior but action—not why your right hand moved thus and so, but why you turned on the stove, why you boiled the water, why you made the tea. To explain why your hand moved in a certain way, it may suffice to advert to causes "in the head," but to explain why you turned on the stove or why you boiled the water, we must invoke wide content states: because you wanted to heat the kettle of water, because you wanted to make a cup of tea for your friend, and so on. Behaviors explained in typical commonsense explanations are given under "wide descriptions," and we need wide content states to explain them. So the point of the reply is that we need wide content to explain "wide behavior." Whether or not this response is sufficient is something to think about. In particular, we might raise questions as to whether the wideness of thoughts and the wideness of behavior are playing any real role in the causal-explanatory relation involved, or whether they merely ride piggyback, so to speak, on an underlying causal-explanatory relationship between the neural states, or narrow content states, and physical behavior. (The issues discussed in an earlier section, "The Metaphysics of Wide Content States," are directly relevant to these causal-explanatory questions about wide content. The reader is encouraged to think about whether the third option described in that section could help the content externalist to formulate a better response. Some of the issues discussed here are covered in chapter 7.)

Wide Content and Self-Knowledge

How do we know that Mary believes that water is wet and that Mary's twin on Twin Earth believes that twater is wet? Because we know that Mary's environment contains water and that Mary's twin's environment contains twater.

Now consider the matter from Mary's point of view: How does she know that she believes that water is wet? How does she know the content of her own thoughts?

We believe that a subject has special, direct access to her own mental states (see chapters 1 and 8). Perhaps the access is not infallible and does not extend to all mental states, but it is uncontroversial that there is special first-person authority in regard to one's own occurrent thoughts. When you reflect on what you are thinking, you know directly, without further evidence or reasoning, what you think; the content of your thought is immediately and directly accessible to you, and the question of having evidence or doing research does not arise. If you think that the shuttle bus is late and you might miss your flight, you know, in the very act of thinking, that that is what you are thinking. First-person knowledge of the contents of one's own current thoughts is direct and immediate and carries a special sort of authority (see chapters 1 and 8).

Return now to Mary and her knowledge of the content of her belief that water is wet. It seems plausible to think that in order for her to know that her thought is about water, not about twater, she is in the same epistemic situation that we are in with respect to the content of her thought. We know that her thought is about water, not twater, because we know, from observation, that her environment is water-inclusive, not twater-inclusive. But why doesn't she too have to know that if she is to know that her thought is about water, not twater, and how can she know something like that without observation or evidence? It looks like she may very well lose her specially privileged epistemic access to the content of her own thought, because her knowledge of her thought content is now put on the same footing as third-person knowledge of it.

To make this more vivid, suppose that Twin Earth exists in a nearby planetary system and we can travel between Earth and Twin Earth. It is plausible to suppose that if one spends a sufficient amount of time on Earth (or Twin Earth), one's word "water" becomes locally acclimatized and begins to refer to the local stuff, water or twater, as the case may be. Now, Mary, an inveterate space traveler, forgets on which planet she has been living for the past several years, whether it is Earth or Twin Earth; surely that is something she cannot know directly without evidence or observation. Now ask: Can she know, directly and without further investigation, whether her thoughts (say, the thought she expresses when she mutters to herself, "The tap water in this fancy hotel doesn't taste so good") are about water or twater? It prima facie makes sense to think that just as she cannot know, without additional evidence, whether her present use of the word "*water*" refers to water or twa-ter, she cannot know, without investigating her environment, whether her thought about the steaming liquid in her kettle has the content that the water is boiling or that the twater is boiling. If something like this is right, then content externalism would seem to have the consequence that most of our knowledge of our own intentional states is not direct and, like most other kinds of knowledge, must be based on evidence. That is to say, content externalism appears to be prima facie incompatible with privileged first-person access to one's own mind. Content externalists are, of course, not without answers, but an examination of these is beyond the scope of this chapter (see "Further Readings").

*   *   *

These issues concerning wide and narrow content—especially the second concerning externalism and self-knowledge—are being vigorously debated and are likely to be with us for some time. Their importance can hardly be exaggerated: Content-carrying states—that is, intentional states like belief, desire, and the reset—constitute the central core of our commonsense ("folk") psychological practices, providing us with a framework for formulating explanations and predictions of what we and our fellow humans do. Without this essential tool for understanding and anticipating human action and behavior, a communal life would be unthinkable. Moreover, the issues go beyond commonsense psychology. There is, for example, this important question about scientific psychology and cognitive science: Should the sciences of human behavior and cognition make use of content-carrying intentional states like belief and desire, or their more refined and precise scientific analogues, in formulating its laws and explanations? Or should they, or could they, transcend the intentional idiom by couching their theories and explanations in purely nonintentional (perhaps, ultimately neurobiological) terms? These questions concern the centrality of content-bearing, representational states to the explanation of human action and behavior—both in everyday psychological practices and in theory construction in scientific psychology.

Further Readings

On interpretation theory, see the works by Davidson, Quine, and Lewis cited in note 1; see also Daniel C. Dennett, "Intentional Systems" and "True Believers."

On causal-correlational theories of content, see the works cited in note 7; see also Robert Cummins, *Meaning and Mental Representation*, especially chapters 4 through 6. Another useful book on issues of mental content, including some not discussed in this chapter, is Lynne Rudder Baker, *Explaining Attitudes*. There are several helpful essays in *Meaning in Mind*, edited by Barry Loewer and Georges Rey.

On teleological accounts of mental content, see Fred Dretske, "Misrepresentation," and Ruth Millikan, "Biosemantics." Karen Neader's "Teleological Theories of Mental Content" is a comprehensive survey and analysis.

On narrow and wide content, the two classic texts that introduced the issues are Hilary Putnam, "The Meaning of 'Meaning,'" and Tyler Burge, "Individualism and the Mental." See also Fodor's *Psychosemantics* and "A Modal Argument for Narrow Content"; and Stephen White, "Partial Character and the Language of Thought." For a defense of content internalism, Gabriel Segal, *A Slim Book About Narrow Content*, is recommended. For a discussion of these issues in relation to scientific psychology, see Frances Egan, "Must Psychology Be Individualistic?"

Concerning content and causation, the reader may wish to consult the following: Colin Allen, "It Isn't What You Think: A New Idea About Intentional Causation"; Lynne Rudder Baker, *Explaining Attitudes*; Tim Crane, "The Causal Efficacy of Content: A Functionalist Theory"; Fred Dretske, *Explaining Behavior* and "Minds, Machines, and Money: What Really Explains Behavior"; Jerry Fodor, *Psychosemantics* and "Making Mind Matter More"; and Pierre Jacob, *What Minds Can Do*.

On wide content and self-knowledge, see Donald Davidson, "Knowing One's Own Mind"; Tyler Burge, "Individualism and Self-Knowledge"; Paul Boghossian, "Content and Self-Knowledge"; and John Heil, *The Nature of True Minds*, chapter 5. Three recent collections of useful essays on the issue are *Externalism and Self-Knowledge*, edited by Peter Ludlow and Norah Martin; *Knowing Our Own Minds*, edited by Crispin Wright, Barry C. Smith, and Cynthia Macdonald; and *New Essays on Semantic Externalism and Self-Knowledge*, edited by Susan Nuccetelli.

Notes

1. The discussion in this section is based on the works of W. V. Quine and Donald Davidson—especially Davidson's. See Quine on "radical translation" in his *Word and Object*, ch. 2. Davidson's principal essays on interpretation are included in his *Inquiries into Truth and Interpretation*; see, in particular, "Radical Interpretation," "Thought and Talk," and "Belief and the Basis of Meaning."

2. Here we are making the plausible assumption that we can determine, on the basis of observation of Karl's behavior, that he affirmatively utters, or holds true, a sentence S, without our knowing what S means or what belief Karl expresses by uttering S. (The account would be circular otherwise.) It can be granted that holding true a sentence, or affirmatively uttering one, is a psychological attitude or event. For further discussion of this point, see Davidson, "Thought and Talk," pp. 161–162.

3. The parenthetical part is often assumed without being explicitly stated. Some writers state it as a separate principle, sometimes called the "requirement of rationality." There are many inequivalent versions of the charity principle in the literature. Some restrictions on the class of beliefs to which charity is to be bestowed is almost certainly necessary. For our examples, all we need is to say that speakers' beliefs about observable features of their immediate environment are generally true; that is, we restrict the application of charity to "occasion sentences" whose utterances are sensitive to the observable change in the environment.

4. Such a position seems implicit in, for example, Daniel Dennett's "True Believers."

5. The following statement from Davidson, who has often avowed himself to be a mental realist, seems to have seemingly irrealist implications: "For until the triangle is completed connecting two creatures [the interpreter and the subject being interpreted], and each creature with common features of the world, there can be no answer to the question whether a creature, in discriminating between stimuli, is discriminating stimuli at sensory surfaces or somewhere further out, or further in. Without this sharing of reactions to common stimuli, thought and speech would have no particular content—that is, no content at all. It takes two points of view to give a location to the cause of a thought, and thus, to define its content." See Davidson, "Three Varieties of Knowledge," pp. 212–213.

6. To use Robert Stalnaker's term in his *Inquiry*, p. 18. Fred Dretske uses "indicator" and its cognates for similar purposes in his writings on representation and content.

7. This version captures the gist of the correlational approach, which has many diverse versions. Important sources include Fred Dretske, *Knowledge and the Flow of Information* and "Misrepresentation"; Robert Stalnaker, *Inquiry*; and Jerry A. Fodor, *Psychosemantics* and *A Theory of Content and Other Essays*. Dennis Stampe is usually credited with initiating this approach in "Toward a Causal Theory of Linguistic Representation." For discussion and criticisms, see Brian McLaughlin, "What Is Wrong with Correlational Psychosemantics?" (to which I am indebted in this section); and Louise Antony and Joseph Levine, "The Nomic and the Robust"; Lynne Rudder Baker, "Has Content Been Naturalized?"; and Paul Boghossian, "Naturalizing Content" in *Meaning in Mind*, edited by Barry Loewer and Georges Rey.

8. For discussion of this issue, see the works cited in note 6.

9. This is not to say that the teleological approach is necessarily the only solution to the problem of misrepresentation or the disjunction problem. See Jerry A. Fodor, *A Theory of Content and Other Essays*.

10. Hilary Putnam, "The Meaning of 'Meaning'"; Tyler Burge, "Individualism and the Mental." The terms "narrow" and "wide" are due to Putnam.

11. Most notably Descartes and Davidson. See Davidson's "Thought and Talk."

12. Hilary Putnam, "The Meaning of 'Meaning,'" p. 227.

13. This idea was first introduced by Paul M. Churchland in "Eliminative Materialism and the Propositional Attitudes." It has been systematically elaborated by Robert Matthews in "The Measure of Mind." However, these authors do not relate this approach to the issues of content externalism. For another perspective on the issues, see Ernest Sosa, "Between Internalism and Externalism."

14. This point concerning content sentences is made by Burge in "Individualism and the Mental."

15. In this connection, see Roderick Chisholm's theory in *The First Person*, which does not take beliefs as relations to propositions but construes them as attributions of properties. David Lewis has independently proposed a similar approach in "Attitudes *De Dicto* and *De Se*."

16. See Stephen White, "Partial Character and the Language of Thought," and Jerry A. Fodor, *Psychosemantics*. See also Gabriel Segal, *A Slim Book About Narrow Content*.

10

Reduction, Reductive Explanation,

and Physicalism

As we have seen (chapter 2), the classic dualism of Descartes was substance dualism, a position that countenances two distinct domains of entities, one consisting of immaterial minds ("mental substances") and the other comprising physical things ("material substances"). Associated with these two domains are two disjoint families of properties, one consisting of mental properties (thinking, consciousness) and the other of physical properties (extension, motion), which serve to characterize the entities of the two domains, minds and bodies, respectively. Thus, Descartes' dualism combines a dualism of substances with a dualism of properties: two disparate domains of substances and two mutually exclusive families of properties. Arguably, substance dualism entails property dualism: It would be pointless and perhaps also incoherent to posit substances of two fundamentally different kinds and yet hold at the same time that a unitary system of properties suffices to characterize all of them.

Substance dualism has been little discussed in contemporary philosophy of mind; for several decades the position has largely been ignored or forgotten rather than overtly scrutinized and criticized. The idea that there are nonphysical substances outside the spacetime frame and yet in causal interaction with material things within spacetime would now strike many philosophers as a bit quaint and bizarre, not as a viable alternative to be taken seriously. The idea is far from moribund (see chapter 2), however, and the feasibility of substance dualism should not be ruled out of court. Still, it is up to its defenders to show that immaterial substances provide us with concrete help with some of the pressing problems about the mind, such as consciousness and the explanatory gap, mental causation, puzzles about mental content and self-knowledge, and the rest. Criticizing physicalism—for example, for its apparent inability to deal with phenomenal consciousness—does not go far enough; what is needed to bring back substance dualism is a *positive* argument that shows that this venerable position brings with it concrete benefits in dealing with the central issues of philosophy of mind and metaphysics. More likely, most philosophers today will regard immaterial minds as only getting in their way, complicating their problems rather than giving them the help they need.

Thus, like it or not, ontological physicalism[1]—the view that there are no concrete individuals, or substances, in the world other than material particles and their aggregates—has in effect become the default position in the study of the mind, serving as a framework within which specific issues about the mind are formulated and investigated. In most contemporary debates, ontological physicalism is the starting point of discussion rather than a conclusion in need of defense. In consequence, the most intensely contested issue—in fact, the only substantive remaining issue about the mind-body problem—has centered on *mental* and *physical properties*, that is, the status of mental properties in relation to physical properties. For several decades the crux of the debate has been—and it continues to be—the contentious disputes between reductionism and antireductionism. The reductionist, or reductive physicalist, takes the view that mental properties are reducible to physical properties and hence turn out to be "nothing over and above" physical properties. On this position, then, there are no nonphysical properties in this world; all properties are ultimately reducible to the properties investigated in fundamental physics. In discussions of the mind-body problem, "physical" properties are broadly construed so as to include behavioral-neural-biological properties (sometimes including computational properties) as well as those of basic physics. The thought seems to be that if the question of reducibility of the mental to behavioral-neural-biological properties can be settled, the remaining question whether these properties are in turn reducible to fundamental physical properties is of secondary importance as far as philosophy of mind is concerned. In any case, behaviorism and the psychoneural identity theory (see chapters 3 and 4) are prime examples of reductionist physicalism.

Since the 1970s, reductionism has had a rough time of it, although of late it has shown signs of renewed vigor and strength. As reductionism's fortunes declined, *nonreductive physicalism* rapidly gained strength and influence, and it has reigned as the dominant and virtually unchallenged position on the mind-body problem for the past several decades. This is the view that mental properties, along with other "higher-level" properties of the special sciences, resist reduction to the physical domain. An antireductionist view of this kind has also served as an influential philosophical foundation of psychology and cognitive science, providing support for the claim that these sciences are autonomous, each with its own distinctive methodology and system of concepts and not answerable to the methodological or explanatory constraints of more fundamental sciences. Thus, the most widely accepted form of physicalism today combines ontological physicalism with property dualism: All concrete individual things in this world are physical, but complex physical systems can, and sometimes do, exhibit properties that are not reducible to "lower-level" physical properties. Among these irreducible properties are, most notably, mental properties, including those investigated in the psychological and cognitive sciences.

What Is Reduction?
Three Models of Reduction

In debating the issues concerning reduction, we need a tolerably clear understanding of what "reduction" is supposed to be. Reduction is one of those concepts, used in philosophy and science, for which there seems to exist a fairly robust shared meaning for most purposes, but whose shared meaning turns out to be not precise enough when the discussion reaches a certain level of depth and complexity. We are now reaching that kind of level with reduction, and it is time to pay closer attention to the concept. Reductions of all kinds must have something in common: They must "reduce" whatever it is that they aim to reduce. But the entities that are the target of reduction may differ from one reductive project to another (sentences, concepts, facts, properties, and so on), and there may be more than one way of reducing entities of a given kind. For our purposes, it is useful to take J. J. C. Smart's expression "nothing over and above" as expressing the core idea of reduction. Smart puts his reductionist physicalism this way: "Sensations are nothing over and above brain processes."[2] If Xs are reduced, or reducible, to Ys, there are no Xs *over and above* Ys—to put it another way, there are no Xs *in addition to* Ys. If numbers are reduced to sets, there are no numbers over and above sets, and if macrophysical properties, like ductility and electrical conductivity, are reduced to microphysical properties at the atomic-molecular level, there are no macrophysical properties over and above microphysical properties. Notice that this does not mean that the reduced Xs no longer exist; it only says that there are no Xs in addition to Ys—that is, when you have got the Ys, you have all you need. Notice too that we did not say that when Xs are reduced to Ys, you always find the Xs among the Ys. Smart's slogan is also consistent with what is called "eliminative" reduction, whereby the reduced entities (say, witches, phlogiston) are eliminated or replaced. When witches were shown to be only psychotic women, witches were eliminated; there are no witches and there never were. So it follows trivially that there are no witches over and above psychotic women. Reductions that are not eliminative, ones in which the reduced Xs are now found among the Ys, are called "conservative" (or "preservative," or "retentive") reductions; when heat was reduced to a more basic physical quantity, it was not eliminated but conserved (as molecular kinetic energy). The idea of "nothing over and above" therefore is consistent with both conservative and eliminative reduction, and it seems nicely to capture the intuitive idea of reduction.

We consider here three models of reduction: bridge-law reduction, identity reduction, and functional reduction.[3] There is no need to view these three distinct ways of carrying out reductions as competitors or rivals; they simply are three ways in which reduction can be executed. Reduction in accordance with one model may work for a given subject matter but not for another. More than one model may work to reduce a subject matter; perhaps some subject matters cannot be reduced in any way at all. We must also keep in mind that reduction is a relation—a relation to a specific "reduction base." Conscious mental states may be reducible to the neural but not to the behavioral; intentional mental states may be reducible to functional states but not to neural states; and so on. What is important is the philosophical—and scientific—significance of the success or failure of reduction of a given kind. For example, a bridge-law reduction of consciousness to neural processes and an identity reduction of the same may have vastly different philosophical implications about the status of consciousness. If you prefer, you could call the three models three "senses" of reduction—three "concepts" that can be associated with the term "reduction." But it would be more proper and less misleading to consider them as specifying three different kinds of reduction; for the "sense" or "meaning" of reduction, we can always fall back on Smart's "nothing over and above."[4]

With these preliminaries out of the way, we now take up the models in turn.

Bridge-Law Reduction

The bridge-law model of reduction, developed by Ernest Nagel in the 1950s, is designed as an account of reduction of scientific *theories*—the reduction of a higher-level theory to a more fundamental theory.[5] For example, the reduction of optics to electromagnetic theory, of gas laws to statistical molecular physics (Nagel's favorite example), and of genetics to molecular biology would count as instances of theory reduction.[6] In this context, a theory is considered to be a set of laws—its "basic" laws *plus* those derivable from them (like the axioms and theorems in a formalized mathematical system). Nagel conceives of reduction of theory T_2 to theory T_1 as consisting essentially in the logical-mathematical derivation of the laws of T_2 from those of T_1. Since each theory is expected to have its own proprietary vocabulary (for example, "temperature" and "pressure," which appear in gas laws, do not occur in molecular physics), it is thought that in order to enable the derivation of T_2-laws from T_1 laws, special principles connecting T_2-terms with T_1-terms, called "bridge laws" or "bridge principles," are required as auxiliary premises of the derivation. This requirement is standardly understood in the following way:

> *Bridge-Law Requirement.* For each primitive (or basic) predicate P of T_2, there is a predicate (possibly complex) Q of T_1 such that it holds as a matter of law that for anything x, x has P at t iff x has Q at t.

Bridge laws are thought to be a posteriori and contingent, and of course they are laws—that is, they hold with nomological necessity. If we are reducing a theory of pain (and other sensations) to neurophysiology, the following could be one of the required bridge laws:

(B$_1$) For every x, x is in pain at t iff x is in brain state N_1 at t.

Suppose that the following is a law of the pain theory:

(L) Anyone who is in pain feels distressed.

Suppose further that we have this bridge law:

(B$_2$) For every x, x feels distressed at t iff x is in brain state N$_2$ at t.

Assume that the neurophysiological theory includes the following law:

(L*) Brain state N$_1$ is regularly followed by brain state N$_2$.

It is easy to see that, given the two bridge laws (B$_1$) and (B$_2$), the law (L) of the pain theory can be derived from neurophysiological law (L*).

Formally, the role of bridge laws in a reductive derivation is to serve as definitions in the following sense: They allow us to *rewrite* any law of the theory to be reduced as a statement in the vocabulary of the reduction base theory, by replacing each higher-level predicate with the lower-level predicate with which it is correlated by a bridge law. In our example, (B$_1$) and (B$_2$) enable us to rewrite (L) as (L*). Given this is what happens, we can now see that if the bridge-law requirement is met, that is sufficient for a Nagel reduction of T$_2$ to T$_1$. Let L be any law in T$_2$. Using the bridge laws, rewrite L in the vocabulary of T$_1$; call the rewrite L#. Either L# is a law of T$_1$ or it is not. If it is, L can be derived from L# with the bridge laws as auxiliary premises. If L# is not a law of T$_1$, add it to T$_1$ as a new basic law—this is permissible (in fact, required) in that L# is a lawlike statement wholly in the language of T$_1$, and in missing it, T$_1$ is missing a general law in its domain. (This assumes that the theory being reduced is true.) We can then derive L from L# as before. In either case, L is derivable from T$_1$-laws *plus* bridge laws. So the satisfaction of the bridge-law requirement is sufficient for Nagelian reduction, and this makes bridge laws the heart of this form of reduction. (Of course, that is why we call it "bridge-law" reduction.)

Bridge-law reduction has dominated philosophical thinking concerning reduction and reductionism for several decades. Many antireductionist arguments are based on the premise that the bridge-law requirement cannot be met.[7] But would a bridge-law reduction of pain theory to neurophysiology help close the "explanatory gap" between pain (and other sensory states) and neural properties and help solve the "hard" problem of consciousness (chapter 8)? We consider this question in a later section, but first let us attend to another, more pressing, problem. As was just noted, the satisfaction of the bridge-law requirement is sufficient to a reduction of this kind. But all sorts of mind-body theories, some of them manifestly dualistic and antiphysical-ist, are consistent with, and in fact entail, a pervasive system of mind-body bridge laws. The doctrines of preestablished harmony, double-aspect theory, emergentism, and epiphenomenalism are all committed to there being psychophysical correlation laws, and there is nothing in substance dualism as such that precludes psychophysical correlation laws to enable a full bridge-law reduction of mentality. It is evident that there being a correlation law between pain and neural N_1 does not suffice for the reduction of pain to N_1; it does not render pain "nothing over and above" neural state N_1. This is why philosophers began looking for something stronger than bridge laws to underwrite reductions.

Identity Reduction

There has been a fairly wide agreement that in order to generate genuine reductions, bridge laws must be strengthened into *identities*. That is, instead of the likes of (B_1) and (B_2), what we need are these:

(I_1) Pain = brain state N_1.
(I_2) Distress = brain state N_2.

Return to the idea of "nothing over and above"; if pain and other qualitative states of consciousness have been reduced to neural states, they should be "nothing over and above" neural states. Evidently, (I_1) and (I_2) warrant us to say just that: Pain is nothing over and above N_1, and distress is nothing over and above N_2. Correlations like (B_1) and (B_2) are not nearly strong enough; we cannot go from "Xs correlate with Ys" to "Xs are nothing over and above Ys."

More generally, we can say that a domain of entities is identity-reducible to another domain just in case each item in the first can be identified with some item in the second. Thus, if mental properties are to be identity-reduced to neural properties, we must be able to identify each mental property with some neural property, as in (I_1) and (I_2).

Given these identities, we can readily derive laws about pain from laws of neurophysiology. Our sample pain law, (L), can be derived from (L*) by "putting equals for equals"—"pain" for "brain state N_1" and "distress" for "brain state N_2." In general, we can see that identity reduction can do everything bridge-law reduction does—and more. In fact, (L) can now be regarded as just another way of stating the regularity described by (L*), something that a bridge-law reduction does not sanction. In any case, it is clear that these identities suffice for the claim that pain and distress have been reduced to neural states. But does an identity reduction solve the explanatory gap problem, and if it does, how does it do it? We consider this question in a later section.

Functional Reduction

Consider the gene and the DNA-molecule. Genes have been identified as DNA-molecules, and we can say that genes have been reduced to them. How does a reduction of this kind work? The first point to be noted is that the concept of a gene is a *functional concept*, a concept defined in terms of a "job description" or "causal role" (chapter 5). The gene is, by definition, whatever mechanism in an organism encodes genetic information and transmits it from parent to offspring. When Mendel, the Austrian botanist who founded the science of genetics, talked of "genetic factors," he had no idea what molecular-biological mechanisms actually did the work he had in mind, but he was quite certain that there had to be mechanisms that would explain facts and regularities about heredity—such as patterns of transmission of phenotypic features from generation to generation. Many years later, in the twentieth century, research in molecular genetics was able to identify DNA-molecules as the mechanisms that execute the causal work assigned to the gene.

Schematically, we can think of reductions of this kind in the following three steps:

Step 1. Property, F, to be reduced is given a functional definition, or characterization, of the following form:
Having F = $_{def}$ having some property, or mechanism, P such that C(P), where C specifies the causal task to be performed by P.
Step 2. Find the property, or mechanism, that does the causal work specified by C—that is, identify the "realizer" (or "realizers") of F, in the system, or population of systems, under investigation.
Step 3. Develop a theory that explains how the realizer(s) of F so identified perform the causal task C in the given system or population.

We can see how a reduction of this form might work for mental states. Take pain. Assume, as an illustrative example, that pain can be given the following functional characterization:

To be in pain = $_{def}$ to be in state S such that S is caused by tissue damage and S in turn causes winces, groans, and avoidance behavior.

Suppose that in humans and higher mammals, it is C-fiber stimulation that realizes pain as defined—that is, C-fiber stimulation is what is caused by tissue damage and what causes winces, groans, and avoidance behavior. For a human to be in pain is, by definition, for her to be in a state that is caused by tissue damage and that in turn causes her to wince, groan, and so on, and having her C-fibers stimulated turns out to be just this kind of state. So there is no more to her being in pain over and above her C-fiber stimulation. Besides, we have in hand a neurophysiological theory, let us suppose, that explains how all these causal processes work—how tissue damage causes C-fiber stimulation, and so on. When all this is in, we can plausibly claim that we have reduced pains in humans and mammals to the stimulation of their C-fibers and that we now understand pain phenomena in terms of their underlying neural processes. That, at any rate, is the idea of functional reduction.

Step 1 represents conceptual work (though it is highly likely that conceptual decisions are made with a view toward the theoretical fruitfulness of the resulting concepts): The property to be reduced is given a functional interpretation in terms of a causal role. Step 2 represents empirical scientific research; no armchair cogitation or analysis will identify the mechanisms that actually perform the causal task involved. As was noted earlier (chapter 5), realizers of a functionally characterized property may differ from species to species and may even differ among conspecifics—in fact, it may change within a single organism as it matures and develops. Multiple realization can be seen to be perfectly consistent with functional reduction.

Does functional reduction meet Smart's "nothing over and above" criterion of reduction? We can at least defend a qualified yes, as briefly indicated earlier: Suppose C-fiber stimulation is the realizer of pain in humans. Then it seems perfectly warranted to reason as follows: For a human to be in pain is, by definition, for her to be in a state that is caused by tissue damage and that in turn causes winces, groans, and aversive behavior; in a human, C-fiber stimulation is precisely the state that is caused by tissue damage and that causes winces, groans and aversive behavior; hence, for a human to be in pain is to be in a C-fiber stimulation state. We can also say that for an octopus to be in pain is for its "O-fibers" to be stimulated; for a Martian to be in pain is for its "M-fibers" to be stimulated; and so on.[8] In general, then, for an organism to be in pain at time t is nothing over and above its being, at t, in a state that realizes pain in organisms of its kind. (Remember that we assumed, purely for illustrative purposes, that pain can be functionally defined, but that may not be true—in fact, it may well be false, as we will see later in this chapter.) From the philosophical point of view, a functional characterization of the property to be reduced, or its "functionalization," is the key; the rest is up to science. If an organism instantiates a functional property at a time, it logically follows that it does so in virtue of the fact that, at that time, it instantiates the realizer (or one of the realizers) of the property in organisms relevantly like it. It is up to scientific research to identify the particular realizer involved and tell us a story about how it manages to perform its assigned causal role. We will see later how functional reduction can give us a reductive understanding of phenomena and, in particular, how a functional reduction of consciousness, if only available, could help close the explanatory gap.

Reduction and Reductive Explanation

The "hard" problem of consciousness is sometimes put in terms of *reductive explanation* rather than reduction. The question then becomes this: Can we reductively explain consciousness in terms of neural processes? Someone who favors this formulation of the problem is apt to do so because of the thought that reductive explanation is possible even where reduction is not. David Chalmers writes:

> In a certain sense, phenomena that can be realized in many different physical substrates—learning, for example—might not be reducible in that we cannot *identify* learning with any specific lower-level phenomena. But this multiple realizability does not stand in the way of reductively explaining any instance of learning in terms of lower-level phenomena.[9]

Chalmers apparently takes the multiple realizability of learning to rule out an identity reduction of learning, but this does not preclude, he is saying, a reductive explanation of the phenomenon.

Jerry Fodor, a tireless and influential critic of reductionism, appears to be driving at the same point when he writes:

> The point of reduction is *not* primarily to find some natural kind predicate of physics coextensive with each kind predicate of a special science. It is, rather, to explicate the physical mechanisms whereby events conform to the laws of the special sciences.[10]

In his first sentence, Fodor is saying that the point of reduction is not to find bridge laws connecting special science predicates with physical predicates—that is, it is not to produce bridge-law reductions of special science theories. Rather, it is to generate reductive explanations of special science phenomena in terms of underlying "physical mechanisms." Multiple realizability makes bridge-law reduction impossible by making bridge laws unavailable, but that should not prevent reductive explanation of higher-level phenomena.

A perspective like this raises a host of questions. What is a reductive explanation, and how does it work? How does a reductive explanation differ from an ordinary, nonreductive explanation? Is reductive explanation really possible without reduction? Does reduction always give us reductive explanation? Let us begin by considering the last question—whether, and how, reductions conforming to our models can generate reductive explanations.

Consider first bridge-law reduction. Given that pain has been bridge-law-reduced to neural state N_1, how might we reductively explain why Jones is in pain at time t? It seems that the best we can muster is something like this:

(α) Jones is in neural state N_1 at t.
    A person is in pain at t iff she is in neural state N_1 at t.
    Therefore, Jones is in pain at t

The second line of this derivation is a bridge law connecting pain with N_1. It allows us to derive a fact about Jones's consciousness from a fact about her brain state. We can grant that (α) is an explanation: It has the form of so-called deductive-nomological explanation—that is, an explanation in which a statement of the event to be explained is derived from antecedent conditions together with laws.[11] But is it a reductive explanation, one that gives us an understanding of pain in terms of neural processes and the laws governing these processes?

The answer: Definitely not. The difficulty lies with the second line, the pain-N_1 correlation law used as a premise of the explanatory derivation. When we want a reductive understanding of conscious states on the basis of neural processes, we want to know how sensations like pain and feelings like distress arise out of neural states—or as some put it, why these conscious states correlate with the neural states with which they correlate (chapter 8). Why does pain correlate with N_1, not N_2, and distress with N_2, not N_1? Instead of attempting to answer these questions, (α) simply assumes the pain-N_1 correlation law as an unexplained premise of the explanation. To put it another way, psychoneural bridge laws are exactly what need to be explained if we are to gain a reductive understanding of consciousness in brain science. You may recall William James's despairing of ever gaining an insight into why thoughts and sensations "accompany" the neural states that they do (chapter 8). In the same vein, T. H. Huxley likened emergence of consciousness to the magical appearance of Djin when Aladdin rubs his lamp. In speaking of sensations "accompanying" states of the brain, James is acknowledging that there are psychoneural correlation laws and that we know at least some of them. That is not the issue. According to James, Huxley, the emergentists, and many others, what we need but do not have as yet (and perhaps we never will) is an *explanation* of these correlations. Only such an explanation would dispel the "mystery" of consciousness and solve the "hard" problem.

As you have perhaps noticed, this complaint is closely related to the reservations we registered earlier concerning bridge-law reduction, to the effect that a bridge-law reduction of mentality to neural states is consistent with a host of dualist and antiphysicalist positions on the mind-body problem, such as double-aspect theory, epiphenomenalism, and emergentism. Like James and Huxley, the emergentists famously denied the possibility of explaining facts of emergence—explaining why pain arises out of N_1, not N_2, and so on. Like James, they were aware that there are "trans-ordinal" laws that connect phenomena at different levels (or "orders"), like the mental and the neural. These are precisely Nagelian bridge laws. Emergentists thought that these trans-ordinal correlations are basic and brute and not further explainable; they counseled us to accept them with "natural piety."

Another way in which the emergentists framed their challenge is this question: Knowing all the facts about the brain and knowing only that, could we know anything about consciousness? If we knew all that is going on in Jones's brain, could we know what conscious experience she is having? Could we even know that Jones is conscious? (We might call this the "predictive" criterion.) The emergentists, of course, answered these questions with a definite no. To make such predictions, we need to derive a statement about consciousness (for instance, "Jones is in pain") from statements exclusively about Jones's neural states, and such derivations are manifestly impossible. Evidently, bridge-law reductions of conscious states do not meet this predictive criterion, on account of the fact that psychoneural bridge laws, which are *not* exclusively about neural facts, are assumed as extra premises.

It should be clear by now that bridge-law reduction is a nonstarter as a way of achieving a reductive understanding of consciousness—or of anything else. Let us now turn to identity reduction.

Where a bridge-law reduction has "pain occurs iff neural state N_1 occurs," an identity reduction has the stronger statement "pain = N_1." If pain is indeed identical with brain state N_1, here there is one thing, not two, and it makes no sense to speak of pain "correlating" with N_1, or pain "emerging from" N_1—or to speak of N_1 as the neural "substrate" of pain. That would make as much sense as speaking of pain as its own neural substrate. This means that it makes no sense to ask for an "explanation" of why pain correlates with, or emerges from, neural state N_1. Consider the following derivation:

(β) Jones is in neural state N_1.
       Pain = N_1.
       Therefore, Jones is in pain.

There is no question that (β) is a valid derivation: The conclusion is obtained by putting "equals for equals" in the first (and only) premise. But is it any sort of explanation? The answer has to be in the negative. The best way of understanding what is going on in this derivation is to see that the conclusion is nothing but a "rewrite" of the premise, with the identity "pain = N_1" sanctioning the rewriting. As such, the conclusion states no new fact over and beyond what is stated in the premise: Given that pain = N_1, the fact stated by "Jones is in N_1" is the very same fact stated by "Jones is in pain," (β) is no more explanatory than something like this:

(β*) Tully gave a moving speech.
        Tully = Cicero.
        Therefore, Cicero gave a moving speech.

If this were offered as an "explanation" of why Cicero gave a moving speech, it would rightly be taken as a joke. If these remarks are on the right track, how does identity reduction fare with reductive explanation and the explanatory gap?

There are two ways of dealing with an explanatory request "Why is it the case that p?" The first is to produce a *correct answer* to the question—that is, to provide an explanation of why it is the case that p. But it may well be that p is false and there is no correct answer to "Why p?" If someone asks you, "Why did Brutus stab Caesar?" you may be able to come up with a correct answer and meet the explanatory request. In contrast, should a misinformed person ask you, "Why did Caesar stab Brutus?" you cannot provide him with a correct answer, for there is none. Rather, you will have to disabuse him of the idea that Caesar stabbed Brutus. The question "Why *p*?" *presupposes* that *p* is the case, and when the presupposition is false, the question has no correct answer, and here there is nothing to be explained. Similar remarks apply to "How *p*?" "Where *p*?" and so on. If a child asks you, "How does Santa visit so many millions of homes in one night?" you will have to tell her that there is no Santa and he does not visit any homes. You may have to break her heart, but that is the only appropriate response.

The same goes for the question "Why does pain correlate with brain state N_1, not N_2?" This question presupposes that pain correlates with N_1, a supposition that is false—if it is indeed the case that pain = N_1. This means that given an identity reduction of mentality—that is, the psychoneural identity theory—it is improper to ask for an explanation of why psychoneural correlations hold. This point is aptly put by Block and Stalnaker:

> If we believe that heat is correlated with but not identical with molecular kinetic energy, we should regard as legitimate the question of why the correlation exists and what its mechanism is. But once we realize that heat *is* molecular kinetic energy, questions like this can be seen as wrongheaded.[12]

The same goes, Block and Stalnaker will say, for pain and neural state N_1, and distress and neural state N_2.

What then of the explanatory gap between consciousness and the brain, between pain and N_1? Again, the identity reductionist will respond: There is no such gap to be closed, and to think that such a gap exists is a mistake—it is the false assumption on which the so-called problem of the explanatory gap rests. You need two things to have a gap. If identity reduction goes through, that will show that there is no gap, and never was. The idea that there is any gap to be closed is just a myth—a piece of myth-mongering abetted by covert dualist thinking.

So the identity reduction of consciousness can handle the explanatory gap, not by closing it but by showing that there is no such gap. And psychoneural identities can be effectively used to bring brain science to bear on the explanation of facts stated in the vernacular psychological vocabulary. Why did Jones lose consciousness? Consider the following derivation:

(γ) Jones was given an injection of sodium pentothal.
Administration of sodium pentothal causes pyramidal cell activity to cease.

Therefore, pyramidal cell activity ceased in Jones.
Consciousness = pyramidal cell activity.
Therefore, Jones lost consciousness.

This looks like a perfectly fine explanation of why Jones lost consciousness. But as we saw earlier (chapter 4), the explanatory activity is over when the third line, "pyramidal activity ceased in Jones," is derived from the first two lines. These two premises explain why pyramidal cell activity ceased in Jones. What the identity "consciousness = pyramidal cell activity" enables us to do is to rewrite in the vernacular what has already been explained. Since the first two premises give a neurophysiological explanation of why pyramidal cell activity stopped in Jones, we can claim that they give a neurophysiological explanation of why Jones lost consciousness, because the fact that pyramidal cell activity ceased in Jones is the very same fact as the fact that Jones lost consciousness.

Given this, you may, if you like, call (γ) a "reductive" explanation of why Jones lost consciousness, but you should be mindful of the fact that the explanation represented in (γ) takes place wholly *within* neurophysiology. If the idea of reductive explanation conjures up for you an image of facts and laws at a "lower" level (neurophysiology) being invoked to explain facts at a "higher" level (vernacular psychology), then you should *not* consider (γ) a reductive explanation. This is only to be expected, because reductive identities, like "pain = C-fiber stimulation" and "consciousness = pyramidal cell activity," make levels collapse onto each other. It is not the case that there is a "higher" level where we find pain and consciousness and a "lower" level where we find C-fiber stimulation and pyramidal cell activity. There is only one level that includes both pain and C-fiber stimulation, both consciousness and pyramidal cell activity. It is precisely the job of identity reduction to abolish multiple levels.

Recall inference (β). As we noted, (β) cannot be considered an explanation, reductive or otherwise, of Jones's being in pain. Given that pain = neural state N_1, there is no explanation of pain in terms of N_1 any more than there is an explanation of N_1 in terms of pain. If you should continue to worry why there is such a thing as pain in this world, you might as well worry about why there is such a thing as neural state N_1. So identity reductions do not provide us with reductive explanations so much as show us that there are no genuine "reductive" explanations to be had.

But one questions remains: Where do we get these psychoneural identities like "pain = C-fiber stimulation" and "consciousness = pyramidal cell activity"?

They would be handy things to have: They would let us deal with the explanatory gap problem and help seal the case for physicalism. Their availability, however, has to be shown on independent grounds; it would be question-begging to argue that we can earn our entitlement to them simply from their ability to handle the explanatory gap and solve the "hard" problem. We discussed this issue in chapter 4; we briefly return to it later in this chapter.

Functional Reduction and the Explanatory Gap

Let us now see how a functional reduction of qualia might give us a reductive explanation of why they correlate with the neural states with which they correlate and thereby solve the hard problem. Again, let us suppose that being in pain can be functionally characterized as follows:

> x is in pain = $_{\text{def}}$ x is in some state P such that P is caused to instantiate by tissue damage and traumas, and the instantiation of P causes x to emit aversive behavior.

In a population of interest to us, say, humans, suppose that neural state N_1 is the realizer of pain as defined—that is, N_1 is the state that is caused to instantiate by tissue damage and traumas and that causes aversive behavior. Consider the following derivation:

> (δ) Jones is in neural state N_1.
>> In Jones and organisms like Jones (that is, humans), N_1 is caused to instantiate by tissue damage and traumas, and it in turn causes winces, groans, and aversive behavior.
>> To be in pain = $_{\text{def}}$ to be in a state that is caused by tissue damage and traumas and that in turn causes winces, groans, and aversive behavior.
>> Therefore, Jones is in pain.

The derivation is valid, and it seems plausible to view it as a reductive explanation of why Jones is in pain in terms of her being in a certain neural state.

Note how (δ) differs from (α) and (β), offered, respectively, by bridge-law reduction and identity reduction. Unlike (α), which appeals to an empirical bridge law to make the transition from the neural to the mental, (δ) invokes a definition, in its third line, to make the transition. As may be recalled, it was the use of an empirical bridge law as a premise that doomed (α) as a reductive explanation. In contrast, definitions do not count as extra premises; they come free in proofs and derivations. To put this another way, the third line of (δ) is not a fact about pains; if it is about anything, it is about the meaning of the word "pain", or the concept of pain. This means that (δ) passes the emergentist's predictive criterion: We can predict that Jones will be in pain solely on the basis of knowledge of neural-biological facts—from knowledge of a neural-physiological law about N_1 and the fact that Jones is in N_1.

Next, compare (δ) with (β): As we saw, in (β) the conclusion "Jones is in pain" is a mere rewrite of "Jones is in neural state N_1" via the identity "pain = neural state N_1." No laws are involved here, whereas we would expect explanations of events and facts to make use of laws. In contrast, the derivation (δ) makes essential use of a law in its second line; in fact, it is a causal law, and it underwrites the explanatory transition from Jones's neural state to her pain. The functional definition of pain is, of course, also crucial, but without the law, the derivation does not go through.

A functional reduction of pain, with N_1 as its realizer, seems also capable of generating an explanation of why pain correlates with N_1. This can be seen in the following derivation:

(ε) x is in neural state N_1.
    In x (and systems like x), N_1 is caused to instantiate by tissue damage and traumas, and an instantiation of N_1 causes x to emit aversive behavior.
    Being in pain $=_{\text{def}}$ being in a state that is caused to instantiate by tissue damage and traumas and that causes aversive behavior.
    Therefore, x is in pain.
    Therefore, whenever x is in neural state N_1, x is in pain.

This seems like a perfectly good explanation of the correlation between pain and neural state N_1. Note that, as in (δ), this explanatory derivation invokes a law in its second premise, satisfying the nomological requirement standardly placed on scientific explanations.[13]

But all this is contingent on the availability of functional definitions of mental states, especially states of phenomenal consciousness, or qualia. At this point the situation with functional reduction is similar to the situation facing identity reduction. Both types of reduction can handle the explanatory gap problem, each in its own way. Identity reduction promises to make the explanatory gap disappear by disallowing the demand for an explanation of why pain correlates with the neural state with which it correlates; functional reduction tries to meet the explanatory demand head-on, providing a reductive explanation of why the correlation holds. But just as identity reduction must come up with psychoneural identities to turn its promises into reality, functional reduction will remain an empty schema if the mental turns out to systematically resist functionalization. Before we turn to these questions in the final section, let us pause to examine the feasibility of nonreductive physicalism, the most widely influential form of physicalism.

Nonreductive Physicalism and Emergentism

If you accept ontological physicalism and yet reject the thesis that all properties possessed by physical systems are physical properties—the properties investigated in basic physics and those reducible to them—you are embracing physicalist property dualism. Nonreductive physicalism, however, is not merely a form of property dualism. Although the nonreductive physicalist denies the physical reducibility of the mental, she accepts a robust and intimate relationship between mental properties and physical properties, and this is mind-body supervenience (chapter 1). In this, the nonreductive physicalism goes beyond some versions of property dualism; it should be clear that property dualism as such does not require the thesis that the mental character of a being is dependent on, or determined by, its physical nature, as mind-body supervenience requires.

Moreover, nonreductive physicalists are mental realists who believe in the reality of mental properties; they regard mental properties as genuine properties the possession of which makes a difference—a causal difference. Part of believing in the reality of mental properties is to believe in their causal efficacy. An organism, in virtue of having a mental property (say, wanting a drink of water or being in pain), acquires powers and propensities to act or be acted upon in certain ways. Summarizing all this, nonreductive physicalism, as standardly understood, comprises the following four claims:

Ontological Physicalism. The spacetime world consists exclusively of bits of matter and their aggregates.
Irreducibility of the Mental. Mental properties are not reducible to physical properties.

Mind-body Supervenience. Mental properties supervene on physical properties.

Mental Causal Efficacy. Mental properties are causally efficacious; mental events are sometimes causes of other events, both physical and mental.

Nonreductive physicalism, understood as the conjunction of these four theses, has been the most influential position on the relation between the mental and the physical. We can think of property dualism as the conjunction of the first, second, and fourth doctrines—that is, all but mind-body supervenience. This makes nonreductive physicalism a form of property dualism, but it is not the only form, since one might very well reject mind-body supervenience while accepting the rest. What makes nonreductive physicalism a form of physicalism is its commitment to mind-body supervenience (in this context, ontological physicalism is taken for granted): The mental world is the way it is because the physical world is the way it is, and this gives primacy, both ontological and explanatory, to the physical.

In accepting the irreducibility thesis, however, nonreductive physicalism honors the special position that thought and consciousness enjoy in our conception of ourselves among the things of this world. The irreducibility thesis is also a philosophical affirmation of the autonomy of psychology and cognitive science as independent sciences, not constrained by more basic sciences. In accepting the causal efficacy of the mental, the nonreductive physicalist not only acknowledges what seems so familiar and obvious to common sense, but at the same time, it declares psychology and cognitive science to be genuine sciences capable of generating law-based causal explanations and predictions. All in all, it is an attractive package, and it is not difficult to appreciate its appeal and understand its staying power.

Emergentism, which flourished during the first half of the twentieth century, was the first systematic formulation of nonreductive physicalism. Its main proponents included not only academic philosophers such as Samuel Alexander and C. D. Broad but also those, like C. Lloyd Morgan, who were scientists by training.[14] The idea of emergence has continued to hold a special fascination for practicing scientists who have an interest in the philosophical issues arising within their disciplines, as witness Roger Sperry, the noted Nobel laureate neurophysiologist.[15]

Ontological physicalism was at the foundation of classical emergentism. The emergentists agree with contemporary physicalists in the claim that material particles and their aggregates distributed over spacetime exhaust all of concrete reality. There are to be no spirits (which some supposed necessary to explain mentality) and no vital forces or "entelechies" (which, according to neo-vitalists, made biological phenomena possible). As we ascend to higher levels from the level of basic physical particles, no new entities or forces make their appearance; we only find increasingly more complex structures and configurations of the basic particles. The central tenet of emergentism is the following claim:

Doctrine of Property Emergence. When aggregates of material particles attain an appropriate level of structural complexity ("relatedness"), genuinely novel properties emerge to characterize these systems.

The emergentist distinguishes between two types of properties of a whole: those that are merely "resultant" and those that are "emergent." Resultant properties are "additive" or "subtractive"; for example, the weight of this table is merely the arithmetic sum of the weight of its top and the weight of its base, and hence it is predictable from the properties of its parts. For this reason, weight is a resultant property. This would be so even if nothing had existed that had exactly the weight of this table before the table came into being. Thus, the property of weighing, say, exactly 314.159265358979323 pounds might be a "new" property, a property that has never been instantiated by anything until now, but it still would not count as a "genuinely novel" property in the sense the emergentist has in mind.

An example that emergentists sometimes used as a novel emergent property is the transparency of water: This property is alien to hydrogen and oxygen atoms and not predictable from the properties of these atoms as they exist in themselves. You can know all about the intrinsic properties of hydrogen and oxygen atoms and not know that when they are combined in a certain way, they result in a transparent substance. Or so some emergentists argued. However, this probably was not a good example; perhaps it is possible to predict, on the basis of what we now know in particle physics, that quantities of H_2O molecules will have the property of letting light beams pass through intact. But the example gives us a serviceable idea of what the emergentists had in mind. There is now a near-consensus that the best candidates for emergent properties are mental properties, in particular, phenomenal properties of consciousness.[16]

In contemporary idiom, the emergentists' distinction between emergent and resultant properties seems best interpreted as the distinction between properties that are irreducible and those that are irreducible to the properties of the constituent parts of a system. (The favorite emergentist slogan is "The whole is more than the sum of its parts.") But what sort of reduction is involved here? Three types of reduction were distinguished and described earlier. Which kind of reduction is appropriate for a proper understanding of emergentism? This question also arises for our statement of nonreductive physicalism. What makes this doctrine nonreductive is the irreducibility thesis, the claim that mental properties are not reducible to physical properties. But what sort of reduction is involved here? Is the mental supposed to be irreducible in all of the three ways, or only in some? We turn to these questions shortly, but let us first fully set out the doctrines that make up emergentism. We have the following thesis as a companion to the doctrine of emergent properties:

> *Irreducibility of Emergent Properties.* Emergent properties are not reducible to their "basal conditions"—the underlying conditions from which they emerge.

Classical British emergentists regarded emergent properties not only as irreducibly distinct from lower-level properties but also as representing richer and fuller levels of reality, toward which the universe is thought to be approaching in its "emergent evolution." Thus, with the successive emergence of life and mind, the world has reached a stage beyond where it was as a mere chaotic assemblage of atoms and molecules moving and jostling against one another in the void.

Classical emergentists accepted the supervenience of emergent properties on their basal properties, and mind-body supervenience as a special case of it.[17] If an emergent property emerges from a given set of basal conditions at a time, then if the same configuration of basal conditions recurs at another time, or in another system, the same emergent property will of necessity emerge. C. D. Broad writes:

> Put in abstract terms the emergent theory asserts that there are certain wholes, composed (say) of constituents A, B, and C in a relation R to each other; that all wholes composed of constituents of the same kind as A, B, and C in relations of the same kind as R have certain characteristic [emergent] properties. . . .
>
> No doubt the properties of silver-chloride are completely determined by those of silver and of chlorine; in the sense that whenever you have a whole

composed of these two elements in certain proportions and relations you have something with the characteristic properties of silver chloride.[18]

Emergentists also believed that emergent phenomena, once they have emerged, acquire causal life of their own and begin to exert their causal powers to influence events and processes at the lower levels. This is the famous, or notorious, thesis of "downward" causation:

Doctrine of "Downward" Causation. Emergent properties have causal powers to influence phenomena at the level from which they have emerged.

Life, consciousness, and rational thought, having all emerged ultimately from physicochemical conditions, can causally loop downward to bring about changes in the physical world. This doctrine is an essential component of emergentism; if emergents had no causal powers to affect the course of events in the physical world, there would be little point in acknowledging them. Downward causation, therefore, is the raison d'être of emergence. It should be clear that the doctrine of downward causation is a generalized version of the thesis of causal efficacy of the mental, a component of nonreductive physicalism.

The upshot, then, is that emergentism is a form of nonreductive physicalism. Many emergentists thought that biological phenomena were emergent, irreducible to physicochemical properties. Though the point is not undisputed, biological phenomena may well be physically reducible; molecular biology promises to give us a reductive understanding of life in terms of underlying physicochemical processes. If, therefore, we restrict the scope of emergentism to mental properties, emergentism appears to coincide, almost exactly, with nonreductive physicalism. The only point where an exact coincidence may fail concerns the type of reduction involved when the irreducibility claim involved in the two positions is spelled out.

Let us first consider the sense of reduction appropriate to emergentism. Why do the emergentists think that emergent properties are irreducible to lower-level properties? Why are mental properties "emergent," and not merely "resultant," from physicochemical or biological properties? Notice, first of all, that the emergentist would have had no problem with laws connecting emergent properties and their underlying lower-level bases. Indeed, they were committed to there being such laws: When appropriate "basal conditions" are present, emergent properties must emerge. More generally, there is no reason why the emergentist would have had any problem with bridge laws connecting emergent properties with lower-level properties. This means that the emergentist's rejection of the physical reducibility of the mental had nothing to do with the question of whether the mental is bridge-law-reducible to the physical. Bridge-law reduction simply does not meet the requirement of reduction that the emergentist had in mind.

Suppose that pain emerges from C-fiber excitation. To reduce pain to C-fiber excitation, the emergentist would require us to answer the following two sets of questions:

1. Why does pain emerge just when C-fibers are excited? What is it about C-fibers that makes it the case that pain, not itch or tickle, emerges from it? Why does pain emerge from C-fiber excitation, not from a different neural state?
2. Can we predict the occurrence of pain from an ideally complete biological-physical knowledge of C-fiber excitation? Knowing all about the neurophysiology of a brain, can we predict what conscious experience, if any, is going on in that brain?

You will recognize the first question as raising the explanatory gap problem. And the second question, of course, is the "predictive" criterion discussed earlier in connection with reductive explanation. Evidently, the second question can be affirmatively answered if, say, the statement "Jones is in pain" can be logically derived from statements concerning Jones's brain states and laws about brain states. Moreover, closing the "predictive gap" this way is also a way of closing the explanatory gap: We can explain why Jones is in pain by deriving "Jones is in pain" from "Jones's C-fibers are stimulated" along with other neural-biological facts (including laws). Itch does not arise from C-fiber stimulation because "Jones is itching" is not derivable from "Jones's C-fibers are stimulated." And so on. It seems clear that what the emergentist is demanding for reduction is that the explanatory gap between pain and C-fiber stimulation be closed by logical derivation of pain from C-fiber stimulation.

We have already rejected bridge-law reduction as an appropriate model for characterizing the emergentist idea of reduction. We now see that identity reduction has to be ruled out as well. The reason is simple: The identity reduction of pain to C-fiber stimulation consists in the identification of pain with C-fiber stimulation—that is, the claim "pain = C-fiber stimulation." According to the identity reductionist, however, this identity is an empirical, a posteriori identity. So it is not a premise we are entitled to use to support an affirmative answer to the question "Can we know that Jones is in pain solely on the basis of knowledge of what is going on in her brain?" For knowing the identity "pain = C-fiber stimulation" goes beyond knowing all about the neural-biological goings-on in Jones's brain.

We now come to functional reduction. Can functional reduction meet the emergentist's demand? Consider an earlier derivation based on a functional reduction of pain ("N_1" has been replaced with "C-fiber stimulation"):

(δ) Jones's C-fibers are stimulated.
In Jones and organisms like Jones (that is, humans), C-fiber stimulation is caused by tissue damage and traumas, and it in turn causes winces, groans, and aversive behavior.
To be in pain = $_{def}$ to be in a state that is caused by tissue damage and traumas, and that in turn causes winces, groans, and aversive behavior.
Therefore, Jones is in pain.

This derivation apparently meets the emergentist's requirement that a pain statement be derived solely from neural-physical statements. (Again note that the third line is a definition and that, as such, it is not about pains but only about the meaning of the word "pain.") We argued earlier that it is also an explanatory derivation; it explains why Jones is in pain on the basis of her being in the neural state of C-fiber stimulation. It tells us what it is about C-fiber stimulation that makes it an emergence base of pain, not of itch or tickle. Functional reduction, therefore, is the only form of reduction appropriate for interpreting the irreducibility claim as a component of emergentism. Identity reduction and bridge-law reduction do not meet the need.

Returning briefly to nonreductive physicalism, how should we interpret its irreducibility claim? It seems that we can again rule out bridge-law reduction. We have already sufficiently cataloged the problems with bridge-law reduction—for example, its compatibility with a host of dualistic mind-body theories and its inability to deal with the explanatory gap. We are left, then, with identity reduction and functional reduction, and we have seen how each is able to handle the explanatory gap, each in its own way. This shows that there are two versions of nonreductive physicalism, depending on whether its irreducibility thesis is interpreted as meaning that the mental is not identity-reducible to the physical or as meaning that the mental is not functionally reducible to the physical. Our earlier discussion of emergentism shows that emergentism coincides with the second version of nonreductive physicalism.

The Problem of Downward Causation

For emergent properties to emerge, the presence of appropriate basal conditions is required, and this means that mental properties emerge only when the right neurobiological and other types of conditions obtain. In this sense, mental properties are dependent on neurobiological properties. But the emergentist holds that once they have emerged, these higher-level properties begin to manifest their powers by causally affecting lower-level phenomena. This is the "downward causation" noted earlier. Evidently, nonreductive physicalism is no less committed to downward causation. The thesis of the causal efficacy of the mental, one of the four components of nonreductive physicalism, is essentially the doctrine of downward causation. This means that any difficulties with downward causation are difficulties for both nonreductive physicalism and emergentism—an unsurprising conclusion since emergentism all but coincides with nonreductive physicalism. "Downward" is only a metaphor in this context, and there is no need to associate it with a literal meaning. The only point to keep in mind about downward causation is this: The existence and character of the mental (or the emergents) depend on, and are determined by, the presence of appropriate conditions (their basal conditions) in the physical domain, and yet they are able to causally influence processes in that very domain.

Earlier (chapter 7), we saw how mental causation combines with certain further reasonable assumptions to create pressures toward reductionism. Here we only briefly recapitulate the arguments and conclusions. First, any form of property dualism—any version of dualism that implies that mental phenomena, events, and states (that is, instantiations of mental properties) are distinct from physical ones (instantiations of physical properties)—runs into difficulties with the principle of the causal closure of the physical domain. This principle, to the effect that the physical domain is causally closed and explanatorily self-sufficient, enjoys wide acceptance and appears to have ample justification. In particular, anyone who calls himself a physicalist must respect it. It is straightforward to see that physical causal closure prohibits the injection of any causal influence from outside the physical domain (though exactly how the reasoning proceeds toward this conclusion depends on how physical causal closure is stated; for details, see chapter 7). This means that unless the emergentist can find a way to reject physical causal closure, her doctrine of downward causation cannot be sustained. Given the closure principle, the nonreductive physicalist is in the same boat: The mental cannot have causal efficacy with respect to the physical—that is, mental-to-physical causation is not possible. This is the "exclusion" argument.

Next, any version of property dualism that also accepts mind-body supervenience, like nonreductive physicalism and emergentism, encounters a further difficulty, the "supervenience" argument. Suppose that an instantiation of mental property M causes another mental property M* to instantiate. But M* is supervenient on physical properties, and M* is instantiated on this occasion in virtue of the fact that one of its supervenience bases, say, P*, is instantiated on this occasion. Now, there are plausible considerations for the claim that whatever event causes a supervenient property to instantiate must do so by causing one of its base properties to instantiate. If so, the instantiation of M can cause M* to instantiate only if it causes P* to instantiate. But this is a case of mental-to-physical causation, something that our preceding argument, if correct, has shown to be an impossibility. It follows then that we have to retract the initial supposition that an instance of mental property M causes another mental property M* to instantiate. This means that there can be no mental-to-mental causation any more than there can be mental-to-physical causation. The upshot of all this is that given the causal closure of the physical, the four theses of nonreductive physicalism—and the corresponding four doctrines of emergentism—form an inconsistent set. The nonreductive physicalist and the emergentist must reject at least one of the four.

The emergentist appears to have two choices to consider. First, she can opt to abandon physical causal closure. Given the overall orientation of emergentism, that seems like the most natural direction to take. For the emergentist, ontological physicalism may be physicalism enough. Whether or not the rejection of physical causal closure can be justified is an independent question, a question that the emergentist must take seriously. This is so especially because this principle in itself does not imply physical monism. As far as it is concerned, there could well be nonphysical domains; its only imperative is that there be no causal interference in the physical domain from outside. Thus, one cannot simply invoke one's antiphysicalist sympathies to reject physical causal closure. A second alternative is to reject mind-body supervenience.[19] However, this falls far short of a full solution for the emergentist. The reason is that the exclusion argument, which is at odds with downward causation, does not invoke mind-body supervenience as a premise; it is the supervenience argument that does. Downward causation is an essential component of emergentism, something without which emergentism would lose its rationale. It seems, then, that the emergentist has no choice but to disavow physical causal closure.

For the nonreductive physicalist, choices are more limited: Abandoning physical causal closure or mind-body supervenience is not an option. That would take physicalism out of nonreductive physicalism. The options, therefore, are now reduced to giving up one of the remaining two theses: the irreducibility of the mental or mental causal efficacy. If you abandon the first, you embrace reductionism; if you let go of the second, you embrace epiphenomenalism. Most contemporary physicalists find neither option tolerable; instead, many of them do their best to resist the exclusion-supervenience arguments. Further discussion of the complex dialectic in this area is beyond the scope of this book. In the section to follow, we focus on how the reductionist option can play out.

The Limits of Physicalism

We have seen how the two types of reduction—identity reduction and functional reduction—could deal with the explanatory gap problem or the hard problem of consciousness. It is also easily seen how they could deal with the problem of mental causation and fight off the threat of epiphenomenalism. If identity reduction can be upheld and we are in a position to affirm "pain = C-fiber stimulation," "consciousness = pyramidal cell activity," and the like, there will be no special problem about how pain, or consciousness, can cause, and be caused by, other events. For pain will have exactly the causal powers of C-fiber stimulation, and similarly for consciousness and pyramidal cell activity. Under identity reduction, all causal actions take place in the physical domain and the mental is part of that domain.

Let us see how things work under functional reduction. We argued earlier that functional reduction meets Smart's "nothing over and above" criterion for individual mental events (or "event-tokens"). If Jones is in pain in virtue of instantiating a neural realizer of pain—say, C-fiber stimulation—her being in pain on this occasion can be identified with her instantiating this pain realizer (that is, her C-fibers' being stimulated). If so, her pain has the same causal powers that her C-fiber stimulation has, and this solves the problem of mental causation for her pains. In general, the same is true of all individual instances of functionally reduced mental properties: Each such instance is identified with the instance of the neural-physical realizer involved, and the individual mental event has the causal power of its physical realizer.[20]

To take stock: Either type of psychoneural reduction takes care of both mental causation and the explanatory gap. If we are to avoid epiphenomenalism, reductionism is the only alternative; we should be prepared to embrace the view that mentality is ultimately reducible to physical-biological-behavioral processes. But our willingness to embrace reductionism does not in itself show that reductionism is true—that is, that either kind of reduction is really possible for the mental. The reducibility of the mental has to be shown on independent grounds. If, in spite of our lately found enthusiasm for reductionism, the mental turns out not to be physically reducible, epiphenomenalism cannot be avoided. So is the mental reducible, and if so how?

In considering these questions, one pitfall to avoid is the tendency to think that the mental in its entirely must be either reducible or irreducible. It may well be that some mental properties are reducible while others are not. For the would-be reductionist, it would be better if the former were to outnumber the latter. The main point to remember is that the reductionist project need not be a total success or a total failure. The more it succeeds, the more we succeed in saving mentality from epiphenomenalism; the less successful it is, the fewer the mental properties we can save from causal impotence.

You may recall a broad classification of mental phenomena into two kinds (chapter 1): phenomenal mental events, or experiences, with sensory and qualitative characters, like bodily sensations, seeing yellow, smelling ammonia, and the rest, on the one hand; and intentional-cognitive states (or propositional attitudes), like belief, desire, intention, thought, and the like. The former are states with "qualia"; there is a "what it is like" quality to having them or being in them. The latter have propositional contents expressed by subordinate that-clauses ("George believes that there are lions in Africa," "Ann hopes the winter will be mild this year"). You may recall the question of what events and states in these two classes have in common that makes all of them "mental." It may well be that physical reducibility is not among the shared properties of these two mental categories.

In fact, there is a view on the current scene according to which the former, states with qualia, are functionally irreducible, whereas the latter, intentional-cognitive states, are so reducible.[21] Let us take up the second class of mental events first. Why should we think beliefs, desires, and such are so reducible, and if so, according to which model of reduction? It would seem that these states cannot be reduced by identity reduction—namely, that it is not possible to identify them with neural-physical states. The reason for this is the old and familiar nemesis of reductionism, the multiple realizability of these states (see chapter 5). As you will recall, however, functional reduction can accommodate multiple realization. Can these states then be functionally reduced?

To reduce a property functionally, the property must first be functionalized; that is, it must be given a functional characterization or interpretation. That is the required conceptual preliminary. After a property has been functionalized, it is the job of science to discover its realizers (in populations of interest). So the question for us is this: Can intentional-cognitive states, like beliefs and desires, be given functional characterization? Can we define belief as an internal state defined in terms of its serving as a causal intermediary between inputs and outputs? In short, can belief be functionally defined?

It is fair to say, as critics of functional reduction point out, that no one has as yet produced a complete functional definition or analysis of belief and that it is rather unlikely that a full functional definition will ever be formulated.[22] However, there are reasons for thinking that belief and other intentional-cognitive states are functionally conceived states—that is, states understood in terms of their "job descriptions." We consider here two such reasons. First, there seems ample ground for believing that intentional-cognitive states are supervenient on the physical-behavioral properties of creatures. Consider the "zombies"—the supposedly conceivable creatures who are just like us both in internal compositional-structural detail and in the functional organization of sensory input and behavioral output but who lack experiences—that is, they have no phenomenal consciousness. Whether such creatures could exist is a question we need not address here. Our immediate question is whether zombies have intentional cognitive states, and a strong case can be made, it seems, for saying that they must have such states. To begin, the zombies are indistinguishable from us, from our fellow humans, behaviorally and physically. If that is the case, we must attribute to them a capacity for speech. Observationally, they emit noises that sound exactly like English sentences, and they seem to communicate among themselves through exchanges of these noises and to be able to coordinate their activities just as we do. Given this, it would be incoherent to deny that they are language users. Making assertions is a fundamental component of speech, and any creature with speech must be able to make utterances and thereby make assertions. To utter "Snow is white" to make an assertion is to express the belief that snow is white. Consider other speech acts, like asking questions and issuing commands. To ask "Is snow white?" is to express a desire to be told whether snow is white. To command "Please shut the window" is to express the desire that the window be shut and the belief that the window is not now shut. It is not conceptually possible to concede that zombies are language users and then refuse to attribute beliefs and desires to them. Once these states are attributed to the zombies and given the assumption that they are behaviorally indistinguishable from us, we must also grant them status as full-fledged agents. Thus, we seem to be driven to the conclusion that belief, desire, intention, agency, and the rest are supervenient on the physical-behavioral aspects of creatures, and that these states cannot go beyond what can be captured in physical-behavioral terms.

Second, suppose we are asked to design and build a device that detects shapes and colors of middle-sized objects around it (perception), processes and stores the information it has gained (information processing, memory, knowledge), and uses it to guide its behavior (action). If that is our assignment, we would know how to go about executing it; in fact, there may already be robots with such capabilities in rudimentary form. We know how to proceed with the design of such a machine because processes and states like perception, memory, information processing, using information to guide behavior, and action are defined by job descriptions. A device, or creature, that has the capacity to do certain specified work under specified conditions is a system that perceives, processes and stores information, make inferences, and so on. All these capacities are capacities for performing specific tasks, and systems that have such capacities are ipso facto systems that are capable of having information-bearing states, learning, remembering, and reasoning. Again, the main point to note here is that these intentional states and processes are closely tied to having capacities of certain kinds—capacities to interact and cope with the environment. The only difference between such states of our simple machine and real-life intentional-cognitive states is that the causal tasks associated with the former are exactly specified whereas those associated with the latter are less precisely defined and, more importantly, open-ended.

It may be true, as critics of functional reduction of intentional-cognitive states have argued, that we will never have complete functional specifications of intentional states like belief, desire, and intention. But that is only because, as just noted, the causal tasks involved with belief are open-ended and perhaps essentially so. It does not show that these are not functional, task-oriented states; as far as supervenience holds, there cannot be extra factors beyond functional-behavioral facts that define or constitute them. Moreover, it is not necessary to have full and complete definitions of these states before scientific research can begin to identify their physical realizers—the neural mechanisms that do the causal work so far specified. The fact is that these intentional states are multitask states; their cores may be fairly easily identifiable, but they may have no clear definitional boundaries. As scientific research makes progress, we may add or subtract from their initial job descriptions; that is one way in which our concepts change and evolve.

Compare this with the situation involving qualia—or the phenomenal, qualitative states of consciousness. Suppose that you are now given an assignment to design a "pain box," a device that can be implanted in your robot that not only will detect damage to its body and then trigger appropriate avoidance behavior but also will enable the robot to experience the sensation of pain when the box is activated. Building a damage detector is an engineering problem, and our engineers, we may presume, know how to go about designing such a device. But what about making the robot experience pain when the device is activated? It seems clear that even the best and brightest engineers would not know where to begin. What would you need to do to make it a pain box rather than an itch box, and how would you know you had succeeded? The functional aspect of pain can be designed and engineered into a system. But the qualitative aspect of pain, or pain as a quale, seems like a wholly different game. The only way we know how to build a pain-experiencing system may well be to make an exact replica of a system known to have the capacity to experience pain—that is, to make a replica of a human or animal brain.

Let us return to the zombies. Some philosophers have argued that zombies (without inner experiences) are metaphysically possible and therefore that the qualitative states of consciousness are beyond the reach of physicalism. The zombie hypothesis has been controversial, and we do not need the zombies to see that qualia are not functionally definable. All we need is the possibility of qualia inversion—for example, visual spectrum inversion (chapter 8). When you and I gaze at a bunch of spinach leaves, both of us say "Green," and when we are presented with ripe tomatoes, we say "Red." However, the visual qualia we experience are exactly reversed: When you look at spinach your visual quale is like mine when I look at ripe tomatoes, and vice versa. This surely is conceivable, and it is hard to see how we could show that to be not "really" (that is, metaphysically) possible. If qualia inversion is possible, it follows that qualia cannot be captured by functional definitions. We cannot define qualia in terms of the tasks they perform. Pain certainly has a function, the important biological function of separating us from sources of harm, teaching us to avoid potentially noxious stimuli, and so forth. However, its function is not, it may be argued, what makes pain

pain, or what constitutes pain; rather, it is the way it feels—nothing can be a pain unless it *hurts*.

If qualia resist functionalization, as they seem to, they cannot be functionally reduced. And a functional reduction of qualia is not available to solve the explanatory gap problem or fend off the threat of epiphenomenalism. So what about the prospect of an identity reduction of qualia? Earlier (chapter 4), we discussed several positive arguments for psychoneural identities and found all of them seriously wanting. The argument from simplicity, of the sort J. C. C. Smart originally appealed to, does not have enough weight behind it to be convincing, and we saw how the two explanatory arguments, one by McLaughlin and Hill and the other by Block and Stalnaker, fall short of the mark. The causal argument seems to work better, but it does not go the full distance; in effect, it only shows the conditional proposition that if mental causation is to be saved, the mental must be brought into the physical domain—that is, physically reduced. And this exactly is the issue we are now grappling with. We have to conclude that an identity reduction of qualia is no more promising than their functional reduction and that qualia epiphenomenalism is looming as a real threat.

We should note, however, that saving intentional-cognitive states from epiphenomenalism is not a small accomplishment. In saving them, we have saved ourselves as agents and cognizers, for cognition and agency are located in the realm of the intentional-cognitive. Recall Fodor's lament about the possible loss of mental causation:

> I'm not really convinced that it matters very much whether the mental is physical; still less that it matters very much whether we can prove that it is. Whereas, if it isn't literally true that my wanting is causally responsible for my reaching, and my itching is causally responsible for my scratching, and my believing is causally responsible for my saying . . . , if none of that is literally true, then practically everything I believe about anything is false and it's the end of the world.[23]

Three mental items are on Fodor's wish list: wanting, itching, and believing. Fodor's world is not coming to an end, at least not entirely; we have saved for him wanting and believing. That is, we have saved agency and cognition.

But what about itching? There are reductive approaches to consciousness that attempt to reduce it to intentional-representational states. Two such approaches, the higher-state thought-perception theory and qualia representationalism, were reviewed earlier (chapter 8). If these theories work and we can reduce qualia to intentional-representational states, these latter states could in turn be functionalized, as we just saw, and that would yield a solution to both the mental causation problem and the explanatory gap problem. But that is a big if. Just because these approaches to qualia would do something nice for us, perhaps something very important, that is not a reason to think that they must work. They must first be shown to be correct approaches, and we have seen some serious difficulties with them—although, of course, the issues are far from closed.

Returning to the model of functional reduction, we can go a little more distance toward saving qualia. Begin with an analogy: the traffic lights. Everywhere in the world red means "stop," green means "go," and yellow means "slow down." But this is merely a conventional arrangement; as far as traffic management goes, we could do just as well with a system whereby red means "slow down," green means "stop," and yellow means "go"—or any permutation thereof. What is important is our ability to *discriminate* among these colors; the intrinsic color qualities are of no importance. The same holds for qualia. You and your red-green-spectrum-inverted friend do equally well in coping with traffic lights, picking tomatoes out of mounds of lettuce, reporting your experience as "red" or "green," learning about what is out there in your respective surroundings (for instance, that those flowers over there are irises, not roses), and so on. It is the qualia differences and similarities, not qualia as absolutely intrinsic properties, that matter to our perception and cognition of the world. That roses look *this way* and that irises look *that way* cannot be cognitively relevant as long as roses and irises look relevantly different to you. Moreover, qualia differences and similarities are behaviorally manifest, as we just saw, and this opens the way to their potential functionalization.

We can conclude, therefore, that qualia are not entirely lost to epiphenomenalism; we can save qualia differences and similarities, if not qualia as intrinsic qualities. It is the qualia similarities and differences that matter—matter to cognition and action. So what we may lose to epiphenomenalism, and something for which we cannot solve the explanatory gap problem, is this small mental residue, qualia as intrinsic qualities. And that represents the limits of physicalism.

Further Readings

The classic source on bridge-law reduction is Ernest Nagel, *The Structure of Science*. For one interesting variant of this model, see Patricia S. Churchland, *Neurophilosophy*, chapter 7. On identities versus bridge laws, see Robert L. Causey, "Attribute Identities in Microreductions."

On functional reduction, see Jaegwon Kim, *Mind in a Physical World*, and "Making Sense of Emergence." *The Philosophy of Science*, edited by Richard Boyd, Philip Gasper, and J. D. Trout, includes useful articles on the general issue of reduction and reductionism in science.

On nonreductive physicalism, see Donald Davidson, "Mental Events," and Jerry A. Fodor, "Special Sciences, or the Disunity of Science as a Working Hypothesis." For analysis and critique, see Jaegwon Kim, "The Myth of Nonreductive Physicalism," and "Multiple Realization and the Metaphysics of Reduction." For nonreductivist replies, see Derk Pereboom and Hilary Kornblith, "The Metaphysics of Irreducibility"; Robert Van Gulick, "Nonreductive Materialism and the Nature of Intertheoretical Constraint"; Ausonio Marras, "Nonreductive Physicalism and Mental Causation"; John Post, *The Faces of Existence*; Ned Block, "Anti-Reductionism Slaps Back"; and Jerry A. Fodor, "Special Sciences: Still Autonomous After All These Years."

For a recent attempt to formulate a version of nonreductive physicalism, see Derk Pereboom, "Robust Nonreductive Physicalism."

Jeffrey Poland's *Physicalism* is a comprehensive discussion of contemporary physicalism. Both *Objections to Physicalism*, edited by Howard Robinson, and *Contemporary Materialism*, edited by Paul K. Moser and J. D. Trout, include chapters relevant to the issues discussed here. John Dupre's *The Disorder of Things* is a sustained attack on reductionism in science. Recent defenses of the physicalist perspective include John Perry, *Knowledge, Possibility, and Consciousness*; David Papineau, *Thinking About Consciousness*; Andrew Melnyk, *A Physicalist Manifesto*; and Jaegwon Kim, *Physicalism, or Something Near Enough*.

Classic sources of emergentism include C. D. Broad, *The Mind and Its Place in Nature*, and C. Lloyd Morgan, *Emergent Evolution*. Brian McLaughlin's "The Rise and Fall of British Emergentism" is a helpful survey and analysis of classical emergentism. Carl Gillett's anthology *Emergence: Philosophical and Scientific Foundations* includes many important classical and contemporary writings on emergentism.

On the explanatory gap, see Joseph Levine, "Materialism and Qualia: The Explanatory Gap," and "On Leaving Out What It's Like." Levine's *Purple Haze* is his most recent and developed statement on the issue. See also David J. Chalmers, *The Conscious Mind*. For analysis and critique, see Ned Block and Stalnaker, "Conceptual Analysis, Dualism, and the Explanatory Gap," and Ned Block, "The Harder Problem of Consciousness."

Notes

1. "Substance physicalism" would be a more appropriate term (it is used by Noa Latham in his "Substance Physicalism"); however, we follow the common usage here.

2. J. J. C. Smart, "Sensations and Brain Processes," p. 119 in the reprint version of *Philosophy of Mind: A Guide and Anthology*, ed. John Heil.

3. These three models do not exhaust the possibilities; for example, there are "definitional" reductions like philosophical behaviorism (chapter 3), phenomenalism, and ethical naturalism. Some philosophers speak of "ontological reductions," reduction of entities (like material things or numbers) that do not easily fit any of the three models. The models to be considered are those that are relevant to our present purposes.

4. Beagles, German shepherds, and poodles are not different "senses" of the word "dog" or different "concepts" of a dog; rather, they are different kinds (breeds) of dogs.

5. Ernest Nagel, *The Structure of Science*, ch. 11.

6. These examples are not uncontroversial; in particular, some strongly deny that genetics is reducible to molecular biology.

7. For example, the Putnam-Fodor multiple realization argument (see chapters 4 and 5) and Davidson's anomalist argument in his "Mental Events" (see chapter 7).

8. What about pain itself? Given the multiple realization of pain, is there a neural-biological property P such that being in pain is "nothing over and above" having P? See note 20.

9. David Chalmers, *The Conscious Mind*, p. 43 (emphasis in original).

10. Jerry A. Fodor, "Special Sciences, or the Disunity of Science as a Working Hypothesis," p. 131 of the reprint version of *Philosophy in Mind: Classical and Contemporary Readings*, ed. David J. Chalmers.

11. For more details on scientific explanation, see Carl G. Hempel, *Philosophy of Natural Science*.

12. Ned Block and Robert Stalnaker, "Conceptual Analysis, Dualism, and the Explanatory Gap," p. 24.

13. Carl G. Hempel, *Philosophy of Natural Science*.

14. Samuel Alexander, *Space, Time, and Deity*; C. D. Broad, *The Mind and Its Place in Nature*; and C. Lloyd Morgan, *Emergent Evolution*.

15. See Roger W. Sperry, "A Modified Concept of Consciousness." For a recent example of a scientist attempting to make use of the emergence concept, see Harold J. Morowitz, *The Emergence of Everything*.

16. However, efforts to apply emergence to the purely physical domain continue; see, for example, Paul Humphreys, "How Properties Emerge," and Harold Morowitz, *The Emergence of Everything*. There is now a plethora of emergence concepts on the scene, and this makes it imperative that the reader be attentive to just what concept is being passed off by a writer under the name "emergence" (if indeed there is a single coherent concept being promoted).

17. Here we are referring for the most part to the classic British emergentism of the first half of the twentieth century. There are some contemporary emergentists who deny the supervenience of emergents on their base-level properties. See, for example, Paul Humphreys, "How Properties Emerge," and Timothy O'Connor and Hong Yu Wong, "The Metaphysics of Emergence."

18. C. D. Broad, *The Mind and Its Place in Nature*, pp. 61, 64.

19. See note 17 for emergentists who have chosen to reject supervenience.

20. But what of pain as a mental kind? If pain is functionally reduced, is there a physical-neural property N such that being in pain = having N? And what of the causal powers of pain as such? One reasonably simple solution goes like this: Let P_1, P_2, . . . be all of pain's realizers. We can then identify pain with the *disjunctive* property of having P_1 or P_2 or. . . . This property can be highly heterogeneous and may well be unprojectible, making it relatively useless as a nomic scientific property. But that is only a reflection of the heterogeneity of the realizers of functional properties. On this account, the causal powers of pain as a mental kind would also be highly heterogeneous, as heterogeneous as its diverse physical-neural realizers. We should keep in mind, however, that all causal relations hold between individual events—that is, instantiations of properties, not directly for properties. For further discussion, see Jaegwon Kim, "Multiple Realization and the Metaphysics of Reduction," and "Making Sense of Emergence."

21. See David J. Chalmers, *The Conscious Mind*; and Jaegwon Kim, *Physicalism, or Something Near Enough*.

22. Ned Block and Robert Stalnaker make criticisms of this sort; see their "Conceptual Analysis, Dualism, and the Explanatory Gap."

23. Jerry A. Fodor, "Making Mind Matter More," in Fodor, *A Theory of Content and Other Essays*, p. 156.

References

Alanen, Lilli. *Descartes's Concept of Mind* (Cambridge, MA: Harvard University Press, 2003).

Alexander, Samuel. *Space, Time, and Deity,* 2 vols. (London: Macmillan, 1920).

Allen, Colin. "It Isn't What You Think: A New Idea About Intentional Causation," *Noûs* 29 (1995): 115–126.

Antony, Louise. "Anomalous Monism and the Problem of Explanatory Force," *Philosophical Review* 98 (1989): 153–188.

Antony, Louise, and Joseph Levine. "The Nomic and the Robust," in *Meaning in Mind,* ed. Barry Loewer and Georges Rey, eds. (London: Routledge, 1991).

Armstrong, David. "The Nature of Mind," in *Readings in Philosophy of Psychology*, vol. 1, ed. Ned Block (1970; Cambridge, MA: Harvard University Press, 1980).

Armstrong, David M., and Norman Malcolm. *Consciousness and Causality* (Oxford: Blackwell, 1984).

Baker, Lynne Rudder. *Explaining Attitudes* (Cambridge: Cambridge University Press, 1995).

———. "Has Content Been Naturalized?" in *Meaning in Mind,* ed. Barry Loewer and Georges Rey (London: Routledge, 1991).

Beckermann, Ansgar, Hans Flohr, and Jaegwon Kim, eds. *Emergence or Reduction?* (Berlin: De Gruyter, 1992).

Bennett, Karen. "Why the Exclusion Problem Seems Intractable, and How, Just Maybe, to Tract It," *Noûs* 37 (2003): 471–497.

Bickle, John. *Psychoneural Reduction: The New Wave* (Cambridge, MA: MIT Press, 1998).

Block, Ned. "Troubles with Functionalism," in *Readings in Philosophy of Psychology*, vol. 1, ed. Ned Block (Cambridge, MA: Harvard University Press, 1980). An excerpted version appears in *Philosophy of Mind: Classical and Contemporary Readings*, ed. David J. Chalmers (Oxford: Oxford University Press, 2002); and in *Philosophy of Mind: Contemporary Readings*, ed. Timothy O'Connor and David Robb (London: Routledge, 2003).

———. "Are Absent Qualia Impossible?" *Philosophical Review* 89 (1980): 257–274.

———. "What Is Functionalism?" in *Readings in Philosophy of Psychology*, vol. 1, ed. Ned Block (Cambridge, MA: Harvard University Press, 1980). Reprinted in *Philosophy of Mind: A Guide and Anthology*, ed. John Heil (Oxford: Oxford University Press, 2004).

————, ed. *Readings in Philosophy of Psychology*, vol. 1 (Cambridge, MA: Harvard University Press, 1980).

————. "Psychologism and Behaviorism," *Philosophical Review* 90 (1981): 5–43.

————. "Can the Mind Change the World?" in *Meaning and Method*, ed. George Boolos (Cambridge: Cambridge University Press, 1990).

————. "Inverted Earth," *Philosophical Perspectives* 4 (1990): 51–79.

————. "On a Confusion About a Function of Consciousness," *Behavioral and Brain Sciences* 18 (1995): 1–41. Reprinted in *The Nature of Consciousness,* ed. Ned Block, Owen Flanagan, and Güven Güzeldere (Cambridge, MA: MIT Press, 1999).

————. "The Mind as Software in the Brain," in *An Invitation to Cognitive Science*, ed. Daniel N. Osherson (Cambridge, MA: MIT Press, 1995).

————. "Anti-Reductionism Slaps Back," *Philosophical Perspectives* 11 (1997): 107–132.

————. "The Harder Problem of Consciousness," *Journal of Philosophy* 94 (2002): 1–35.

————. "Mental Paint," in *Reflections and Replies*, ed. Martin Hahn and Bjorn Ramberg (Cambridge, MA: MIT Press, 2003).

Block, Ned, Owen Flanagan, and Güven Güzeldere, eds. *The Nature of Consciousness: Philosophical and Scientific Essays* (Cambridge, MA: MIT Press, 1999).

Block, Ned, and Robert Stalnaker. "Conceptual Analysis, Dualism, and the Explanatory Gap," *Philosophical Review* 108 (1999): 1–46. Reprinted in *Philosophy of Mind: Classical and Contemporary Readings*, ed. David J. Chalmers (Oxford: Oxford University Press, 2002).

Boolos, George S., John Burgess, and Richard C. Jeffrey. *Computability and Logic*, 4th ed. (Cambridge: Cambridge University Press, 2002).

Boghossian, Paul. "Content and Self-Knowledge," *Philosophical Topics* 17 (1989): 5–26.

————. "Naturalizing Content," in *Meaning in Mind*, ed. Barry Loewer and Georges Rey, (London: Routledge, 1991).

Borchert, Donald, ed. *The Macmillan Encyclopedia of Philosophy*, 2nd ed. (New York: Macmillan, forthcoming).

Boyd, Richard, Philip Gasper, and J. D. Trout, eds. *The Philosophy of Science* (Cambridge, MA: MIT Press, 1991).

Brentano, Franz. *Psychology from an Empirical Standpoint*, trans. Antos C. Rancurello, D. B. Terrell, and Linda L. McAlister (New York: Humanities Press, 1973).

Broad, C. D. *The Mind and Its Place in Nature* (London: Routledge & Kegan Paul, 1962).

Burge, Tyler. "Individualism and the Mental," *Midwest Studies in Philosophy* 4 (1979): 73–121. Reprinted in *Philosophy of Mind: A Guide and Anthology*, ed. John Heil (Oxford: Oxford University Press, 2004). An excerpted version appears in *Philosophy of Mind: Classical and Contemporary Readings*, ed. David. J. Chalmers (Oxford: Oxford University Press, 2002).

————. "Individualism and Self-Knowledge," *Journal of Philosophy* 85 (1988): 654–655. Reprinted in *Philosophy of Mind: A Guide and Anthology*, ed. John Heil (Oxford: Oxford University Press, 2004).

Carnap, Rudolf. "Psychology in Physical Language," in *Logical Positivism*, ed. A. J. Ayer (1932, in German; New York: Free Press, 1959).

Castaneda, Hector-Neri. "On the Phenomeno-Logic of the I" (1969), reprinted in *Self-Knowledge*, ed. Quassim Cassam (Oxford: Oxford University Press, 1994).

Causey, Robert L. "Attribute Identities in Microreductions," *Journal of Philosophy* 69 (1972): 407–422.

Chalmers, David. *The Conscious Mind* (New York: Oxford University Press, 1996).

————, ed. *Philosophy of Mind: Classical and Contemporary Readings* (Oxford: Oxford University Press, 2002).

Chisholm, Roderick M. *Perceiving* (Ithaca, NY: Cornell University Press, 1957).

————. *The First Person* (Minneapolis: University of Minnesota Press, 1981).

Chomsky, Noam. Review of *Verbal Behavior* by B. F. Skinner. *Language* 35 (1959): 26–58.

Churchland, Patricia S. *Neurophilosophy* (Cambridge, MA: MIT Press, 1986).

Churchland, Paul M. "Eliminative Materialism and the Propositional Attitudes," *Journal of Philosophy* 78 (1981): 67–90. Reprinted in *Philosophy of Mind: Classical and Contemporary Readings*, ed. David J. Chalmers (Oxford: Oxford University Press, 2002); and in *Philosophy of Mind: A Guide and Anthology*, ed. John Heil (Oxford: Oxford University Press, 2004).

Cottingham, John, Robert Stoothoff, and Dugald Murdoch, eds. *The Philosophical Writings of Descartes*, 3 vols. (Cambridge: Cambridge University Press, 1985).

Craig, Edward, ed. *The Routledge Encyclopedia of Philosophy* (London: Routledge, 1998).

Crane, Tim. "The Causal Efficacy of Content: A Functionalist Theory," in *Human Action, Deliberation, and Causation*, ed. Jan Bransen and Stefaan E. Cuypers (Dordrecht: Kluwer, 1998).

————. "Mental Substances," in *Minds and Persons*, ed. Anthony O'Hear (Cambridge: Cambridge University Press, 2003)

Crumley II, Jack S., ed. *Problems in Mind* (Mountain View, CA: Mayfield, 2000).

Cummins, Denise Dellarosa, and Robert Cummins, eds. *Minds, Brains, and Computers: An Anthology* (Oxford: Blackwell, 2000).

Cummins, Robert. *Meaning and Mental Representation* (Cambridge, MA: MIT Press, 1989).

Davidson, Donald. "Actions, Reasons, and Causes" (1963), reprinted in *Essays on Actions and Events*, ed. Donald Davidson (New York: Oxford University Press, 1980).

————. "The Individuation of Events" (1969), reprinted in *Essays on Actions and Events*, ed. Donald Davidson (New York: Oxford University Press, 1980).

————. "Mental Events" (1970), reprinted in *Essays on Actions and Events*, ed. Donald Davidson (New York: Oxford University Press, 1980); in *Philosophy of Mind: Classical and Contemporary Readings*, ed. David J. Chalmers (Oxford: Oxford University Press, 2002); and in *Philosophy of Mind: A Guide and Anthology*, ed. John Heil (Oxford: Oxford University Press, 2004).

————. "Radical Interpretation" (1973), reprinted in *Inquiries into Truth and Interpretation* by Donald Davidson (New York: Oxford University Press, 1984); and in *Philosophy of Mind: A Guide and Anthology*, ed. John Heil (Oxford: Oxford University Press, 2004).

————. "Belief and the Basis of Meaning" (1974), reprinted in *Inquiries into Truth and Interpretation* by Donald Davidson (New York: Oxford University Press, 1984).

————. "Thought and Talk" (1974), reprinted in *Inquiries into Truth and Interpretation* by Donald Davidson (New York: Oxford University Press, 1984); and in *Philosophy of Mind: A Guide and Anthology*, ed. John Heil (Oxford: Oxford University Press, 2004).

————. *Essays on Actions and Events* (New York: Oxford University Press, 1980).

————. "Rational Animals" (1982), reprinted in *Subjective, Intersubjective, Objective* by Donald Davidson (Oxford: Clarendon, 2001).

————. *Inquiries into Truth and Interpretation* (New York: Oxford University Press, 1984).

————. "Knowing One's Own Mind" (1987), reprinted in *Subjective, Intersubjective, Objective* by Donald Davidson (Oxford: Clarendon, 2001).

————. "Three Varieties of Knowledge" (1991), reprinted in *Subjective, Intersubjective Objective* by Donald Davidson (Oxford: Clarendon, 2001).

———. "Thinking Causes," in *Mental Causation*, ed. John Heil and Alfred Mele (Oxford: Clarendon Press, 1993).

———. *Subjective, Intersubjective, Objective* (Oxford: Clarendon, 2001).

Davis, Martin. *Computability and Unsolvability* (New York: McGraw-Hill, 1958).

Dennett, Daniel C. *Brainstorms* (Montgomery, VT: Bradford Books, 1978).

———. "Intentional Systems," reprinted in Dennett, *Brainstorms* (Montgomery, VT: Bradford Books, 1978).

———. "Evolution, Error, and Intentionality" (1987), reprinted in *The Intentional Stance* by Daniel C. Dennett (Cambridge, MA: MIT Press, 1987).

———. "True Believers," in *Intentional Stance* by Daniel C. Dennett (Cambridge, MA: MIT Press, 1987); reprinted in *The Nature of Mind*, ed. David Rosenthal (New York: Oxford University Press, 1991); and in *Philosophy of Mind: Classical and Contemporary Readings*, ed. David J. Chalmers (Oxford: Oxford University Press, 2002).

———. "Quining Qualia," in *Consciousness in Contemporary Science*, ed. A. J. Marcel and E. Bisiach (Oxford: Oxford University Press, 1988); reprinted in *The Nature of Consciousness*, ed. Ned Block, Owen Flanagan, and Güven Güzeldere (Cambridge, MA: MIT Press, 1999); and in *Readings in Philosophy and Cognitive Science*, ed. Alvin Goldman (Cambridge, MA: MIT Press, 1993).

———. *Consciousness Explained* (Boston: Little, Brown, 1991).

Descartes, René. *Meditations on First Philosophy*, in *The Philosophical Writings of Descartes*, vol. 2, ed. John Cottingham, Robert Stoothoff, and Dugald Murdoch (Cambridge: Cambridge University Press, 1985).

———. *The Passions of the Soul*, book 1, in *The Philosophical Writings of Descartes*, vol. 1, ed. John Cottingham, Robert Stoothoff, and Dugald Murdoch (Cambridge: Cambridge University Press, 1984).

———. "Author's Replies to the Second Set of Objections," in *The Philosophical Writings of Descartes*, vol. 2, ed. John Cottingham, Robert Stoothoff, and Dugald Murdoch (Cambridge: Cambridge University Press, 1985).

———. "Author's Replies to the Fourth Set of Objections," in *The Philosophical Writings of Descartes*, vol. 2, ed. John Cottingham, Robert Stoothoff, and Dugald Murdoch (Cambridge: Cambridge University Press, 1985).

Dretske, Fred. *Knowledge and the Flow of Information* (Cambridge, MA: MIT Press, 1981).

———. "Misrepresentation," in *Belief*, ed. Radu Bogdan (Oxford: Oxford University Press, 1986); reprinted in *Readings in Philosophy and Cognitive Science*, ed. Alvin Goldman (Cambridge, MA: MIT Press, 1993).

———. *Explaining Behavior* (Cambridge, MA: MIT Press, 1988).

———. *Naturalizing the Mind* (Cambridge, MA: MIT Press, 1995).

———. "Minds, Machines, and Money: What Really Explains Behavior," in *Human Action, Deliberation, and Causation*, ed. Jan Bransen and Stefaan E. Cuypers (Dordrecht: Kluwer, 1998).

Dupre, John. *The Disorder of Things* (Cambridge, MA: Harvard University Press, 1993).

Egan, Frances. "Must Psychology Be Individualistic?" *Philosophical Review* 100 (1991): 179–203.

Enc, Berent. "Redundancy, Degeneracy, and Deviance in Action," *Philosophical Studies* 48 (1985): 353–374.

Feigl, Herbert. "The 'Mental' and the 'Physical,'" in *Minnesota Studies in the Philosophy of Science*, vol. 2, ed. Herbert Feigl, Michael Scriven, and Grover Maxwell (Minneapolis: University of Minnesota Press, 1958).

Flanagan, Owen. *Consciousness Reconsidered* (Cambridge, MA: MIT Press, 1992).

Fodor, Jerry A. "Special Sciences, or the Disunity of Science as a Working Hypothesis," *Synthese* 28 (1974): 97–115; reprinted in *Philosophy of Mind: Classical and Contemporary Readings*, ed. David J. Chalmers (Oxford: Oxford University Press, 2002).

———. *Psychosemantics* (Cambridge, MA: MIT Press, 1987).

———. *A Theory of Content and Other Essays* (Cambridge, MA: MIT Press, 1990).

———. "Making Mind Matter More," in *A Theory of Content and Other Essays* by Jerry A. Fodor (Cambridge, MA: MIT Press, 1990); reprinted in *Problems in Mind*, ed. Jack S. Crumley II (Mountain View, CA: Mayfield, 2000).

———. "A Modal Argument for Narrow Content," *Journal of Philosophy* 88 (1991): 5–26.

———. "Special Sciences: Still Autonomous After All These Years," *Philosophical Perspectives* 11 (1997): 149–163; reprinted in *In Critical Condition* by Jerry A. Fodor (Cambridge, MA: MIT Press, 1998).

———. *In Critical Condition* (Cambridge, MA: MIT Press, 1998).

Foster, John. *The Case for Idealism*, (London: Routledge, 1982).

———. *The Immaterial Self* (London: Routledge, 1991).

———. "A Defense of Dualism," in *The Case for Dualism*, ed. John R. Smythies and John Beloff (Charlottesville: University Press of Virginia, 1989); reprinted in *Problems in Mind*, ed. Jack S. Crumley II (Mountain View, CA: Mayfield, 2000).

———. "A Brief Defense of the Cartesian View," in *Soul, Body, and Survival*, ed. Kevin Corcoran (Ithaca, NY: Cornell University Press, 2001).

Garber, Daniel. "Understanding Interaction: What Descartes Should Have Told Elisabeth," in *Descartes Embodied* by Daniel Garber (Cambridge: Cambridge University Press, 2001).

———. *Descartes Embodied* (Cambridge: Cambridge University Press, 2001).

Gendler, Tamar Szabo, and John Hawthorne, eds. *Conceivability and Possibility* (Oxford: Oxford University Press, 2002).

Gillett, Carl. "The Metaphysics of Realization, Multiple Realizability, and the Special Sciences," *Journal of Philosophy* 100 (2003): 591–603.

Gillett, Carl, ed. *Emergence: Philosophical and Scientific Foundations* (Oxford: Oxford University Press, forthcoming).

Ginet, Carl. *On Action* (Cambridge: Cambridge University Press, 1990).

Goldman, Alvin I. "Interpretation Psychologized," in *Liaisons* by Alvin I. Goldman (1989; Cambridge, MA: MIT Press, 1992).

———, ed. *Readings in Philosophy and Cognitive Science* (Cambridge, MA: MIT Press, 1993).

Gopnik, Alison. "How We Know Our Minds: The Illusion of First-Person Knowledge of Intentionality," *Behavioral and Brain Sciences* 16 (1993): 1–14; reprinted in *Readings in Philosophy and Cognitive Science*, ed. Alvin I. Goldman (Cambridge, MA: MIT Press, 1993).

Gordon, Robert M. "Folk Psychology as Simulation," *Mind and Language* 1 (1986): 159–171.

Guttenplan, Samuel, ed. *A Companion to Philosophy of Mind* (Oxford: Blackwell, 1994).

Hardin, C. L. *Color for Philosophers* (Indianapolis, IN: Hackett, 1988).

Harman, Gilbert. "The Inference to the Best Explanation," *Philosophical Review* 74 (1966): 88–95.

———. "The Intrinsic Quality of Experience," *Philosophical Perspectives* 4 (1990): 31–52; reprinted in *The Nature of Consciousness*, ed. Ned Block, Owen Flanagan, and Güven Güzeldere (Cambridge, MA: MIT Press, 1999).

Harnish, Robert M. *Minds, Brains, Computers: An Historical Introduction to the Foundations of Cognitive Science* (Oxford: Blackwell, 2002).

Hart, W. D. *The Engines of the Soul* (Cambridge: Cambridge University Press, 1988).

Heil, John. *The Nature of True Minds* (Cambridge: Cambridge University Press, 1992).

———, ed. *Philosophy of Mind: A Guide and Anthology* (Oxford: Oxford University Press, 2004).

Heil, John, and Alfred Mele, eds. *Mental Causation* (Oxford: Clarendon Press, 1993).

Hempel, Carl G. "The Logical Analysis of Psychology" (1935), in *Philosophy of Mind: A Guide and Anthology*, ed. John Heil (Oxford: Oxford University Press, 2004).

———. *Philosophy of Natural Science* (Englewood Cliffs, NJ: Prentice-Hall, 1966).

Hill, Christopher S. *Sensations: A Defense of Type Materialism* (Cambridge: Cambridge University Press, 1991).

Horgan, Terence. "Supervenient Qualia," *Philosophical Review* 96 (1987): 491–520.

———. "Mental Quausation," *Philosophical Perspectives* 3 (1989): 47–76.

Humphreys, Paul. "How Properties Emerge," *Philosophy of Science* 64 (1997): 53–70.

Huxley, Thomas H. *Lessons in Elementary Physiology* (London: Macmillan, 1885).

———. "On the Hypothesis That Animals Are Automata, and Its History," excerpted in *Philosophy of Mind: Classical and Contemporary Readings*, ed. David J. Chalmers (Oxford: Oxford University Press, 2002). A full version of the paper appears in *Methods and Results: Essays* by Thomas H. Huxley (New York: D. Appleton, 1901).

Jackson, Frank. "Finding the Mind in the Natural World" (1994), reprinted in *The Nature of Consciousness,* ed. Ned Block, Owen Flanagan, and Güven Güzeldere (Cambridge, MA: MIT Press, 1999).

Jacob, Pierre. *What Minds Can Do* (Cambridge: Cambridge University Press, 1997).

James, William. *The Principles of Psychology* (1890; Cambridge, MA: Harvard University Press, 1981).

Kim, Jaegwon. "Events as Property Exemplifications" (1976), reprinted in *Supervenience and Mind* by Jaegwon Kim (Cambridge: Cambridge University Press, 1993).

———. "Psychophysical Laws" (1985), reprinted in *Supervenience and Mind* by Jaegwon Kim (Cambridge: Cambridge University Press, 1993).

———. "The Myth of Nonreductive Physicalism" (1989), reprinted in *Supervenience and Mind* (Cambridge: Cambridge University Press, 1993).

———. "Multiple Realization and the Metaphysics of Reduction" (1992), reprinted in *Supervenience and Mind* by Jaegwon Kim (Cambridge: Cambridge University Press, 1993); in *Philosophy of Mind: Classical and Contemporary Readings*, ed. David J. Chalmers (Oxford: Oxford University Press, 2002); and in *Philosophy of Mind: A Guide and Anthology*, ed. John Heil (Oxford: Oxford University Press, 2004).

———. *Supervenience and Mind* (Cambridge: Cambridge University Press, 1993).

———. *Mind in a Physical World* (Cambridge, MA: MIT Press, 1998).

———. "Making Sense of Emergence," *Philosophical Studies* 95 (1999): 3–36.

———. *Physicalism, or Something Near Enough* (Princeton, NJ: Princeton University Press, 2005).

Kripke, Saul. *Naming and Necessity* (Cambridge, MA: Harvard University Press, 1980).

Lashley, Karl. *Brain Mechanisms and Intelligence* (New York: Hafner, 1963).

Latham, Noa. "Substance Physicalism," in *Physicalism and Its Discontents*, ed. Carl Gillett and Barry Loewer (Cambridge: Cambridge University Press, 2001).

LePore, Ernest, and Barry Loewer. "Mind Matters," *Journal of Philosophy* 84 (1987): 630–642.

Levine, Joseph. "Materialism and Qualia: The Explanatory Gap," *Pacific Philosophical Quarterly* 64 (1983): 354–361; reprinted in *Philosophy of Mind: Classical and Contemporary*

Readings, ed. David J. Chalmers (Oxford: Oxford University Press, 2002); *Philosophy of Mind: Contemporary Readings,* ed. Timothy O'Connor and David Robb (London: Routledge, 2003).

———. "On Leaving Out What It's Like," in *Consciousness,* ed. Martin Davies and Glyn W. Humphreys (Oxford: Blackwell, 1993).

———. *Purple Haze* (Oxford: Oxford University Press, 2000).

Lewis, David. "How to Define Theoretical Terms" (1970), reprinted in *Philosophical Papers* by David Lewis, vol. 1 (New York: Oxford University Press, 1983).

———. *Counterfactuals* (Cambridge, MA: Harvard University Press, 1973).

———. "Psychophysical and Theoretical Identifications" (1972), reprinted in *Readings in Philosophy of Psychology,* vol. 1, ed. Ned Block (Cambridge, MA: Harvard University Press, 1980).

———. "Causation" (1973), reprinted, with "Postscripts," in *Philosophical Papers* by David Lewis, vol. 2 (New York: Oxford University Press, 1986).

———. *Philosophical Papers,* vol. 1 (New York: Oxford University Press, 1983).

———. "Attitudes *De Dicto* and *De Se,*" *Philosophical Review* 88 (1979): 513–543. Reprinted in Lewis, *Philosophical Papers,* vol. 1.

Loar, Brian. "Phenomenal States," *Philosophical Perspectives* (1990): 81–108; reprinted in *The Nature of Consciousness,* ed. Ned Block, Owen Flanagan, and Güven Güzeldere (Cambridge, MA: MIT Press, 1999).

Loewer, Barry, and Georges Rey, eds. *Meaning in Mind* (London: Routledge, 1991).

Ludlow, Peter, and Norah Martin, eds. *Externalism and Self-Knowledge* (Stanford, CA: CSLI Publications, 1998).

Lycan, William G. *Consciousness* (Cambridge, MA: MIT Press, 1987).

———. *Consciousness and Experience* (Cambridge, MA: MIT Press, 1996).

———, ed. *Mind and Cognition,* 2nd ed. (Oxford: Blackwell, 1999).

Marcel, A. J., and E. Bisiach, eds. *Consciousness in Contemporary Science* (Oxford: Oxford University Press, 1988).

Marras, Ausonio. "Nonreductive Physicalism and Mental Causation," *Canadian Journal of Philosophy* 24 (1994): 465–493.

Matthews, Robert. "The Measure of Mind," *Mind* 103 (1994): 131–146.

McGinn, Colin. *The Problem of Consciousness* (Oxford: Blackwell, 1991).

McLaughlin, Brian. "What Is Wrong with Correlational Psychosemantics?" *Synthese* 70 (1987): 271–286.

———. "Type Epiphenomenalism, Type Dualism, and the Causal Priority of the Physical," *Philosophical Perspectives* 3 (1989): 109–136.

———. "The Rise and Fall of British Emergentism," in *Emergence or Reduction?* ed. Ansgar Beckermann, Hans Flohr, and Jaegwon Kim (Berlin: De Gruyter, 1992).

———. "Varieties of Supervenience," in *Supervenience: New Essays,* ed. Elias Savellos and Umit Yalcin (Cambridge: Cambridge University Press, 1995).

———. "In Defense of New Wave Materialism: A Response to Horgan and Tienson," in *Physicalism and Its Discontents,* ed. Carl Gillett and Barry Loewer (Cambridge: Cambridge University Press, 2001).

McLaughlin, Brian, and Ansgar Beckermann, eds. *The Oxford Handbook of Philosophy of Mind* (Oxford: Oxford University Press, forthcoming).

Melzack, Ronald. *The Puzzle of Pain* (New York: Basic Books, 1973).

Melnyk, Andrew. *A Physicalist Manifesto* (Cambridge: Cambridge University Press, 2003).

Millikan, Ruth G. *Language, Thought, and Other Biological Categories* (Cambridge, MA: MIT Press, 1984).

———. "Biosemantics," *Journal of Philosophy* 86 (1989): 281–97; reprinted in *Problems in Mind*, ed. Jack S. Crumley II (Mountain View, CA: Mayfield, 2000); and in *Philosophy of Mind: Classical and Contemporary Readings*, ed. David J. Chalmers (Oxford: Oxford University Press, 2002).

Morgan, C. Lloyd. *Emergent Evolution* (London: Williams & Norgate, 1923).

Morowitz, Harold J. *The Emergence of Everything* (Oxford: Oxford University Press, 2002).

Moser, Paul K., and J. D. Trout, eds. *Contemporary Materialism: A Reader* (New York: Routledge, 1995).

Nagel, Ernest. *The Structure of Science* (New York: Harcourt, Brace & World, 1961).

Nagel, Thomas. "What Is It Like to Be a Bat?" *Philosophical Review* 83 (1974): 435–450; reprinted in *Philosophy of Mind: A Guide and Anthology*, ed. John Heil (Oxford: Oxford University Press, 2004).

———. "Subjective and Objective," in *Mortal Questions* by Thomas Nagel (Cambridge: Cambridge University Press, 1979).

Neader, Karen. "Teleological Theories of Mental Content," in *Stanford Online Encyclopedia of Philosophy* (http://plato.stanford.edu/).

Nida-Rümelin, Martine. "Pseudo-Normal Vision: An Actual Case of Qualia Inversion?" *Philosophical Studies* 82 (1996): 145–157; reprinted in *Philosophy of Mind: Classical and Contemporary Readings*, ed. David J. Chalmers (Oxford: Oxford University Press, 2002).

Nuccetelli, Susan, ed. *New Essays on Semantic Externalism and Self-Knowledge* (Cambridge, MA: MIT Press, 2003).

O'Connor, Timothy, and David Robb, eds. *Philosophy of Mind: Contemporary Readings* (London: Routledge, 2003).

O'Connor, Timothy, and Hong Yu Wong. "The Metaphysics of Emergence," *Noûs* (forthcoming).

Olson, Eric T. *The Human Animal: Personal Identity Without Psychology* (Oxford: Oxford University Press, 1997).

Papineau, David. *Thinking About Consciousness* (Oxford: Oxford University Press, 2002).

Pereboom, Derk. "Robust Nonreductive Physicalism," *Journal of Philosophy* 99 (2002): 499–531.

Pereboom, Derk, and Hilary Kornblith. "The Metaphysics of Irreducibility," *Philosophical Studies* 63 (1991): 125–145.

Perry, John. *Knowledge, Possibility, and Consciousness* (Cambridge, MA: MIT Press, 2001).

Place, U. T. "Is Consciousness a Brain Process?" in *Philosophy of Mind: Classical and Contemporary Readings*, ed. David J. Chalmers (Oxford: Oxford University Press, 2002).

Poland, Jeffrey. *Physicalism: The Philosophical Foundation* (Oxford: Clarendon Press, 1994).

Polger, Thomas W. *Natural Minds* (Cambridge, MA: MIT Press, 2004).

Post, John. *The Faces of Existence* (Ithaca, NY: Cornell University Press, 1987).

Putnam, Hilary. "Brains and Behavior" (1965), reprinted in *Philosophy of Mind: A Guide and Anthology*, ed. John Heil (Oxford: Oxford University Press, 2004); and in *Philosophy of Mind: Classical and Contemporary Readings*, ed. David. J. Chalmers (Oxford: Oxford University Press, 2002).

———. "Psychological Predicates," in *Art, Mind, and Religion*, ed. W. H. Capitan and D. D. Merrill (Pittsburgh: University of Pittsburgh Press, 1967); reprinted and retitled "The Nature of Mental States," in *Mind, Language, and Reality: Philosophical Papers*, vol. 2, 2nd ed., ed. Hilary Putnam (Cambridge: Cambridge University Press, 1979); also reprinted in *Phi-*

losophy of Mind: A Guide and Anthology, ed. John Heil (Oxford: Oxford University Press, 2004); and in *Philosophy of Mind: Contemporary Readings*, ed. Timothy O'Connor and David Robb (London: Routledge, 2003).

———. "Robots: Machines or Artificially Created Life?" (1964), in *Mind, Language, and Reality: Philosophical Papers*, vol. 2, 2nd ed., by Hilary Putnam (Cambridge: Cambridge University Press, 1979).

———. "The Meaning of 'Meaning'" (1975), reprinted in *Mind, Language, and Reality: Philosophical Papers*, vol. 2, 2nd ed., ed. Hilary Putnam (Cambridge: Cambridge University Press, 1979). An excerpted version appears in *Philosophy of Mind: Classical and Contemporary Readings*, ed. David J. Chalmers (Oxford: Oxford University Press, 2002).

———. *Mind, Language, and Reality: Philosophical Papers*, vol. 2, 2nd ed. (Cambridge: Cambridge University Press, 1979).

———. *Representation and Reality* (Cambridge, MA: MIT Press, 1988).

Quine, W. V. *Word and Object* (Cambridge and New York: Technology Press of MIT and John Wiley & Sons, 1960).

Rimbaud, Arthur. "Voyelles," in *Arthur Rimbaud: Complete Works*, translated from the French by Paul Schmidt (New York: Harper & Row, 1976)

Robinson, Howard, ed. *Objections to Physicalism* (Oxford: Clarendon Press, 1993).

Rosenthal, David M. "The Independence of Consciousness and Sensory Quality," *Philosophical Issues* 1 (1991): 15–36.

———, ed. *The Nature of Mind* (New York: Oxford University Press, 1991).

———. "Explaining Consciousness," in *Philosophy of Mind: Classical and Contemporary Readings*, ed. David J. Chalmers (Oxford: Oxford University Press, 2002).

Ross, Don, and David Spurrett. "What to Say to a Skeptical Metaphysician: A Defense Manual for Cognitive and Behavioral Scientists," *Behavioral and Brain Sciences* (forthcoming).

Rozemond, Marleen. *Descartes' Dualism* (Cambridge, MA: Harvard University Press, 1998).

Ryle, Gilbert. *The Concept of Mind* (New York: Barnes and Noble, 1949)

Searle, John. "Minds, Brains, and Programs" (1980), reprinted in *Philosophy of Mind: A Guide and Anthology*, ed. John Heil (Oxford: Oxford University Press, 2004); and in *Philosophy of Mind: Contemporary Readings*, ed. Timothy O'Connor and David Robb (London: Routledge, 2003).

———. *Intentionality* (Cambridge: Cambridge University Press, 1983).

———. *The Rediscovery of the Mind* (Cambridge, MA: MIT Press, 1992).

Segal, Gabriel M. A. *A Slim Book About Narrow Content* (Cambridge, MA: MIT Press, 2000).

Sellars, Wilfrid. "Chisholm-Sellars Correspondence on Intentionality," *Minnesota Studies in the Philosophy of Science*, vol. 2 (Minneapolis: University of Minnesota Press, 1958).

Shaffer, Jerome. "Mental Events and the Brain," *Journal of Philosophy* 60 (1963): 160–166; reprinted in *The Nature of Mind*, ed. David M. Rosenthal (New York: Oxford University Press, 1991).

Shapiro, Lawrence. *The Mind Incarnate* (Cambridge, MA: MIT Press, 2004).

Shoemaker, Sydney. "The Inverted Spectrum," *Journal of Philosophy* 79 (1982): 357–382; reprinted in *Identity, Cause and Mind* by Sydney Shoemaker (Cambridge: Cambridge University Press, 1984).

———. "Some Varieties of Functionalism," in *Identity, Cause, and Mind* by Sydney Shoemaker (Cambridge: Cambridge University Press, 1984).

———. "Absent Qualia Are Impossible—A Reply to Block," in *Identity, Cause, and Mind* by Sydney Shoemaker (Cambridge: Cambridge University Press, 1984).

———. *Identity, Cause, and Mind* (Cambridge: Cambridge University Press, 1984).

————. "Realization, Microrealization, and Coincidence," *Philosophy and Phenomenological Research* 67 (2003): 1–23.

Skinner, B. F. "Selections from *Science and Human Behavior*" (1953), reprinted in *Readings in Philosophy of Psychology*, vol. 1, ed. Ned Block (Cambridge, MA: Harvard University Press, 1980).

————. *Science and Human Behavior* (New York: Macmillan, 1953).

————. *About Behaviorism* (New York: Alfred A. Knopf, 1974).

Smart, J. J. C. "Sensations and Brain Processes" (1959), reprinted in *The Nature of Mind*, ed. David M. Rosenthal (New York: Oxford University Press, 1991); in *Philosophy of Mind: A Guide and Anthology*, ed. John Heil (Oxford: Oxford University Press, 2004); and in *Philosophy of Mind: Classical and Contemporary Readings*, ed. David J. Chalmers (Oxford: Oxford University Press, 2002).

Smith, Michael. "The Possibility of Philosophy of Action," in *Human Action, Deliberation, and Causation*, ed. Jan Bransen and Stefaane E. Cuypers (Dordrecht: Kluwer, 1998).

Smith, Quentin, and Aleksandar Jokic, eds. *Consciousness: New Perspectives* (Oxford: Clarendon, 2003).

Sosa, Ernest. "Mind-Body Interaction and Supervenient Causation," *Midwest Studies in Philosophy* 9 (1984): 271–281.

————. "Between Internalism and Externalism," *Philosophical Issues* 1 (1991): 179–195.

Sperry, Roger W. "A Modified Concept of Consciousness," *Psychological Review* 76 (1969): 532–536.

Stalnaker, Robert. *Inquiry* (Cambridge, MA: MIT Press, 1984).

Stampe, Dennis. "Toward a Causal Theory of Linguistic Representation," *Midwest Studies in Philosophy* 2 (1977): 42–63.

Stanford Online Encyclopedia of Philosophy (http://plato.stanford.edu/).

Stoutland, Frederick. "Oblique Causation and Reasons for Action," *Synthese* 43 (1980): 351–67.

————. "Real Reasons," in *Human Action, Deliberation, and Causation*, ed. Jan Bransen and Stefaane E. Cuypers (Dordrecht: Kluwer, 1998).

Swinburne, Richard. *The Evolution of the Soul* (Oxford: Clarendon, 1986).

Thagard, Paul. *Mind: Introduction to Cognitive Science* (Cambridge, MA: MIT Press, 1999).

Turing, Alan M. "Computing Machinery and Intelligence," *Mind* 59 (1950): 433–460; reprinted in *Philosophy of Mind: A Guide and Anthology*, ed. John Heil (Oxford: Oxford University Press, 2004).

Tye, Michael. "Qualia, Content, and the Inverted Spectrum," *Noûs* 28 (1994): 159–183.

————. *Ten Problems of Consciousness* (Cambridge, MA: MIT Press, 1995).

Van Fraassen, Bas. *The Scientific Image* (Oxford: Clarendon, 1980).

————. *Laws and Symmetry* (Oxford: Oxford University Press, 1989).

Van Gulick, Robert. "Nonreductive Materialism and the Nature of Intertheoretical Constraint," in *Emergence or Reduction?* ed. Ansgar Beckermann, Hans Flohr, and Jaegwon Kim (Berlin: De Gruyter, 1992).

Von Eckardt, Barbara. *What Is Cognitive Science?* (Cambridge, MA: MIT Press, 1993).

Walter, Sven, and Heinz-Dieter Heckmann, eds. *Physicalism and Mental Causation: The Metaphysics of Mind and Action* (Charlottesville, VA: Imprint Academic, 2003).

Watson, J. B. "Psychology as the Behaviorist Views It," *Psychological Review* 20 (1913): 158–177.

Watson, Richard A. *The Breakdown of Cartesian Metaphysics* (Atlantic Highlands, NJ: Humanities Press International, 1987).

White, Stephen. "Partial Character and the Language of Thought," *Pacific Philosophical Quarterly* 63 (1982): 347–365.

Wilson, Robert A., and Frank C. Keil, eds. *The MIT Encyclopedia of the Cognitive Sciences* (Cambridge, MA: MIT Press, 1999).

Wittgenstein, Ludwig. *Philosophical Investigations*, trans. G. E. M. Anscombe (Oxford: Blackwell, 1953).

Wright, Crispin, Barry C. Smith, and Cynthia Macdonald, eds. *Knowing Our Own Minds* (Oxford: Clarendon Press, 1998).

Yablo, Stephen. "Mental Causation," *Philosophical Review* 101 (1992): 245–280.

Index